PREPPER'S OFF GRID ULTIMATE SURVIVAL HANDBOOK

8 BOOKS IN 1

The Comprehensive Guide to Off Grid Living | Includes Medical Emergencies, Solar Power, Backyard Homestead, Food Canning and So Much More

BY

BRADLEY STONE

CONTENTS

YOUR FREE GIFT!

As a way of saying thanks for reading, I'm offering the self-sufficiency 6 book bundle to my readers for FREE!

To get instant access click the link below or scan the QR Code:

bradley.brainfoodpress.com

SCAN ME

Sustainable Living Made Easy:

Creating a Healthier Future for Your Family and Protecting the Planet One Step at a Time

We all know the planet is in trouble and needs our help. But sometimes our effort seems wasted. This guide will show you simples steps that make a huge difference and so much more...

Discover;

- ✓ What to expect from sustainable living
- ✓ How to take the first steps to grow your own food
- ✓ Best practices for taking care of animals in your backyard
- ✓ Simple tips for producing and conserving energy in your home
- ✓ How to sustain the Earth while managing your waste
- ✓ Why it's important to keep poisons out of the landfill
- ✓ Techniques for getting kids involved with your new lifestyle

Survival Prepping on A Budget:

The Essential Guide to Prepare for Disaster on A Budget

What do you do when disaster hits? Well, that depends on if you're prepared or not. This guide will ensure you are thoroughly prepared.

Discover;

- ✓ Why preparation is always the key to surviving whatever life throws at you
- ✓ How to plan so you don't buy haphazardly
- ✓ The importance of being picky what you splurge on
- ✓ Reasons for buying in bulk to cut costs
- ✓ Steps to add to your stock a little at a time
- ✓ How to buy at certain times to save money

Using Animals in Your Homestead:

A Beginners Introduction to Raising and Caring For Animals in Your Backyard

There are several ways you can us animals to be become more self-reliant and self-sufficient. This guide is a great resource on your journey.

Discover;

- ✓ Why it's important to honour the animal

- ✓ Which animals are great for different locations

- ✓ How to research your best options

- ✓ Why rabbits are a homestead hidden gem

- ✓ Why it's important to not let any part of the animal go to waste

Solar Panel:

An Introduction for Beginners

This guide contains 5 articles that have been combined to provide an excellent starting point on your solar power quest.

Discover;

- ✓ What a solar panel is
- ✓ What solar power can do for you
- ✓ The key things to look for in a home solar panel
- ✓ Why you can benefit from solar panel cells
- ✓ The true cost of solar
- ✓ And much more…

A Simple Living Guide to Rainwater Usage:

7 Tips For Harvesting, Storing and Using Rainwater in Your Off Grid Homestead

As the demand for clean water grows every year and water bills are on the rise, it is imperative that you harness the power of the sky and collect rainwater.

Discover;

- ✓ The benefits of storing and using rainwater
- ✓ How to create a storage system for rainwater
- ✓ The importance of first flush systems for the cleanest water
- ✓ The details of rain barrel maintenance
- ✓ How much you can collect
- ✓ The many different uses of stored rainwater

Homeschooling:

A Beginners Guide

Living off the gird can cause serious worries for parents with regards to their children's education. This eBook aims to eliminate those concerns.

Discover;

- ✓ The different methods of homeschooling
- ✓ What it costs to homeschool your child
- ✓ What to keep in your child's homeschool portfolio
- ✓ How to ensure your homeschool child gets socialization
- ✓ Faith based versus secular homeschooling

If you want to fast track your way to self-sufficiency, scan the QR Code below and grab the 6-book bundle for Free!

SCAN ME

bradley.brainfoodpress.com

FOOD PRESERVATION AND CANNING FOR BEGINNERS

── BOOK 1 ──

7 Essential Food Preservation Tips For Off Grid Survival and The Homestead | Includes Recipes

BY

BRADLEY STONE

Introduction:
Why Is Canning An Important Aspect Of Off Grid Living?

"Food that is necessary for man's existence is as sacred as life itself. Everything that is indispensable for its preservation is the common property of society as a whole."

- Maximilien Robespierre

There is a lot to learn regarding off grid living, and you may wonder why home canning should be high up on the list. It might seem like one of the things to eventually get under your belt. However, according to the USDA, between 30 and 40% of food is wasted every year; This adds up to $161 billion on food in 2010 alone.[i]

Reducing your food waste can bring down your carbon footprint significantly. Nonetheless, when you grow your fruits and vegetables, you will probably find that you struggle to use up gluts of food in time. You might end up with fifty zucchinis all at once, three hundred plums, or buckets and buckets of blackberries., and then none until the following season.

It is just part of growing food; it involves cropping in a relatively short time, providing large quantities that do not last for long. Resulting in waste during the times of plenty, and then months in which you wish you had that particular fruit or vegetable again. When you can't depend on a store with big freezers or food being shipped in from other countries, this causes three fundamental problems:

A) How do you enjoy the food for a long time, especially if it is a staple food for you?

B) How do you prevent food waste so that you are making the most of your growing efforts?

C) How do you minimize the impact of your storage so that it is not using up large amounts of power (e.g., freezing)?

Even if you have both unlimited freezer space and unlimited power (unlikely in an off-the-grid living arrangement), freezing is not a planet-friendly solution to storing food – but nor is letting that food go to waste. Ergo, besides trying to eat your way through the surpluses and missing out on your favorite foods when they aren't in season, *what can you do?*

Home canning is the answer. It involves sealing food in sterile containers so that it lasts for months, or sometimes for years. These containers need no refrigeration or freezing (until opened), meaning that they are ideal for anyone with limited power access.

It is imperative to get home canning right. Food-borne bacteria are microorganisms that you do not want to mess around with, and if you don't store your food correctly, it will very quickly rot or turn moldy. If this happens, you will have wasted the food, your time and energy, and the ingredients used for home canning – so it's crucial to avoid this issue.

That's why this book is going to explore the challenges associated with home canning, the different kinds of canning, how to make enough time to do it, and some top recipes for preserving produce using this method. With this guide, you will soon have pantry shelves stocked with homegrown, home-preserved foods, keeping you and your family fed with delicious fruits and vegetables year-round, without having to depend on the seasons.

I've done home canning for many kinds of foods, including chutneys for apples and green tomatoes and syrupy plums as a perfect winter treat that brings out the deep almond flavor in the stones. I believe food is valuable, and homegrown food should never be wasted. The problem of too much of one thing and too little of another is easy to overcome with home canning. It will give you more control over what you eat and when.

In the next chapter, I will cover some of the top methods that people use for preserving food, including curing, pickling, fermenting, freezing, and – of course – canning. We look at the pros and cons of each and where the different methods come into their own.

1

The Top Food Preservation Methods

"You don't need a silver fork to eat good food."

- Paul Prudhomme

The problem of preserving food has followed humans throughout history, and the issue of having an excess of one kind of food, followed by a dearth of that food, is ongoing. Some plants have longer fruiting seasons than others, but it has always been the case that every kind of food has a season, and it is difficult to enjoy that food outside of its season.

Even foods that are available throughout the year, such as meat, have needed preserving. Before the advent of freezing, inventive techniques helped different kinds of foods last for longer. These techniques include:

- Pickling
- Drying
- Fermenting
- Curing
- Cellaring
- Canning
- Sealing

Freezing is the last to have been added to this list (except in countries with cold enough weather to freeze food without a home freezer), and all of these methods remain in use today. Indeed, they have brought us some of the foods that we love most, such as pickles, chutneys, jerky, dried fruit, alcohol, and vinegar.

Without these processes, vast swathes of the food on the shelves would disappear, and even using modern methods such as freezing would not help us overcome the problems we would face if we couldn't use them.

With that in mind, let's look at how these techniques work and the pros and cons.

Pickling

Pickling refers to two different preservation methods. You can either pickle foods by submerging them in vinegar or fermenting them in brine (this is done anaerobically, which means no oxygen is involved). Pickling infuses the foods with a strong flavor of either salt or vinegar.

Pros:

1. Food is preserved, usually in glass jars, without the need for power or freezer space. It can last for many years, and even once the jar has been opened, pickled food tends to have a long shelf-life without the need for refrigeration.
2. Pickled foods can have more exciting and intense flavors. They are often used as side dishes because of their intensity – such as olives and gherkins – but they bring a lot to our tables in texture and taste.
3. Depending on what you pickle, it can offer some good health benefits. Many pickled products contain healthy bacteria, amino acids, and vitamins. However, bear in mind that this does depend on the food, and pickled foods are not automatically more nutritious because of brine or vinegar.

Cons:

1. The original taste of the food is often lost and can be overwhelmed by the strong flavor of brine or vinegar; This is great for adding interest to meals, but it does prevent you from enjoying the original product. For example, a pickled gherkin does not taste like fresh cucumber, and it does not even resemble the texture that much. When you pickle a product, you make new food rather than helping the old food last longer. You can rarely use pickled foods as substitutes for fresh foods in a recipe.
2. Although they are healthy in moderation, pickles cannot be eaten in large quantities. The level of sodium or acid in them will be harmful. You should not drink brine or pickle juice because you might make yourself ill. For example, consuming a lot of salt from the brine can increase your blood pressure.
3. You will need to purchase suitable jars that can be sealed to preserve the integrity of the food. These carry a few disadvantages, such as being bulky to store (as they are round) and easy to break (almost always be made of glass).

Drying

Drying food involves removing the water from it to prevent the growth of mold. It is often referred to as dehydrating, and it is a technique that has been used for a long time. It may be the oldest food preservation method and dates back to 12,000 B.C. in the Middle East.[ii] Fruits, vegetables, and meats have been dried using the sun, wind, and fire as heat sources.

Pros:

1. If properly stored, dried food should last indefinitely.
2. Dried foods weigh far less, so they are easier to ship around the planet. They will also take up slightly less storage space in the home.
3. Dried foods often taste comparable to fresh foods, and they can sometimes be used as substitutes for that food in a recipe (for example, dried herbs).
4. This method is particularly suitable for preserving fruits for consumption at times of the year when fruit does not grow.
5. It is easy to transport dried food with you, and it is clean enough to eat. Dried food is excellent for traveling because it is not messy, requires no fork or plate, and is not very bulky.

Cons:

1. Dried foods do not taste the same as the fresh version, and they are often less satisfying to eat.
2. Small amounts of moisture can ruin the dried product, either because it was not appropriately dried or because it gets wet afterward, making it unsafe to eat.
3. This kind of preservation method can lead to inedible food if it is allowed to get too dry, and it is not reversible. Food may become tough and unappetizing.
4. Dried food often leaves you thirsty, and you need to carry water and increase your fluid intake because you aren't getting liquid from your meals.

Fermenting

Fermentation crosses over with some other categories of food preservation, such as pickling, but it is worth listing it as a separate category. It creates many foods, including yogurt, kimchi, kombucha, and beverages such as beer and wine. It involves encouraging certain kinds of bacteria in your food and keeping other types of bacteria out.

Pros:

1. You can create foods that are very different from their raw ingredients – e.g., yogurt and cheese from milk – and add variety to your diet as a result.
2. There are many health benefits associated with eating the right bacteria, such as improving the microorganisms in your gut; This has led to a recent increase in the number of people eating kimchi.
3. Fermented foods tend to last very well, although some require careful storage (e.g., yogurt) to maximize their shelf life.

Cons:

1. Fermented products tend to have a strong taste, and they do not preserve the food in its original form – they change it considerably. While that does make your diet more varied, as mentioned above, it also means you often cannot preserve the original food through fermentation.
2. Fermentation requires careful and knowledgeable input. You must know precisely how to encourage the correct bacteria strains and keep the dangerous ones out. Getting it wrong could lead to bacteria such as botulism infecting the food, which will then make you very sick.
3. It is difficult to tell if something has gone wrong with the fermentation process. Unless you can visibly see an unwelcome mold growing on the surface, it's easy to consume something dangerous unknowingly because the bacteria are not visible to the naked eye.

Curing

Curing is very similar to dehydrating in that it involves removing the moisture from the food, but it uses salt to do this rather than heat. The salt is spread upon the surface of the food (usually meat), and it draws moisture up out of that food, leaving it dehydrated.

Sometimes, foods are cured using sugar or smoke as alternatives to salt.

Pros:

1. Food that has been cured with salt, sugar, or smoke tastes excellent. It has a strong flavor, but this does not obscure the taste of the food in the way that pickling or brining can. Instead, it enhances it. (Think about smoked meats or honeyed ham, for example.)
2. Cured food needs minimal packaging. Unlike the pickling and fermenting options, it does not require glass jars or rubber seals. After all, the food is preserved by removing

all the moisture, making it compact, easy to store, and transport.

3. Curing is often a simple method for preserving food. It is not hard to cure meats with salt, for example, which increases the chances of the preservation is done correctly and reduces the risks of food poisoning or food waste; This does not apply if you use smoke for curing – see the cons list for more details.

Cons:

1. There is an issue with how much salt or sugar needs to be used in the curing process. It can lead to high blood pressure, diabetes, or hypertension if people eat too many foods that have been cured with salt or sugar.

2. Using smoke to cure food does not have these problems, but it is much more complicated and requires a lot of attention and careful calculations about time and temperature. It also reduces the amount of nutrients in the food.

3. Many foods cannot be cured, and some are spoiled by being cured, because of the salt. For example, while meats can be cured, things like fruit need to be preserved in other ways.

Cellaring

Cellaring, often known as root cellaring, requires a special space. Rooms built underground are naturally cool all the time because the ground pulls heat away from the walls. They also tend to be damp. A root cellar uses these conditions to help keep foods cool without the need for a fridge or freezer. It can store all kinds of foods but is usually best for fruits and vegetables.

Pros:

1. This preservation method helps you to extend the lifespan of fresh produce. This is unusual; most preservation methods significantly change the food that is being preserved. With this technique, you can enjoy fresh fruits and vegetables for far longer than usual without committing fridge space to them.

2. You have dedicated storage spaces for lots of fruits and vegetables so you can keep food from all your late harvests to feed you through the winter.

3. There are minimal (if any) ongoing costs once the system is set up.

Cons:

1. There is a high upfront cost if you don't already have this cellar in place. They can cost thousands to build, even if you do some of the work yourself.

2. You need to understand how to store vegetables because almost every kind will have different requirements. Some vegetables, such as onions, need to be cured before they are stored.
3. A rotten vegetable can ruin a whole crop if you do not notice it and remove it quickly.
4. You must understand what good conditions are and maintain these. For example, high humidity levels will keep vegetables from drying out and must be kept high, but light levels must be kept low. Learning about how to use a root cellar effectively can be a long process.

Canning

One of the last forms of preservation to be developed, canning, involves heating jars (or cans) to a hot enough temperature to destroy bacteria. When the jar cools, a vacuum is formed, sealing the jar. This prevents new bacteria from entering the jar and contaminating the food.

Pros:

1. Canned food keeps exceptionally well and can last for two years or even longer.
2. Canned food often retains some of the original flavors, although sauces/syrups may alter the taste in some foods.

Cons:

Canning requires quite a bit of time and precision in heating jars and transferring food quickly to avoid the jars cooling before they are sealed.

1. This sort of food tends to be less nutritious.
2. You need equipment to can food effectively.

Sealing

Vacuum sealing helps preserve some foods, removing the air so that bacteria cannot grow on the food's surface.

Pros:

1. This method saves a lot of food storage space and can be quite simple.
2. It keeps moisture in the food and ensures it retains most of its original nutrients and flavor.

Cons:

1. You need expensive equipment to seal the bags.
2. Many foods, particularly fresh produce, do not benefit from being vacuum sealed. Some will degrade faster because the ethylene gas will build up inside the bag.
3. Some kinds of anaerobic bacteria (those that do not need oxygen) thrive in a vacuum-sealed bag.

Takeaway From Chapter 1

In this chapter, we've covered:

- The many different kinds of food preservation
- Some of the advantages and the disadvantages of each option
- Why canning has some clear benefits over other options, especially for storing fruits and vegetables

In the next chapter, I will detail the two different kinds of canning and how you can use them.

2

Water Bath Canning And Pressure Canning

"It's difficult to think anything but pleasant thoughts
while eating a homegrown tomato."

- Lewis Grizzard

Let's look at water bath canning vs. pressure canning and break these down. We will explore how the different methods work and the advantages and disadvantages of each one. This should help you determine which is most suitable for you and the food you wish to preserve.

Before you make any decisions, it's crucial to understand that you must match the canning method to the food that you are preserving. If you do not do this correctly, the preservation method will not work, and your food is at risk of being infected with bacteria. Fortunately, with just a couple of simple rules, you'll always know what kind of canning method to use!

It should be noted that the term "canning" is somewhat misleading. Many people think of cans in terms of the sealed metal cans that can be bought in stores. However, home canning is almost always done using glass jars with metal lids. Store-bought canned food is created via canning, but you can't really make these sealed metal cans in your home – so when you think of home canning, think glass jars with metal lids.

Water Bath Canning

Many people consider this the easier of the two canning methods, and this may be partly because it does not require any special equipment, as long as you have some suitable glass jars and a large pot to boil them in. This makes this method much more accessible than pressure canning.

You need to be careful about the kinds of foods you preserve using this method because it does not reach such a high temperature. Although the temperature it does reach 212 ° F will be sufficient to kill many kinds of bacteria, it will not kill all of them – and the spores of a bacteria called botulism will survive, even if you boil the food for a long time. However, botulism spores do not survive in acidic foods.

Hence you should only preserve acidic foods, such as tomatoes, pickled vegetables, fruits, and sugary preserves, using the water bath canning option. The acidity of the food, combined with the heat sealing, will be sufficient to keep bacteria out. However, non-acidic foods may still harbor botulism spores, and these will spread inside the jar and make the food unsafe to eat. Do not try to can non-acidic foods using this method.

Often, even with acidic foods, you will want to add a little more acidity. You can do this by adding some food-safe citric acid, vinegar, or lemon juice. By adding these to the jar, you will increase the acidity and reduce the risk of bacterial infections, but you will also alter the taste of the canned food to a degree.

The water bath method involves filling clean jars with hot food, cold food, and hot liquid, placing the lid back on the jar, and tightening it. The jar should then be placed in boiling water for a certain period while the jar and its contents heat up, and then the stove will be turned off and the jar removed from the water to cool.

So, what are the advantages and disadvantages of the water bath method?

Pros:

- You do not need a lot of special equipment
- It is a relatively easy method to get right, and so many people can do this at home
- You can give it a try before spending money on equipment
- It allows for the preservation of some foods in a sealed, safe environment

Cons:

- You can never heat the food over 212 °F because that is the temperature at which water boils
- You cannot preserve certain foods using this method; if the food is not acidic, you must use pressure canning

You can see why many people use water bath canning in their homes, but it is crucial to remember that you can only use it for acidic foods. So many people are still using this for the wrong kinds of foods and putting themselves at risk of food poisoning. Foods that are above 4.6 pH are not suitable for water bath canning.

Below, you'll find a list of foods that are usually safe for this canning method, and then we will move on to pressure canning.

You can use water bath canning for:

- Tomatoes, although some modern varieties of tomatoes, are less acidic. If in doubt, get a pH testing kit, and add extra acid to the jar if your tomatoes are not acidic enough to be safely canned using the water bath method
- Fruits, such as plums, pears, peaches, and berries
- Jellies, marmalades, and fruit conserves
- Foods that you have added vinegar to. For example, pickled eggs, pickled cucumbers, pickled onions, pickled beets
- Fermented foods, such as sauerkraut and kimchi

You may find other suitable foods, but this list covers most of them. Do not try to preserve vegetables via the water bath canning method unless you have added sufficient quantities of vinegar.

Pressure Canning

Pressure canning is the best way to ensure that your food is free from *Clostridium Botulinum. This toxin* spreads throughout non-acidic foods and can cause food poisoning and even death in some situations. It thrives at room temperature, and although the bacteria itself is killed by boiling, its spores are not killed until temperatures reach 240 degrees F, which means that water bath canning does not get hot enough to destroy them.

Even at such temperatures, it can take up to 100 minutes for the bacteria's spores to be eradicated. You will need to pay attention to your altitude to set up your pressure canner for safe operation.

You will need to depend heavily on the dial gauge on your pressure canner to let you know what pressure your food is being processed at. You should have this tested every year to ensure that it is still accurate. A local university may offer this testing, or you may have to source a local business to do it. Testing takes just a few minutes and is not expensive.

Pressure canning is the way to go if you are serious about preserving large quantities of not acidic foods. It will let you safely preserve both meat and vegetables at room temperature, provided you follow the proper techniques and can them under enough pressure.

Note that a pressure cooker is not the same as a pressure canner, and a pressure cooker should not be used for this preservation method. Although it bears some similarities to a pressure canner, it is made differently, and there are no current guidelines on how to use one for canning food safely – so it is best to have a dedicated piece of equipment just for this job.

Let's explore the pros and cons of this method.

Pros:

- You can preserve all kinds of foods, not just pickled or acidic foods
- It is safer because it kills almost all types of bacteria and their spores
- You can still preserve acidic foods using this method, so it is suitable for all your canning needs
- You can sometimes process raw vegetables without needing to cook them first because the pressure canning process will cook these; This cuts down on prep time considerably and simplifies the whole process

Cons:

- You have to buy special equipment, so there is an upfront cost
- You must learn how to use a pressure canner safely, following the instructions; This can be a little harder than learning the water bath canning method because it involves calculating the pressure that you need to can under, based on your location, and then setting the equipment up accordingly
- Because it is more complicated and there is a greater risk of botulism due to the food being processed, there is more chance of the food being incorrectly processed and becoming infected with bacteria

Pressure canning is more complicated for people to learn at home, but it opens up a whole range of foods that you can learn how to preserve and allows you to keep vegetables and meats, and fruits. If you grow a lot of your food, this is one of the most viable preservation methods to enjoy vegetables out of season.

It means you do not have to pickle foods to keep them viable, and this massively opens up the range of foods you can enjoy throughout the year. Instead of eating seasonally or heavily acidic foods, you can enjoy pressure canned food of all types and know that it is safe to eat – provided you have followed the instructions.

Foods that are suitable for pressure canning include:

- Meat sauces
- Meats of almost any variety, including poultry and seafood, as well as pork and beef

- Stews
- Soups
- Vegetables, regardless of their acidity
- Mixes of foods

Takeaway From Chapter 2:

In this chapter, we've covered:

- The differences between water bath canning and pressure canning
- The advantages and disadvantages of each method
- Why pressure canning has some significant benefits when it comes to food preservation

In the next chapter, we will look at how you can make space in a busy schedule for canning food. It isn't easy to find time for everything that needs to be done when you're living off the grid, and you may find that food gets wasted more often than you would like – so we will talk about some top techniques for changing that.

3

Making Space In Your Life For Canning

"One cannot think well, love well, sleep well, if one has not dined well."

- Virginia Woolf

Life is busy for everyone, and it isn't easy to make time for everything we want to do, no matter how dedicated we are to schedules and time management. However, making room to can your food can save you time if you produce a lot of it yourself – because reducing wastage means reducing the amount that you need to grow, which gives you time in later years.

It will also help keep your indoor space-efficient because you won't have lingering vegetables that need using up or the chaos of trying to fit different kinds of foods into meals that don't call for them, just so that those foods don't get wasted.

Additionally, it will give you more freedom in cooking throughout the year because you will have the ingredients you want, not just the seasonally available ingredients – and those foods will already be processed and cooked and ready to go. What could be better?

However, it is still a challenge to make room in a busy schedule for canning food, so let's look at some techniques to help you start this process and make it more efficient. There is no doubt that it will take time, but you will save yourself hours in the future and prevent your labor in the vegetable garden from going to waste.

Tip 1: Set Aside A Day

Although that might sound like a massive chunk of time to suddenly dedicate to a project, it is essential to try and clear a whole day in your schedule for canning. There is a lot of work involved, and it is so much more efficient to do one big session than to try and do a little here and a little there. Because you need a sterile environment, you are better off working in big batches rather than small ones.

You will still need to do this multiple times throughout a season, but you can make your process far more efficient by creating dedicated canning days. If you discover you don't need the whole day, that's great, but at least you won't find that you are stuck in the kitchen at four in the morning, still trying to get everything finished because you didn't start early enough.

Early in the day, go and pick a good harvest of vegetables. You want to fill as many jars at once as possible, and it's a good idea to use freshly harvested vegetables. Bring the vegetables indoors to wash and cut them, and sterilize the surfaces you will be working on. You are well on the way to a successful canning session!

Tip 2: Work With A Tidy Kitchen

When you're canning, you need space. You do not want to be tripping over toys or fighting with clutter that has built on the work surfaces in your kitchen. Do not start with a kitchen that is in chaos. Before you even pick your harvest, make sure that your kitchen is clean and organized, and you have everything you need set out and ready.

This will make it so much easier to enjoy the canning process because it will massively reduce the amount of stress. Instead of constantly struggling to find what you need when you need it, everything will be at your fingertips. It cannot be overstated what a difference this makes to the canning process.

It also reduces any risk of cross-contamination. By cleaning the kitchen before you start preparing the food and the jars, you make everything more accessible and safer. Organization is key to home canning.

Tip 3: Skip Sterilizing The Jars

Many home canners mistakenly think that they need to boil their jars for long periods of time before adding food to them to kill off any bacteria in the jars. However, this is not necessary and eats up time that could be spent better elsewhere.

You do not need to sterilize your jars before adding food **if you are at an altitude of less than 1000 feet, and your preservation process will take more than ten minutes.** This is because the preservation process will sterilize the jars as it happens, ensuring any bacteria is destroyed. However, if your preservation process will take less than ten minutes, make sure you sterilize the jars in advance.

It is best to use this when you already have some experience of home canning. Sterilizing the jars does not carry any disadvantages and may feel safer to some, but it can be skipped if you want to save time, and your process allows for this. This information comes directly from the USDA's 2015 recommendations.[iii]

Do note that your jars must still be clean before using them, so always wash them in hot, soapy water. A clean jar is not the same as a sterilized jar.

Tip 4: Buy An Electric Water Bath Canner

You can use any large pot for water bath canning. This may be preferable when you start and get used to the process, but once you are a dedicated home canner, having an electric water bath can make the process much easier.

This allows you to move canning off your stove and to any convenient place. You can preserve food outdoors if you want to, as long as you have an extension cord. If your kitchen space is small or you have other family members wanting to use it, an electric water bath canner is a great way to make canning easier – and that makes you more likely to do it.

Tip 5: Don't Pre-Warm The Lids

Most home canners believe that they need to warm the lids up before canning, and this is just another step that makes the whole canning process slower and more complicated. However, it is unnecessary.

It used to be recommended that you heat the lids in water to soften the sealing agent. People thought that this made for a better bond and improved the seal between the jar and the lid. However, the manufacturers of the popular home canning jar brand Ball (also known as Kerr in some countries) say that their lids now perform as well at room temperature as they do when pre-warmed.

Make sure that the lids have been thoroughly washed and are clean before using them for home canning.

Tip 6: Keep Your Pantry Organized

As an ongoing way to make home canning a part of your life, you must keep your pantry or food storage space in order. This is particularly important during the canning season, but it is an aspect of everyday life and is something that you should get all of your family members involved with.

Ordered food storage makes home canning easier and ensures that food is getting used up in the proper order, rather than new food being used up before old food. Take some time to order your pantry before canning anything; this will make it easier to put away the jars after. It also adds an element of satisfaction that is important for home canning – a tidy, ordered food storage space makes you feel good.

To keep your food storage tidy, give everything a place, and make sure everyone knows what its place is. Label the shelves if this helps; it will encourage people to put the right things in the right positions and minimize the time needed to sort out jars and bottles. Being organized throughout the year will massively reduce the job you need to do before you start canning tidy up.

Before you start canning, check out your food storage space and look at what has got out of place. Pull old jars of food to the front so that you can slip the new jars you are making in behind them. Reorganize boxes and shelves, and dispose of food that is no longer suitable for consumption.

This will make the end of your canning process – when you are probably feeling hot and tired – so much easier because you will be able to simply put the jars on the shelves in the right places. The last thing you want is to try and sort out your food storage when you have just done a full day of canning.

Remember, if you need overflow space, you can keep jars anywhere, including in cup-boards. They will do best if kept in the dark, however, so don't store them on open shelves – but make use of other parts of your kitchen for home-canned food if necessary

Tip 7: Use Your Freezer

If you haven't got time to can things like berries immediately, you can freeze them instead. They will make good jellies, and you may not even be able to tell the difference between jellies made with fresh fruit and jellies made with frozen fruit.

This gives you more control over the canning process and takes away some of the pressure. If you don't have time to deal with food right away, make use of your freezer, and give yourself a break. Come back to it when you have a free day.

Tip 8: Enjoy It

There is no way to make room for canning in your life if you hate it; you will always find excuses not to do it. If you are struggling, sit down and work out what makes the canning process difficult for you. *Is it a lack of organization? Is your kitchen too small? Do you need fewer interruptions? Is your equipment scattered? Have you run out of space to put the food?*

Once you have identified the pain points, work on overcoming them and make canning more fun. Play music, involve your family members where possible, or even put on the T.V. or an audiobook. Get an electric water bath canner so you can free up the kitchen or sit outside, or encourage a family member to help you out with organizing the food storage.

By making canning more fun, you will increase the chances of finding time for it in your life. Try to start small and just can a few crops per year (or even just one) to not get overwhelmed by it. You can always build up to preserving other crops later!

Takeaway From Chapter 3:

In this chapter, we've covered:

- Top tips for making it easier to preserve food in your home
- Ways to reduce the time you need to spend canning food
- Ideas for making canning more fun, so you feel encouraged to do it

Next, we're going to cover some tips that should help you select a home canner, so you can get one that is right for you and then actually start doing some home canning.

4

Tips For Choosing A Home Canner

"When a man's stomach is full, it makes no difference whether he is rich or poor."

- Euripides

Getting the right kind of home canner can be a challenge, and getting the wrong kind of one can be disastrous. Home canners aren't cheap, so it's better to get it right the first time, rather than ending up with one you hate or wasting money and resources buying multiple different kinds.

So, how do you choose a home canner that is right for you? While you can use almost any kind of large pot for water bath canning, provided you can put a rack in the base, you must have a proper pressure canner if you wish to pressure can your food.

Which Kind Of Canner Do You Need?

The first thing to consider is the kind of canner you want. Are you going to be doing water bath canning or pressure canning? You will need to think about the types of foods you wish to preserve to make this decision.

If you are only looking to preserve tomatoes and fruits, you can buy any pot that is large enough to hold your jars while you boil them (preferably with a rack at the base to reduce the risk of the jars cracking). If you are looking to preserve other vegetables, you must buy a dedicated pressure canner.

We will cover top tips for helping you choose the pressure canner that is right for you and your family.

Tip 1: Think About Size

Size is probably the most crucial consideration when choosing a pressure canner. If you are a single-person household with small harvests, you do not need a big pressure canner. However, big is almost always better (except that you must work out where to store it) because it allows you to grow according to your needs.

It is only a little more work to make larger batches of canned foods. If you are already going to the trouble of canning four jars of tomatoes, you might as well can eight. Look at how many jars the pressure canner can hold, and then choose the larger of the two sizes you are considering. It is better to have too much space than too little.

You should also look at the kind of jars that it will hold. Pressure canners are usually measured in either pint jars or quart jars, but some are measured in terms of both. It is best to choose one that will hold both kinds of jars, as this makes it more flexible if you change jars in the future.

Tip 2: Think About Your Stove

Some stovetops specifically say that they are not suitable for use with heavier pressure canners. Make sure you consider this when choosing your pressure canner, and do not buy one that is not safe for your stove.

Read the instructions for both the stove and the pressure canner, and ensure that they are compatible with each other. It is not safe to use a pressure canner that is not compatible with your stove.

Tip 3: Think About Replacement Parts

It's always a good idea to check whether the manufacturer provides replacement parts for its pressure canners. Hopefully, your pressure canner will last you for years, and you want to know you can buy parts for it as they degrade, rather than replacing the whole canner. The gasket is a vital part to replace. Still, you may also want to have a secondary pressure release valve, so make sure these parts are available.

Tip 4: Look At Price

Price is often a huge factor in any buying decision, so don't forget to weigh it up when choosing your pressure cooker. Pressure canners save you money in the long term because they allow you to enjoy your food throughout the year and massively reduce the amount of waste, but they are an upfront cost.

If funds are tight, go for one of the cheaper pressure canners and start saving up for a more expensive option. You do not have to splash out on the costliest immediately, and you can always donate your current one when you can afford the one you prefer.

Takeaway From Chapter 4:

In this chapter, we've covered:

- How to decide whether to buy a water bath canner or a pressure canner
- Top tips to consider when you are choosing a pressure canner

In the next chapter, we're going to look at some of the commonest mistakes made when canning food so that you can avoid these when you get started with your canning journey and become a canning pro in no time.

5

The Top Canning Mistakes To Avoid

"Ask not what you can do for your country. Ask what's for lunch."

- Orson Wells

There is no getting away from the fact that canning is a somewhat challenging process, and when you first do it, there is a lot to take in. You will probably be very aware of the risks of making mistakes and perhaps a little nervous about the whole thing. That's why we will cover the top mistakes made when home canning, so you can avoid these common pitfalls.

Mistake 1: Not Washing The Jars

Many people assume that when they first open their canning jars, they will be clean and sterile. They are not. Canning jars contain contamination from the factory where they were made, and they should not be used without being cleaned first.

Your jar may contain dust, bacteria, and even tiny bits of glass. Always wash jars in hot, soapy water before you use them to preserve food.

Mistake 2: Not Adjusting For Altitude

It might seem odd that canning pressures vary depending on where you are located, but you must not ignore this fact. You need to add time to your canning process to allow for different altitudes. A good rule of thumb is to add one minute for every 1000 feet above sea level.[iv]

That means that if you are 0-1000 feet above sea level, you need ten minutes to sterilize a jar. If you are 1001-2000 feet above sea level, you need eleven minutes. At 7001-8000 feet above sea level, you would need a full seventeen minutes to sterilize the same jar that would only take ten minutes at sea level.

Do not ignore this; it is crucial to ensure your food is safe to eat.

Mistake 3: Not Removing The Air

Air will inevitably get trapped in the food when you can, but you must remove as much of this air as possible before sealing the jars. The air will add to the "headspace" in the jar (how much air is left at the top, between the food and the lid) and spoil the seal. Remember, you need a vacuum.

You should always run a plastic or wooden tool around the inside of the jar once you have packed the food in it, allowing the air to be freed. Do not use a metal tool, as this can scratch the inside of the jar and damage it over time. This increases the risk of it breaking in the future.

Mistake 4: Using A Bigger Jar

If you are using a canning recipe, make sure you use a jar of the correct size to know how much processing time it needs. Do not increase the jar size because it will need more processing time to be safely sterilized. You can decrease the jar size and retain the processing time, but do not simply increase the amount of food and expect the processing time to remain the same.

Mistake 5: Not Leaving Headspace

The amount of space between the food and the jar's lid is crucial, because this is the space that will form the vacuum as the jar cools. The space needed will vary depending on the food you are preserving, so use a recipe to ensure you get this right.

As a rough rule, leave an inch of space for low acid foods you are pressure canning, although some meats and vegetables require an inch and a quarter, or even an inch and a half. If you are using the water canning process, leave a quarter of an inch for jellies and half an inch for pickles and tomatoes.

Takeaway From Chapter 5:

In this chapter, we've covered:

- Five of the commonest mistakes of home canning, which apply to both water bath can-

ning and pressure canning
- Ways that you can avoid these issues and what to do instead

In the next chapter, we're going to explore how to preserve the different kinds of foods, so you know how to process the different kinds of harvests you might have.

6

How To Preserve Different Kinds Of Foods

"Let food be thy medicine and medicine be thy food."

- Hippocrates

Knowing how to preserve your foods correctly is crucial because otherwise, you will have a lot of food waste on your hands. You will also have a lot of time wastage, which is extremely frustrating, especially if you are a busy person. Whenever you are preserving food, think about its pH value and whether it is suitable for water bath canning or pressure canning.

We are going to cover:

- Which foods you can put in your water bath canner, and how to do it
- Which foods you can put in your pressure canner, and how to do it

Water Bath Canner Foods

We have already discussed that foods that are safe for water bath canning must be quite acidic and have a pH value of 4.6 or lower. You should not use water bath canning for fresh vegetables such as zucchinis, carrots, potatoes, onions, etc. You can only add these foods to jars for water bath canning if you also include an acidic ingredient such as vinegar – which is why pickles were invented.

To can these foods using a water bath, you should follow the method below.

Step 1) Check the pH value of your food and make sure it is suitable for water bath canning.

Step 2) Clean the jars and the lids with hot, soapy water, and then sterilize the jars if your recipe has a processing time of less than 10 minutes.

Step 3) Cook the foods if necessary, or pack them into the jars and pour the boiling liquid in on top, leaving the appropriate amount of headspace. Do not pour hot liquids into cold jars, or they may crack.

Step 4) Remove the air bubbles by running an implement between the jar and the food and then tapping the top.

Step 5) Use a clean, damp cloth to wipe the rim of the jar. Remember that sticky residue or any dust/debris will prevent the jar from sealing as it should.

Step 6) Screw on the lids until you meet resistance, but do not tighten too much.

Step 7) Put the jars in the canner on top of a rack. They should not touch the base of the pan.

Step 8) Cover the jars with water to an inch above the top of the jar. Do not leave the level of the water below the top of the jar.

Step 9) Bring the water to a full boil, and then start your timer. When the time is up, follow the directions for allowing the canner to cool and remove the jars. Be careful and do not burn yourself.

Step 10) Leave the jars to cool for up to 24 hours without moving them. Once they are cool, test that they have sealed. If the top of the lid does not flex, the seal has worked, and you can store the jar in a cool, dark place. If the top flexes, the jar is not sealed. You should place it in the fridge and use the food quickly because it is not safe for long-term storage.

Pressure Canner Foods

You can put many more kinds of foods in your pressure canner, and you may wish to add meat or raw vegetables so that you can store them at room temperature. Poultry, pork, beef, fish, and many kinds of vegetables are suitable for pressure canning. Follow the below directions for creating pressure canner foods.

Step 1) Clean the jars and the lids with hot, soapy water, and then sterilize the jars if necessary.

Step 2) Cook the foods if necessary, or pack them into the jars and pour the boiling liquid in on top, leaving the appropriate amount of headspace.

Step 3) Remove the air bubbles.

Step 4) Use a clean, damp cloth to wipe the rim of the jar.

Step 5) Screw on the lids until you meet resistance, but do not tighten too much.

Step 6) Place your jars in the canner and follow the manufacturer's directions about the amount of water to use.

Step 7) Lock the canner's lid in place, but don't turn the pressure control on immediately. Instead, allow the steam to vent for 10 minutes. This lets the pressure build-up, and it is crucial.

Step 8) When 10 minutes have passed, select the pounds of pressure required by the recipe, and engage the controller. When it is jiggling and hissing several times per minute, you can start your timer.

Step 9) Once the time is up, allow the canner to cool according to the instruction manual, and then remove the jars.

Step 10) Leave the jars to cool for up to 24 hours without moving them, and then test for a seal. As above, if the lids do not flex, they have sealed and are ready for storage. If a lid turns, put the food in the fridge and consume it quickly.

Takeaway From Chapter 6:

In this chapter, we've covered:

- Foods that can be canned using a water bath canner, and the proper method
- Foods that can be canned using a pressure canner, and the appropriate method

In the final chapter, we will look at some top recipes for home canning, and then you can give it a go yourself!

7

Top Recipes For Canning

"What I say is that, if a man likes potatoes, he must be a pretty decent sort of fellow."

- A. A. Milne

Knowing where to start with your new canner can be a challenge – so what should you preserve first? You might already have a crop in mind, but if not, we're going to look at two top recipes you can try out.

Recipe 1: Canned Potatoes (Pressure Canner)

Note: you should use peeled potatoes for this recipe and not leave the skin on; This is because potatoes with intact peels will need different processing times.

It takes about 2-3 pounds of potatoes to fill a quart jar.

Step 1) Peel your potatoes and chop them into 2-inch pieces. Place them in water to stop them from browning while bringing a pot of water to a boil. Boil the potatoes for 10 minutes, and then strain and discard the water.

Step 2) Pack the potatoes into your clean canning jars, leaving an inch of headspace. Cover the potatoes with fresh boiling water. Wipe the jar rims and tighten the lids gently.

Step 3) Set up your pressure canner and add 2 inches of boiling water to the bottom, along with the canning rack. Add the jars, close the lid and let the steam vent for 10 minutes before sealing.

Step 4) Calculate the necessary pressure. At under 1000 feet, you want 10 pounds of pressure and 35 minutes of processing for pints or 40 minutes for quarts. Increase this accordingly for other altitudes. Begin timing once the pressure has been reached.

Recipe 2: Canned Tomatoes (Water Bath Canner)

Note: this recipe is for 15 pounds of tomatoes and requires bottled lemon juice (not fresh) or food-grade citric acid.

Step 1) Wash your jars and lids.

Step 2) Wash your tomatoes and then dip them into a pan of clean, boiling water for about 50 seconds. The skins should loosen. Place the tomatoes in ice water, and then peel them once they have cooled.

Step 3) Quarter about 12 tomatoes and add them to a saucepan. Heat until soft, and then crush with a potato masher.

Step 4) Bring the pot to a boil and then quarter the rest of the tomatoes and add them. Stir frequently and boil for 5 minutes.

Step 5) Lift your canning jars out and dry them with a clean towel. Add 2 tablespoons of lemon juice or ½ teaspoon of citric acid to each quart jar (1 tablespoon of lemon juice or ¼ teaspoon of citric acid for a pint jar).

Step 6) Use a funnel and ladle to add the tomatoes to the jars, leaving ½ inch headspace. Release the air bubbles and clean the rims. Screw on the lids gently.

Step 7) Transfer the jars to the canner and add water to an inch above the jar tops. Put the lid on the canner and bring it to a boil. Pint jars need 35 minutes and quart jars need 45 minutes at an altitude of 1000 feet or less.

Step 8) Turn off the heat, remove the canner lid, and allow to cool for 5 minutes. Lift out the jars and leave them untouched for up to 24 hours. Check the seals, store all successfully sealed jars, and use up any that have not been sealed correctly.

Takeaway From Chapter 7:

In this chapter, we've covered:

- A recipe for canned potatoes using a pressure canner
- A recipe for canned tomatoes using a water bath canner
-

Conclusion

"If more of us valued food and cheer and song above hoarded gold, it would be a merrier world."

- J. R. R. Tolkien

Hopefully, this book has helped you get to grips with the basics of canning at home and allowed you to understand how this process works and which kinds of foods require which kinds of preservation.

Canning should always be treated as a science. Where most cooking allows you to estimate and guess your way through recipes, canning must be treated with more care. It is not okay to just go with your instincts and assume it will be fine because this will result in food waste and even in severe cases of food poisoning.

Always be careful when you preserve food at home, no matter how experienced you are. This book should have given you the tools to:

- Understand the different preservation methods that have developed over time
- Choose the suitable canning method
- Make canning an efficient and viable part of your life, year after year
- Choose the correct home canner for your situation
- Avoid the commonest home canning mistakes
- Understand the differences between water bath canning and pressure canning and how these methods work
- Complete a simple recipe for each kind of canning

With these tools, you are now ready to try your hand at home canning in your own kitchen. It is a good idea to start with a small batch, to begin with. Although large batches of food are much easier to do in the long term, starting with a little batch ensures that you don't get overwhelmed. It also allows you to test your method and check you are doing it correctly without risking a lot of wasted food.

It is crucial to check your jar seals 24 hours after you have completed the canning process. If a jar has not been sealed, place it in the fridge and use its contents quickly; they are not safe from bacterial infection. Alternatively, freeze the contents. Jars that have successfully sealed should be stored in a cool, dark place and rotated each year to be used up. Canned food is not preserved indefinitely, so label and date foods clearly.

With all that said, I wish you the very best with your home canning journey! Go and make the most of the food that you put so much energy and work into growing so that you can enjoy eating it throughout the year!

OFF-GRID LIVING BIBLE:

BOOK 2

The Ultimate Beginners Guide to Become Fully Self-Sufficient in 7 Steps

BY

BRADLEY STONE

Introduction

"Going back to a simpler life is not a step backward."

- Yvon Chouinard

Surrounding yourself with nature has been proven to boost productivity, creativity, cognitive function and positively impact our health overall.

In this day and age where we are super attached to technology and modern conveniences, it is hard for many people to tear away from the life-sucking, fast pace of urban areas to enjoy nature.

Of course, some make up for life in the concrete jungle by having flowers and plants in their apartments or offices. However, that doesn't make up for the lack of nature in our surroundings.

The living off the grid movement was triggered by a San Diego journalist by the name of Richard Louv. Louv wrote a book titled "Last Child in the Woods," in which he talks about how nature-deficiency in children directly contributes to the disturbing childhood trends the world is experiencing. These trends include attention deficit disorders, obesity, and depression in minors.

The 2005 book largely created an awareness that the absence of nature in kids' lives was impacting them negatively.

According to estimates by the Conservation Institute, more than 1.7 billion people live off the grid. In the United States, Home Power magazine placed the number of American families living off the grid to be 180,000 and counting in 2013.

A growing body of research suggests that living in nature can lower stress and blood pressure, enhance your immune function, reduce anxiety and boost your mood and self-esteem.

Living off the grid and away from the constant anxiety caused by overstimulation in negative news cycles, the bombardment of calls and text messages, and the stress of traffic and commutes can eliminate the direct causes of health conditions like anxiety and high blood pressure.

This book will look at how to make the transition into off the grid living, including:

- How to know if it is the right move for you
- What to expect when living off the grid
- How to identify the right location for your needs
- How to source for food, power, water, and other essentials
- The right mindset to have to live off the grid

You are not alone in finding the rigors of urban living overwhelming.

Famous singer John Mayer opts to live on a farm in Montana instead of cramming himself into the Hollywood facade. And he is not alone. Bruce Willis has a ranch in Idaho to escape from prying eyes that come with his job, and Micheal Keaton has a ranch in Montana to allow him to fish, hike, and canoe.

Tina Turner lives near Lake Zurich in Switzerland, while Woody Harrelson, the actor/environmentalist, prefers to make Maui in Hawaii his home.

You are in great company if you are thinking along the same lines as some of these greats. Although, to be fair, they are not living the roughing-it version of off-grid living.

It is hard to determine where the best place is for you to live off the grid and whether you should completely go off the grid or rely on some services.

Use this book as a resource to let you know where you can find the best off-the-grid living community in the United States and other places outside the US. It will also help you determine which type of off-grid is best for you.

This book will walk you through all you need to know about moving to an off-grid area. It will show the challenges without glossing over them because this is a life-changing move.

Nonetheless, the benefits are numerous and life-giving/affirming compared with the rat race of city life.

As David Russel aptly puts it, *"Sometimes the hardest thing in life is to know which bridge to cross and which to burn."*

The fear of walking away from urban living is real. But, the truth is that it is more natural for us to be surrounded by wilderness and nature than to be surrounded by concrete, pollution, and processed foods.

Let this book be a step-by-step guide to cross over to health and natural wealth.

Let's get into it!

1

Is Off-Grid Living The Best Choice for You?

"Building an off-the-grid home is one of the hardest but also one of the most reward-ing things you will ever do."

- Gary Collins, author of Going Off the Grid:
The How-To Book of Simple Living and Happiness

It may sound novel and even romantic to think of living in nature and away from the con-gestion of most cities.

The truth is that you are not the first person to romanticize the idea of living off the grid. But you must approach this lifestyle change with the full scope of the advantages and disadvantages.

This chapter will explore what living off the grid is and outline what to expect so that you make an informed decision.

What is Off-Grid Living

Off-Grid living means living a sustainable life while operating independently of the orga-nized electrical power, water, and sewerage grids.

Self-reliance goes beyond creating your utilities. You also have to:

• Home-school your kids.
• Grow your food and rear animals for consumption.
• Know how to attend to minor medical needs.

When you live off-grid, you are autonomous; therefore, you do not depend on the munic-ipal sewer systems, water, natural gas, or power.

That is the official meaning of off-grid living. But the good news is that you can decide your interpretation of living off the grid.

Here are the three options for living off the grid:

a) Roughing It

Roughing it is off-grid living where you **completely** go off the grid. That means that you do not rely on any of the government utilities at all.

You have your source of water, a septic tank for waste, and a renewable source of power like solar or wind. You may even choose to go without electricity entirely.

You may have to build a dry shelter, meaning it has no running water, electricity, or plumbing. You will have an outhouse for toilet use, a river, well or borehole for water, and a garden for growing your food.

Roughing-it usually means starting with a small cabin and creating a homestead to sustain the family's needs.

Your ability to refrigerate food is limited, so you only have to prepare what you can eat at a time. This type of off-grid living is popular with survivalists.

Roughing it is the extreme version of off-grid living, and you have to be ready to overcome these challenges.

Advantages of Roughing it Off-Grid Living

- You wholly reduce your expense.
- It is an environmentally friendly option.
- You learn how to survive using nature as a daily resource.

Disadvantages of Roughing it Off-Grid Living

- You are entirely cut off from all amenities.
- It takes time to become completely self-reliant to enjoy roughing it.

b) Half Off/Half On the Grid

There is the option **not to go entirely off the grid**. Instead, you can **rely on the modern infrastructure for some of the essential services you need to run your home.**

However, the reliance is not as heavy as it would be if you were in the city.

For example, you could use the municipal sewer system for sewerage needs but pump water from the borehole for bathing and cooking needs.

The combination of half-on-half off-grid living is entirely up to you and your needs. The point is that you will have moderate reliance on the government utilities in your area.

Advantages of Half On/Half Off-grid Living

1. You live more comfortably than roughing it.
2. Your expenses are still minimal compared to city living.
3. It allows you to test the waters of off-grid living before committing fully with your family.

Disadvantages of Half on/Half Off-grid Living

1. You are still reliant on municipal systems.

c) Modern Off-Grid Living

This is by far the most popular form of off-grid living. *You still have almost all the trappings of a modern lifestyle, but you choose only to use them to stay self-sufficient.*

Modern Off-Grid Living means your home has a way to harness electric power with generators, solar panels, or wind/water power. You will also have a pump to harness water from the underground water table.

Your home also needs a septic tank and pump to remove the waste from your home to the tank. That allows you to run your bathroom and kitchen the same way you would if you were reliant on municipal utilities.

The running water, electricity, and waste disposal systems that you put in place to live a modern off-grid lifestyle also allow you to use modern appliances.

You may still choose to grow your own food, rear animals, and make your own washing and hygiene products.

Advantages of Modern Off-Grid Living:

- You still maintain the same lifestyle despite going off the grid.
- It is cheaper than living off municipal utilities.

Disadvantages of Modern Off-Grid Living:

- It is expensive to put in place all the amenities to keep you completely off the grid.

How Do I Know Off-Grid Living is For Me?

It may be a good idea to try out the off-grid lifestyle if you are yearning for the following things:

Simplicity in Your life

How simple you want your life to be is dependent on what you would like. For example, simplicity for you may mean no more traffic jams and the hurried pace of life that comes with city living.

With the hustle and bustle of the city far away, you can enjoy the simple things in life like long walks/hikes, a peaceful day without constant and stressful text messages and calls, or more time with your loved ones.

Eliminating Reliance on State-Provided Resources

Over-reliance on state-provided resources can leave you vulnerable if any of these resources are not available for one reason or another.

For example, if there is a state-wide power blackout, you, along with the thousands of other citizens, are left with no way to cook, cool, or heat your home or even power critical devices and appliances in the home.

However, off the grid, you have your own power source from reliable renewable sources like solar, water, and wind. Your daily processes are not affected.

The coronavirus showed the world how easy it is to go from having plenty to being cloistered and unable to access even the essentials. Still, when you are allowed to go shopping, basics are missing from supermarket shops because manufacturers cannot produce enough necessary items.

Chicken and meat plants were shut down due to workers coming down with Covid-19 and that led to less production of these meats for urban dwellers.

However, those people living off the grid found that their food supply was not affected in any way. They were still able to have enough to eat and even a surplus despite the pandemic bearing down on the entire world.

This self-reliance gives you security allowing you to enjoy your life regardless of where you are living.

A Natural and Healthier Quality of Life

Many people are attracted to off-grid living by the idea of growing their own food and rearing animals for their consumption.

Which allows you to move away from processed foods and also to be sure of the quality of the food you are consuming. Unfortunately, you cannot ascertain the source and quality of food on grocery store shelves.

Homesteading ensures you eat fresh, high-quality food at every meal.

To Cut Down the Cost of Living

Living off the grid is very economical because you spend little to nothing paying bills or buying food.

The initial cost of setting up a self-reliant homestead may be quite high because you have to get your source of power, water, and cooking going. That requires capital to buy solar panels, dig the well or borehole and set up a septic tank.

But once the home is set up, your costs go down to almost nothing.

According to the website USNews.com, states like Indiana, Michigan, Missouri, Tennessee, Oklahoma, and Ohio, among others, are the cheapest states in the country.

But even in affordable places like this, life can be expensive. For example, the price of an average four-bedroom house in Ohio could be a little over $260,000. It seems like a steal compared to Atlanta, where a similar house could be as much as $1.2 million.

However, if you opt to build your house off-grid and homestead, you can eliminate that $260,000.

Living off the grid guarantees low costs and little to no surprise expenses.

Conserving the Environment

Off-grid living is excellent for the planet because you draw less from the environment and give back more. Off-grid homes, especially the tiny home trend, consume little energy, and you also end up living a minimalist lifestyle.

You do not need to use coal, petroleum, or natural gas, which reduces your carbon foot-print in your environment.

You also do not take more than you need. For example, without a refrigerator, you only need to catch fish to eat at one meal.

How Do I Test Off-Grid Living?

If you are still on the fence about this lifestyle, it is a good idea to begin by going on vacation at off-grid Airbnb spots.

There are plenty of homestead rentals available on Airbnb. These rentals allow you to experience off-grid living without committing to the lifestyle just yet.

It is an excellent way to see which type of off-grid living is good for you: Roughing it, half on/half off, or modern off-grid living.

I recommend trying out all three. You can rough it in an isolated cabin in the woods, and then try the half-on/half-off experience and finally the high-tech off-grid home.

The point of this exercise is to enable you to meet the off-grid living experience where you are most comfortable.

If after you have experienced the off-grid living vacation and decided which one you best prefer, it is time to reframe your mindset and attitude.

The Take-Away

- Off-grid living means you either do not use state utilities or limit your use of said utilities.
- There are three ways to enjoy off-grid living: Roughing it, half-on/half-off grid living, and modern off-grid living.
- Write down the type of off-grid you would like.
- Test out each of the three off-grid lifestyles before making the big move.

2

Finding the Best Off-Grid Location

"When you leave your old neighborhood, the city streets and business will almost instantly fade from your mind. The chirping of birds will replace the yelling of people."

**- Norm Geddis, Off the Grid Financed Land Online:
The Ultimate Guide to Seller Financed Land Ownership for Homes, Cabins, Hunting, and Investment.**

How to Choose the Ideal Off-Grid Living Location

Since off-grid living involves relying on the land, the ideal location should have the following essential resources to ensure you survive and thrive.

Water:

It is impossible to survive anywhere without water. Water is life. This may sound like common sense, but you may find yourself swayed by the low cost of the land, outstanding scenery, or other perks of the land that you overlook the inaccessibility of water.

There are arid places in the country where the land may be cheaper, but you have to haul water for miles to your property.

And the cost of getting water onto your property under such circumstances is astronomical.

Think of it like this: You may have to leave your home to go and find water. Sometimes for days and your home is in a remote area. Speaking from a security point of view, you leave the rest of your family vulnerable and without your protection. If you take the vehicle to get water, they have no way to move around.

Hauling water is not sustainable, and you are at risk of unsanitary conditions, disease, and dehydration.

The location you choose needs to be close to a water source, and it should be easy for you to get the water to your property. But more than that, make sure that you have a water storage tank and filtration system on the property as well. That ensures that your water is safe to consume in the home.

Climate:

Choose the climate wisely, ensuring it is weather that you can weather (pun intended), even at its worst.

Several things go into choosing the ideal climate for you. They include:

- Source of renewable energy.
- Health.
- Safety.
- Accessibility

Choose a climate that supports the type of renewable energy you intend to harness. For example, if you are keen on using solar energy, make sure your location offers plenty of sunshine for the better part of the year.

If you prefer hydropower, it is best to have a sustainable water source nearby. And if you want to use a windmill, ensure your location experiences strong enough winds to support the turbines.

It is also crucial to ensure that the climate doesn't affect your or your family's health. Very cold areas carry a risk of hypothermia. If you keep your livestock outdoors, you could lose the animals to cold weather.

In humans, cold weather has been linked to an increased risk of a heart attack. You are not immune to hypothermia either, especially if your heating system has a problem.

You also need to choose areas with a safe climate. For example, living off-grid in a location prone to hurricanes, flash floods, and tornadoes puts your life at risk.

Finally, ensure the location is accessible even in the worst weather. Some off-grid places experience landslides, cutting off the roads and rendering it impossible to leave or enter the area. That means you are trapped without a safe way out.

Building Materials

Living off the grid means you have to build a house to live in. Strive to find a location where you can access natural building materials to build the type of home you would like.

It is very costly to bring in other materials from elsewhere for the building.

So pick an area where construction is going to be cheaper. Depending on your preferred building material, consider a location that has:

Wood

Wood is necessary for all types of construction. Buying it from a lumberyard or a big box store is very costly. So, ensure that your chosen location has access to a wooded area nearby that can be a source of cheap lumber for building.

Earth

Constructing using earth is a technique as old as time itself. It is a building technique that uses earth, limestone, chalk, and gravel. Building using earth has lived through history, and in this case, you will use a mixture of different aggregates.

Did you know that rammed earth is found in many luxury homes because it is an excellent thermal material? It allows the sun to warm it in the day and releases the warmth slowly in the evening.

It is cheap to access the materials that go into rammed earth when you live near them. This low carbon technique requires the earth materials to be placed in layers together with a binder. The layers are then applied using pressure into a durable, hard surface.

Some people also use the same concept to create building blocks from waste materials derived from quarries.

Straw Bale

Straw bales have become popular once again in the west after being used centuries ago. For example, 400 years ago, many houses in Europe either featured a straw-thatched roof, or the entire house was straw bales. Even when European settlers first came to America, they would put straw on the teepees to insulate the tents from the cold, especially in the cold season.

In this age, straw bales provide excellent load-bearing structural support to buildings, and they can be used simultaneously with other natural building materials like wood.

Not only is straw cheap and available, but it is also an excellent insulation material because it makes the walls thicker. And the straw bales can be made fire-resistant making them an excellent substitute for wood.

Strawbale buildings are warmer in the cold months and cool in the hot months.

A big part of off-grid living is building a sustainable, eco-friendly home using natural building materials, including the ones mentioned above.

You will notice all the materials mentioned above were used centuries ago when human beings existed in tandem with nature and wilderness. They thrived, were safe and comfortable in homes built with these materials.

But you can have a modern twist if you do not want to use natural materials. For example,

Container Home

You can use a shipping container and have it refitted to create a wonderful home for you.

A container home is an instant solution, and there is little to no labor in the building from your end. You can place it anywhere on your land, and it will be immediately usable.

It can also be an option to use as you prepare to build an eco-friendly structure using natural materials. If you are relocating to an off-grid location with many containers, you may find the best way to conserve the environment is by recycling the shipping containers.

There are different types of containers ranging from grade A to grade D. For a safe and eco-friendly option, opt for grades A and B.

Access to Roads

Just because you live off the grid doesn't mean that you should become absolutely inaccessible. Ensuring that the place you choose has access to roads means that if you have an emergency, you can reach a hospital, police station, or fire station quickly.

Also, if your car has a problem, help can reach you easily.

Before delving into the best states to live off the grid, here is a quick look at the legality of living off-grid in the United States:

It is technically utterly legal in all the 50 states in America. But legal problems can arise when you try to install a septic tank that doesn't pass the health department inspection. Or if you decided to put a composting commode in your home that doesn't pass the building code.

However, there is a silver lining. If you do everything according to the book, pass health inspections and build your home and infrastructure according to the International Residential Code, then you will not have any problems with the law.

Here are some of the laws and restrictions you must be prepared for when considering off-grid living:

- Rainwater collections laws.
- Laws regarding complete disconnection from the electricity grid.
- Solar energy laws and regulations.
- Composting toilet laws and codes.

1. Rainwater Collection Laws

Rainwater collection codes stipulate that it is legal to collect rainwater in all 50 states (or most areas of the 50 states) if you are on private property.

However, setting up a rainwater collection barrel system is not legal. Such a system may be a violation of the local or state ordinances in the area. You may need to get a permit to engage in such an activity.

Before you settle on a location, it is crucial to determine the rainwater collection laws. Some states have simple laws, while others have a lot of exclusions.

2. Composting Toilet Codes

All the states have stringent rules and ordinances governing the disposal of raw sewage. These codes are found on the state or municipality websites, and they offer guidelines on septic tanks and sewage disposal.

Some states may allow a composting commode while at the same time being against an off-the-grid septic system. That is because the American building codes require that your living situation should feature a flush toilet that drains to a government-approved sewer or septic system.

But there is some good news regarding composting toilets for off-grid living families. An Oregon activist group by the name of ReCode worked hard to legalize sustainable sanitation systems all around the country. They drafted the code with the help of composting commode experts in the US. This code is now part of the 2017 Water Efficiency Standard.

That may prove helpful when it comes to composting toilets.

3. Solar Energy Laws and Regulations and Disconnecting from the Electrical Grid

You can legally install solar energy panels on your home and not have to use power from the state-provided electrical grid. In some states, you can utilize solar energy without needing a permit.

However, some states require you to have a permit before you can go completely solar. Some have rules about the placement of solar panels.

In other states, you may have no choice but to remain on the main electrical grid and pay a small connection fee even if you are primarily using solar energy. These laws may be in line with building codes, and they are more common if you are trying to live off the grid in an urban or suburban municipality.

But here is some good news:

If you harness more energy than you need, you can sell it back to electrical power companies for a tidy sum.

If you go to rural areas where building codes do not have an effect, you are less likely to run into stringent laws and ordinances regarding using solar energy.

You can find out if you can disengage from the municipal power grid in your area by checking whether the International Property Maintenance Code applies in your municipality. If it does, review the building codes for the state and the municipality. But if not, you have no hindrance to using solar energy undisturbed.

Additional rules and laws to consider include:

- How to build permanent homes because using a mobile home or a tent is against the law resulting in eviction and fines.
- The size of your house must be built to state size specifications.
- Restrictions on selling raw milk from your homestead.
- Restrictions that may arise about livestock.
- Disposing or use of composting toilet waste.

These laws, rules, and ordinances vary from one state to another. For example, in Alabama, the state considers harvesting rainwater to be a property right. This state even offers technical instructions and guidelines to help residents safely and sustainably collect water off-grid.

On the other hand, the state of Georgia has laws that highly regulate rainwater collection. It also stipulates that any collected rainwater must be used outdoors only.

That brings us to the best states for off-grid living with all the above laws and legal issues considered.

Keep in mind that there are laws that prohibit you from off-grid living in urban or suburban areas.

You cannot live off the grid in these areas, so it is crucial to find the ideal location for off-grid living. Living off the grid is better to pursue in the countryside. So, it is best to look for a state that has a rural county.

Rural counties tend not to have zoning laws, and you can get away with installing infrastructure like solar panels or windmills without interfering with government machinery.

Best States for Off-Grid Living

The top ten states for off-grid living are in the following order:

1. Alabama
2. Missouri
3. Georgia
4. Tennessee
5. Texas
6. Louisiana
7. Indiana
8. Hawaii
9. Colorado
10. Arkansas

These states are the creme-del-a-creme of off-grid living because they offer the most freedom to live off the grid. The cost of living is low, the lifestyle is sustainable, and they have an excellent off-grid living community, among other considerations.

They also are excellent and sustainable for agriculture, energy, and water.

The cheapest states are:

1. New Mexico
2. Louisiana
3. Alabama
4. Mississippi
5. Wyoming
6. Arkansas
7. Oklahoma
8. Arizona
9. Utah
10. South Carolina

From the property taxes to the cost of land, purchasing and maintaining land in these states is more affordable than in other states. That means that beginning the journey to off-grid living in these states may be more accessible if you are on a budget.

You may also find that shopping for food and other costs of living issues are more affordable in these states.

The following states have more freedom for off-grid lovers, including allowing you to build without adhering to a building code. They include:

1. Alabama
2. Tennessee
3. Georgia
4. Missouri
5. Indiana
6. Maine
7. Texas
8. Wyoming
9. Colorado
10. Idaho
11. Montana
12. Nevada
13. Alaska

Most of the counties in these states allow you to build a structure without a building code. That means you have the freedom to create a septic tank, composite commode, and get off the power grid entirely.

Some of these states, like Alabama, Tennessee, and Georgia, allow "riparian water rights," meaning they allocate you water if the river passes through your land. In other states, they offer you a "hybrid solution" so that you have several sources of water.

Finally, other states accept the prior "appropriation of water rights," which means that the first person to divert or use water for beneficial use can get full rights to that water.

If you purchase a new piece of land with a river running through it, you have rights to the river and its waters.

These states are excellent options if you want to build a tiny house, an off-grid cabin, a container home, or embark on natural building using materials like straw bale and others.

Here are states that have exceptional off-grid water access if you want to live in an area where you can not only harvest rainwater but also enjoy water sports or income-generating water activities:

1. Hawaii
2. Mississippi
3. Alabama
4. Louisiana
5. Florida
6. Kentucky
7. Tennessee
8. Connecticut
9. North Carolina
10. Arkansas

In these states, it is legal to harvest off-grid water, and some even go further and make it an unrestricted activity.

With no legislation curtailing water harvesting efforts, you can do a lot with rainwater and underground water as well.

If you are looking for states that permit off-grid agricultural productivity, here are the top ten to consider.

1. Florida
2. Louisiana
3. Hawaii
4. Alabama

5. Texas
6. Georgia
7. Missouri
8. Arizona
9. South Carolina

The climate in these states is warm with a lot of Growing Degree Days (GDD). GDD refers to the number of days that support the growth and development of plants during the growing season.

The more the GDD, the larger the period within a year you have to grow plants and the bigger your harvest. If you have large acres of land, the more GDD you have, the more food you produce per acre.

These are the states with the most off-grid power potential. If you choose one of these states, you can enjoy uninterrupted solar or wind power because of the availability of wind or sun for most of the year.

1. Colorado
2. Kansas
3. Nebraska
4. Hawaii
5. South Dakota
6. North Dakota
7. Oklahoma
8. New Mexico
9. Texas
10. Wyoming

You can take advantage of the natural sources of energy and live fully off the power grid, especially in states that allow the unrestricted use of sustainable energy.

Finally, you may be looking for a state where there is a large off-grid living community. Here are some considerations to look at. After all, off the grid is not an excuse to be isolated:

1. California
2. Oregon
3. North Carolina
4. Virginia
5. Missouri

6. New Mexico
7. Washington
8. Colorado
9. New Hampshire
10. New York

It may be harder to live off-grid in places like New Jersey, Illinois, Massachusetts, and Rhode Island, among others.

Off-grid living can become illegal in all the 50 states if you do the following:

a) Squat On Someone else's Land

If you plan to live off the grid, you must purchase the piece of land you intend to live off. It is illegal to squat in abandoned buildings or live off any land that may seem unclaimed.

The police have a mandate to remove you physically from the land where you may be squatting. It is not trampling on your freedom when the police evicts you.

You cannot build a home and infrastructure on land that doesn't belong to you only to have it torn down because you were squatting.

b) If You Disregard Building Codes or Zoning Restrictions

Zoning restrictions and building codes are not suggestions that you can choose not to abide by. If they are in place, it is mandatory to follow them to the latter to stay on the right side of the law.

Check out these codes and restrictions and ensure that any structure you build on your property is in line with them.

For example, it is illegal to dump sewage anywhere except the designated areas. Building codes stipulate what types of toilets you should have (flushing toilets) and how they should be built.

c) Fail to Pay Your Taxes

Even when you live off the grid, you still have to pay your taxes. Paying taxes is mandatory for all law-abiding citizens. If you have property, you must pay property tax regardless of how remotely placed your lot is. Find out the taxes applicable to your property from the state you are in.

The taxes also apply to livestock keeping, crop production, craft-making, and any income-generating services you may render locally. All income is taxable by the government.

The IRS is still watching you, even as you live off the grid.

Best Places to Live Off the Grid Outside the United States

Australia

Australia is a survivalist paradise. There is a lot of outback that can accommodate off-grid living; This is one of the places where you can completely get off the national energy grid.

However, there are laws and regulations concerning off-grid living in Australia. Each town and country has permits that control zoning and housing. If you do not want to deal with tedious zoning rules and permits, you can opt to go wholly remote, but that means you are away from schools, hospitals, and other critical infrastructure. Areas that do not have zoning rules and permits tend to be very remote and secluded.

Also, you need to purchase land for your home and get the relevant building permits from the local council. For example, one of the building requirements, if you intend to live off the grid in Australia, is that you must install high-volume batteries to store electricity from your solar systems.

This is one of the numerous standards and regulations governing off-grid power installations.

Some states in Australia have embraced off-grid living more than others. They include Queensland and New South Wales, among others.

The good news is that you can receive rebates and incentives from the Australian government for choosing to adopt off-grid living. Such incentives help to mitigate the initial cost of setting yourself up for off-grid living.

United Kingdom

The United Kingdom has some of the best country-sides in Europe: Picturesque, peaceful, and self-sustaining. It is legal to live off the grid in the United Kingdom.

But, be prepared because some local authorities may have special rules that apply to places of natural beauty within the locale. If your off-grid living interferes with such places, you may find yourself on the wrong side of the law.

If you are considering off-grid living in the United Kingdom, you must get planning permissions for the following building scenarios:

- If you intend to change the use of the building.
- If you intend to build something entirely new.
- If you need to make massive renovations.

For people that want to dig a borehole, they must carry out a geological survey to ensure the process is safe and sustainable for you and the environment.

Canada

Depending on the state you are considering, you must look out for local building codes, which vary from one place to another.

If you are building any house off the grid, you must have smoke detectors and ventilation, among other things. For example, you may be interested in leaving no carbon footprint; however you may not be able to achieve that because the building codes require appliances and devices that leave a high carbon footprint.

Canadian law doesn't recognize squatter rights, and their postal service doesn't play the off-grid seeking game. If you are off the grid, you have to find a way to receive your parcels or online purchases.

All companies need a legal street address which may be a challenge for purist off-gridders in Canada.

You also have to be prepared for property taxes and income taxes. You will find a lot of similarities in off-grid living laws and ordinances between the United States and Canada.

Polynesia

Polynesia encompasses the Hawaiian Islands, New Zealand, Samoa, Tonga, Cook Islands, and Tahiti, among other islands.

You can grow your own food, fish, catch other seafood and build using natural materials; because of the frequency of rain, rainwater collection is commonplace. Plus, Polynesian islands remain some of the most undisturbed areas of the world, so activities like fishing and hunting are not only feasible but sustainable as well.

Some islands may have more stringent building regulations compared to others. You also need to research and educate yourself on any conservation efforts on your island of choice.

Europe

Italy is a great country that sustains off-grid living in places like Abbruzzo and Torri Superiore. You can also enjoy the off-grid lifestyle in France in areas like the Mid-Pyrenees and Hameau des Buis. In Denmark and the Netherlands, you have options like Fertile Soils and Amsterdam, respectively.

Sweden has Suderbyn and Kolarbyn Eco-lodge, which feature island and mountainous lifestyles, while rural Romania is all about off-grid agricultural living. Scotland has several regions like the Findhorn Eco Village, while Northern Ireland has Leitrim. Inhabitants of both places are interested in reducing their carbon footprint. For example, people living in Findhorn Eco Village build their properties using recycled whiskey barrels.

Spain and Portugal also have excellent off-grid living regions Arterra Bizimodu and Tamera in that order.

If you want remote living, you have the option of Scoraig in Scotland, where residents live off the land and use wind turbines for power; This is similar to Tinker's bubble in England, which is a well-established off-grid community. Residents use solar panels and wind turbines, and no fossil fuels are allowed.

At Tinker's Bubble, you will find people are self-sufficient by developing tools and implements to build their houses and other vessels.

If you want to live off-grid and away from national utilities but still retain the modern off-grid living model, you can opt for Matavenero. Matavenero was once a ghost town that has been repopulated by off-grid enthusiasts, who have built amenities like a library, free school, bar, bakery,; They even have a community social media account.

You must put a lot of thought into the reasons for transitioning to off-grid living.

Five main reasons cut across the board for many people making this move. They determine the location they choose. They are:

To Live a Sustainable Life

If you want to be near nature and live a natural life where you sustain all aspects of your existence, then roughing it may be the best option for you.

That means you are not reliant on state-provided utility systems, and you find ways to survive in nature.

In this case, you can live in a remote area even with forest cover. But, it is essential to ensure that you are near a water source. That could be a river or the underground water table.

Look for a location that takes you away from the sheltered life you are used to and provides an environment where you can thrive off nature. Ensure that it enables you to build your survival skills, and you are safe doing so.

To Enjoy a Stress-free Lifestyle

In this case, the location has to be removed from the stressful urban influences. You can opt for modern off-grid living where you are removed from the city, but you can still enjoy the comforts that you are used to.

Or you can opt for roughing it where you cut off contact with your previous lifestyle and opt to live a survivalist life.

In both cases, you need to look for a remote place or community.

Half-on/half-off grid living may not work because, if you are still plugged into any of the state-provided utilities, you have not broken free of the stressful bills at the end of every month.

To Lessen the Cost of Living

If you are moving off the grid, for this reason, you probably still want to retain some of the modern trappings but just at a lesser cost. You may be best served by a half-on/half-off grid living or modern off-grid living.

In both cases, you still have access to the modern utilities that you are used to, making the off-grid life more palatable.

If you opt for the half-on/half-off option, you can use limited municipal resources like sewerage only and figure out how to power your appliances using renewable energy. You have saved on the high electricity bills you would usually expect at the end of every month.

You may choose to remain on the state electric grid but build a septic tank for sewerage and dig a borehole for water. Even in this scenario, you have saved on the water and sewerage bills.

If you decide to adopt modern off-grid living, you need to rig your homestead with pumps for pumping water, waste, and solar panels/windmills for electrical energy. It may be expensive to put all these amenities in place but once installed, your cost of living goes to near zero while you enjoy the same modern living you are accustomed to.

You also have to make off-grid living choices more often. For example, if it is cloudy and wet, you learn to make do with little to no power as you conserve the solar energy until the sun re-emerges.

That means you cannot power large appliances like a washing machine, so you wash by hand. Or learn other food preservation methods like salting and drying because you cannot use the refrigerator.

If you are interested in half-on/half-off, you need to find a location within reach of the utilities you still want to continue using. That means you cannot go very remote.

However, if you are going for modern off-grid living or roughing it, you can afford to go remote since you will be completely self-reliant.

But in both cases, you need a place with plenty of water and sun to sustain your lifestyle.

To Preserve the Environment

If you are interested in keeping the planet safe and preserving the environment, roughing-it is the best option.

Roughing it requires no state-provided infrastructure. You will learn to survive and keep your carbon footprint low so that the environment doesn't suffer.

Overall, when choosing a location, consider practicality and quality over price.

"The bitterness of poor quality is remembered long after the sweetness of a low price has faded from memory."

- Aldo Gucci.

The Take-Away

- Determine your needs to ascertain what is the best off-grid location for you and your family. For example, *do you still need access to schools, or do you want to homeschool? Does a member of your family have a pre-existing health condition? Are you interested in enjoying a modern social life, or do you want a complete disconnection from the urban social setting?*

- Consider your budget when it comes to building and standard of living. The quality of life in an off-grid setting can be determined by which state you choose. For instance, if you live off the grid in a remote county in Mississippi, your quality of life will be very different from if you were doing the same in Georgia or Florida.

- Research the climate to figure out what is the worst-case scenario climate-wise to expect. For example, you shouldn't choose to live off-grid in a remote place where tornadoes and hurricanes are common.

- Research local, state, and federal laws that apply to the off-grid location of your choice so that you always remain on the right side of the law. That requires staying up to date with lawful off-grid living practices.

- Refer to the list above for the best states and countries for off-grid living.

3

Types of Sustainable Off-Grid Water Systems to Consider

"What makes a desert beautiful is that somewhere it hides a well."

- Antoine de Saint

There are four main types of popular off-grid water systems that you can choose from. Unless you are living in a place with particular criteria for how you source your water, the following options should work for any off-grid lifestyle:

1. Wells And Boreholes

Wells and boreholes are vertical holes that penetrate the aquifer to reach and exploit the water from the water table.

A borehole is usually machine-drilled with a small diameter, while a well is sunk by hands and has a larger diameter.

There is a reserve of water underneath the ground surface that is surrounded by rock, gravel, and soil. The water sits in the pore spaces of the gravel, rock, and soil. This water is from rain or melted snow, and it moves down into these spaces because of gravity. As more water seeps into the ground, the pore spaces become saturated, forming what we know as groundwater.

The water sits in aquifers which are geological formations of soil and rock.

Boring a borehole or digging a well allows you to reach said groundwater, and it becomes your source of water. The digging and boring releases water from the aquifers, and they fill the holes created. That means that even if you use up the water in the well or borehole, the water from the aquifers will keep filling up the well/borehole.

How deep you have to dig or drill the hole for your borehole or well depends on how deep or shallow the water table is. The shallower it is, the less digging you have to do, and the deeper it is, the more you have to do. In wet areas, the water table may be shallow and deeper in arid places.

In arid areas, it is not uncommon for the water table to be as low as 1000 feet off the ground surface.

Many modern wells feature a pipe or casing in the hole and grouting at the surface that prevents the water in the hole from getting contaminated by surface water.

Things to Look Out for When Considering A Well Or Borehole

i) Location

Ensure that the well/borehole is located in an area away from animals or farming implements. The wellhead should not be accessible to animals to avoid accidents like animals falling in or defecating near the well.

It should also not be too close to a road, but it must be close enough to the house to facilitate easy plumbing connections.

Unfortunately, when it comes to boreholes and wells, there is no guarantee that you will hit water. Nevertheless, there are well-drilling companies that can perform a water survey of your area and let you know if you can successfully get water from the water table. They may rely on water maps of your area that show how far the water table is.

The most reliable water map is from the United States Geological Survey (USGS), which shows where underground water aquifers are available countrywide.

ii) The Drilling Method

There are primarily two drilling methods:

- Hiring a drilling company.
- Water witching.

Hiring a drilling company is convenient because the company comes with all the equipment and the employees have the best expertise.

As mentioned, the company can conduct an onsite survey to find out where the water may lie. This is an expensive option because you may spend $350 to $700 to acquire a permit and up to $60 per foot for the drilling.

In addition, there is the cost of installing a filtration system, pumping and housing the pump, and the labor. You may be looking at a range of $6000 to $7000 just to drill a depth of 300 feet. Overall, you may find yourself looking at fees of over $10,000.

You need to apply for a permit from the building permits office before hiring a drilling company.

Water witching, on the other hand, is a do-it-yourself way of hunting down water aquifers. The practice is also known as dowsing. You take a Y-shaped piece of metal or twig and hold each end. The twig or piece of metal will twist towards the nearest underground water aquifer.

You can also use two separate rods of metal, and if you are standing on top of underground water, they cross over each other. But make sure that the rods are L-shaped and held loosely close to each other.

Now, keep in mind that this is not a scientific method, so no data is backing it up. But, many people swear by it, and it has been a go-to method for thousands of years before drilling companies came into the picture.

Some people opt to drill themselves without hiring a drilling company. This may work if the land doesn't have any bedrock to drill through or very few rocks form a formidable obstacle.

If you decide to take this route, you will need to purchase some drilling equipment. Some kits are hand-turned, and some that you can put on a three-point hitch on your tractor.

However, remember that it is a laborious process to drill.

iii) Ensure the Water is Safe

Some water tables are contaminated, making the water unsafe for human consumption. Just because it is underground water doesn't mean it is safe.

You can tell the water is not safe if it has the scent of rotten garbage or eggs. That is an indicator that the water is probably contaminated by high sulfur content. Unfortunately, hydrogen Sulfide is formed within the ground, and it can make its way into the water table, contaminating the water.

Ensure that your water is tested to ascertain safety, including unseen metals like lead, arsenic, and mercury. These don't smell or taste bad, but they are deadly. Companies that test the water will offer the best filtration solutions

iv) Invest In a Pump and Sand Filter

The pump is essential to help you move the water from the depth it is to the house. Such pumps can be dropped through the casing in the well/borehole into the depths of the well. The pump will need to use power, so if you are not connected to the national power grid. It will require solar energy to work.

It may be a good idea to consider a dedicated solar panel for the sole purpose of running the pump when required. That means it doesn't power anything else in the homestead.

Before placing the pump, you must place a sand filter which looks like a screen at the bottom of the well. The sand screen prevents small rocks and sand from entering the pump and blocking it. Also, at the top of the well/borehole, you must install a well cap. This cap allows the pump's wiring to run safely down the depth of the hole while keeping the debris from rain runoff from entering your well/borehole.

The casing for your borehole/well must be at least 12 inches off the ground to meet the legal requirement for this structure.

It is not uncommon for people with boreholes and wells to utilize water pressure tanks. These tanks fill up with water and automatically cut off the supply when full. However, when you open your faucet, the water pressure is more because the water is coming from the tank instead of the depths of the well.

Water pressure tanks come with an air diaphragm that creates the necessary pressure to push water out and into the faucet with the normal pressure you are used to.

2. Springs

If your land is close to a natural spring or one is passing through it, that is an excellent water source. Water from natural springs is underground water that has seeped through the cracks and bubbled to the ground surface.

The good news is that springs can offer you a consistent supply of water, and they cost you nothing to draw to the surface. All you need to do is hook up some pipes and divert the water into a storage tank.

But natural springs are rare, and most affordable off-grid lots don't have them. Also, there are higher chances that the natural springs may dry up or cease flowing depending on environmental factors.

Things to Look Out for When Considering Natural Springs

i) Animal Coverage

Animals can smell water much better than human beings. That means that they may lead you to a hidden water spring.

Look out for footprints or your animal digging the area. For example, if your dog constantly comes through the door with muddy paws and snout, you can follow it and see where it is getting the mud from. Once on the site, you can step on the ground and see if water seeps out of the ground and also look around to see if there are any animal footprints left behind.

If you are convinced that there is water or a natural spring, you should dig around to ascertain. Insects and birds tend to also gather near a water source, so keep an eye out for them. Look for birds and insects early in the morning and late in the evening.

ii) Flourishing Vegetation

The water causes greenery to become lush, green, and healthy. Look for a patch of greenery flourishing and growing in a dry patch of land.

A small spring may be the source of the water supply to the green patch. Once again, you can test the patch around the greenery by stepping on the area and watching for any seepage.

iii) Look for Areas That Do Not Dry

Muddy sections without visible water sources may be the area where the natural spring is bubbling to the surface.

The water will bubble to the surface and then seep back into the ground.

Take a shovel and remove any standing water, then dig into the soil for a few inches. Study the place to see if any water will seep back and take the place of the standing water you just removed.

If you do not have any burst pipes causing the pooling water, then you should explore the possibility of an underground natural spring.

3. Rainwater

Rainwater is a leading source of water in off-grid living situations. Rainfall comes for a couple of months every year.

If you live in an area with adequate and consistent rainfall, you should have a lot of rainwater. This scenario especially applies to people who live off the grid in Polynesian countries or near a water body.

Creating a simple system of harnessing water will allow you to make this a consistent water source.

Things to Look Out For When Considering Rainwater Catchment

i) The Amount of Rainfall

Rainwater is the cleanest source of water that you can harness. An easy way to capture this water is to use your roof to channel the water into a storage area.

The amount of rain will determine just how effective this option will be as a source of water. If you are living in an arid area, this may not be an option for you.

Measuring the amount of rainfall you can expect in a year is simple: Use a rain gauge.

The rain gauge is a cylinder that catches rain to let you know how many inches of rain has fallen on a given day. If it catches one inch of rain, then only an inch has fallen. A standard rain gauge features a funnel at the top and calibration along the length of the cylinder to help you determine the amount of rainfall.

According to the calibration, one-tenth of an inch of rainwater denotes one inch.

Here is a simple technique if you do not have a rain gauge:

- Place a bucket outdoors during the rainy season to capture rain.
- Measure the diameter of the bucket at the level of the rainwater collected. (However, you must subtract the thickness of the bucket walls to get an accurate water diameter).
- Measure the diameter of the bucket at the bottom.
- Next, divide the two diameters by two for an average radius.
- Next, get the area of the rainfall by multiplying the radius by 3.14.

Finally, the rain volume is averaged by multiplying the depth of the bucket by 3.14 by the radius. Therein lies the amount of average rainfall volume; This is a more time-consuming and labor-intensive process, so the rain gauge may be your best bet if you cannot go through this entire process.

ii) Roof Space

The amount of water you collect depends on the roofing system you have in place and the size of your house. A tiny house may offer you about 125 gallons of water, which is enough to cater to your needs if you are alone or just two people.

A house with a larger roof provides more water catchment opportunities resulting in more water in storage.

Consider the roofing materials. You can collect the water from a shingled roof but make sure your storage tank has an inlet screen to filter any debris and gravel from entering the water. The asphalt composition in shingles is inert, which makes them safe for water collection.

Standing seam metal and corrugated metal are also considered excellent roofing options for collecting rainwater. Standing seam metal features an enamel or powder coat which ensures that the water is safe from zinc and aluminum.

However, corrugated metal doesn't have the same coating, so you must be careful not to be ingesting zinc that leeches off the roof and into the water.

You can test your water for acceptable zinc levels even if you are using a corrugated roof. Just because you have a corrugated roof doesn't mean it is the end of the road for your water catchment

Solar panels also make an excellent water collection surface. So, if you have solar panels, you are not limited in your rainwater catchment activities.

Rivers, Ponds, and Streams

Some lots of land already have a river, stream, or even a pond on them. That provides a natural source of water immediately.

But you must take some of the water to be tested to detect any contamination or other problems. Rivers, ponds, and streams may be contaminated by wild animals drinking from them or even from the underground water table if that is their source.

Things to Look Out for When Considering River

i) Animal Traffic

There are many waterborne diseases that wildlife carry and that can contaminate fresh-water sources. For example, Leptospirosis and Campylobacteriosis are carried by both wildlife and domestic animals.

Your pigs, horse, dogs, cat, and poultry can also transmit diseases like Salmonellosis, Yersiniosis, Rinderpest, Paratuberculosis, Anthrax, and Actinomycosis.

ii) Test the Water

Make sure there is no arsenic in the water. Arsenic is scentless and tasteless, making it a very silent killer.

Some facilities will test your water for free for a wide range of metals.

iii) Water Rights

Make sure that you know if you have any water rights before using the water running through your land. In some states and countries, just because the water runs through your land doesn't give you the right to claim the water source.

Of course, you may not be punished for using up a few hundred gallons of water annually. But, if you decide to divert the river or stream. You may find yourself facing serious legal issues.

The Best Way to Store Water

Water tanks are an excellent water storage facility if you are living off the grid. It can be gravity-fed storage. That means that the tank relies on gravity to feed the water into the tank so that the tank only sits there and receives.

There is also the option of an underground cistern storage tank that stores water directly from the water table.

Look for the following qualities in a storage tank:

Size:

You should choose the size depending on your needs. If you want a storage tank that fits in the house, you should consider a water closet tank; This is a tank that can fit through a 29-inch doorway, and they are portable. So you can carry them in your RV as you move around. This type of tank is used as an emergency water source in the house.

The alternative is using a stationary water tank is another option. This type of tank is used as the primary water storage facility. Stationary water tanks are typically plastic, and they come in various widths and heights.

The use of this type of water tank is to take care of the daily running of your home, while the smaller closet tank keeps more water to use in case this runs out. That means that the stationary tank gives you more storage space compared to the closet tank.

Design

You have the option of the underground cistern storage tank being specially designed only for underground use. You cannot use this tank for over-the-ground use because it will become deformed and may fail to work.

A closet tank is small and compact to make it portable and a good fit for indoors.

On the other hand, a stationary tank is designed with sturdy plastic that can withstand the weather elements, and it also takes up a lot of room. You need to create the best possible outdoor space to accommodate it to provide long service life.

A pillow or bladder tank is a low-profile collapsible tank that you can fit in crawl spaces. Most people living off the grid prefer to store fuel in it, but it can also come in handy for storing water occasionally. If you have to go and buy water or fetch from far away, this could be an excellent option.

If you have outdoor use like watering animals and plants, there is the option of a trough. A trough is designed to remain open, and it is easier to clean and fill up daily.

Material

The material used in making the tank is critical. Most storage tanks are made from plastic. It is crucial to ensure that you buy a tank made from safe plastic material. Look out for 100% virgin polymer as the plastic of use.

Virgin polymer is new and meets industry standards when it comes to the quality of resin used. The material is durable and robust, meaning the tank can serve you for long, even when placed outside.

Some plastics leach into the water, and that can be a health hazard. So, ensure that the plastic is not only virgin but also food grade. Since the container will come into contact with the water and the water will be used for direct and indirect consumption, this is not something you can afford to overlook.

Water quality will degrade if you use non-food-grade plastic storage containers. Particularly beware of BPA plastic. BPA stands for Bisphenol A, an industrial chemical that has been in circulation since the 60s and is associated with health effects on possible elevated blood pressure, cardiovascular disease, and type 2 diabetes. It has been associated with behavioral problems, brain development issues, and even prostate health issues in infants and fetuses, and children.

If you opt for a metal storage tank, ensure that it is corrosion-proof so that it doesn't deteriorate quickly and contaminate the water within with rust.

Specific Gravity

Specific gravity refers to the tank's ability to hold the amount of water you intend to store in it. Ensure that you choose the right specific gravity for the needs in your home. Storage tanks feature specific gravity from 1.0 to more than 1.9 depending on use.

The higher the specific gravity, the better the ability for the tank to withstand hydrostatic stress from the water within.

UV Stability

Many of the storage tanks on the market, especially those intended for stationary, outdoor use, feature UV stability. The manufacturer should ensure that no UV rays can get inside the tank. UV rays promote faster deterioration of the tank, which in turn contaminates the water inside the tanks.

UV stability is done using UV stabilizers that prevent the photodegradation process. Photodegradation is a chemical process that causes chemical bonds to collapse within the polymer. The stabilizers absorb the harmful UV light stopping it from interfering with the water quality within by turning it into harmless low-level heat.

Corrosion Resistance

You should look for a storage tank that features both leak-proof and corrosion-proof properties. These properties ensure that you do not have to keep replacing your tanks after just a few weeks of use.

It is essential to look out for these two qualities if you want your tank to last for a long time. These are the most critical qualities to look for to ensure durability.

Color

Color may seem like a trivial matter, but it plays a role in the temperature and quality of the water inside the tank. Darker colored tanks tend to retain heat leaving the water inside the tank warm to hot depending on the intensity of the sun.

If the tank is lighter colored, it will be cooler as the color deflects the heat away from the tank instead of retaining it.

Before purchasing a tank, it is best to know exactly where you intend to place it so that you can opt for a darker or lighter color.

If you do not have the time or expertise to seek out a storage tank with the above qualities, you can ask a plumbing expert to accompany you shopping and check your list of requirements.

The Take-Away

- Find out the existing water sources and collection options in the location you have in mind for off-grid living.
- Save sufficiently to be able to harness water and channel it close to your space.
- Ensure that you have your water source tested for contamination and safe human consumption before you begin to use it. That applies even if it is a freshwater source.
- Find out how sustainable your water source is. Even if you will rely on rainfall, it is best to measure the amount of rain to know if it is reliable and enough for your needs.
- Always have more than one source of water in case one dries up or it becomes contaminated.
- Educate yourself on water rights if you own a piece of land with a water body on it or running through it.
- Invest properly in water storage facilities that will hold enough water for your needs while also preserving the water quality within.

4

Sustainable Energy Options for Off-grid Living

"Solar power is the last energy resource that isn't owned yet-nobody taxes the sun yet."

- Bonnie Rait.

The beauty of living off the grid is understanding and enjoying sustainable energy. Sustainable energy is renewable, meaning that nature replenishes your source of power naturally.

For example, solar energy comes from the sun, which is a natural ball of energy. There is nothing that you can do to limit the energy that comes from the sun. Even when there is cloud cover, you can find a way to save energy harnessed for later use.

The good news is that sustainable energy options have a zero-carbon footprint. That means that they leave no adverse effect on the environment.

There are several sources of sustainable energy. They are:

1. Solar.
2. Hydro.
3. Geothermal.
4. Wind.
5. Biomass.
6. Tidal.

Solar Energy

Solar energy comes from the sun. This is perhaps the most well-known source of sustainable energy that is affordable and accessible to people that are considering off-grid living.

It involves harnessing power directly from the sun by capturing the sunrays and storing them in solar panels.

Sunlight is abundant in arid and semi-arid areas. You can also access it in tropical regions at certain times of the day.

Fun fact about solar energy: The amount of solar energy reaching planet earth in an hour can handle the entire planet's total energy needs for a year.

How Does Solar Power Work?

Solar panels come with a technology that converts sunlight into electric energy. When the sun shines on the solar panels installed on your roof, the energy is absorbed by the photo-voltaic cells (PV cells); Once the energy is converted into electrical charges that respond to the electrical field inside the cell. As a result, an electrical current is formed, which then flows out into appliances and for use around the house.

The electric charges are transported to an inverter that converts the direct current into usable AC.

You can use a battery bank to store some of the energy. A solar battery bank acts as an emergency storage unit for your energy, especially during those times when it is not very sunny.

You see, solar energy is not like gas or water, which can live in distribution lines. Once the energy is converted into direct current, it needs to be utilized or stored in the battery bank for future use. The good news is that if you do not have a solar battery bank, you can consider selling your excess power to a power company in an exercise known as net metering.

You can maximize your investment in your solar panel by net metering.

Look out for any incentives offered by local power companies or the government for people with solar power systems.

Some tax incentives include federal and state tax breaks if you decide to invest in solar energy as your home or business's sole power source. In some states, you can even get a rebate on past electrical bills just for choosing to go solar.

You have the choice of two types of solar panels:

PV Solar Panels

The PV panels are the most commonly used option. They catch the solar energy and convert it to electricity. These types of panels are usually connected to each other to form a large unit which is referred to as a module.

Thermal Solar Panels

These solar panels are installed onto the roof with the intention of heating water. Hence, these types of panels cannot power appliances but are designed to heat water.

They turn the sunlight into heat instead of power.

Even if you have to remain on the state power grid for one reason or another, thermal solar panels can be instrumental in bringing down your monthly electric bills.

When installing a solar panel, here are some best practices to follow:

➤ Find the best, long-lasting solar panels.
➤ You need a south-facing roof for the best result. Although it is not a necessity, it is a good idea.
➤ Consider a 30-degree angle for the best year-round solar production. If you cannot achieve 30 degrees, you can settle on an angle between 15 and 45 degrees.
➤ Install the panels vertically for better placement. Horizontally laid panels tend to protrude off the roof. However, both vertical and horizontal panel orientation is acceptable.
➤ Install the panels on a rack instead of laying them flat. The racks will tilt the panels at an angle of about 10 degrees. Panels that sit flat on the roof tend to trap water underneath after it rains. That can interfere with their operation in time.
➤ Only use a qualified installer to onboard your solar panels. Make sure they offer a warranty for their work so that you can call them if the panels act up. In some states, the only way to qualify for some tax breaks, your system needs to be installed by accredited installers.

Geothermal energy ties in with solar energy because it is the use of solar energy trapped in the ground. You can utilize this energy in tandem with solar energy, using them interchangeably.

Hydro Energy

As the word hydro suggests, this type of energy is harnessed from water.

Did you know that the 7% of the power that you enjoy on the national grid in the United States is generated by water?

Hydro is also known as hydroelectric power. This power requires you to divert the flow of the river or dam to generate power.

However, hydropower requires a constant, never wavering supply of water. That means that your supply of water must never run out.

Also, you have to contend with water rights in your area if you want to use hydro energy. It is one thing to use several hundred gallons of water for home use and quite another to divert the water source to generate electricity.

If you have water rights, you can use the river water on your land without any legal ramifications. But, ensure that you have prior appropriation water rights.

Fun fact about hydro energy: Ancient Greeks used water to produce energy for running the wheels on age-old grain-grinding machines.

How Does Hydropower Work?

When the water flows downstream, it utilizes kinetic energy to turn the turbines. The amount of energy generated will depend on the volume of water flowing and the elevation from one point to another.

The more the flow and greater the elevation, the more electricity you will generate.

The water flows through a pipe, and as it gushes out, it turns the blades of the turbine by pushing against them. As the turbine blades turn, they spin a generator, producing electricity. If you intend to use hydropower, you have to harness the water's power at the river's source, where the force of the river's current is at its highest.

The primary role of the hydraulic turbines is to convert the energy imparted by the moving water into mechanical energy that the hydroelectric generator turns into electricity.

For hydropower to work, the water has to be running fast or falling at great speed. Countries like Kenya continue to use hydroelectric power to power the entire country and sustain its economy. It is one of the countries in the world with a small carbon footprint when it comes to energy production.

Because water is a sustainable source, it can be banked on for as long as it is available.

However, you have to remember that, unlike the sun, which is never wavering, water can dry out, or the source can get depleted.

Here are the best practices to adhere to when using hydropower:

➤ Make sure the water source is sustainable. It is irresponsible to use water from a source that can be depleted.
➤ Check the local conservation efforts. If harnessing the water will cause harm to flora and fauna near the river source, you may land in trouble with local conservationists or conservation laws. For example, hydropower harnessing can cause low dissolved oxygen levels, which endanger the lives of plants and animals living in the water or around it. Dams to harness hydropower also affect fish like salmon by preventing them from swimming upstream.
➤ Make sure you use the correct turbines and generators to harness the power
➤ Harnessing water power is an expensive venture. Therefore ensure that you put away enough to build one.
➤ Make sure that you work with a small hydro system that can break down the air in the water to solve the problem of low dissolved oxygen levels.

Hydropower offers you three main advantages. They are:

• Low to little carbon emissions since it is a natural source of energy.
• Sustainability because it is a renewable source of energy.
• It can be a great way to utilize contaminated river water.

Wind Energy

If you live in an area with high winds, you may have the privilege of using wind energy. Wind energy is simply the power that is produced when the kinetic energy of wind creates mechanical energy that is then turned into electricity by a generator.

Wind energy remains one of humanity's technological breakthroughs that we can be proud of to help our planet thrive. The future of wind energy appears sustainable and safe because it releases no air pollutants.

Offshore winds blow more uniformly and harder than winds on land which means that if you live close to a water body, you may be at a greater advantage than someone on land.

How Does Wind Energy Work?

Wind patterns differ all around the world, and they tend to be modified by the presence and absence of water bodies. In areas where the wind is a lot, you will experience consistent wind power.

A wind turbine converts the wind energy into electric energy using aerodynamic force like the energy from a helicopter rotor blade. The rotor on the turbine is connected to the generator so that aerodynamic force in rotation creates electricity.

Wind turbines can be built on land or offshore.

There are two types of turbines:

- Horizontal-axis turbines.
- Vertical-axis turbines.

Horizontal axis turbines are the most common wind turbines that many people associate with wind power. These turbines feature three blades and are typically placed upwind to harness wind energy. The turbine pivots at the top of the tower facing its blades towards the wind.

Vertical axis turbines are omnidirectional, meaning they do not have to be placed upwind or facing a particular direction to harness the wind's energy.

An example of a vertical axis turbine is the Darrieus Model, which features the eggbeater design.

Land-based wind turbines can produce as little as 100 kilowatts to as much as several megawatts. They are the most affordable option, and they tend to be clumped together to provide bulk power.

If you are working with off-shore turbines, they can be quite large. You may be looking at one turbine being the size of the statue of liberty. These are the type of turbines that can be used for commercial or communal purposes if you have a large off-grid community living together.

They capture the powerful ocean/sea winds and use them to generate massive amounts of clean energy.

Small turbines, whether land or offshore-based, that are installed near where their energy is utilized are also called distributed wind turbines. These tend to be the small turbines that are used to facilitate agricultural, residential, and small commercial applications. They can even support small industrial use.

The good news is that if you do not want to rely entirely on wind power, you can use it in conjunction with other energy resources like diesel generators, photovoltaics, and batteries in a hybrid system.

Such a hybrid system works best for the off-grid living application.

Here are some best practices to consider when it comes to wind turbines

➢ Ensure that you have a space that is undisturbed by human traffic. That is why wind energy works very well in remote areas because they work undisturbed.
➢ Ensure that you build at a good distance from the turbines because some of this equipment generates a lot of noise.
➢ Carve out a place where the turbines do not interfere with your view if that is possible.

Biomass Energy

Biomass energy refers to the use of organic matter as a form of fuel in electricity generation. If you live in an off-grid area, you are lucky enough to have access to several biomass resources around you.

There are six primary resources of biomass that you can depend on if you are living off the grid in remote and semi-remote areas:

• Dedicated energy crops.
• Agricultural crop residue.
• Forestry residues.
• Algae.
• Wood processing residue.
• Wet waste.

There is also the option of using sorted municipal waste like residential and commercial garbage, paper, food wastes from factories, textiles, and leathers. This option will work if you live near a town or city where you have access to recyclable material and sorted municipal waste.

Burning biomass returns the carbon dioxide that was used by the plants during growth back into the environment. That is unlike burning fossil fuels which just release carbon dioxide into the atmosphere resulting in an imbalance in the CO_2 concentration in the air.

1. Dedicated Energy Crops

These are non-food crops explicitly grown to provide biomass. They are typically grown on marginal land, which is not suitable for growing food crops like corn, among others. Marginal land has little profit value mainly because of a poor agricultural profile or its prohibitive farness from human traffic.

Dedicated energy crops can be broken down into two categories: Woody and herbaceous plants. Herbaceous plants are perennial, meaning that they will continue being productive for over two years. You can harvest from them for two to three years if they continue to reach full maturity.

Herbaceous plants used as dedicated energy crops include:

❖ Kochia.
❖ Tall fescue.
❖ Miscanthus.
❖ Switchgrass.
❖ Bamboo.
❖ Sweet sorghum.

The alternative dedicated energy crops are the short-rotation wood plants. These are fast-growing woody plants that require five to eight years to grow and mature. Within this time, they help to improve the soil and air profile.

Some short-rotation wood crops include:

❖ Black walnut.
❖ Silver maple.
❖ Eastern cottonwood.
❖ Sycamore.
❖ Sweetgum.
❖ Hybrid poplar.
❖ Willow.

You will notice the above list features a mixture of soft and hardwoods. You can mix the harrowing and softwoods to balance their strengths. Hardwoods contain less carbon and are not as dense as softwoods which feature more energy with higher carbon content. Fuelwood, in the form of short-rotation woody crops, produces heat that can generate electricity for residential, commercial, and even industrial use.

Herbaceous crops have little to no woody content, but they have a high carbon and energy content. You must have a harvesting strategy for both the herbaceous and short-rotation woody crops.

That entails making sure that the plants are harvested on time to allow the possibility of regrowth during the growing season. Also, make sure that you have a plan to replace nutrients in the soil after harvesting to promote new growth. To do that, you should consider fertilizer application and get rid of life-choking weeds.

All the above, and more, plants have a proven resilience that guarantees you successive annual harvests over several years.

Dedicated energy crop material can be used in the following way to generate energy:

★ Direct combustion

Direct combustion entails burning the waste materials to heat water that generates steam. The steam turns turbines connected to a generator which produces electricity. The steam comes out of the boiler at high pressure to turn the turbines that rotate and drive an electricity-producing generator.

★ Gasification of the dry matter

Gasification produces syngas that is used to turn the turbines which power the generator producing electricity. You need gas turbines if you intend to use the gasification process because syngas is in gaseous form.

You will also need a gasifier, a steel tank that is carefully engineered to process the waste matter, allow the precise amount of oxygen, and create the best gas for end-use. Having a gasifier eliminates the human error that comes with trying to do this process manually.

Advantages

- You can make good use of marginal land.
- Combustion of organic crops is easy on the environment because of the carbon dioxide released is absorbed by the plants.

Disadvantages

- It can lead to deforestation as people look for hard and softwood for this purpose.
- You need space to accommodate a digester.

2. Agricultural Land Residue

Agricultural land residue refers to all the plant material left on the surface and within the soil after all the food crop has been harvested. The residue includes:

1. The stem.
2. The stalks.
3. The leaves.
4. Pods of the plants.
5. Husks.
6. Cobs.

Using agricultural land residue allows you to leverage the land without interfering with the annual cultivation, growth, and harvest of essential food crops.

Sources of agricultural land residue include:

1. Corn stover.
2. Oat straw.
3. Wheat straw.
4. Rice straw.
5. Barley straw.
6. Sorghum stubble.

Not only can you use these crops for personal biomass production, but you can also sell any excess residue that you may have to places like the local biorefinery or other off-grid community members.

That is a great way to generate additional income from agricultural products if you are an off-grid farmer.

There are several ways to generate electricity from agricultural land residue

★ Direct Burning and Co-firing:

This type of waste material can be burned to generate heat that converts water into steam. The steam powers a turbine connected to a generator which produces electricity.

But, you can also co-fire the agricultural land residue and fossil fuel which eases the need for coal. Burning this residue with fossil fuel reduces the amount of carbon dioxide and greenhouse gases produced by fossil fuel.

★ Pyrolysis:

This means that the waste is heated to a degree of between 200 and 300 degrees Celsius without oxygen so that it doesn't combust. The process of pyrolysis causes a chemical alteration of the waste material to create pyrolysis oil, a dark cooled bio-fuel oil. Pyrolysis oil, also known as bio-crude or bio-oil, can be burned to generate electric power.

The process of pyrolysis is also responsible for producing syngas which can be converted to methane, a better replacement for natural gas.

Pyrolysis also applies to dedicated energy crops

★ Gasification

Syngas is also produced through the process of gasification. The waste is heated to more than 700 degrees Celsius within an environment with a very controlled amount of oxygen. Carbon monoxide and hydrogen (syngas), and slag are produced from this process. The syngas is cleaned to remove sulfur, mercury, particles, and other pollutants.

The cleaned gas is used to power turbines that help generate electricity.

★ Anaerobic Decomposition

You can opt for anaerobic decomposition, which utilizes bacteria to break down the agricultural land residue and produce methane gas. The methane gas can be used to replace natural gas. The anaerobic activity must take place in an oxygen-deprived setting.

Methane gas can replace fossil fuels in heating and cooling your home.

★ Black Liquor

If you live near a paper mill, you can access the black liquor produced at the mill due to wood being processed into paper.

This is a biofuel that retains over 50% of wood's biomass energy. It can be recycled using a recovery boiler and used to power machinery in your home instead of using electricity. It can also be used to produce syngas that works to generate electricity.

★ Hydrogen Fuel cells

Agricultural land residue is pretty rich in hydrogen, which can generate electricity from stationary hydrogen fuel cells.

For example, the Yosemite National Park in the United States uses hydrogen fuel cells for electricity and to heat water. According to the United States Department of Energy, biomass can produce 40 million tons of hydrogen annually.

Advantages

- Agricultural land residue is readily available after every harvest season making it affordable.
- The waste produced doesn't compete with food production.
- It can be used sustainably in remote agricultural areas.
- It doesn't produce excessive carbon dioxide even when burning.

Disadvantages

- It works well for people who own their land, so it may not apply to modern off-grid living.
- It takes expertise to work with anaerobic digestion and other science-related areas.

3. Wood Processing Residue

Wood processing residue is material that comes from the woodwork in carpentries, mills, and lumber yards, among other wood-related industries. That includes residue like sawdust, tree barks, tree pulp, leaves, and roots.

The best part of using wood processing residue is that all the material is collected at one point as the woodwork continues. You can collect this residue from wood mills or logging cabins where there is a lot of wood being processed.

For example, in the lumbering process, the tree bark, shavings, sawdust, and trimmings are removed. They can be immediately used to generate electricity.

There are three primary ways to generate electric power using wood-processing residue. They are:

★ Direct Combustion

This is where you burn the wood residue to heat water that produces steam. The steam drives steam turbines which are connected to an electricity-producing generator.

★ Thermal Gasification

The waste is subjected to high temperatures (without combustion) in an environment with controlled amounts of oxygen or steam. The process produces carbon monoxide, hydrogen, and carbon dioxide. The waste must be carbon-based for this process to work, so softwood with high carbon content is the best option. Syngas is the direct result of thermal gasification.

The syngas produced runs a gas engine or gas turbines, which in turn drives the generator responsible for generating electricity.

★ Fast Pyrolysis

The fast pyrolysis process also produces syngas in addition to liquid fuels similar to diesel. Fast pyrolysis is the process in which the wood material is heated quickly in the absence of oxygen at temperatures of between 450 and 600 degrees Celsius.

The heated material produces vapors that are condensed to form biofuel. This biofuel is used to turn turbines attached to a generator that produces electricity. The best part is that wood is an excellent choice for rapid thermal decomposition.

Advantages

- There are multiple ways to generate renewable energy to produce electricity: fast pyrolysis, thermal gasification, and direct combustion.
- The carbon dioxide produced by this biomass is not too much, so the growing plants quickly reabsorb it.
- It is an excellent way of disposing of wood waste material that can cause wildfires if left unchecked in remote areas.
- You can find biomass combustions chambers that are self-cleaning/

Disadvantages

- The biomass boiler needed for the job tends to be bulky, and you also need a large space to store the wood processing residue waste.

- The wood residue must remain dry to burn efficiently, meaning you have to consider creating a storage facility.
- The boilers need to be cleaned out every week.
- You have to find a supplier for the wood residue close to you to reduce the inconvenience of going far and wide to collect it.

Sorted Municipal Waste

Solid municipal waste can be used as biomass material while at the same time keeping the environment in urban areas cleaner and safer. Because sorted municipal waste poses a continuous disposal problem for urban and suburban areas, municipalities are more than happy to hand this waste material to off—gridders interested in using them for biomass.

If you use sorted municipal waste as a biomass resource, feed the waste into a combustion chamber to burn. The heat released by the burning waste will convert water to steam which turns a turbine connected to a generator. That causes the generator to produce electricity.

You can also use the gasification and pyrolysis processes with solid municipal waste to generate energy, electricity, and other forms of power.

Advantages

- It is a cost-effective way to dispose of municipal waste in localities.
- You can utilize safe fermenting organisms to help biologically convert the biomass to biofuel.

Disadvantages

- Municipal solid waste is a complex mixture of all manner of waste that has to be handled with care.
- This waste has low energy content, which presents a problem for high energy production
- You have to invest in a highly effective anaerobic facility which can be expensive.

Other Energy Options

Tidal Energy

Tidal energy works by harnessing the kinetic energy found in the rise and fall of ocean current and tide. It is also called tidal flow, which can be converted into electricity.

There has to be a large tidal range. That means that the height difference in the high and low sea level tides should be significant. The more the height difference, the more energy you can expect to harness. The tides are determined by the gravitational pull of the moon and sun.

The good news is that tidal energy can be harnessed day and night, unlike solar energy, which depends on the hours when the sun is out, the same as wind energy.

Tidal energy is not your typical off-grid option for power generation. Unfortunately, tidal energy is only applicable for large-scale applications, so it may not be something you can explore if you are living off the grid on your own. Typically, it is explored for commercial applications. We mention it here because as research around it grows, it may become an option for electricity companies to offer to people living off-grid.

The tides hold a vast amount of energy that it is estimated that they can generate enough electricity to cater for a third of America's electricity needs.

How Does Tidal Energy Work?

There are three primary approaches to harnessing tidal energy:

- Using tidal barrages.
- Using tidal turbines.
- Using tidal fences.

★ Tidal Barrages:

A tidal barrage is a dam with low walls. It is placed at the estuaries or inlets where the tides come in and out. They work like a traditional hydroelectric dam because they feature sluice gates to create a reservoir on one side of the dam/barrage.

The barrage is securely fitted to the bottom of the sea/ocean floor, with its top peeping just slightly above the water at the point where the flow comes in at its highest tide. There are turbines inside a tunnel at the bottom of the barrage. The tunnel allows water to flow into the barrage.

As the tides come in and out, the turbines continually turn. As the turbines turn, they are connected to a generator which produces electricity. During high tide, the water covers the turbines, and during low tide, they may become slightly exposed.

The barrage is constructed with concrete, and they wall off the area where the turbines are located so fish and other sea creatures cannot pass through.

★ Tidal Turbines:

These turbines work similarly to wind turbines, with the only difference being the location. Tidal turbines are placed underwater, and they turn as the water current pushes against their blades.

The blades are connected to a generator that produces electricity for use. Because water is denser than wind, tidal turbines do a much better job of producing electricity than wind turbines. But these turbines need to be much stronger to withstand the density of water.

The good news is that, unlike tidal barrages, they do not alter the marine ecosystem they find in place because fish can still swim through them safely. However, they tend to emit a low hum as they turn, which may scare away marine life.

★ Tidal Fences:

The tidal fence is a hybrid of the tidal turbine and tidal barrage. It features turnstiles placed next to each other to form a fence-like wall. The fence also spins like turnstiles, and the process generates energy that is converted to electricity in the attached generator.

You can expect to see vertical blades on a tidal fence, and although they are close together, they do not form an impenetrable wall like the tidal barrage.

Tidal fences are typically found at inlets or where there are fast-moving streams. They will be completely submerged in water.

Currently, there are only nine tidal power stations globally. These are for research purposes, but as the technology surrounding tidal power grows, there are increasing chances of commercial energy applications.

The cost of installing tidal power plants is expected to decrease as technology grows. Maybe in the future, this may be a viable option for communities of off-gridders but with the help of power companies or major corporations interested in investing.

The Take-Away

- Choose the area where you want to settle with the sustainable energy source of your preference in mind.

- Do not be afraid to explore multiple energy sources and create a hybrid energy solution for your needs. For example, you may be near a sustainable water source, and the area also has ample sunshine all year round. You can opt to harness both solar and hydro energy.
- Consider your energy options according to your budget. But you can also opt to join an off-grid living community with an already established renewable energy grid to reduce the cost of having to do all the installation yourself.
- Do not waste agricultural land residue and other sources. Instead, use them for biomass. But be careful about deforestation, which devastates the environment.
- Tidal energy is a great option, but it may be out of range for regular off-grid living.

5
Nutrition and Feeding Yourself While Off-Griding

"I don't understand why asking people to eat a well-balanced vegetarian diet is considered drastic, while it is conservative to cut people open or put them on powerful cholesterol-lowering drugs the rest of their lives."

-Dean Omish, MD

No matter the settings you are in, on or off the grid, healthy nutrition rings true. Living off the grid is not convenient for most, but it has its perks that positively affect health. The beauty of nature and living off the land does something special for the soul. That feeling is hard to replicate in the urban jungle.

But then anyone looking at off-grid living is already ready to tap into that mystic of nature.

Even for the skeptic, there is no denying that waking up to the chirping of birds, morning dew on the grass, and a full-blown sunrise can change your perspective.

A breakfast of home-baked bread or substituted with corn, arrowroots or sweet potatoes, and groundnuts with a mug of tea laced with lemongrass picked from your backyard garden sure beats a Macdonald's breakfast on the go any day. The nutritional health benefits of such "country meals" are distinctly superior in the long run.

Besides, the level of activity you have to put in to make things work daily will get you fit and healthy. While a lifestyle of homesteading is no walk in the park and certainly not for the faint-hearted, it contributes and encourages healthy living. There is a lot of walking, hauling, pulling, pushing and other grunt work involved.

Bottom line:

You will find that you need healthy meals to sustain the life of a successful homesteader. And, even if you are not into homesteading, you cannot afford to live on junk food when living off the grid because of the lack of accessibility to fast food joints.

Living off the grid means that you may have little to no access to the conveniences that one usually takes for granted when living on the grid. These include things such as grocery stores where you can buy over-processed foods and fizzy sugary drinks.

But look on the bright side: It is the beginning of weaning yourself off life-threatening food choices and eating straight from the earth.

Successfully living off the grid boils down to meticulous planning and patient execution that ensures you have enough food to not only survive but thrive. In the process, you learn to tap into the natural resources and the bounty that nature provides you with and take advantage of it. Most people may think that living off the grid means eating less, but not necessarily. It often means being mindful of what you eat and that you don't run out of food. Besides, it is hard work to hunt, gather and plant food. You learn to be more careful with your supplies. No more unnecessary leftovers to throw away every night. You learn to cook what you will consume.

With proper long-term planning, you will be feasting on fresh vegetables, herbs, nuts, homegrown or hunted fresh meat, and fruits in season, all organically grown. In this chapter, we shall explore how you can eat like a king and have your stores full for a rainy day. Living in the boondocks can have you eating better, healthier than you ever did without compromising on the amount of food you consume.

Growing Your Food

If you plan on living off the grid, the convenience of passing by a grocery store and grabbing veggies and supplies every other day goes out the window. And, while you may drive to town once in a while to reload on essentials such as medical supplies, salt, matches, and other survival essentials, you need to learn to live entirely off the land on your property.

That will ensure you bring down the cost of living as you intended by moving off the grid.

A big part of happiness and healthy living off the grid is nutrition. So, now that the convenience store is not an option, what do you do for food? This is an essential question when considering living away from the typical urban setting. Initially, for most homesteaders with an urban background, this can be a hard lesson to wrap their heads around.

That is a massive leap and needs adequate mental preparation and plenty of research.

But, if you have lived a portion of your life in the countryside, that may not seem like a foreign concept.

While to some, the cavalier idea of living off the grid might seem appealing and even romantic, a lot of thought must go into it. It may, in some aspects, seem similar to camping out in the wild, but that is only a part of the true presentation of actually living off the grid and being entirely dependent on the land.

For many people, such romanticism is shattered when they run out of milk or meat goes bad due to poor storage. What if you run out of food in the middle of nowhere? Living off the grid goes hand in hand with learning to work the land.

But as Gordon Hinckley so aptly puts it:

"You can't plow a field simply by turning it over in your mind."

What can you grow if you had to depend on the piece of land that you are living on?

There are plenty of options that you can grow on your piece of land, no matter how big or small. But, before you begin mapping out the plants you want to grow, there are a few factors to consider and have in place to grow food successfully:

- Water.
- Compost.
- Climate.

Water

The presence of water and access to it is crucial to growing your food. If you are contemplating going off the grid in a remote place, it is fundamental that the property you acquire has or is near a reliable water source. That's because your survival will depend on your ability to plant and irrigate the food crops you need for sustenance.

A nearby river, lake, or dam can effectively serve as a water source. Alternatively, if the water table on your property is high enough, you can sink a borehole or dig a well. Building a water reservoir or using a rugged storage water tank can also help you trap plenty of rainwater during the rainy season. That provides water to help you make do in times of drought.

These water catchment options should be explored while scouting potential properties.

Also, look at the viability of the water source. Some sources may appear to be viable, but they fizzle out with time and use. Research the origins and sustainability of any nearby water sources to determine how long they can serve your agricultural purposes.

It is best to set an irrigation system that works for you for better efficiency and minimize the daily chore of watering your plants. Drip irrigation is a splendid way to irrigate your garden and is pretty easy to set up.

Drip irrigation involves delivering water to the plants by dripping slowly. Not only does it not flood the crops unnecessarily, but it also saves water. It is essential to use irrigation methods that conserve water when living in a remote area.

Compost Manure

The whole idea of living off the grid is to cut down costs to a minimum while still making your living space as comfortable as possible. Naturally, producing your food and having more than enough to survive on is a vital and integral process to thriving away from the comforts of urban living. For that, you need fertilizer. But why depend on commercial fertilizer that is expensive and sometimes may not be a good fit for your soil profile?

Instead, work to make your compost manure.

Fertilizers can be expensive and inaccessible when living off the grid. Making your compost will be sufficient for growing your plants as it enriches your soil with the correct nutrients that your plants can feed off.

Making compost is reasonably easy. All you have to do is dig a shallow pit and throw in organic matter such as plant matter such as twigs, leaves, branches. Throwing leftovers such as fruits, vegetable leaves, eggshells, and other organic material into the pit adds to the composting nutrients.

It also helps balance the carbon and nitrogen levels of the compost.

If you rear some animals, you can add the dung into the compost pit for an even more potent compost pit mix that your plants will thrive on. But, do not add fecal matter from dogs and cats because they contain harmful bacteria and parasites that find their way into crops meant for human consumption.

Thought out off-the-grid living ecosystems can be low cost after the initial expenses of setting up.

That's because very little goes to waste. Rearing some animals and growing your sources of protein also helps provide you with meat protein in your diet. Some poultry like ducks, chickens, and geese are very good foragers that eat and clean pests from your compound.

Chicken, for instance, will eat worms, grass, and bugs on your compound, while ducks such as the hardy Muscovy breed will eat mosquito larvae from stagnant puddles and rid your compound of snails and slugs. Over and above that, a chicken and duck coop will provide you with eggs and plenty of manure to add to your compost pile. Some vegetable leftovers, such as kale, spinach, or cabbage stalks and leaves, make excellent feed for chicken.

The chicken and ducks will forage for food, control pests, and eat your house leftovers while providing your household with eggs, meat, and manure. Just make sure you find a way to keep them away from your garden by using something like a netted fence.

Climate

When growing your food, you want to grow plants that are agreeable with the climate of your area. If you are in an area that experiences winter, then you will have to plan around planting in the spring and harvesting in the fall and in between.

Depending on the climate of your region, plants that have a short turnaround growth period are recommended. Here are some options to consider:

- Green beans (55 to 65 days)
- Carrots (30 to 40 days)
- Kale (55 to 65 days)
- English peas (50 – 60 days)
- Spinach (40 – 50 days)
- Potatoes (3 to 4 months)

While you may want to plant grain like maize, your climate may not permit it. Maize requires six months of sunshine to grow well and a decent rainfall to deliver a good harvest. However, if the climate in your area permits, then you can opt to grow the grain. Corn is an excellent grain due to its longevity in storage once harvested and dried.

Growing Your Own Protein

Maximizing the amount of land that you have will make your homestead self-sustaining. The beauty of homesteading is that once you figure out what your needs are and what your environment throws at you in terms of natural resources and inhibitions, you are in a position to plan better and become self-sustaining. While a sizable chunk of land is welcomed, one does not necessarily need a massive piece of land to live off the land successfully.

It's astounding what you can achieve with a small parcel of land as little as 1/8 of an acre (50 feet x 100 feet) in terms of food production. Not only can you build a sizable and comfortable house using locally available material, but you are also able to grow a survival garden that keeps you and your family nourished all year round.

But beyond that, you can also be able to effectively and sustainably grow meat protein sources by rearing rabbits, poultry, and goats. First of all, these animals do not require a lot of commercial feed and can live on pasture if you have the space to let them wander and forage for themselves.

Secondly, construction for their housing can be simple and highly efficient in allowing them to graze and feed on worms and bugs off the earth, such as is the case of poultry like chickens, ducks, and geese. If you don't have space and materials to construct a barn, you can build simple mobile cages for use in the summer and a well-constructed small coop that will shield your birds during the winter months.

Mobile Cages

These can be square or rectangle in shape and are ideal for the spring, autumn and fall when there is vegetation and plenty of bugs. When you cannot free-range because of land space constraints or lurking predators, this method of rearing poultry is quite effective in saving space, land management, and cost-effectiveness.

You can make the cages as big as you see fit, but typically, dimensions of 6-8ft L x 4ft W x 2ft H are adequate to house eight chickens comfortably with plenty of room to roam around graze and feed on bugs. The cage can be made from a wooden frame, covered with chicken mesh on the sides and the top with an open bottom. It is advisable to have half the top covered with an iron sheet to shade the scorching sun or shelter from sudden rain.

The cage should also have a drinker with fresh water and a perch to keep your chicken comfortable when they want to roost. The cage can stay in the same spot for several days. In favorable weather, you do not have to move the chickens at night as they can sleep there protected from wild animals.

When you feel they have grazed that cage area sufficiently, you simply drag the cage to the next spot of fresh grass and bugs for your chicken to feed on. In the meantime, the previous area they had been grazing on is left to regenerate and be ready for use another time. So, you never run out of space for your chicken to feed on and continue to grow.

You can make as many of these cages as your land allows you to and grow as many chickens as your space allows at a meager cost. That ensures that you have a constant supply of chicken and duck meat for your meat protein needs. When rearing chicken and ducks, you can expect them to be ready for butchering anywhere from weeks to months.

If you are homesteading in a small parcel of land and want to keep all your chickens contained but still foraging, you can also build a chicken tunnel around an area of choice on your compound—Along the fence of your compound is usually a good idea.

A chicken tunnel is about 3 feet high from the ground to the highest point of its roof and can be about 3 feet wide. The tunnel can be the length of your entire compound or a section that is most convenient. Like the mobile cages, the chicken and ducks can forage for bugs and nibble on available vegetation with the tunnel.

The tunnel can be connected directly to the chicken coop so that in the mornings, the birds can easily access the tunnel, and in the evening, they can make their way back to the coop from the tunnel without a fuss.

These simple yet effective homesteading methods of growing poultry kill two birds with one stone. They serve to protect your precious vegetable garden from invasion by your chickens and ducks, and they also protect the chicks from being preyed upon by hawks. The third angle to this rearing methodology is that they are less dependent on commercial animal feed as the birds can free-range within confinement for their protection and land management.

Rearing rabbits is another excellent way of producing your own organically grown meat protein. Rabbits are remarkably prolific breeders and are relatively easy to manage. They are another excellent choice for growing your own meat. Hatches are quite simple to build, and they do not take up much space. You can breed rabbits in several sections of your off-the-grid home.

If you have a spacious garage with decent ventilation, you can set up a few cages in there. An enclosed space such as a garage offers good protection from the cold winter months and can help you get started right away before building another housing structure elsewhere in the compound. Typically, one rabbit cage can house a large breed about 3 feet L x 2 feet D x 2 feet high. Cages can be constructed from wood, wood offcuts, or you can invest in some steel ones that can be mounted on chains and stacked against a wall.

They are an exceptional choice for growing your own meat because one female rabbit gives birth to a litter of 6-10 bunnies. Their gestation period is short at 28-30 days, meaning they can provide an endless supply of meat. They carry a pregnancy for only a month and give birth to many kits that replace the ones you may be feeding on currently. What's even more remarkable is that they can get pregnant again immediately after birth.

However, you want to rest your female rabbits for a month before giving them over to the buck. This will allow your doe to live longer and reproduce healthily. The bunnies feed primarily on hay and any other edible leafy greens such as those leftover greens from your food prep. The cost of raising them is very low, and they are not labor-intensive. Bunnies are ready for butchering within 5 months at a good weight of about 3kgs.

If you have five female rabbits and one or two bucks, breeding them means that you stand to have 30 bunnies at the end of 30 days. That is with a conservative survival rate of five bunnies in every litter. Given that a female rabbit can comfortably give you four to five litters in a year, all things square, you can have more than a hundred bunnies in a given year. You should never lack meat protein with rabbits when living off the grid.

Rabbits need constant clean water, clean cages, and be sheltered away from the cold or too much sunlight. Their primary food is hay and weeds, such as blackjacks. Rearing rabbits of the grid work well because they also provide your garden with nitrogen-rich manure.

Milk is another source of protein and calcium that can be quite a luxury if you are living off the grid. If you have a huge swath of land and plenty of pasture, rearing cows is an option. Then you won't have to worry about milk as much.

However, if your property is small, rearing a cow is probably out of the question. But goats are not. They occupy minimal space, eat a fraction of what a cow would eat, and they will provide you with meat and highly nutritious milk that is rich in vitamin A.

Goats thrive on pasture and brush and will survive even in areas where there is little vegetation. They are good foragers and require minimal care, and their housing is easy to construct with locally available material. However, they should be sheltered from direct wind, and their cages should be raised from the floor. The flooring of their housing should have struts so that their pebble-like manure and urine find their way out of the cage. This way, the cage remains reasonably clean and disease-free.

While there is always so much to learn when rearing animals, these animals are easier to rear, even for someone new to breeding animals. If you have them, you can be sure of a good supply of protein from their meat, milk, and eggs to complement the produce from your vegetable garden. So, as you can see, it is possible to live off the grid and still have plenty to eat. With adequate planning, you should have food that meets the nutritional value you require for a healthy lifestyle.

And who knows, you may even acquire new skills like becoming a great cheesemaker with all the goat milk supply at your disposal.

Rearing animals and growing your food organically guarantees that the food you are eating is clean and healthy, produced from compost manure, watered sustainably, and favorable for the soil profile you have.

Food Stock Expectations

When starting off-the-grid living, one must understand and account for the time that plants and animals will grow and become mature for harvest; This means that when starting, you must have a plan for the long haul stocking up, allowing yourself time enough to settle in and execute the strategies to start cultivating a garden and rearing easy to manage animals

You can stock up your pantry with canned foods, powdered milk, and preserved meat such as beef jerky to help you make the transition as you start to grow your produce in the homestead. The first harvests may not be as bountiful as you would want due to many factors. The soil in your garden may not be as rich when you first start, but that improves as you till and start growing crops using compost.

You may also be a complete novice in growing plants and rearing animals. But through research and learning from your mistakes, you will soon become quite adept at what to do; and when to do it, leading to better yield down the road.

All things considered, even in the beginning, the food supply from your homestead should sustain you sufficiently if you have made the above plans for food.

In fact, as you begin to sustain yourself from food grown and reared in the homestead, you will quickly realize that producing the food is not the most significant challenge when you have all the essential resources such as water, compost, and good seed quality.

The main challenge becomes how to preserve surplus food so that it keeps during the summer and into the winter.

As you depend on your garden for food sustenance, you must learn how to plant in a cycle that keeps your garden feeding you consistently for as long as the weather seasons will allow. For instance, allocating two portions for lettuce and planting them three weeks apart is a good idea.

Why is that? That's because the first portion will be ready for harvest in 30 days.

When the first portion is ready, you can harvest from the garden directly as you need by plucking the amount you need for the day while leaving the rest in the garden. By 3 weeks, you may have depleted the first portion, and by then, the next portion is ready for harvesting.

If you plant kales, spinach, broccoli, cauliflower, cabbage, and lettuce at the same time, the lettuce and spinach will be ready before all the others. By the time you and your family finish consuming the lettuces, the kales should be about ready at 55- 65days. By the time you are done with those, the cabbages are fully grown at 70 days and ready for consumption. In between, carrots, onion, and tomatoes also come to maturity for flavoring your meals and providing excellent nutrition for you and your family.

So as you can see, you can have plenty to eat from your garden if you plant as soon as spring hits. A well-planned and successful off-the-grid garden ensures produce does not all yield at the same time.

Being off-grid is all well and good when the climate is favorable, and your garden has plenty of food. But the question begs, what do you do when the weather turns, and your garden cannot produce such bounty? This is where natural food preservation methods come in to save the day and keep you alive at a time of scarcity.

Besides, you need to understand food storage to prepare for eventualities like drought, locust invasions, or floods which you have no control over.

So how can you naturally preserve some of the bounty harvest experienced when the weather is favorable to carry over to the lean times of drought or winter, depending on which region you live in?

Borrow a leaf from ancient civilizations that did not have the benefit of hi-tech technology such as refrigeration to preserve their food; Their reliance on natural methods guaranteed that they remained well-fed even during lean seasons.

When living off the grid, these natural methods are still practical and very applicable even today in helping you keep your food stockpile high, especially when the weather is not favorable for gardening. These methods are as described below.

Canning

For most people, canning is the most popular way of preserving food. The fortunate thing is that today, there are numerous "indefinitely reusable" canning lid options on the market that make this process a whole lot easier.

The idea behind canning food is simple yet fairly effective. Canning food works under the premise that when items such as partially cooked vegetables, fruits, meats, jams, soups, or milk are stored in an airtight jar. It is boiled long enough to kill anything inside that could spoil the contents; the items can keep for a long duration of time.

Canning food items works for the most part. However, when not done correctly, there is the concern of contracting botulism; This is a rare disease that is caused by bacteria known as Clostridium botulinum. The disease causes difficulty breathing, muscle paralysis and can be fatal.

The bacteria thrive in low oxygen conditions like the inside of canning jars. Fortunately, it cannot survive in sugar, acidic solution, or salt; This is the reason why some foods like jam and salsa can be safely canned in boiling water. Items like meats, vegetables, and soups must be sterilized in the higher temperatures of a pressure cooker to ascertain safety. When living off the grid, you want to have a trusted source or manual on how to safely can your food for long-term off-grid storage.

Going to local farmer's markets can help you learn a thing or two from local farmers who bring their canned goods to sell. Make a farm visit to see the process or take an online course before you make a move to your off-grid home.

Smoking / Salting / Drying

There are two methods of food preservation through smoking: Hot or cold smoking. When living off the grid, butchering an animal should occur perhaps once a week to sustain your protein nutritional needs. Simply because most off-grid living will have no refrigeration, smoking is the next best option for preserving meat.

During hot smoking, the meat is salted and hung in the kitchen rafters to dry and get smoked. The process begins with salting which helps draw water out of the meat. Hot smoking also means that the meat will cook as it is smoked. Salt and the smoke permeate the meat, speeding the drying process and bringing a slight acidic element to the flesh and that helps the meat to keep for long.

Cold smoking means exposing the meat to cool smoke, and the meat does not cook. However, it needs to go through a curing process to enable it to be kept for long.

Drying can be done on a table out in the sun. Just be sure to tie or hood the meat properly on the table to prevent hawks from clawing and flying away with it as it dries out in the open.

Pickling

This age-old art is terrific for preserving vegetables. However, like canning, it poses the danger of causing Botulism. The ingredients used in pickling usually include salt, water, vinegar (acetic acid), sugar, and spices.

The pickling process is pretty straightforward. The food should be cleaned, peeled, and diced, or sliced where necessary, then immersed in a brine solution containing vinegar. Be sure to have a reliable resource on the process to ensure that you get it right and your food keeps without going bad. Equally important, you want to get the process right so that you don't contact Botulism after consuming a pickled batch of vegetables.

Well stipulated instructions on quantities and ratios from a reliable source will help you achieve the correct pH of 4.6 that pickled storage should have. With that pH, the bacteria Clostridium botulinum has zero chance of survival. It is best to go to a cooking class to learn some of these life skills before moving to off-grid living. The reason for that is because you do not have the luxury of learning on the job due to the wastage and risk of getting ill from poorly pickled veggies.

Only firm and almost ripe fruit or vegetables should be pickled. To give them a good chance at staying preserved, they should not have blemishes such as rot or mold. Below are vegetables from your garden that can be pickled for off-grid storage:

- Asparagus.
- Beetroot.
- Pears.
- Peaches.
- Figs.
- Garlic.
- Capsicums and chilies.
- Cauliflower.

- Cucumber and gherkins.
- Tomatoes.
- Onions.

During winter, stored food keeps well because the temperatures are low anyway. In areas with barely any winter, and there is sun almost all year round, you can harness solar energy to run a low-tech refrigeration unit.

Root Cellar

Root cellars are underground or partially underground cold damp rooms in which some select foods store very well. Foods that keep well in a root cellar include:

- Pears.
- Potatoes.
- Rutabagas.
- Turnips.
- Radishes.
- Apples.
- Beets.
- Broccoli.
- Brussels Sprouts.
- Cabbage.
- Carrots.
- Artichokes.
- Leaks.
- Parsnips.

Dry Storage

Dried items such as onions, dried chilies, grains in protective containers, and sweet potatoes can be kept in a dry and cool pantry.

Honey

Storing fruits is just as critical as preserving meat and vegetables. Having a good supply of honey in your homestead will serve many purposes for creating tonics that you can use in the home. It is also helpful in the preservation of fruits when you are off the grid. If you have a freezer in your home, you can glaze the fruit of choice with honey and then freeze it for long-term storage.

Feed Yourself Without Relying on Power

If you do not have electric power in your homestead, a pantry and a root cellar will help you preserve your produce from the garden both in the summer months as well as in winter. As we noted earlier, food preservation in winter is much easier because the temperatures are already low. Therefore, food keeps for longer.

Planting nutritious crops in your garden that overlap each other is the best way to ensure food safety. Apart from your pantry and root cellar that you can use to store your surplus, you can live off the land by picking what you need while leaving the rest in the garden to be consumed another day.

Drying meats, smoking, and salting is another effective way of preserving food for the long term without using power.

Living Off the Land

Living off the land is dependent on where you are settled. Various geographical areas have different advantages and disadvantages to be exploited and overcome. Your property may mean that you have abundant wildlife to hunt, including wild geese, ducks, fish, or deer. It may also mean that there are plenty of fruits, berries, and mushrooms to be harvested just because of the climate and ecosystem that surrounds you.

In other areas, off-gridding may mean farming a garden and rearing animals for your diet and nutrition. In both scenarios, you are living off the land. However, by default, off-gridding means that different weather seasons may offer plenty of food to eat and scarcity in others. The key to living off the land is to know how to spread out your food resources when there is plenty in a way that they carry over to the period of scarcity.

This applies whether you are hunting and gathering or farming crops and rearing animals for your subsistence. Nature can be harsh, but it's also very generous once you learn to understand and work with its laws.

For most people, the discovery of how nature works and the generosity it possesses is often a refreshing revelation once they move off the grid. It makes you wonder why you did not make the switch from city dwellings to the off-grid living way earlier.

The Take-Away

• Part of successful off-grid living is being prepared to become self-sufficient when it comes to feeding yourself.

- Proper long term planning will keep you on a sustainable fresh food supply for a long time
- Consider the climate, ability to compost, and water source situation of your location if you grow your food.
- You can grow crops and rear animals
- Find out about laws governing farming and farm produce in your locale. For example, it is illegal to sell milk from your homesteading venture to other people around you.
- Research on the best food preservation option for your location. For example, drying may not work for wet areas, but salting might.
- Choose the type of food you plant carefully with consideration of the climate and weather. Also, put a lot of thought into the storage options you go with. That will ensure the food remains safe for you and your family's consumption.
- Prepare for living off the land by taking classes on food storage and best planting practices to keep your soil productive for longer. Do not move to an off-grid location without this essential know-how. Investing in this knowledge is investing in your survival.

6

Heating and Cooling Your Off-Grid Space Efficiently

"The sun—that power plant in the sky—bathes Earth in ample energy to fulfill all the world's power needs many times over. It doesn't fire off carbon dioxide emissions. It won't run out. And it is free."

- Susannah Locke

Throughout the year, you need cooling and heating to stay comfortably in the house. That applies even when you are living off the grid. So how do you live off the grid with the comfort of everyday cooling and heating through all seasons?

There are five ways to have the best heating and cooling while living an off-grid lifestyle. They include:

- Passive solar design
- Solar-powered air conditioners and heating pumps
- Roman-style water cooling
- Ground cooling loops
- Heating and Cooling by Passive Solar Design

Let's start with the passive solar design because it is by far the simplest option. To begin with, all you have to do is consider the placement of the windows in your space.

Heating and Cooling with Passive Solar Design

Earlier, this book highlighted how you could place the solar panels on the south side of your roof to capture the most solar energy. Now you can place fewer windows on that side and have plant cover to prevent the sun's heat from overwhelming you.

If you get this placement correct, you do not have to worry about cooling because the sun will always stay in the same place, and your house isn't moving either.

All you have to do is to minimize energy use without having to expend any other energy. Good design and insulation in the walls alone can keep a building cool and comfortable.

Use temperature regulating materials to help you control the temperature in your house.

Here are four elements of passive solar design for this approach to cooling and heating to be successful.

#1 Properly Oriented Windows

It is best to have the windows facing off the true south by five to ten degrees. That means the solar efficiency of the window decreases, leaving the house a lot cooler.

If your windows are within 30 degrees of the south-facing face, you are likely to experience a lot of heat between 9 am and 3 pm. To mitigate the heat during summer, you can use trees and plant cover to shade the area.

To make the most of natural light, you should consider north-facing windows. But for comfortable heating and warmth, a southwest-facing window orientation will work well. This orientation combines a little sun and warmth that filters in from the south and soft light and cool temperatures from the west. As a result, you can enjoy a temperature-regulated space.

Depending on how you would like to regulate the temperature in your home, here is a small guide to follow in window orientation.

North facing windows: This window orientation means that you have little to no sun coming into the house. The space will be evenly lit, but it will also appear darker than other rooms in the house. If you do not want to experience too much sun, this is the perfect window placement.

South-facing windows: This orientation floods your house with tons of sunlight and warmth. It makes the space the brightest and hottest in the daytime. You can expect the temperature to be high in your house if you have some south-facing windows.

East/West facing windows: The sunlight pours through east and west-facing windows early in the morning and evening as the sun rises and sets. However, during the day, the temperatures are cool with warm golden tones. The golden tone persists in this room throughout the day.

East facing windows: your space will be warm in the mornings as the sun rises but cool down as the day progresses.

West-facing windows: This type of window allows sunlight during the day and becomes warm as the day progresses and the sunsets.

#2 Heat Distribution Mechanisms

Solar energy is typically transferred all over the house by convection, conduction, and radiation. A passive design uses these three natural methods exclusively without adding an air conditioner that runs on electricity.

Conduction is where the heat from the sun travels through objects in contact with each other. For example, between your feet and a sun-warmed floor.

Radiation is whereby you feel the sun's warmth radiating from a sunny window or a sun-kissed wall even if you are not in direct contact with it. The heat retained by the wall or window warms the home as it radiates some of the heat trapped within the air.

Convection is the transfer of heat through air or fluid into the rest of the house. Some people use a blower, ducts, or fans to distribute the heat throughout the house.

#3 Thermal Mass

Thermal mass refers to heat absorption from sunlight during hot months and similar absorption from warm air during cold months. Masonry is one of the primary ways to achieve excellent thermal mass in a moderate climate. If you use heat absorbent masonry material like concrete, brick, stone, and tiles, you do not need to invest in additional thermal storage regardless of the year.

You can use the mentioned masonry material in conjunction with other thermal mass materials like water. The water can store and distribute heat throughout your space, depending on the time of the year. For example, you can have water pipes with heated water passing under your tiles to heat the floor. We will look further at how this geothermal concept works in the geothermal concept of HVAC.

The water can be heated underground through geothermal and distributed into underground ducts strategically placed under the house.

If you want to use natural thermal mass in your passive design, you should consider things like how dark or light your walls should be to facilitate the absorption of sun rays. Dark-colored walls and furnishings tend to absorb heat better, making them better conductors for thermal mass.

Avoid anything that will shade the thermal mass material from absorbing heat. For example, do not have any plant cover on walls that you would like to use as a thermal mass material. In a moderate climate, you can get away with using furnishings and drywall to achieve sufficient thermal mass, eliminating the need to use walls or intricate underground water pipe systems.

#4 Control Mechanisms

These are mechanisms that ensure that you control the amount of heat and light entering the house. Roof overhangs can offer shade, especially to south-facing windows mitigating the amount of sunlight and heat getting into your space.

Another option is using a differential thermostat that alerts you to high temperatures and signals a fan to go on and cool the space. Some people prefer to use insulating shutters, low-emissivity blinds, or vents that restrict heat flow.

These mechanisms allow you to create a sustainable passive design.

There are three concepts of passive solar design.

1. The sunlight enters your house through the south-facing windows and heats the masonry (floors and walls). The masonry absorbs the heat and stores it to later release it as the temperatures cool in the evening and night. The stored heat warms the air in the house naturally. It is called the direct gain passive solar design. Some homeowners incorporate water-filled containers to absorb and store the solar heat because water stores two times more heat than masonry.
2. The sunlight enters your home through the south side, but it encounters a Trombe wall. That is an 8- to 16-inch-thick dark-colored wall that stores the heat in its mass. The heat then slowly radiates into the living room, heating the room. Since heat travels through masonry at an average rate of one inch per hour, you will begin to feel the heating effects in the evening if the heat is absorbed late morning to late afternoon. A single or double glass mounted an inch or less in front of the Trombe wall absorbs the heat before migrating it into the wall. It is known as the indirect gain passive solar design.

3. Alternatively, you can opt to build a sunroom, also known as a solarium or solar room. That is a space with operable openings like doors and windows to allow heat into the room. They make a pleasant space for relaxing and soaking up the heat, and you can also grow a plant or two. It is commonly referred to as an isolated gain passive solar design.

Heating and Cooling Using Solar Powered Air Conditioners and Heating Pumps

A solar-powered air conditioner or heating pump relies on electric current produced by photovoltaic panels, which harness solar energy.

These air conditioners and heating pumps use direct current, which comes directly from the PV panels. That means that there is no current conversion from DC to AC, which typically results in power loss.

A small home off the grid can use three solar panels of 320 watts each to power the air conditioner.

If you want to use solar-powered air source heat pumps during the cooler season, you need solar panels that give you between 500 to 1400 watts each, depending on your needs.

Did you know that a standard air-source heat pump can use 50% less energy than a window air

conditioning unit?

Heating and Cooling Using Roman Style Water Cooling

The Romans suffered unbearable heat between July and August. So they had a "frigidarium," a large pool of cold water to help them cool down. In our modern setting, we can use a pool to cool down during the day. An outdoor swimming pool with regulated water temperature is an excellent option.

The good news is that cool water from the pool has a way of cooling the immediate surroundings. If you live near a river, lake, pond, or dam, you will notice this more because the winds passing over the water surface are cooled, bringing a breeze with them.

The most sophisticated cooling method in Roman society was pumping water through the walls of their houses to keep the interior cool during the summer months. But this was a privilege for well-off Romans. The rest of the population had to contend with snow shops and frigidarium.

Romans indulged in eating snow to cool off. Wealthy members of society kept snow at home for this purpose, but ordinary citizens would go to the snow shop for a quick fill.

That is similar to using ice cream, a cold drink, or chomping on crushed ice.

Heating and Cooling Using Ground Cooling Loops

Four to six feet underground, the temperatures remain cool and constant all year round. A buried system of pipes connected to an indoor handling unit creates what is known as an earth/ground loop.

The pipes are buried underground horizontally or vertically, and they may be fed by water from an underground aquifer. The water is heated by the stored heat absorbed by the ground from the sun. The heated water makes its rounds throughout the loop in the house, and then it is reinjected back to the same aquifer it came from.

These geothermal HVAC systems do not typically require electricity or fossil fuel to generate heat.

In the winter, they simply use heat naturally stored in the ground to heat the water. In the summer months, these systems pull heat from the building and deposit it in the earth or the aquifer. Those units that require electricity consume very little of it.

Unfortunately, a geothermal HVAC system can be costly to install. But with time, they pay themselves back.

Geothermal HVAC systems are becoming more popular as part of the green building movement dedicated to building eco-friendly homes.

Types of Ground Loop Systems

There are two categories of ground loop systems: Open and closed ground loop systems.

Open-Loop System

There is only one type of open-loop system. It extracts water directly from your well or artificial pond and runs it through a water-refrigerant heat exchanger found in the geothermal heat pump unit.

Heat is transferred from the heat pump to the water before expelling the water back to the pond or well to heat the house.

This system is also known as the pump and dump loop. Local environmental personnel must be consulted when installing this type of system to ensure the installation is per the local laws.

You may encounter problems with this system if the water quality is poor. That means the water features too much dissolved solid content or high mineral content.

This type of ground loop works well when there is plenty of underground water.

Closed-Loop System

This system comes in three formations

1. Horizontal Closed-Loop System

The horizontal closed-loop system requires lots of space because of its sprawling design. The pipes can go for hundreds of feet horizontally and six to ten feet deep. This system works for people living off the grid in remote areas with lots of land to work with.

Also, you have to ensure that the land can accommodate trenches. Rocky areas are not a good fit for this type of ground loop system.

The ground is dug up with trenches going five to ten feet underground. A series of small plastic pipes is entrenched. The pipes have a geothermal heat exchanger to facilitate the heating and cooling process.

2. Vertical Closed-Loop System

This system features pipes running vertically instead of horizontally, and it works for people with limited land sizes. The installers digs one or more boreholes, each around 200 or 500 feet deep into the ground. The boreholes must each be five to six inches in diameter, and they should be 20 feet away from each other.

The next step is to insert a pipe connected at the bottom by a u-shaped bend to create a loop. The vertical looped line is grouted then connected to a horizontal pipe. The horizontal pipe is placed in the trenches and connected to a geothermal heat exchanger.

Due to grouting, contact between the pipe and the earth is guaranteed, meaning heat will be constantly transferred to the water in the pipes to heat your space.

You will encounter vertically closed-loop systems in schools and commercial buildings because of the limited space. However, this ground loop system is more expensive to install than its horizontal counterpart due to excessive drilling.

3. Pond/Lake Ground Loop System

This option works if you have a water body on your land. The installing team runs a supply pipeline from your house and underground into the water; The pipework coils into circles that run at least eight feet underground. That depth eliminates the chances of the water freezing.

However, the pond or lake must meet local minimum volume, quality, and depth requirements before the installation of the coiled pipework.

This ground loop system is the cheapest option.

Advantages of Using Off-Grid Heating and Cooling Solutions

Affordable

The good news is that the solar panels pay for themselves after a while because they save you a lot on your electricity and other utility bills. Generating your electricity mitigates the amount you spend on bills throughout all the seasons.

Once you have finished paying for the solar panel system, your electricity production is completely free. So it doesn't matter if national oil and gas prices go up, impacting the cost of electricity. You are exempt from the price hikes.

Eco-friendliness

Traditional heating and cooling methods can release greenhouse emissions in their operations, especially if they run on fossil fuels. Pair the solar panels with your air source heat pump to cool and heat your home with little to no carbon footprint.

In the United States, most of the electricity on the national grid uses fossil fuel. But, by using solar-powered cooling and heating systems, you reduce reliance on fossil fuel and reduce pollutants and emissions in your little corner of the world.

Incentives

Most governments, state, and private utility companies offer incentives to people who produce and use clean energy. The incentives can be rebates on previous bills or financial payments. You can find out what tax credits or production-based incentives are available in your local area.

Myths about Ground Loop Systems

- ### *Geothermal HVAC heat pumps make a lot of noise*

These systems are typically quiet. Besides, they are located outside and underground, where any sound would be muffled.

- ### *They have a short service life*

This myth is perpetuated; there is a higher likelihood of deterioration due to the elements by the belief that by being underground and outdoors. However, ground loops can last for decades without any further intervention in the running of the system. There are new guidelines in place to ensure the complete efficiency of the system. The materials used include durable plastic that can weather the elements for years.

- ### *Geothermal HVAC use a lot of electricity*

These HVAC systems use one unit of electricity to move five units of heating and cooling from the ground to your house. That is highly efficient.

Geothermal HVAC systems can remove more kilowatts of electricity consumption from the electric grid compared to solar and wind energy.

- ### *The systems only work in heating mode*

They work in both cooling and heating mode. These systems use loops and lines in the ground for this purpose.

- ### *They use a lot of water*

These HVAC systems do not use any water. For example, if the water is derived from an aquifer, it is returned to the exact aquifer after running through the pipes. This process is known as re-injection.

The Take-Away

- Cooling and heating can be achieved without using electricity which is cheaper in the long run.

- Decide on which cooling or heating option you would like before you begin building your house.
- Look out for incentives in your locale that apply to some of the HVAC solutions you have in mind. Rebates and the like can save you some money.
- Solar and geothermal HVAC systems tend to have very high installation expenses, but they eventually pay themselves back.
- Take advantage of the benefits of off-grid heating and cooling solutions to mitigate the high cost of utility bills.

7

The Best Waste Management Practices Off-Grid

"I have become quite good at repurposing and reusing much of what comes into the house. The goal is to generate as little waste as possible."

- Anna Getty, philanthropist and activist.

Life off-the-grid allows you to repurpose almost anything to be used for something else. That leads to minimal wastage of virtually everything. When resources are not as abundant as they might have been when you lived on the grid, you have no choice but to think outside the box and live with utmost frugality. You can be frugal and still have plenty of food and a homestead that looks great, clean, and green.

On the grid, waste management is a challenge for almost any city. Given the high-density populations that generate loads of waste every day, it is not surprising that vast mounds of garbage are visible outside cities where the trash is disposed of.

These massive garbage heaps often become unmanageable, foul the surrounding air for several miles and become a cesspool for disease, all while contributing to global warming. This occurs because when such massive heaps of trash decompose in a landfill, they release lots of methane gas.

Methane is a potent greenhouse gas that plays a role in heating the planet. Eliminating this gas at the source by cultivating habits such as composting is very effective in conserving the environment.

Most city dwellers who have become conscious of these environmental challenges have adopted the concept of recycling to clean up the environment and leave decent and healthy earth for posterity.

When living off the grid, waste management becomes far much easier, depending on how your homestead runs. Food leftovers are fed to animals such as poultry, pigs, and rabbits, and plant residue is used as biomass.

Most of the remaining organic material in the trash are remains that are out in the pit to become compost manure in a few days. When ready, the compost manure is then fed to the garden to enrich the soil and nourish the plants for robust health and yield. The recycling concept also applies in a homestead environment for items such as plastics and glass bottles.

And, because you are aware of your environment, you also make organic choices that can undergo natural decomposition and leave little to no carbon footprint.

Conservation and efficient use of water in a homestead is a part of the puzzle that needs solving to live off the grid successfully. Forming a system that utilizes gray water for your lawn, live fence, or garden sees to it that your homestead remains green, beautiful, and productive even through dry periods. You can do so by raising the efficiency of your water usage and conserving your clean water.

In this chapter, we shall explore how you can utilize waste in a way that enriches your homestead and conserves vital resources such as water and the air.

Trash and Composting

When living off-grid, keeping your costs low and using materials at your disposal to create solutions to common problems is at the center of off-grid living. Growing your food is crucial to your survival.

Composting then becomes a vital part of your homestead's ecosystem that keeps your compound and household clean while generating essential manure for plant growing and soil enrichment.

Did you know that organic wastes, such as yard and food waste, account for 25 to 50% of what you throw away? You may not be able to compost all of the organic waste you generate, but composting does significantly cut down on your overall trash.

Frequently asked questions about composting include:

❖ What exactly should be thrown into the compost pit?
❖ What shouldn't be thrown into composting manure?
❖ How long does it take for composting materials to be broken down and be ready for

use?

We shall answer these questions further in the chapter but first, let's see how you would go about setting up a compost pit in your yard.

You don't need any specialized training to set up a compost pit. The first thing you need to do is choose a suitable site in your compound where you can dig a pit. The pit can be any size, including 3 x 5 feet with a depth that goes one to two feet deep. It is as simple as that. It should not be too deep.

A shallow depth allows you to manage the compost with ease on occasions when you need to turn and aerate the heap. The alternative to digging a pit is to build a compost bin that can either be stationary or portable, depending on preference.

A pallet bin is also a great idea. However, you must be mindful of changing the bottom pallet every one to two years because of rot. The side panels can be replaced as needed, but they will last anywhere from four to six years before you have to do any replacing. Digging a compost pit, on the other hand, offers less maintenance.

There are several general rules to observe to achieve a good outcome when setting up a compost pit for your homestead.

- Choose a site that is not too close to the house but also not too far away. That ensures that the occasional odor coming from the pit does not foul the air in your house. On the other hand, the trip to the compost to dump litter should not be too long for the sake of convenience.
- Install the compost pit in well-drained ground that is level and near a water container. You can always put a drum filled with water next to the compost pit. That makes it easy and convenient when you need to pour water into the pit to keep it moist.
- The area where you set up the compost pit should be free of shallow tree roots for a uniform composting process.
- As you pile material into the pit, remember to moisten the pit's contents by occasionally adding water to the pile. If you have water close by, such as a tap or drum full of water, the chore becomes less tedious and keeps your compost moist with little effort. You should also ensure that you form a concave space in the middle to capture rainwater when it rains.
- The ideal moisture level of a compost pit should resemble the moistness of a wrung sponge. In the rainy season, it becomes a good idea to cover your compost pit with a polythene cover to prevent excess moisture.
- It is good practice to turn the compost heap once every week. That keeps the pile well aerated, promoting decomposition while minimizing putrid smells.

- A heap of compost is ready and fully decomposed in 3-6 months. By this time, the pile's contents are sweet-smelling, crumbly, and assume a dark brown almost black hue. Another indication that composting is complete is a rise in the temperature of the heap that shoots up from 48 to about 66 degrees centigrade.
- While you can use the compost directly from the pit, you should remove the manure from the pit and let it age for a month before use in your soil or on your plants.

If you are new to composting, you are likely to run into a few challenges. These are the most common ones you can expect to face and how to overcome them.

Bad Odor

This is a common problem with compost heaps. It usually means that your pile is not well aerated, and the moisture level is low. If your pile appears dry, moistening it by adding water to the pile helps resolve the smell issue.

Turning the heap once a week will ensure that the aeration is good and will play a part in alleviating strong odor from the heap. The odor attracts all manner of flies. By doing the above, you will also be discouraging flies from your compost. You can also add more browns to the heap to control smell

The Pile is Too Wet

In case of excess rain that results in too much moisture in your compost heap, you can add more browns to the pile and turn more frequently to help the water get absorbed and dissipate to acceptable moisture levels.

No Decomposition

If you notice that the contents of your heap are not degrading, then you need to rectify one or several of the following things; turn the heap more frequently, at least once a week. Adding more greens will help catalyze the decomposition process.

Ensure the moisture levels are good by either adding more water to increase moisture or adding more browns and turning it frequently to lessen moisture. Adding urea, fresh manure, or blood meal to the pile can also act as a catalyst to degrade the pile.

Compost Not Getting Hot

The degrading process will naturally cause a rise in temperature in your pile over time. If your compost is not getting hot, it means that your heap is too small, and therefore, you need to pour on more materials to increase the size of the heap.

Pets

If you have pets like a dog or a cat, they are likely to frequently visit the pile for a chance at spotting a piece of meat or bone. To prevent pets from accessing the heap, you can cover the top of the pit with a pallet, or you can take to burying foodstuff at least a foot deep into the pile.

Insects

Insects love a heap of degrading material. To prevent an influx of insects from setting up shop on your compost pit, be sure to keep it moist and turn it in more frequently.

Now we revisit the questions posed earlier.

After how long is your compost ready for use?

The answer is three to six months. When throwing items for composting into the pit, you need to ensure that they are in small pieces or sizes to lessen the time it takes to break down and fully degrade or decompose.

The other common question concerns the material you should dump in your compost heap. Here's an exhaustive list of what can go into your compost pile;

- Inedible plant materials such as flowers, twigs, and leaves due to trimming the hedge or fence. Items such as banana peels, corn cobs, and grass clippings are suitable for your compost. Just be sure to chop them into smaller pieces before adding them to your compost heap.
- Fruits and vegetables.
- Non-recyclables such as shredded paper.
- Used paper products such as napkins, tissues, towels, and plates.
- Eggs and eggshells.
- Natural loose fibers such as hemp and jute.
- Nuts and grains.
- Coffee grinds.
- Teabags.
- Cardboard.
- Bread.

- Pasta.
- Rice.
- Chips.

A common misconception when it comes to composting is the difference between compostable and biodegradable items. Most people misconstrue this to mean the same thing. Biodegradable items can be broken down by the soil, even if it may take a long time to do so. They include items like paper and cardboard. These items are also compostable when cut down to smaller pieces.

When composting natural paper products, it is essential to leave out glossy papers. That's because the glossy paper has an overwhelming amount of chemicals that take far too long to break down and may end up negatively affecting the quality of your soil as well as your plants.

Therein lies the difference: Glossy paper is biodegradable but not ideal for composting, while regular paper is biodegradable and excellent for compost. Just because a material is biodegradable doesn't mean it is a good choice for composting.

When living off the grid, what items should you consider keeping out of your compost and why?

There are a few animal products that are compostable, but you may want to think twice before throwing them into your compost heap. These include cheese, milk, and meat or meat products.

These products result in a putrid smell as they decompose, which attracts tons of flies and rodents. Other items to avoid in your compost heap include the following;

- Animal waste such as that of dog and cat feces— That's because they develop a foul smell and often contain parasites, and play a role in attracting pests such as rodents.
- Yard trimmings may be compostable. However, if they have chemical pesticides, it is best to avoid them because they will kill beneficial composting organisms in your heap
- Coal ashes feature with excessive amounts of sulfur and high iron content to damage plants

Here is an exhaustive list of what not to throw into your compost heap;

1. Meats of any sort such as poultry, fish, and so forth.
2. Dairy products milk, cheese, and yogurt.
3. Animal or human feces and urine should not be composted.
4. Any item with inseparable plastic/ metal/glass or rubber.

5. Styrofoam.
6. Items made from rubber or latex such as rubber gloves or condoms.

Other items that are likely to form part of your trash and should not find their way into the compost but should be recycled instead include the below:

1. Aluminum cans.
2. Glass bottles.
3. Plastic containers.
4. Plastic bags.

How does composting stand to serve you when living off-grid?

- It helps keep your compound neat and clean.
- It increases organic matter in your soil.
- It promotes the absorption of nutrients in the soil and in the plants in your garden.
- It improves aeration and drainage in clay soils.
- It helps sandy soils retain water that normally runs through.
- It makes clay and other soils more friable. That translates to a garden with improved soil that's easier to crumble and dig in.
- It contributes to the pH balance in your soil.
- It helps control soil erosion
- It extends the growing season by moderating soil temperature.

Gray Water

In many cases, when living off-grid, water is often one resource that can become scarce and should be managed with utmost care. Whether you harness rainwater, dig a well or use a nearby river or lake, water conservation in a homestead is paramount.

We have already established that, indeed, water is life. For that reason, you will find that for you to be happy and in a position to carry out other chores that keep your homestead in the state that you desire, water is at the very heart of sustaining your life and all in the homestead.

That includes the crops in your garden and the animals that you rear. Since the water demand is high, tapping into a system that helps you recycle some of the used water from laundry and the kitchen to cater to needs like cleaning the driveway, watering a live fence, and watering the garden can help conserve your freshwater reservoirs. Adopting such a practice will significantly minimize the overall amount of liters you consume in your homestead.

That brings us to gray water. What is gray water? This is gently used water from your homestead's kitchen, bathroom, showers, washing machine, and tubs. It is essential to note the distinction between gray water and black water.

Simply put, the distinction between the two is that black water is water that has come into contact with feces, either from the toilet or from washing diapers. In contrast, gray water is from the above-mentioned sources, such as the kitchen and bathrooms, and has not come into contact with feces.

Gray water will contain varying degrees of soap, food particles, hair and will look "dirty." However, this water can still be repurposed for safe use in the homestead instead of being sent and lost directly to the sewer. Keeping gray water out of the sewer or septic system reduces the chance that it will pollute local water bodies. Gray water can be repurposed to water the yard and flush the toilet(s) in the house.

The idea of using gray water is to help conserve your freshwater resource in your off-grid home. If you stop to think about it, you will realize that the shower and laundry take up most of your freshwater. Here's a table showing the general breakdown of how freshwater is used in an average off-grid home.

Section of house	Water usage
Bathroom	50%
Laundry	22%
Garden	19%
Kitchen	8%

As you can see, harnessing gray water from the bathroom and laundry area alone for watering the yard and the garden can positively help you conserve your freshwater. Using gray water will also help you cut down on the cost, energy, and effort of fetching freshwater, especially if you use a pump to pull the freshwater from a well, river, lake, or dam.

Just for clarification, as we have pointed out, gray water is not clean or freshwater. If it runs off to the river or lake, it is a pollutant owing to the various soap and detergent chemicals it carries from human use. Chemicals in gray water are dependent on how harsh and toxic the soaps you use are. Gray water can be harmful to your plants and your yard.

The solution to this is to use mild soaps that have fewer chemicals and are environmentally friendly. Occasionally, water your garden and yard with fresh water to help the soil break down the process of the trace chemical found in gray water. In the rainy season, give your yard and plants a break from the gray water.

In dry weather, gray water comes in handy in keeping your garden and compound lush without depleting your freshwater resource. For as long you use organic soaps, the gray water from your house is absorbed into your yard and garden without harming the plants.

Ideally, gray water should flow toward fruit trees and ornamental plants in the yard. When directed to the garden, the water should only touch the base of the plant and into the soil. The soil will be able to break down the gentle chemicals. Toxic soap residue in gray water can overwhelm the soil with chemicals and ruin your plants. If you intend to use gray water for your garden and yard, use environmentally friendly soaps for your laundry, dishes, and shower.

Simple Gray Water Systems

When living off the grid, systems that conserve your water work to your advantage and help you to manage other resources such as energy and time efficiently. Gray water systems can be low-tech and inexpensive or highly sophisticated and expensive depending on what you want to use them on and for.

Drum or Barrel System

This system is low cost, and you can install it yourself with relative ease. All you need is a drum or barrel that is placed strategically out of the house where your laundry machine drains the wash water.

The drum connects to an outlet hose which goes all the way to the yard and can be held to plants for manual watering. The water can also be used to water your lawn. It is recommended that you strap the drum to a wall or strong post for safety purposes. That prevents any accidental toppling of the drum.

Washing machines are excellent sources of gray water for two reasons; water volume and pressure. Given that washing machines have an internal pump that automatically pumps out the water, the water surge or pressure that results can work to your advantage. You can do that by ensuring your system does not connect into the existing plumbing but goes right into the drum, through the outlet hose, and directly diverted into the yard or selected trees and plants of choice in your compound.

If your house is on the upper side of a gradient and your yard below, this works perfectly.

In addition to the surge generated by the washing machine dispensing the laundry water, the gray water will flow by gravity to the desired areas of the yard.

However, with this method, you will have to manually hold and constantly move the hose over the plants you want to water. The upside is, this system is simple to install, low cost, and hardly requires any maintenance.

Landscape Irrigation System

If you prefer a more automated system for irrigating the plants in your yard, then the laundry to landscape system should help make use of gray water from your laundry. This system automatically diverts the water to selected sections of the lawn or garden of specific plants based on how you have set it up.

The beauty of this system is it does not interfere with your existing plumbing. The installation is pretty simple and straight forward allowing you to do it yourself. You will directly attach the washing machine drain hose to a diverter valve; This offers you flexibility and control over where you want the gray water to go. When the weather is hot and dry, the gray water is beneficial as you can direct it towards the yard or specific plants through the diverter valve.

When there is plenty of rain, you can divert the gray water directly to the septic or sewer system. That allows your yard and garden to breathe, flourish and enjoy the freshness of rainwater. This gray water irrigation system utilizes a 1 tubing with 1/2 outlets for directing water to specific plants. If you want a decent element with low tech flexibility for irrigation, this gray water system is a good choice as it is easy to set up, low cost, and requires minimal maintenance.

When it comes to low-tech and low-cost irrigation systems, you want to avoid components like filters and pumps for as long as your setup and the land gradient allows you to.

Kitchen and Bathroom Gray Water System

As you can see in the table above, these two areas generate a decent amount of gray water that can be directed into watering shrubs and trees in your yard. Gray water from the kitchen is rich in organic material such as greases and food particles, while water from the bathroom may have hair.

The particles will quickly clog up your system over a short period and will force frequent maintenance issues. To avoid clogging, a branched drain system with mulch basins is recommended. Since the kitchen and bathroom do not generate too much water, you can opt to harness the water from the two areas using one system.

In this system, you can opt to use 1" and 1/2 size drainage pipes. Use gravity on a slope with a ¼" drop for every foot traveled horizontally. Because the water goes through plumbing fittings that split the flow, it is divided into smaller and smaller quantities which helps prevent blockages.

Your trees and shrubs will remain evergreen even in drought periods because their root zone is continually being fed by gray water throughout. The only glaring con to this system is that it consumes a great deal of time when setting up. But, the upside is that very little maintenance is required once complete.

For off-grid homes, gray water systems are meant to conserve water and maximize the efficiency of water usage. The above options are low-tech but practical and effective with low-cost installation.

If your yard is sloped with your home being uphill and everything else downhill, we recommend that you consider using gravity to transport gray water through your system to the yard and garden.

If your land is sloped uphill with your house at the bottom of the slope, or your land is flat, then you have no option but to employ the use of filters and pumps. While pumps work well and are a solution, they do add to the cost of running your homestead, and they will inevitably break down from time to time.

If the lay of your land allows it, it is best to avoid them altogether. But, if the gradient of your land does not favor gravity, then you have no choice but to incorporate pump(s) into your gray water system.

Everything You Need to Know about Gray Water

While gray water will alleviate the pressure of freshwater use in some instances, it is essential to note that it is to be handled differently from freshwater. Below are some of the guidelines to adhere to when using gray water in your off-grid home.

- Do not store gray water for more than 24 hours. That's because the organic particles, dirt, and chemicals from the soap will start to break down and emit an unpleasant odor. For this reason, it should be used immediately or within 24 hours.
- This type of water is not fit for humans or animals to drink. As such, your system should be designed in a way that allows the water to soak into the ground without pooling.
- Match our gray water system to the irrigation needs of your yard and plants.

- Ensure the water does not pool anywhere in your compound to avoid creating breeding grounds for mosquitoes.
- Avoid pumps and filters in your gray water system. The simpler the system, the better because of low cost, ease of maintenance, and durability.
- Installing a 3-way valve is recommended for easy switching between the gray water system and the sewer.

Septic System

The reason why living in urban areas is known as on-grid living is because most basic and vital utilities are tied to the grid. That means utilities such as water, electricity, and sewage systems are part of public facilities served by the government. Naturally, you will receive a weekly or monthly bill for the above services.

Living off the grid means that you have to find a solution for your water, energy, and sewerage. One of the solutions to the latter lies in installing a septic tank that collects and disposes of your wastewater. A septic tank can be a metal tank or plastic tank that is placed underground for that purpose. There are numerous types of septic systems such as;

- Conventional system.
- Aerobic system.
- The recirculating sand filter system.
- Chamber system.

The septic tank system that will be suitable for your off-grid home will be determined by several factors that include;

- Soil type.
- Lot size.
- Site slope.
- Household size.
- Weather conditions.
- Water bodies in the immediate area.
- Local regulations.

A septic tank works by collecting water in a metal tank and then being acted upon by bacteria. The bacteria break down everything in the tank resulting in the natural separation of the waste into a bottom sludge layer, top scum layer, and liquid in the middle layer. When new wastewater flows into the tanks, the liquid in the middle layer flows out of the tank into underground perforated pipes that run a distance into what is called a drain field. In the drain field, the released water is absorbed and treated by the soil.

Septic tanks are excellent off-grid sewer solutions. However, they do need a thorough inspection and maintenance by a professional once a year. If you have an efficient self-cleaning system, maintenance can be every three years.

Advantages of a Septic Tank

Environment friendly because they do not need power or chemicals to clean the wastewater.

You are in charge of the upkeep and maintenance of the sewerage system.

You want simple systems that are easily manageable and require minimal to no maintenance. That keeps your cost of living low and allows your homestead to function seamlessly. A good and efficient septic system is of utmost importance for a healthy off-grid space.

Outhouse

Depending on where you are from, it can be easy to confuse an outhouse with a latrine. But then again, these toilets share some similarities. A latrine may comprise a trench or dug-out pit for waste disposal.

It can have a bench or stone seating that can serve multiple individuals simultaneously. The unit housing can be made from wood or other building materials, depending on how temporary the latrine is. In some cases, the pit or trench is not housed. That concept was popular with the military decades ago.

Outhouses, on the other hand, take after the same concept of a deep pit for waste disposal but offer more privacy. The outhouse exterior can also be made from wood. The seating area has a hole in the middle and is designed for one person hence the privacy aspect. When the pit is full, the housing or shell can be transferred and placed on a freshly dug pit.

An outhouse is a practical and hustle-free low-cost option when living off the grid for several reasons, as outlined below:

Advantages of Outhouses

- No need to flush.
- Saves on water.
- Easy cleaning.

- Odors are kept outside.
- Little to Zero maintenance.

Composting Toilet

So what is a composting toilet? It is an environmentally friendly sewerage option that is waterless and requires no plumbing. The composting toilet device effectively turns solid waste into compost by creating an oxygen-rich environment that allows aerobic bacteria to break down waste.

For an off-grid setting and for someone who is environmentally conscious, a composting toilet is a practical solution to waste disposal. One of the misgivings that people may have about a composting toilet is the aesthetic of the units.

However, modern composting toilets look very much like a conventional toilet and therefore bode well in with a décor of a conventional modern bathroom. Such a design is self-contained and houses the entire composting system.

This is ideal for a household that does inhabit many people. You can also use it in a small home, boat, or RV. A point of consideration is that this composting type of toilet has to be emptied by hand.

The second type of composting toilet is referred to as the central or remote toilet. In this version, the composted material does not have to be emptied by hand; instead, this version diverts solid and sometimes liquid waste to a remote composter situated elsewhere on the compound.

This option is ideal for bigger off-grid households and can even serve an off-grid compound with several homes and multiple toilets as all the waste is directed to a central compost pile or septic tank of sorts.

Irrespective of which composting toilet you settle for in your off-grid home, both work using the same composting principle that is waterless and odorless. But, for composting to happen seamlessly, the conditions have to be favorable for the aerobic bacteria to thrive and break down the waste. Favorable conditions for aerobic bacteria mean:

- Optimal moisture levels.
- Optimal nitrogen levels.
- Ideal temperatures of 60-100 degrees Fahrenheit.

You will notice that most composting toilets will tend to have a separate urine compartment that is emptied once it fills up or may have a drain pipe that drains the urine elsewhere or incorporate a mechanism to evaporate the urine.

Proper disposal of urine helps keep and maintain optimal moisture without wetness and manages the nitrogen levels in the composting chamber.

Wetness and high nitrogen levels in the composting chamber will kill the aerobic bacteria, and therefore, the waste will not be broken down, leading to odor in the toilet.

Modern composting toilets are easy to use because they come with sensors, thermostats, and automatic mixers that make it easy for you to ensure optimal conditions are maintained for the composting process to work as needed.

You can use this toilet just as you would a regular toilet. The difference is, instead of flushing using water, as is the case of solid waste, you will need to turn the handle at the base of the unit. Spray the bowl with a mixture of water and vinegar whenever it gets dirty.

Advantages of composting toilets

- Easy to install.
- Eco-friendly.
- Save on water.
- Odorless.

Modern times have come with many innovations that make off-grid living quite possible and manageable. For many people, the idea and concept of off-the-grid living are becoming more appealing and a real possibility. A good number of people work online anyway and can live anywhere where there is an internet signal. Escaping the high cost and tyranny of urban life is no longer impossible.

With such water conservation ideas, you can maximize;
- Repurposing gray water.
- Growing your organic food on the cheap by utilizing compost manure from household trash.
- Having a sewerage system that is affordable and eco-friendly.

The Take-Away

- Make arrangements for your sewerage needs before you move to your new off-grid home.
- Choose the best option depending on your immediate needs.
- Ensure you choose the right location for your septic tank, compost toilet, or outhouse to avoid water contamination.

Final Words

Living off the grid is not for everyone. It requires dedication and discipline. But, the benefits are irrefutable and life-changing.

In this book, you get to learn how to survive off-grid as you begin this life-transforming change; How to look for the best location for your needs, what type of off-grid lifestyle is best suited to you and how you can live sustainably off the land.

Make no mistake; this resource doesn't guarantee that off-grid living will be easy. However, it does make it clear that you can do it and how you can achieve a successful off-grid life.

Use this book every step of the way to learn more and research what you need to do before making the transition. Make visits to some of the off-grid places mentioned in the book where possible and see how others are making it work for themselves.

There are many off-grid communities in and out of the United States that love sharing their lifestyle with potential off-gridders. Alternatively, you can make Airbnb arrangements to experience the different off-grid lifestyles.

As you contemplate this journey, let these words from Abraham Lincoln, the 16th president of the United States of America, inspire you:

"The greatest fine art of the future will be the making of a comfortable living from a small piece of land."

OFF-GRID SOLAR POWER HANDBOOK:

BOOK 3

The Ultimate Beginners Guide to Power Your RV, Van, Cabin, Boat and Tiny Home in 7 Simplified Steps

BY

BRADLEY STONE

Introduction

"We are like tenant farmers chopping down the fence around our house for fuel when we should be using Nature's inexhaustible sources of energy – sun, wind and tide... I'd put my money on the sun and solar energy. What a source of power! I hope we don't have to wait until oil and coal run out before we tackle that."

-Thomas Edison

Have you been thinking about setting up solar power in your off-grid home or wondered about the feasibility of setting up a fully powered off-grid home with solar panels? No matter what stage you have reached, you might have questions and concerns about solar panels, their installation, and the setup you want to achieve.

First, let's briefly look at why you might want to install solar panels in the first place. For most people, this stems from a desire to live more simply and reduce their dependency on fossil fuels. We are all becoming increasingly aware of how damaging fossil fuels are and how destructive the extraction of fossil fuels can be. Still, few people currently feel that they have viable alternatives.

Every aspect of our daily lives revolves around the use of fossil fuels. Our cars, homes, and jobs are driven by coal, oil, gas, etc. We are utterly dependent upon these resources, yet we know they are also in minimal supply.

Americans use a startling amount of oil every year.

Did you know that if the whole world used the same amount, we would run out in just nine years?[v] That's a significant subject that many people wonder how to solve. Reducing our usage is only a start, and it does not go far enough to solve the problem – although it's certainly not wrong to reduce where you can!

You are probably already aware that there are no "easy fixes" to this issue. They are complicated and nuanced, and we have to acknowledge such if we want to get anywhere. Often, solutions involve compromise, and a perfect outcome rarely exists.

Even great technology like solar power is not perfect. There are environmental costs in creating and disposing of the panels, and they suffer from certain drawbacks. They are not, by themselves, a solution to climate change. However, we need to do what we can to improve the situation, even if the best outcome we can achieve is far from perfect.

There is no doubt that solar power is an excellent start to generating electricity and powering off-grid living for all its flaws. In many cases, installing solar panels on the roofs of houses generates almost enough for the household. If you are reducing your power usage because you're moving to off-grid living, you're even more likely to be able to achieve this.

For readers who can't cut back on the amount of power they use, know that you will still be massively reducing the strain placed on oil and gas when installing solar panels. An imperfect solution is preferable to no solution at all. Even halving your dependency on fossil fuels has a significant impact on your overall footprint.

One of the biggest issues you have probably encountered if you've started looking into setting up solar panels for an off-grid situation is that the whole thing is surprisingly complicated. If you've started to feel like you need a degree in electrical engineering by just thinking about it, you are not alone; This puts many people off trying to install solar panels before they have even started. It seems daunting.

Nevertheless, I've spent a lot of time looking into and analyzing solar panels, their use in off-grid setups of all kinds (boats, cabins, tiny homes, caravans, and more), and how you can make them work for you. I'm going to cover everything you need to know about them, including the batteries, the fuses, the inverters, how to build your solar system, and the best panels to consider.

You should then have all the knowledge necessary to design and build a system that works for you at a fraction of the cost of one you might buy from a company. Ideally, you will be able to adapt much of the information held in this book to your situation and ensure that you can create a working and efficient system no matter what kind of off-grid home you are working on.

Of course, it is a good idea to look at your budget for adding solar panels before you start.

Installing a solar system is not cheap, regardless of your approach. However, it will represent immediate savings in electricity if you no longer use power from the grid. It will allow you to move off-grid and reduce your dependency on society. You should see lower ongoing costs for the energy you generate in either scenario.

I'm passionate about making solar more accessible to everyday people because I believe everyone should be able to add a functional and reasonably inexpensive solar setup to their homes. With more and more people moving off-grid and trying to soften their impact on the planet, this is becoming increasingly important.

It also seems to be one of the few ways in which America, and the world as a whole, can tackle some of the problems with fossil fuels. Almost all individuals can install solar in some form or another, and if everyone does so, we can massively reduce our need for fossil fuels. Because so many individuals can take this step, it is feasible to represent a fundamental change to the problems we face. A mass, joint move toward solar – even with a small population – would result in extraordinary shifts in the requirements for energy.

If you are thinking of setting up an off-grid system or improving a current system that you have already set up, don't be daunted by the amount of information that's out there. It is not the simplest thing in the world, but it does not have to be so complicated that you can't do it. Don't be put off solar just because it is challenging; this system is well worth setting up.

We will start the next chapter by looking at the benefits of solar power, how it works and how solar panels generate energy, the components that a basic solar system requires, and the phases you will go through when you install solar panels.

Let's start unlocking solar power!

1

Explanation of Solar Power

"Solar energy will not pollute our air or water. We will not run short of it. No one can ever embargo the sun or interrupt its delivery to us. But we must work together to turn our vision and our dream into a solar reality... I dedicate, this afternoon, this solar heater, harnessing the rays of the sun to the benefit of those who serve our country at the White House."

-Jimmy Carter

In 1979, American President Jimmy Carter acknowledged how vital and robust solar energy is. He recognized many things in his speech on solar power, including the dangers of pollution, the limitlessness and availability of solar power, and the need to work together to make solar power a viable reality in our world.

This speech and the dedication of the solar water heaters on the roof of the White House are indicative of just how significant solar has been in our world, *but where did it first come from? How did we start harnessing the sun, and when?*

It might amaze you to learn that solar power has existed since 1839, when a scientist named Edmond Becquerel experimented with electrolytic cells and realized that the cells would produce more energy if they were placed in sunlight. Technology has come a very long way since then, and indeed since Carter's day.

In recent years, solar panels and our ability to produce energy from the sun have undergone immense development and change, making solar panels a genuine, viable, and promising alternative to the fossil fuels that we have depended upon for so long.

What Is Solar, And How Does It Work?

Solar is the energy that the sun outputs in the form of both light and heat.

We can harvest solar energy in a couple of different ways, including:

- Photovoltaics (PV)
- Concentrating Solar-Thermal Power (CSP)

You are most likely familiar with PV, as CSP is usually only used in big power plants and is not suitable for at-home setups. It involves using mirrors to concentrate sunlight onto receivers. For this book, we will be concentrating on PV solar power, as this is the kind that can be installed in homes and off-grid settings.

PV is the solar technology used for solar panels. It uses materials that naturally produce electricity when sunlight strikes them via an electronic process. These materials are called semiconductors, and they contain electrons freed by the energy contained in solar rays.

When these electrons are freed, they can be channelled into an electrical circuit which can either power a device or send energy into a battery or grid to store or transmit to other homes.

In short, the PV cells in the solar panels have been designed to absorb the energy from sunlight when it falls on them, and this forms an electrical charge we can utilize; This can be done at almost any scale.

You can get small solar panels, which can charge devices such as cell phones, batteries, flashlights, etc. You can also get much bigger solar panels, which generate enough electricity to power computers, heaters, and so on.

Today, we generally use crystalline silicon or thin-film semiconductor material to create solar cells. These have both come down in price significantly since they were developed, bringing solar into the reach of ordinary people. Each material has pros and cons.

The thin-film materials are not as efficient in gathering energy. However, they tend to be cheaper to make, and they are relatively simpler, thus making them more accessible for at-home projects.

Silicon cells have higher efficiency rates, but they are also more expensive to manufacture. They are the better option if you can afford them, but many people still find these are out of their price range.

There is an additional category, but they are highly specialized and only used in military and scientific operations. They are called tandem cells or multi-junction cells, but they will remain too costly for most people to use until the future.

How Can You Harness Solar?

A solar panel made of one of the above categories of cells is needed to harness solar. Which category you use will depend on the application and what is deemed affordable, but you must have either a thin-film or silicon cell panel.

Next, you will need to decide on the size of the solar panel. In general, the bigger a solar panel is, the more energy it can generate. This discrepancy is often one of the biggest weaknesses of a solar panel – it needs space and requires a clear shot at sunlight. Without vast, open areas dedicated to many panels, it is challenging for the human race to generate enough electricity to meet our needs.

To generate enough solar power for our homes and infrastructure, we would have to clear vast swathes of land to install all the panels that would be needed. Despite recent developments in solar panels and improvements in their efficiency, this remains true.

Clearing large amounts of space is problematic because this may mean removing trees and animal habitats and taking up land that could be used for farming. Areas around the solar fields would also need to be cleared to ensure sunlight falls on the panels with minimal interruption.

Rooftop solar panels are the solution to these two issues.

Roofs offer blank, empty canvasses to install panels on without needing to clear any new land, and they are elevated so that the panels will get maximum access to sunlight, with few objects blocking them. They are also located where the power is wanted – alongside buildings – so there is no need to send the electricity through long cable stretches.

How Can Solar Panels Convert Solar Energy Into Electricity?

Solar panels convert solar energy into electricity because the energy makes electrons within the material move, generating electricity with varying efficiency rates.

On average, a single panel will produce somewhere between 250 and 400 watts. A domestic system for a house might have between four and ten solar panels, giving it a capacity between a kW and 4 kW. Over a single year, a 4kW solar panel system could produce almost 3000 kWh of electricity if operating in good conditions.[vi] Of course, off-grid systems are often smaller due to space constraints and reduced consumption needs.

Understanding this allows people to calculate how many solar panels are needed for any given application to power it properly. However, it is essential to note that many domestic solar panels are surprisingly inefficient, although they can still produce plenty of energy in homes.

Even the best residential panels generally only operate at around 20% efficiency. Solar panels can be made far more efficient than this, achieving efficiency rates of up to around 50%, but unfortunately, this technology is still prohibitively expensive. In the future, it is likely to become cheaper, and we may be able to make better use of the sunlight that is available to us.

Overall, therefore, the process of converting solar energy into electricity is pretty inefficient at present but still valuable, especially in off-grid settings where other sources of power may not be applicable. While solar panels are far from perfection, they are certainly a viable option.

Off-Grid VS On Grid Solar Energy

There are three different options you can set up your system with: you can be off the grid, on the grid, or utilizing a hybrid setup. Let's break down these three systems.

1.   Off-Grid Solar Energy Systems

An off-grid system is what you may be interested in developing if you are keen to stop depending on the grid. A boat, an RV, or any other moving vehicle, or a cabin located a long way from the nearest town, will usually be set up using this kind of system because it cannot easily be connected to the primary grid.

An off-grid system will be closed-loop, and the energy you produce will be pumped into your system and stored in your batteries. You will not be contributing any energy to the electricity grid in your area, and you will not be pulling any energy from it either.

The energy that flows from the solar panel will be sent into a large battery, storing the energy and supplying it to your home. The effect will be the same as using energy from the local energy supplier, but your energy will be limited, and once it has been used up, you will need to wait for more to be generated by the solar panels.

Think of an off-grid system like growing your carrots. The carrots you produce in your garden go into your kitchen, feeding you and your family, and none of them goes anywhere else; they are kept in your home. You stock the refrigerator with your garden carrots (just as you stock your batteries with your solar panels). When your fridge is empty, you have to get more carrots from your garden, rather than from a store.

These systems are also known as Stand-Alone Power Systems (SAPS). They are great if you cannot connect to the grid or choose not to, but they have the pronounced disadvantage that if you outstrip the amount of power your system generates, you will simply run out of power.

They also tend to be considerably more expensive than an on-grid system because you need better solar panels and some excellent batteries. They can be prohibitively expensive to set up, and you will need enough room to store the batteries.

A third disadvantage of this system is that it has nowhere to go if you produce more power than you need. The power is wasted once the batteries are fully charged, rather than being fed to other homes.

If you cannot connect to the grid in any way because you are setting up your system in a live-in vehicle or an isolated property, this is your only option. However, it is worth understanding the other two and considering whether they could work for you.

2.   On-Grid Solar Energy Systems

An on-grid solar energy system means that your solar panels are linked up with the nearby energy supply that supplies other homes. Your energy will be fed into this grid instead of into your home, and you will pull power from the grid.

You will not directly use your energy, but this doesn't matter because the overall system will remain the same. The same amount of energy will be produced and used, and it is irrelevant whether this comes from the grid or your solar panels.

Think of this somewhat like supplying carrots to your local store. Instead of carrying the carrots into your kitchen, you carry them to the local store and put them in a big box of carrots. Other people also supply this box (whether individuals or energy companies, both green and fossil fuel dependent).

When you want carrots, you have to take them out of the box. You may not get your carrots back, but you have still contributed eco-friendly carrots to the box and reduced the overall use of "non-green" carrots. Your carrots have made the world greener, even though you are not directly using them.

However, if you use more carrots than grown, you depend on other carrot suppliers to meet your needs. That may mean you are still depending upon non-green carrots – or electricity. The advantage, of course, is that you do not run out of carrots, even if your garden is not currently able to meet your requirements.

Some people would prefer to be using their solar energy before sending it into the grid, however, simply because this "feels" more satisfying. If that's the case, you might be interested in building a Hybrid Solar Energy System.

3. Hybrid Solar Energy Systems

This is a system that utilizes a battery but also feeds into the grid. With this system, energy will first be stored in a battery, and as devices use this energy, they will draw on the battery until the battery levels are depleted.

The grid will also feed into the batteries during the low-demand hours. When electricity is cheap (which is generally between midnight and six in the morning), it will fill the batteries, ensuring that the system has the maximum amount of energy available.

If the battery gets depleted, the system can then tap into the grid and start pulling energy from there to supply your systems. This ensures that you have access to power even in bad weather when your solar panels are not generating much.

In some cases, hybrid systems are organized so that excess solar power can also be fed back into the grid, but not all do this.

Using our carrot analogy, a hybrid system is like growing your carrots, placing them in your fridge, and topping up your fridge from the store. With some systems, if you have excessive carrots and cannot use them all, they will be sold to the store, but only those that will not fit into your fridge (or battery).

Hybrid systems are popular for obvious reasons because they allow you to enjoy the best of both worlds. You can use your solar power, have it topped up by the grid and – in some cases – sell excess power back to the grid.

Of course, a significant disadvantage is that you must connect to the grid to use a hybrid system. If your off-grid setup cannot be joined up to the primary circuit (or you would rather not join it), you cannot utilize a hybrid system, and your only option is an off-grid system.

In this book, we will be looking predominantly at creating an off-grid setup. However, it is worth being aware that the other systems exist because you may utilize them in some situations. Don't dismiss hybrid or grid systems if your setup allows for them; they are often cheaper and better for the planet.

Major Components Of An Off-Grid Solar Power System

So, what do you need to create an off-grid solar power system? Different systems can vary enormously, so we will focus on the most typical kind of setup for a small off-grid system (the sort that you would set up for a van, RV, cabin, etc., as opposed to a large off-grid home).

A small-scale solar off-grid system usually uses MPPT solar charge controllers between the solar panels and the batteries that are being charged. Although instalments may vary, your system will likely include most or all of these components:

- Solar panels
- An MPPT solar charge controller
- HRC fuses
- A battery bank (or single battery)
- Your direct current loads (e.g. lights)
- An inverter
- Your 240V alternating current loads (e.g. laptops)

In some cases, one or the other of these components may be switched for something else that performs a similar job, but generally, all small scale off-grid systems will utilize these components. Let's break them down.

4.   Solar Panels

You need solar panels to run a solar system. You will have to determine the number of panels you require to meet your electricity demands, calculate the size of the panels, the efficiency that the materials offer, and your needs.

Solar panels will generally be installed on a roof, but you should think about their placement and make sure that you have a suitable space.

5.   An MPPT Solar Charge Controller

The MPPT stands for Maximum Power Point Tracking. Its job is to control the high voltage current sent by the solar panels and make sure it is converted into a current that is suitable for your devices. The controller also makes sure that the power coming in from the panels is utilized as efficiently as possible so that your batteries are getting charged.

This is a surprisingly complex process because the panels and the batteries will often be poorly matched. To maximize the efficiency of the power sent by the solar panels, the solar charge controller converts the direct current (DC) into alternating current (AC) and then converts it back to a different DC voltage and current – one that perfectly matches your batteries.

Without an MPPT solar charge controller, your solar panels are not compatible with your batteries or lighting. Usually, an MPPT solar charge controller is wired directly to the solar panels, and from there, linked to:

- The batteries
- The lights
- The inverter

It then makes sure that everything is getting the proper voltage and the right kind of current.

6. An HRC Fuse

High rupturing capacity (HRC) fuses will sit between the batteries and MPPT solar charge controller. These fuses have been designed to carry a short circuit current for a set period. As soon as a fault occurs, the fuse blows, breaking the circuit to prevent damage to the other components.

These fuses are usually made of glass, and they prevent your system from being blown up if the MPPT solar charge controller fails to do its job correctly.

7. A Battery Bank

Obviously, for solar panels, you will need batteries. These store energy while your panels generate it and hold it there for use when your panels are not. Not all of the energy your panels produce will go into the batteries in most systems. They are usually wired to supply directly to devices and then simply feed extra energy into the batteries.

Without batteries, you will have no reliable power source. Something as simple as a cloud could knock out your whole system, so it's essential to make sure you have batteries ready to install.

8.   Direct Current Loads

These are loads that work on direct current rather than alternating current. Direct current is what your solar panels supply, so these can be wired in before your inverter (which will swap the DC into AC).

In general, DC loads will be things like your lights, rather than things like laptops, chargers, etc.

9.   A 24V Converter

A battery inverter is crucial for your solar panel setup. Remember, your solar panels produce DC, and your plug-in devices require AC to function. Your battery inverter is one of the most critical parts to spend time selecting because it must be able to meet the needs of every appliance that could be plugged into it at all times and in all circumstances.

Your solar panels will have minimal use if you do not have a battery inverter. Installing an inverter lets you utilize solar energy for all your devices, such as cell phone chargers, toasters, laptops, fridges, etc.

It's important to avoid just buying the cheapest inverter you can find. Spend time researching different inverters, mainly how they handle power surges. When you first turn your system on, there will be a sudden and sharp demand for power as the high-power units (e.g. fridges, water pumps, etc.) turn on. If your inverter cannot handle this surge, it will fail.

We will cover how to choose an inverter suitable for your needs later in the book.

10.   240V Alternating Current Loads

This is anything that you wish to plug into your system. Remember, the more devices you have, the greater the load on the system and the better your components need to be. If you plan to run high-energy devices such as fridges, dishwashers, vacuum cleaners, etc., you will need components that can cope with the demand.

Anything that is not directly wired into your direct current will be on alternating current.

Installation Phases

Phase 1) Check That You Have Space

If you want to use solar power for your off-grid setup, you will need to find a space to install the panels, which can only be done on the roof in a moving vehicle, such as a boat, RV, or van. If you own a small piece of land, you could site the panels elsewhere, but the roof is still likely to be the preferable option.

Phase 2) Calculate Your Energy Needs

Once you know that there is room for solar panels, you need to work out whether you can build a viable system to meet your energy needs and whether you can afford this system; This will involve a bit of math, but it is not too complicated once you make a start.

You will need to begin by making a list of the appliances you want to run and how long per day. Check the appliance's power rating so you can calculate the amount of power it needs; This is done by multiplying the power rating by the number of hours it will run for.

Do this for each appliance you wish to run, always erring on the side of producing too much power. Next, remember that most solar panels cannot run at maximum efficiency most of the time. You will often lose about 30% of your energy or more.

If you are struggling with this, there are many load calculators available on the internet that should help you. Once you have a total for the amount of energy needed, you can move on to the next step.

Phase 3) Choose Your Solar Panels

We will talk about choosing solar panels in a dedicated chapter (Chapter Four), but this is the next installation phase.

You will need to make sure that your solar panels are suitable for charging your batteries.

You will also need to think about the amount of sun the panels will get most days, whether you can afford the more efficient (but more expensive) monocrystalline solar panels, or whether to go with the cheaper and less efficient polycrystalline panels or thin-film panels; This will all be explored in Chapter Four.

Phase 4) Choose Your Batteries

You need batteries for your solar panel setup, even if you only plan to run your appliances during the day. There are a few reasons for this.

1. We tend to use more electricity at night when it is dark. Even if you don't plan to do so, having an emergency supply is wise.
2. Solar panels produce direct current, which won't power any plugin devices. You need

batteries and a converter to get an alternating current.

3. Even if you only want lights (direct current), you should still use batteries because they supply a constant rated voltage. Even in full sun, solar panels may fluctuate depending on what they supply; This is not good for your lights and won't produce a satisfactory system.

We will cover how to choose the best battery in Chapter Three. Be aware that although batteries have come a long way, they still lack efficiency, so you will constantly be losing energy even as your panels are charging the batteries. Therefore, it's essential to take care and choose a battery that will perfectly meet your needs.

Phase 5) Choose Your Solar Charge Controller

Again, you will need to select a solar charge controller that works with the other parts of your system. There are three kinds, but MPPT is the most efficient and will be predominantly focused on in this book.

Phase 6) Choose Your Inverter

You will need an inverter to get any AC appliances running, and again there are several types. The inverter will need to be capable of handling the maximum watt load of your system, including the starting power of any devices (which is often higher than their ongoing power requirements).

Phase 7) Begin Wiring

You will need to decide whether you will create your system with series connections or parallel connections. In general, your wiring system will look something like this:

Solar Panels Solar Charge Controller Battery Inverter AC Load

There will be a further join on the Solar Charge Controller to any direct DC loads (lights). Usually, a breaker is installed between the battery and the inverter, and another breaker is installed between the inverter and the AC load. You may also have one between the solar panels and the charge controller or other places, but that is your basic system.

You will need to ensure that the cables you are using can handle the charge being sent through them and that energy loss is minimized.

Phase 8) Mount The Solar Panels

You can purchase a mounting stand for your solar panels, and then you will need to mount them on an elevated surface (usually a rooftop).

Make sure that the mounting stand is angled so that your panels will capture the maximum amount of sunlight (although this may be challenging if your off-grid home moves). You should also angle the panel based on your latitude, and you can find calculators to help with this online.

If you are mounting panels on a static off-grid home, consider anything that might obscure the sunlight nearby – such as trees, other buildings, etc.

Mount the panel stands according to the manufacturer's instructions, and then mount the panels on them. You can then wire the panels into your main system.

Phase 9) Mount The Batteries And Inverter

You will need to put your batteries and inverter in an out-of-the-way spot. You may wish to put them up on a wall overhead in a covered box; this looks neater and protects them from bumps or damage.

However, remember that the inverter fan will need access to fresh air to keep the system cool and prevent it from overheating. The batteries will also benefit from some ventilation, so drill holes in your mounting box for air circulation and cables.

Mount your box and finish wiring up the system, and once the sunlight falls on your solar panels, you should soon have energy.

Summary

Hopefully, from this chapter, you learned:

- How solar energy works and how we can start harnessing it to power our homes
- The potential power of solar panels
- The difference between on-grid and off-grid solar setups, as well as hybrid setups
- What components an off-grid solar setup requires
- The fundamental phases of installing solar panels

In the next chapter, we will cover some of the basics of electricity, including the differences between power and energy. You can get to grips with what your system is doing and how it works, which will help you choose the correct components for your solar power system.

2
Basics of Electricity

"And God said, 'Let there be light,' and there was light, but the Electricity Board said He would have to wait until Thursday to be connected."

-Spike Milligan

Electricity is something that very few of us stop to think about. It is part of our lives and integral to almost everything we do. *We all know our phones, televisions, and computers are powered by electricity, but what about things like streetlamps, fridges, freezers, stoves, and everything else that we use daily?* Alarms, monitors, printers, emails – electricity is integral to every single aspect of our lives now.

We often have to take it away to understand how much we depend on it. If you have ever experienced a power cut, you have had a taste of this. When I was younger, power cuts were a regular occurrence, and we could lose our electricity for days at a time.

It was an adventure for the first hour or two, and then it became a nuisance. Doing homework by candlelight and eating takeouts because we couldn't cook was frustrating. Going to bed in a freezing bedroom because all of our heating was electric was downright unpleasant.

Anyone who has trialed their mobile home without electricity will be familiar with these challenges and with the sense of panic as a battery is dying and you just haven't quite finished making dinner or sending a work email. As time passes, this becomes truer and truer as our dependency on electricity increases.

Very few people now are happy to live without electricity, but very few of us understand how we get connected and where the power comes from. We flick the switch and watch the device boot up. When I first started to study solar panels and how to utilize them, I was surprised by how little I knew about where the power in the home comes from, what the options for powering homes are, and how it works.

In this chapter, we will run through some of the basics of electricity and how it can be generated.

Solar power is fundamentally about creating the right amount of electricity to power your system and ensuring that it is being utilized efficiently, so this chapter will give you the foundations you need to understand this process.

We are going to cover:

- The basic forms of power that exist
- The differences between power and energy
- The fundamentals of solar power

Basic Forms Of Power

There are many ways in which we can generate electricity. Often, it is generated by burning fossil fuels, and we all know how problematic this is for the environment. More and more people are trying to reduce their use of fossil fuels, but they remain our go-to source for energy. Even in recent years, only around 11% of global primary energy was generated using renewable technology.[vii]

So, what are the basic forms of power that we can use? All of the major ones are as follows:

- Coal (fossil fuel)
- Oil (fossil fuel)
- Natural gas (fossil fuel)
- Nuclear fission
- Wind
- Wave
- Geothermal
- Hydroelectric
- Biomass
- Solar

Some are non-renewables, including coal, oil, natural gas, and nuclear. Others are renewable, including wind, wave, geothermal, hydroelectric, biomass, and solar. We can depend upon these sources in the future because they are not finite resources, and we can generate power from them indefinitely.

If we continue to depend upon non-renewable resources, we will run out, no matter how carefully we use them; This is a simple fact. These resources are not regenerating (or so infinitesimally slowly as to count as non-regenerating). Even if we halve or quarter our use, we will run out.

Every item we use that requires electricity will be generated from one of these sources. They have different pros and cons. Non-renewable sources suffer the significant disadvantage of running out, and they are enormously damaging to the environment – but they are also attractive because they produce lots of power.

Of course, the amount produced does vary depending on the source in question. Coal, oil, and gas produce reasonable amounts of power, whereas nuclear produces massively more for the materials it needs. However, nuclear energy uses rarer materials and has many other drawbacks in disposing of them. Overall, the reward for using fossil fuels and nuclear fuel is high, but the payoff is also very high and not viable in the long term.

Renewable energy has trailed a long way behind fossil fuels in terms of how much power it can produce. Yet, this gap is closing, and recent advancements have meant that renewables are becoming a viable alternative to non-renewable energy in many instances.

So, our options are currently:

- Fossil fuels, with a medium power output but pollution
- Nuclear fission, with superb power output but many disadvantages
- Renewable energy, which currently suffers from either a low (but improving) amount of power output or from being very location specific (geothermal works very well in some areas, but not in others), is a long-term solution

At present, the human population is making compromises and finding a best-case scenario for power use. We depend upon a combination of all of these things. Swapping to one or the other as a global movement is not currently viable. Still, individuals can choose to move toward renewables – and this will usually be solar, which we will discuss a little later in this chapter.

Differences Between Power And Energy

It is essential to understand the difference between power and energy when talking about electricity because they are not the same thing, even though many people use these terms interchangeably.

Energy is the capacity to make something happen, the driving force of change. Moving something uses energy. To do that, you have to expend energy stored in your muscles and convert it into something different – the movement.

Energy is never destroyed or created. When we generate energy from something (like coal or sunlight), we simply convert the energy from one form into another. When we burn coal, we release the energy to produce heat and power. When solar panels create energy, they convert this energy from sunlight into electricity. Although we talk about generating energy, we mean converting it.

As an example, think about how you convert your food into energy. When you go to the gym, you are putting energy into moving something (whether weights, your legs on a treadmill, etc.), which burns energy stored in your body. The energy has not gone, but you have converted it into another source; This is the same with any form of energy. It does not disappear and cannot be destroyed or created.

In physics, energy is usually measured in joules. However, energy is often measured in kilo-watt-hours when working with electrical systems. One kilowatt-hour is equal to 3600000 joules. You will have seen kilowatt-hours on your electricity bill.

Power is a measure of how fast energy is being put into something. It means the amount of energy spent per unit of time; This is why a high power engine can do more work and is needed for situations in which a low power engine would be too slow. The low power engine might still be able to do the job, provided it has enough fuel (energy), but it would take too long to be practical.

Power is usually measured in watts or kilowatts. It is important not to get kilowatts con-fused with kilowatt-hours. A kilowatt-hour is 3600000 joules of energy – the amount of energy that something requiring a kilowatt of power to run would use if it were left running for an hour.

Think of it in this way:

If you want to carry a heavy box from A to B, it takes 10 units of your energy to move the box in one hour. It might take another person 10 units of their energy to move the box in a day. The same amount of energy is required for the box to move, no matter who moves it. However, one of you can carry the box more quickly because you are a more powerful person. Your muscles are stronger. You can therefore do the same job faster.

It does not take less energy, but having more power improves the time ratio. In some cas-es, improvement is needed for the device to function this time. A weak motor might not be able to make something move even slightly. A light bulb provided with insufficient wattage might not just be dimmer; it may fail to light up at all.

Recognizing the distinction between energy and power is crucial because it helps you understand why we need to look at the energy output of something and its power. If you are thinking of using a battery that stores 5 kilowatt-hours, you also need to know how fast it can release this energy to the devices you're running. If it can only output it at a rate of 1 watt, the battery will last a long time without going flat, but it doesn't serve you very well because it won't give your device enough power quickly.

The amount of power that a device needs is often the most relevant factor, and this should be given to you in the manual or on the device. If the device receives 1 watt when it needs 20 watts, it will likely not function at all. To calculate the energy that your solar panels should generate, it is crucial to recognize how much power your devices need and whether the energy your solar panel's output can meet that demand.

Solar Power Basics

Solar power is one of the most promising renewable energy sources, partly because it is applicable wherever you go. It is also improving very quickly, and today's solar power technology is vastly more useful and viable than the technology from fifty years ago.

One of the big myths about solar panels is that you need direct sunlight for them to work at all, and on a cloudy day, you will not get any energy; This is not true. The sun is outputting energy all the time, and less energy does not equate to no energy. Modern solar panels can generate electricity even on cloudy days, and they do not stop working just because of a shadow passing over the panel.

It is vital to recognize if you live in a part of the world that does not enjoy as much sunlight. You can still utilize solar panels, although you may not get as much efficiency from them as someone who lives somewhere with a lot of sunshine.

If you live somewhere with only a limited amount of daylight hours, solar panels will not serve you as well because they are getting less energy, and therefore they will output less power. When the sun no longer falls on them at all, they have nothing to convert, and they cannot charge your batteries.

Of course, solar power does suffer from some other major disadvantages, such as:

- It is an intermittent source of power, as many of the renewables mean unreliable; This is frustrating for a system that you may need to power basic essentials such as cookers, fridges, and lights. If you do not get enough daylight, your panels cannot operate properly.

- It tends to produce the most power when you least need it (when you want your lights on at night, your panels are not producing any power), so energy storage is needed, and this is expensive. When you are using significantly more energy for heating and cooking in cold, dark weather, your panels may struggle to keep up.
- It is fairly expensive still, despite the constantly reducing costs. This puts it out of reach for many people who own tiny homes, despite offering such good cost savings going forward.
- The energy storage solutions are not yet very efficient, so you will have to buy large batteries that need to be stored. This is not ideal when space is already limited in your home. Additionally, these batteries are expensive and may not be very green, and they will have a maximum lifespan, leading to pollution when they are eventually disposed of.
- It takes a significant amount of space to produce enough power for most situations. You will have to dedicate space on your roof, which might have been utilized for additional storage (depending upon your setup).
- The components will not last forever, so there will be future costs to maintaining the system as parts need to be replaced.

However, there are some significant advantages:

- You can have power without being linked up to the grid, which is ideal if you wish to move your home around or live a long distance from society. This provides the freedom that has previously been very limited unless you are happy to live without power.
- You are not dependent on energy production from other companies, so you will not be affected by crises or power cuts outside of your control.
- You will reduce your living costs because you can power your home without buying batteries or paying to charge them regularly. You will not have energy bills and standing charges to pay for the grid's service.
- You can create a more environmentally friendly space because you have moved away from fossil fuels. Adding solar power to your home will massively reduce your carbon footprint. How big this reduction is will depend heavily on your situation.
- You are not affected by rising energy costs, so as fossil fuels become scarcer, and in greater demand, you will not be paying exorbitant prices to keep your power on.
- Almost anyone can fit solar panels, and they can be used almost anywhere, making them ideal for homes that move. Instead of having to access society every few days/ weeks to recharge your batteries, buy new ones, or exchange power sources (e.g. gas canisters), you can go where you please, provided enough light for the panels.

Solar panels are attractive for these reasons and compared with many of the other renewable sources, they are an excellent way to power your home.

Even compared with the non-renewables, they are attractive because they make you independent of society and generate power wherever you are. The ongoing costs are low (although parts will need to be replaced at times), so if you can afford the upfront costs, you will massively reduce your ongoing bills.

In terms of the other renewables, solar tends to win for several reasons, which will be explored below.

Solar VS Wind

Wind is massively more efficient than solar, but it has some major disadvantages that make it inapplicable in most residential situations – especially for tiny homes/mobile homes.

- It is noisy
- It is ugly (in most people's view)
- There is usually not enough steady wind in a residential area to work well
- Wind turbines need more maintenance
- Wind turbines may not be as easy to fit into your mobile setup

In general, wind is vastly more preferable for a large scale setup, but solar wins every time for a small one.

Solar VS Other Renewables

None of the other renewable energy sources can be used in most mobile home setups. Things like wave and hydropower require you to be alongside water, even if we discount the size of the necessary equipment.

Geothermal energy is also impractical, as is biomass. Solar is, therefore, your only option, besides wind, for generating electricity while on the go in most off-grid situations. Of course, there are exceptions, but on the whole, solar is the best method for reducing your dependency on civilization and fossil fuels.

Summary

In this chapter, we've covered:

- How we can currently generate power, including both renewable and non-renewable fuel sources

- The difference between power and energy and why it is key to understand this when creating a solar power setup
- Some of the essential advantages and disadvantages of a solar panel system and why you might use solar power instead of other renewable resources for an at-home setup

In the following chapter, we will start choosing the appropriate battery for your solar power system. Remember, the battery is crucial because it will power your home any time there is not enough daylight to generate electricity.

3

Choosing The Right Battery

"Every great device, gadget, electric car, and robot would be even greater if batteries didn't suck so badly."

-Steven Levy

You are bound to be aware of batteries' impact on our daily lives. Every portable electronic device depends upon them, and many of us find that our lives also – to a degree – depend upon them. *How often have you felt a jolt of horror upon realizing that your cell phone's battery is almost dead and you can't do the important thing that you depended upon it for?*

This can leave you unable to navigate, make an emergency call, submit documents, coordinate with group members, help out a friend, or a whole host of other things. It is a major inconvenience and is becoming more so that we become more dependent on our cell phones every year.

This extends to every area of life that includes batteries. A flat battery on your car, your laptop, your tablet, or even just your remote control can range from devastating to inconvenient, but there's no doubt that when batteries fail, it is never a good time, and it is always frustrating. More than anything, batteries are a technology that we depend upon heavily and very often, they let us down.

However, in each of these scenarios, you are only dealing with one item that has gone flat and become unavailable for use. It might be very important in that instant, but it is still just one thing. However, the batteries in your solar panel system are supporting everything – and that's why it's so crucial to choose as well as you possibly can within your budget.

Getting the right battery will make a massive difference to your experience with solar panels. Batteries are notoriously inefficient and suffer from many other problems, such as how much space they require, the maintenance that is needed, and the end of life disposal issues.

The battery is the store you depend upon most of the time, and it is therefore extremely important to choose correctly, so, in this chapter, we're going to look at:

- Lithium-ion batteries
- Flooded Lead-Acid batteries
- Sealed Lead-Acid batteries
- Nickel-Cadmium batteries

For each, we will explore the advantages and disadvantages associated with them and the setups they are most appropriate for. This should put you in a great position to choose the most viable for your off-grid solar power system.

We'll then cover choosing the best battery and which specs matter the most.

Lithium-ion Batteries

This is one of the newest kinds of battery technology. It has been climbing in popularity recently, especially with the increasing uptake of electric vehicles – which require good energy storage in a very limited space.

They are an excellent option in many applications, and if you can afford them, you may find them good for an off-grid setup. Of course, no battery is perfect, but many people are turning to these as a solution for their power storage. They are currently one of the most widely used in solar battery banks because of the advantages they offer.

Don't be deterred just because they are new technology. As evidenced by their popularity, they are a particularly attractive option at present, and they often outstrip the other batteries for a number of reasons.

Pros:

There are a few major advantages to these batteries, including:

- They are low maintenance
- They do not require as much space as other batteries tend to
- They last for considerably longer than most other batteries (generally at least ten years, usually longer)

Let's break each section down below.

They are low maintenance. In general, batteries require you to look after them and perform a few basic tasks on a regular basis to keep them running (see below for further information). You might be willing to do that, but if you are operating an off-grid setup that you are often away from for long periods of time, this can be very problematic.

Even if you are present, it is annoying to have to keep servicing your batteries, as this is an ongoing chore and one that you must keep track of if you want to keep the batteries in good condition.

They are smaller. A major advantage in an off-grid setup where space is lacking, being smaller makes these batteries a far more attractive option than many of the competing products. Instead of having to dedicate large amounts of space to your battery bank, you can reduce the footprint of the setup and keep it to a contained area.

On a boat or an RV, this is enormously attractive and may be the biggest factor in the popularity of lithium-ion batteries. Anywhere that space is at a premium, the compactness of these batteries makes them extremely attractive.

It should also be noted that this reduction in size and weight may help you to make financial savings in areas like fuel. If you install solar panels on a moving vehicle, adding heavy batteries is not an attractive option. Lithium-ion batteries are considerably lighter.

They last much longer. These batteries allow the system to pull more of the stored energy from them before they require more charge to be put in. This is known as a higher depth of discharge, and it helps to lengthen the battery's lifespan because it is charging in a significantly more efficient way.

This is attractive for very obvious reasons, making you less dependent on society, reducing the environmental footprint of the materials you use, and costing you less money in replacing parts of the system.

Cons:

There are also a few disadvantages associated with these batteries, in spite of their popularity, including:

- They cost significantly more than other batteries
- They are more of a fire risk

Let's explore in more detail.

They are more expensive. Although this is the case, it's important to remember that some of this cost will be offset in the long term by their increased life expectancy. They do cost more to buy, but they should last longer, making them more comparable despite the up-front costs. However, you will still need to be able to afford those upfront costs to install these in your system.

If you are on a tight budget, you may find that you have to purchase a cheaper battery, at least initially. You can then save up for a more efficient battery in the future if you find that this is possible, and choose this option then. In general, this is the biggest reason to avoid purchasing a lithium-ion battery when you first start setting up your system; these batteries are almost always considered superior to the other options in every way except the cost.

They are more of a fire risk. This might sound like a considerable downside, but it should be noted that although lithium-ion batteries do pose a slightly bigger risk of catching fire, this is only the case when they are improperly installed.

The risk is caused by something known as thermal runaway, and in most setups, this will not be an issue. As long as you thoroughly research how to set these systems up or you hire professionals for this part of the job, you should not have any problems. However, it is still wise to have good fire detecting equipment and an alarm that is regularly checked so that you further minimize any risk of fire damage being caused by these batteries.

Don't install lithium-ion batteries without having a good understanding of what you are doing, and you should not have any problems with the fire risk.

Overview:

In general, lithium-ion is the most promising and useful battery for at-home use, especially in off-grid setups where space is very limited. If you don't have room for large battery banks and you are looking to minimize the weight of your home (in a mobile setup, for example), then lithium-ion batteries are certainly the best option in almost every given scenario. This is true despite the cost.

Flooded Lead-Acid Batteries

Also, in common use, lead-acid batteries have been the standard for many years, and although they suffer from quite a few disadvantages, they are a reliable storage solution that has stood the test of time. We'll look at flooded and sealed lead-acid batteries, starting with flooded.

Suppose you cannot afford lithium-ion batteries and you have a stationary off-grid home. In that case, these are certainly a reasonable alternative, and they remain popular in solar panel systems despite their disadvantages. Let's explore the benefits and drawbacks.

Pros:

- They are a reliable and much-tested solution
- They are pretty easy to recycle
- They tend to cost less

They are reliable. These batteries have been used for a long time, partly because they are highly dependable and very stable. This makes them suitable if you are heavily dependent on your power system and have a viable space for them (see the cons list to understand what this entails). In some circumstances, they are the preferable option.

They are easy to recycle. The disposal can be a major issue for some kinds of batteries, and if you are setting up a solar system with the well-being of the planet in mind, this really matters. Fortunately, these batteries are easy to recycle.

They cost less. Cost is probably a huge factor in your setup, and a flooded lead-acid battery is highly appealing if you are on a budget because the upfront cost is far lower than that of other batteries.

Cons:

- They are bulky
- They need to be stored upright in a ventilated, temperature-controlled area
- Their depth of discharge is poor
- They don't last as long as other batteries
- They need maintaining

They are bulky. In many off-grid setups, size really matters, and these batteries are not small. A bank of these will require plenty of space, and because of the poor depth of discharge, you will need more than one battery.

They need special storage conditions. Many off-grid setups will not have a suitable spot for these batteries. They need to be kept in a ventilated space and sensitive to temperature fluctuations. You cannot store the batteries sideways, making them even trickier to assign space. If you own land and have a dedicated building that you can place them in, this may work, but they aren't suitable for off-grid homes in many cases.

They have a poor depth of discharge. As mentioned above, the depth of discharge refers to how much power you can pull from the battery before it needs more power to be put in. With a low depth of discharge, these are inefficient – and will die more quickly.

They don't last well. Contributed to the depth of discharge, they have a relatively short lifespan, which decreases the attractiveness of the low starting cost. The lifespan will depend heavily on the usage and the individual battery, but it can be as low as two years (some batteries lasting more than twelve years).

They need maintenance. You will need to top up the water as it is lost from the battery to keep it operating correctly, which has an ongoing cost in terms of your man-hours and possibly your water supply (if this is limited).

Overview:

There are some scenarios in which a flooded lead-acid battery is the best option, but in general, you will find other solutions better unless you are on an extremely tight budget and you have a suitable space for them – in which case they become attractive.

Sealed Lead-Acid Batteries

In a low-maintenance version, the sealed lead acid batteries don't require you to top up the water and do not have a high risk of toxic gasses escaping while the battery is recharged. Otherwise, these share similar advantages and disadvantages to the flooded lead-acid batteries, although they may be somewhat more expensive and have a reduced lifespan overall.

These batteries are similar to car batteries, although they are usually considerably larger.

Nickel-Cadmium Batteries

Another battery that has stood the test of time and improved significantly in recent years, nickel-cadmium batteries (Ni-Cd batteries), are also an option. Still, they are not allowed in some countries due to high toxicity levels.

They are still available in the USA, but you should consider the environmental impact of selecting one of these batteries; they are generally considered a poor option.

Pros:

- Reliable storage solution
- A very durable battery that should last long
- Not affected by temperature extremes

They are reliable. This technology has existed for over 100 years, so it is considered very reliable, and it has been well-refined.

They are durable. On the whole, these batteries are built to last, and they will handle being bumped occasionally without any issue. Depending upon your setup, this could be significant.

They aren't affected by temperature. If you don't have a means of protecting the batteries and you want to mount them outside, this could be significant, especially if you live in a very cold or very hot place. Protecting other batteries from temperature damage will be critical, but nickel-cadmium batteries are good at coping with temperature changes.

Cons:

- The toxicity levels are high
- The battery is tough to recycle
- The battery must be discharged before it can be recharged, affecting the storage space

They are toxic. Many people have moved away from these batteries for both health and environmental reasons.

They are hard to recycle. Tying in with the above point, the end-of-life of these batteries is very bad for the planet. Few – if any – of the components can be removed and reused, so these batteries tend to end up in landfill sites. Because of the toxicity, this is a massive problem.

They need to be fully discharged. This is another huge issue, as you will generally want your solar panels to top up the battery whenever energy is available. However, nickel-cadmium batteries often "remember" the point from which they were last recharged, preventing them from being recharged effectively by the panels. This massively reduces the storage space that they offer, making them a very unattractive solution.

Overview:

In general, you will find that other options are far more appealing than nickel-cadmium unless your battery bank cannot be protected from the elements by any means. In these scenarios, nickel-cadmium batteries may remain a viable option.

Which Specs Should You Look At?

Even once you have chosen the type of battery for your off-grid home, you will need to look at the various batteries within that category and the specs they can offer you. It is important to narrow down the category first. The comparison is simply too huge to deal with, but now that we've looked at categories, let's explore the specs and which ones are particularly important when you're shopping for a battery.

Capacity:

Potentially the most important element in choosing a battery is its capacity. This means the maximum amount of energy stored in that battery. When the battery is full, your solar panels will not be able to store up any more energy.

It is imperative to look at this number and measure it against your needs. Suppose your battery cannot hold enough power to be helpful. In that case, it will constantly cause problems within the system, and you will find you perpetually run out of power when your solar panels aren't operating (e.g. overnight).

Make sure that your battery can manage for at least one night, or consider the minimum power storage acceptable for you. This calculation should be reasonably easy to do when you know approximately how much power you will use during 24 hours.

Stackability:

If you buy a battery, it is always worth thinking about the future and what you may need then. It is beneficial to expand your energy storage system later, so it is important to look at whether your solar batteries are stackable.

This may not be a deciding factor, but if you want to build a large power bank, it is worth exploring stackability and ensuring that your battery can be expanded when necessary.

Cycles warrantied:

All batteries have a set number of times to recharge and be fully powered. This number varies according to other stats, but it's imperative to consider the number of recharges guaranteed by the manufacturer.

You will constantly be draining and recharging your solar battery, and over time, the amount of power it will hold (and how long it will keep it for) will decrease as the battery becomes less efficient. Usually, manufacturers provide a warranty that tells you how the battery will perform after several charging and discharging cycles.

Looking at this number will give you a good idea of how long the battery should last, which will help you to choose a high-quality product that suits your needs. Remember, batteries with better guarantees are likely to cost more upfront but should not need replacing as quickly and will usually offer protection if something goes wrong with them.

Power rating:

You need to know how much power your battery can supply to your system all at once. A battery may have a significant amount of energy stored in it, but if it only outputs this at a trickle speed, it will not supply all your appliances at once. This is particularly true if you have devices that demand a lot of energy, such as vacuum cleaners or fridges.

You should look at the kilowatts that the battery you consider can provide. Often, you will find two different power ratings: one is an "instantaneous power rating", and the other is a "continuous power rating." As you might expect, the continuous power rating tells you how much the battery can supply if it is steadily drained. The instant power rating tells you how much power the battery can give in one short burst. This is useful if you have appliances that require a lot of power to start up but little while running.

Familiarize yourself with both of these stats and factor them into your equation to know what power rating you need to get the most from your system.

Battery size:

This will matter a lot more in some setups than others, but it is important to bear the size of the battery in mind when you're weighing up your options, especially if space is limited in your home. You need to minimize how much you dedicate to your battery bank, as this will be a permanent feature of the system.

Even if you can tuck it out of the way, it's a good idea to look for small, compact, light-weight batteries, especially if you are operating a mobile home rather than a fixed off-grid setup. Of course, this does cost more, but it's generally worth the extra expense to give yourself long term convenience.

Summary

In this chapter, we've covered:

- The different kinds of batteries, including lithium-ion, flooded lead-acid batteries, sealed lead-acid batteries, and nickel-cadmium batteries
- The advantages and disadvantages offered by each kind of battery, as well as the situations in which they are most likely to be used
- The specs you should pay attention to when choosing a battery to ensure you get the correct one for your needs

In the next chapter, we will move on to looking at solar panels and how you can choose the perfect solar panel for your system. We'll look at the different price options and the different kinds of technology available, simplifying the various kinds you can choose from so that you know which is right for you.

4

Choosing the Right Solar Panel

"Solar power is the last energy resource that isn't owned yet
– nobody taxes the sun yet."

-Bonnie Raitt

You are probably already aware of how important it is to get the right solar panel for your system and energy needs. *Not doing so could undermine your entire system and make it almost useless to you – but how do you pick?*

This technology has advanced at an extraordinary rate. While that means that we have access to technology that has made great leaps in terms of its efficiency, it also means that there is a lot of information out there, and much of it has become quite confusing. In this chapter, I will break down the different kinds of solar panels available and discuss why some are preferable to others, along with the situations you might want to use them for your off-grid solar panel setup.

Whatever kind of solar panel you decide to use, make sure that you do some thorough research around it to check that it exceeds your needs. You should always go for considerably more power than you anticipate needing, as this allows you to scale up if necessary, and the only downside is slightly increased upfront costs.

Aiming to hit the exact need may seem a more economical option because it means you are not purchasing equipment that you don't require. Still, often, this is a false economy because you will find that your system either fails to meet your needs (because you have underestimated them) or that it soon stops meeting your needs (both due to increased needs and degradation of equipment). It is important to remember that solar panels do not offer perfect efficiency and that the rating of the equipment is not what you will achieve on most days, even if you live in an ideal climate with excellent weather.

Provided that you over-estimate your needs, you should find that your solar panels can keep up, but if you under-buy in an attempt to keep your budget down, you may find that you have to completely rebuild the system and buy new panels because your original purchase simply isn't powerful enough. If in doubt, always choose the more powerful option because it is much better to have a system that is over-powered than one that cannot meet demand.

Monocrystalline Solar Panels

The most expensive kind of solar panel, monocrystalline solar panels, are also currently the best option on the home market (although some better ones exist for military use at present). They will offer you the best productivity for the space that they take up, so if you can afford them, these are generally the option that you should go for.

Pros:

- Currently, the best commercially available option for converting light into energy
- They do not need as much space to generate energy
- They last for longer than other panels
- They cope better with reduced levels of sunlight

They are currently the best option for converting sunlight into energy. Because they contain more silicon, they will work better, and they can achieve efficiency levels of up to 20% in some circumstances. This ensures that you get the maximum energy from whatever sunlight is available, which is optimal for your setup.

They need less space. Because the panels are more efficient, you need fewer of them overall. That means that although the panels are more expensive, you may not need as many. You will also be able to maximize the space you do have if it is limited and would not otherwise provide enough power (for example, on a boat's roof).

They last for longer. Like buying the best kind of battery, when you accept a higher up-front cost, you do enjoy reduced ongoing costs because the monocrystalline solar panels should last for considerably longer than other kinds of solar panels. Some manufacturers offer as much as a 25-year warranty, so if you are able to afford this kind of panel, it is well worth the investment and will probably mean that your system lasts for longer overall.

In general, this kind of solar panel should last up to 50 years.

They perform well in cloudy areas. Another advantage of the particularly efficient solar panels is that they will do well even when the weather is cloudy and dim. Where other panels may not produce any power because the weather is too bad, you will still be getting some charge from your panels, making them a significantly more useful piece of equipment, especially in some parts of the world where sunlight is more limited.

Cons:

- The price makes monocrystalline solar panel setups pretty expensive
- This kind of panel has very wasteful manufacturing processes
- They are the most expensive solar cells on the market and so not in everyone's price range
- The performance levels tend to suffer if the weather is hot. However, it is a small loss when compared to other forms of solar cell
- There is a lot of waste material when the silicon is cut during manufacture

The panels are expensive. As the most expensive solar panels on the market, these are not a great option for people on a tight budget. Although you will enjoy a product with a significantly longer lifespan, it is still a problem if you don't have a lot to spend on your solar panels – especially if you need a lot of them.

In general, the panels cost between $300 and $700 each, which can get expensive fast, especially when you take the other component costs into account.

The panels don't like being heated. Getting really hot is not good for any solar panels, so this is not a major con. You will find that solar panels do much better when kept cool, but if you can't avoid the system getting hot occasionally, these should cope better than polycrystalline solar panels do.

The manufacturing process is wasteful. One of the biggest cons of these panels, from an environmental perspective, is that they have a high material cost when it comes to manufacturing them. A lot of silicon is cut off because all four sides of the cells are sliced. This drives up the financial and environmental costs for manufacturing the panels, so if you are looking for both a cheap and a green option, these panels are not the right choice.

However, this balances against the increased efficiency, which means that they will always be creating more energy than their cheaper-to-manufacture alternatives. It isn't possible to do a hard calculation on which is the better option, either environmentally or financially, because it will depend very heavily on the operating circumstances, but it is worth remembering that the high manufacturing costs (environmental and financial) will be offset at least to a degree by the increased efficiency and extended lifespan of the panels.

Overview:

Monocrystalline solar panels are the top technology in terms of solar panels, and that makes them preferable to pretty much every other option if you can afford them. Additionally, their space-saving is enormously attractive for most off-grid setups, as space tends to be more limited in places like RVs and cabins, so maximizing the efficiency is crucial to making solar panels viable.

Polycrystalline Solar Panels

Although they are similar to monocrystalline solar panels, polycrystalline solar panels are a preferable option for many people. They enjoy several advantages, as they are cheaper than monocrystalline solar panels, and they create considerably less waste in terms of their manufacturing.

Instead of silicon being cut away and therefore wasted, polycrystalline solar panels use up all of the silicon that is associated with manufacturing them, which makes them vastly preferable in terms of the "green" impact. Being greener and more affordable, they are an excellent choice, but they are not as efficient. They are still made using silicon solar cells, but these are cooled differently, creating multiple crystals rather than just one (hence polycrystalline vs monocrystalline).

Pros:

- They are a reasonably efficient way of converting sunlight into energy
- The manufacturing process wastes massively less silicon compared with monocrystalline solar panels
- They are considerably cheaper than monocrystalline solar panels
- They should last for at least 25 years

A reasonably efficient way of converting sunlight into energy. Polycrystalline solar panels suffer somewhat from negative associations because they were considered very inefficient in the past. However, they have been massively improved in recent years, and although they are still worse than monocrystalline solar panels, they are an excellent option. They can reach efficiencies of around 15 to 17%.

The reason the efficiency is lower is that having multiple silicon cells within the panel slows down the movement of the electrons, and therefore some energy is constantly being lost due to this resistance.

The fact that the silicon purity is lower also affects the efficiency, but overall, many people find these panels are a great choice.

The manufacturing process is less wasteful. Because the silicon is not as pure, all of the material gets used in the panel, massively reducing the waste. For a product that is often marketed based on its green credentials and as a means of helping the planet, this is vastly preferable to the monocrystalline manufacturing process.

They are cheaper. This is a big factor in choosing the panels because opting for the expensive monocrystalline solar panels can massively increase your costs. In general, polycrystalline solar panels cost around $200-$500 per panel, which is significantly cheaper than the monocrystalline $300-$700, especially if you need multiple panels.

They last long. Like monocrystalline solar panels, polycrystalline solar panels should last pretty well – usually upward of 25 years. Many manufacturers offer guarantees about the lifespan of their products, so make sure you look at this when choosing your panels. Cheap panels with a very short warranty are not usually a safe gamble; choose slightly more expensive ones with a better warranty for peace of mind. You don't want to have to reinstall the whole system a few years down the line!

Cons:

- They are less efficient than monocrystalline solar panels
- They take up more space than monocrystalline solar panels
- They struggle in warm temperatures
- They (often) have a lower power rating
- They can be fragile

They are less efficient. As expressed above, the loss in silicon purity comes at a cost in efficiency. Where monocrystalline solar panels can achieve efficiency levels of 20%, polycrystalline will generally only reach 17% at best. While that may sound like a small difference, it can be surprisingly significant.

However, recent advances have been made in polycrystalline solar panels, and new processes are improving efficiency, closing the gap between the two kinds of panels and making polycrystalline ever more attractive (especially to those concerned about the waste produced by monocrystalline solar panels).

Given a few more years, it is likely that polycrystalline solar panels will draw level with monocrystalline solar panels or come even closer to matching them.

They take up more space. Unfortunately, loss in efficiency means that you will need to dedicate more space to the solar panels in order to generate the same amount of energy. Suppose you have lost 3% efficiency (comparing a top polycrystalline solar panel with a top monocrystalline solar panel). In that case, you will need to either accept less power or build more panels to compensate for that loss.

In a confined setting, such as an RV, this may not be possible, which makes polycrystalline panels somewhat less appealing.

They don't cope well with heat. All solar panels suffer in high temperatures, but polycrystalline solar panels are truer than monocrystalline ones. If temperatures in your area are regularly above 80 degrees F, you will find that polycrystalline solar panels do not perform well at all. They will lose a lot of efficiency whenever the weather is hot, decreasing the value of sunny days and making it hard to generate enough energy. The efficiency can drop by as much as 23% in hot weather.

They are not as powerful. Because polycrystalline solar panels are not as efficient, they are also less powerful on the whole. They will usually only have an output of up to 300 watts, although some expensive ones do have higher power ratings than this. If you need powerful solar panels, you may look at monocrystalline ones.

They can be fragile. Polycrystalline solar panels seem to be more vulnerable to physical damage than many other options. They are more likely to get broken if they get knocked, or something falls onto them, such as a branch.

If you regularly move around, you may be more concerned about physical damage. Equally, if you live in a heavily forested off-grid area, tree branches or even smaller debris brought down by high winds could do damage to your panels. This might lead to the need for expensive repairs or replacements.

Overview:

Polycrystalline solar panels tend to be one of the most popular options for home installations because they combine green manufacturing with low costs. This means they are a realistic financial outlay for many more households, making solar panels viable where monocrystalline would simply prove too expensive.

If you have enough space to set them up, these are likely to be your best option for generating solar power for your home, but you should be aware that they have not yet caught up with the efficiency offered by monocrystalline solar panels yet.

Thin-Film Solar Panels

As the most budget option, thin-film solar panels also lack efficiency (at least for the commercially available options) at present. Up until a few years ago, most had an efficiency rating below 10%, and even now, most are only able to achieve up to 13% efficiency, despite technological advancements.

Few residential installations with limited space will find that thin-film solar panels can generate enough energy to support a household, as they need a large area to make up for the inefficiency. However, if you do have a lot of space (for instance, on or around a fixed abode such as a cabin) and a tight budget, they may be worth considering. They can also be suitable in some limited space setups if you just want to generate a small amount of power – for example, on a boat, they might keep batteries charged and provide emergency power.

They also perform better in high temperatures than any other kind of solar panel, making them viable in warm climates.

It is worth noting that there are four different kinds of thin-film solar panels (Dye-sensitized Solar Cells, Cadmium Telluride, Copper Indium Gallium Selenide, and Amorphous Silicon), but they generally share their advantages and disadvantages, so we will cover them all in this section.

Pros:

- They offer improved temperature performance
- They are a cheaper option
- They can be made on flexible surfaces
- They often look more appealing than other solar panels
- They are lightweight
- They are less susceptible to getting dirty
- They are versatile
- They cope well with indirect light

They have improved temperature performance. Interestingly, although these solar panels are the cheapest, they are your best option if you live in a climate with consistently high temperatures. If you live somewhere like Arizona, with temperatures easily reaching the high 80s even in spring, these are certainly a good option to consider. Unlike monocrystalline and polycrystalline solar panels, they should not lose much efficiency when temperatures climb.

They are cheaper. Thin-film solar panels are often preferable if you are on a very tight budget because they will almost always win in terms of costs. Manufacturers offer shorter warranties for these panels, which reduces their costs, and the process of making them tends to be less pricey.

They generally also use fewer materials, and this makes them attractive from an environmental standpoint. However, it is important to note that the different thin-film panels will have different environmental costs, and Cadmium Telluride, in particular, has some problems. It uses raw tellurium, which is extremely rare on Earth. If you want to consider environmental costs, this needs to be weighed up according to the kind of thin-film that you wish to purchase.

They can be made flexible. This may not prove an advantage in some off-grid setups, but the fact that these panels are not rigid can be a massive bonus in certain niche situations. Unlike the rigid crystalline-based solar panels, they can be wrapped around surfaces and made to conform to rounded shapes. On a boat, this can be very useful.

However, you should note that this flexibility is only applicable during the installation, and once installed, they become rigid. They also do still tend to be installed flat, like other solar panels, so unless your unique situation particularly needs a curved panel setup, you may not find this offers any particular benefits.

They look more appealing. Thin-film solar panels tend to have a homogeneous appearance, making them more attractive to look at. Polycrystalline solar panels, by comparison, create a mosaic of different colors because they are made from slices of silicon, and this makes them look messy and unattractive.

They are light. Depending on what the film is poured onto during the manufacturing process, thin-film solar panels can be very light. This may be appealing if you are in a moving vehicle and you don't want to add to your fuel costs by increasing the load with additional solar panels. Crystalline-based solar panels weigh considerably more, and although they will offset this cost in power savings, it is still worth bearing it in mind as something that adds to the fuel cost of moving and to the wear and tear on your vehicle.

The lightness of thin-film solar panels also means that they can be installed in situations where other solar panels would prove too heavy.

They are versatile. Because the film can be poured onto almost any surface, even something like paper, they are far more versatile than either of the other two panels. The film can be used to coat roofing tiles or roof substances (for RVs, etc.), making it even more subtle on top of your vehicle and taking up less space. However, remember that you won't be able to put things on the roof, even if your tiles/surface are coated, because you will block the light from the solar cells.

You can turn your entire roof into a solar panel using this substance, although it will admittedly be a less efficient solar panel overall, and this may prove fairly expensive.

They are good in indirect light. Although all solar panels require sunlight to operate, these far outstrip the competition when it comes to operating well with indirect light. If your roof is north, east, or west facing, there may not be enough sunlight for the crystalline-based solar panels, which is a good solution.

This also means that they operate better in states (or countries) with less sunlight and more rainy and cloudy weather because they will draw more energy overall, despite the decreased efficiency rating.

Cons:

- They are less efficient
- They require more space
- Other equipment may come at a higher cost
- They often do not last as long and may come with a shorter warranty
- The overall system can cost more, despite lower panel costs
- It is a relatively new technology
- Some of the thin-film substances raise toxicity concerns

They are less efficient. The biggest deterrent from installing thin-film solar panels is that they do not offer a good deal in terms of their efficiency. They are significantly worse than polycrystalline or monocrystalline solar panels. You will not be able to generate nearly as much power using them unless you have vastly more panels.

They need more space. To set up a viable thin-film solar panel system, you will need to install a large number of them, and this requires a wide area of uninterrupted space. This makes them unattractive for many off-grid setups, especially in the tiny home, RV, and boating areas. You are unlikely to have this sort of space to spare, and that means you will only be able to generate small amounts of electricity from your panels – which may not be enough to make the system worthwhile.

Other equipment will cost more. Frequently, the lack of space efficiency will also mean that you require a lot of other equipment, such as longer cables, more support structures, etc. This comes at an increased cost and can further reduce the efficiency, as you will have to transport the electricity over greater distances, which results in a loss. It is important to budget carefully when building a system using thin-film solar panels. Make sure that the apparently cheap solar panel cost doesn't just win you over. Other expenses can add up fast.

They don't last as well. This con may prove false as this technology is still being tested, but at present, it seems that thin-film solar panels do not last as well as either polycrystalline or monocrystalline solar panels. This is evidenced by the fact that they come with a shorter warranty. You are likely to have to replace your system much sooner if you opt for thin-film solar panels, which may mean greater overall costs, even if the upfront costs are lower.

In the future, this may change as improvements in technology are made, but at present, it seems that thin-film solar panels are not a lasting solution.

The overall system is more expensive. Often, you will find that despite the low price for an individual panel, your overall system costs more. This is because you will need so many more panels and the additional cost of equipment mentioned above. You may find that it is more economical to buy polycrystalline solar panels, even if the individual panels cost more.

Of course, this depends upon your setup and the prices in your local area, as well as the kind of thin-film solar panel that you choose. When looking at costs, try to consider the overall system costs, as well as the costs for the individual elements.

The technology is quite new. Thin-film technology is relatively new, and this means that there are quite a few unknowns in terms of operation, longevity, etc. It remains to be seen whether the disadvantages in efficiency can be overcome.

Some of the ingredients may be toxic. This is heavily dependent on the material that you choose, but there are certainly concerns about toxicity for some of these panels, especially Cadmium Telluride. These panels should not have any effect on residents when installed on rooftops, but it is still important not to dismiss the issues of Cadmium, which we discussed in the previous chapter on batteries.

Overview:

Although monocrystalline and polycrystalline solar setups tend to be better, there are situations in which thin-film solar panels are more attractive. They are more versatile and easier to find an installation spot for (if you only need a small amount of power), and they are considerably cheaper in terms of their upfront costs. Crystalline-based panels will be preferable in many situations, but do not dismiss thin-film as unviable because they certainly have their uses.

Summary

In this chapter, we've covered:

- The benefits and drawbacks of monocrystalline solar panels
- The benefits and drawbacks of polycrystalline solar panels
- The benefits and drawbacks of thin-film solar panels
- The different situations in which each panel might be most useful, depending upon your setup and where you are located

In the next chapter, I will move on to the other components required for a solar panel system, so we can break down the things you will need and help you understand how to choose the best of each kind. We'll look at wires, fuses, and inverters so you can fine-tune your system to maximize the power that you get and the convenience you enjoy.

5
Choosing the Best Wires, Fuses, and Inverter

"Watch the little things; a small leak will sink a great ship."

-Benjamin Franklin

The batteries and the panels are the most obvious part of your system that needs to operate well, and unfortunately, it is far too easy to focus on just those parts and forget about all the needed bits to make them run well. When it comes to building a solar panel system, you need to pay attention to the panels and batteries you buy, but you also need to think about every other part that makes your system work properly.

Think of it a little like the human body: you have vital organs such as the heart, the lungs, the kidneys, etc., but if you don't also have the veins connecting them and the blood running through them, they won't work. Similarly, if you don't choose the right wires, fuses, and inverter for your system, it will not work properly, if at all.

It's crucial to pay attention to this part because without these bits and pieces, your system could end up as an actual hazard.

In this chapter, we are going to look at:

- How to choose cables and wires that are the right size
- How to earth your system to make sure it is safe
- What to do about the risk of lightning
- How to specify your inverter and the charge controller
- How to pick fuses that are the right spec for your system

This should put you in a great position to build a functional, efficient, and safe solar panel system that will make life easier for you off the grid.

Choosing Cables And Wires

What Is The Difference Between Cables And Wires?

Many people use these terms interchangeably, but they are not actually the same thing at all, and it's important to understand the distinction.

A wire is a single conductor; it is just one strand of metal. Multiple wires can be twisted together and sometimes have a thin layer of PVC to cover them. Wires are measured according to their diameter, using a gauge number. Smaller gauges indicate thicker wires. Larger wires (with smaller gauges) carry more current, so the thicker your wiring is, the more dangerous it becomes to handle.

Cables, by contrast, are groups of conductors and will usually be covered by an insulation jacket (often thick rubber or something similar) that protects the cable and holds the twisted conductors together. Cables tend to contain a hot wire which transports the current, a grounding wire which makes the system safe, and a neutral wire that completes the loop. The wires making up a cable can have different gauges, and usually, the number of wires will be used to classify the cable.

Why Does It Matter?

Your first question when you start a section on choosing the correct cables and wires is likely to be why it matters what the size is and whether you use cable or wire. It matters because you will minimize both heat issues and energy loss if you choose the correct size. A wire that is not sized correctly will get very hot and could create a fire risk – so it's not safe to use wires or cables until you know what size you need.

How Do You Choose?

The size of the wire will be heavily dependent on the amount of power that your solar panel can generate. Larger amounts of power require bigger wires to carry them, or the wire will get too hot.

The distance also matters a lot. If you are transporting electricity over long distances, you need bigger wires to do it, so if your system is spread out, larger wires will be needed. Be aware that this will usually cost you more, but using small wires is unsafe, so this is not an area where you can cut costs by using different materials. The wires and cables must be sized to match your solar panel if you want the system to be safe.

Often, you will be using a multi-stranded cable with flexible wires inside, and it's a good idea to stick to the standard colors for your country to ensure that there is no confusion for either you or anyone else who looks at it later.

If any of the cabling runs outdoors (at least some is almost certain to do), you need to make sure that its coating is weatherproof and resistant to ultraviolet light to ensure that it will last well.

To calculate the thickness of the cable required for a task, you will need to have two pieces of information: the maximum number of amps it will carry and the distance that it will carry it.

You can calculate the maximum current by inspecting your appliances, which should tell you what you require. If your appliance only offers information about the watts, divide this number by 12 for 12V appliances and 24 for 24V appliances.

To calculate the distance, use a flexible measuring tape to check how long the cable will be. Remember, the longer it is, the greater the power loss will be. There are many tools online that will help you to calculate cable thickness according to these two stats, and you should ensure that your voltage drop is not more than 5% (or you will simply be wasting a lot of power).

Remember, a thicker cable is always preferable to one that is too thin. It will not carry any disadvantages besides slightly increased upfront costs, and it may last better overall. Don't ever opt for cables or wires that are less than what you need because you then have reduced efficiency and an increased risk of fires.

Earthing The System Properly

Even if you live in an area that rarely experiences electrical storms, you must make sure that you correctly ground your solar panel system. Not doing so could lead to the destruction of the system and its components and even fire and further damage to your home. An unearthed system is extremely unsafe and is not something that you should consider installing. As well as lightning strikes, an unearthed system is vulnerable to short circuits, which could also be very dangerous.

Grounding a system means that you create a "path of least resistance" for the electricity to follow when lightning strikes (or surges through a short-circuited system). This prevents the power from racing through your system and creating a surge that will knock out and damage the various components, and instead channels it into a safe area.

To ground a system, you will essentially be connecting every component using a piece of bare copper wire, which is then connected to several copper pipes that are buried in the ground (we will cover grounding mobile systems shortly). When the lightning strikes, it will follow the least resistant route to the earth, and therefore it will run through this copper wire and into the pipes, getting safely channelled away from your equipment and your home.

If you are creating a solar panel system in a home that already has a grounding system established (perhaps because of previous on-grid electrical connections), it is very important to tie the two systems together so that your solar panels use the same grounding system as everything else. Not doing so creates a risk of the electricity behaving in unpredictable and dangerous ways, so make sure you implement this with your setup. Do not create a separate grounding system for solar panels if a grounding system is already in place.

Of course, you cannot use this system for a mobile setup because you are constantly moving, so you can't bury a series of copper pipes 6+ feet underground. Many people do not bother to ground their solar panels when they add them to something like an RV, but it should be noted that this is extremely dangerous, and you should not do it. You are at risk of getting a serious and possibly deadly electric shock if you touch the hull when it is wet, and there is any power leakage from the solar panels.

You will need to attach the panels to your RV's grounding system. To begin with, locate the grounding lug, which is usually near the bottom of each panel and should be marked. Attach your grounding wire to this lug, and connect this to the rest of the panels using a series connection (not a parallel connection).

Next, you will need to connect this to the metal of the chassis (where there is no paint, plastic, or anything else to interrupt the flow of electricity). You should make at least two connections to allow for failures. When you have done so, your system is grounded.

Similar systems can be set up for boats by simply linking the solar panels into the existing ground system.

Never set up and use a solar panel system that is not grounded. Although you may only have a small number of panels on a mobile vehicle, it is still crucial that you protect your system, your home, and yourself from the dangers of surges, and you can only do this by ensuring that the system is earthed correctly.

Reducing The Risk Of Lightning

As well as grounding your system, you should also take steps to try and reduce the risk of lightning striking it in the first place. You may not feel this is necessary for your area, but it is worth doing; climate change creates unusual weather patterns across the globe, and although grounding will make the system safer, a lightning strike could still cause damage.

Fortunately, there are a few things that you can do to reduce the risk of lightning striking your solar panels, so let's explore these next.

One of the first pieces of equipment you may wish to install is a lightning arrestor. These are designed to help the surge bypass all the wiring and equipment, and you should install them at either end of any significantly long pieces of wire in any part of your system. You can get these in various voltages, and they will absorb the spikes, protecting your system from being damaged by having too much power put through it.

You may also wish to install lightning rods, but these will only work if you are looking at a static off-grid setup, as they are again intended to be connected into the ground. Their job is to provide a safe path for the lightning to follow, redirecting it safely into the ground. They also discharge any static electricity that buildings up around the panels, which helps reduce the chance of lightning striking in the first place.

In general, lightning rods will only be used in areas with extreme electrical storms, so you are unlikely to need these for your setup, especially as you will probably only have a relatively small number of solar panels, and they, therefore, may carry a low charge.

Choosing An Inverter And Charge Controller

The inverter and the charge controller are crucial parts of your solar panel system, too, so you need to take the time to choose well.

To recap briefly, the inverter converts DC to AC so that you can attach home devices to it. The charge controller is used to stop the batteries from getting overcharged by your solar panels (overcharging will destroy the battery much more quickly than if it is charged to the correct level).

Inverters

There are a few different kinds of inverters, and they have different pros and cons.

String inverters are the most basic, and they are formed from chains of panels that are all connected up into a series. The panels must all be orientated in the same way to maximize efficiency.

Microinverters have an inverter in every panel, rather than one inverter to all panels. These tend to be hooked up to a computer system to identify and rectify any issues quickly.

Optimized inverter systems are a hybrid version of these two systems. They have optimizers behind each inverter panel, which isolate failures and provide a steady voltage to the central inverter (which increases the efficiency). Again, these are connected to the internet to deal with faults quickly.

As well as the kind of inverter you buy, you also need to think about its size. Often, you will only need a small inverter for an off-grid home because you will be using small amounts of power, but as always, it is better to have a large inverter than one that cannot keep up with your system. However, a huge inverter will cause a reduction in efficiency levels if you don't need it, so you should aim to be as close as you can to your needs.

Inverters are rated both in Continuous Watts and Surge Watts, and you need to pay attention to both of these statistics.

The measure Continuous Watts lets you know how much the inverter can handle consistently. If you have a 1000 watt inverter, it can supply a steady 1000 watts. Larger inverters will supply more.

Of course, you are unlikely to be running just one thing from your inverter, so make sure that you add up the Continuous Watts of all the appliances that you want to use at one time. This will let you know whether your inverter can handle the demand or whether you need a more powerful one.

Surge Watts lets you know how much power your inverter can offer in terms of a surge. This will be higher than the Continuous Watts rating and lets you know what the inverter can handle in a short burst. Many appliances take significantly more power when booting up, which is the "surge" power.

If your inverter struggles when you try to start up an appliance that has a high startup demand, you may need a more powerful inverter. The Surge Watts rating needs to be higher than the greatest draw of your appliances' surge watts rating. This can usually be found on the stickers on the backs of appliances or in the instruction manual.

Add up all the devices that might be powered up at once, and this should help you to calculate the Surge Watts that you need for your inverter. If the surge watts add up to 5000 watts, you will need an inverter with more than 5000 watts.

Charge Controllers

The charge controller is another vital component that needs to be chosen correctly. This serves several jobs, all of which help to make your batteries last longer and function well. Batteries are often among the most expensive components in any solar panel system, so this needs to be chosen with care.

Typically, a charge controller will be placed between the battery bank and the solar panels. It limits the amount of power that goes into the battery and how fast it goes in. This prevents the batteries from getting overcharged, damaging them and reducing their overall life expectancy. A battery that gets overcharged can even explode, so this is a pretty major job, and you must have a reliable charge controller.

Furthermore, the charge controller prevents the battery bank from getting drained too heavily by your system. It does this by measuring the battery's voltage and disconnecting it when it drops below a certain level. This stops the battery from being completely drained (which would reduce its overall capacity and reduce the effectiveness of your system overall).

Finally, a charge controller stops any reverse flow going into your solar panels at night when they are not charging. This prevents damage to them. Therefore, the charge controllers protect the system in several different ways – *so how do you choose the correct unit?*

Your charge controller needs to be able to handle more energy than your solar panels can generate, and again, it is better to have one that allows a bit more than you need, as this will ensure it can cope with any spikes.

As I mentioned in Chapter One, a particularly common kind of charge controller is an MPPT (Multi Power Point Tracking). These are generally used if you have solar panels with much higher voltages than your batteries – up to ten times higher. None of the current will be lost in pulling this down to the right level for the batteries, and this makes the controller very efficient (often between 92 and 95%).

To size an MPPT controller, you just need to select one that is higher than the maximum full potential of the solar panels. Unlike a PWM (Pulse Width Modulation) controller, an undersized MPPT controller will not damage your system, but it will prevent you from getting the full benefit of the energy your solar panel's output.

To maximize efficiency, you need to make sure that the MPPT controller is capable of outputting a voltage at least as high as your battery's rating and that it can handle sufficient current to transfer all the power generated by your panels at that voltage. As the power transferred through a wire is equal to the voltage times the current, you can calculate the necessary current capacity by dividing the power output of your solar panels by the voltage of your batteries.

If your solar panels output a maximum of 1000 watts and your battery can handle a standard 24 volts, the current needed to transfer all of that power to the battery without exceeding the voltage would be calculated by dividing 1000 watts by 24 volts, which equals just under 42 amps. When in doubt, it is best to round up the calculation.

Most standards suggest that you then increase this by an additional 25% in order to handle any spikes in power that may occur, meaning the optimal MPPT controller, in this case, needs to be capable of handling at least 24 volts and 53 amps. This will ensure it functions at maximum efficiency even when your solar panels are outputting the maximum power.

The other option is a PWM controller, but this does only achieve efficiency levels between 75 and 80%. To size a PWM controller, you should look for one that has a voltage rating and an amperage that is higher than both your battery and your solar array. Once you have done this, check what the rated current of your battery is, and again choose a charge controller that exceeds the amp rating for the solar array. 25% is usually a sufficient margin. Multiply the amp rating of your solar panels by 1.25, and then look for a charge controller with a higher number.

Selecting Fuses For The System

To recap, the purpose of a fuse is to break the circuit if something is going wrong and the wiring is getting too hot. A fuse is a means of protecting the system from damage if it short circuits; it is a weak point that ensures the system's circuit will break before doing major damage to any of your expensive components.

You do not have to use fuses for a system to work, but they are key to safety and to protect your equipment. A system without fuses won't blow if something goes wrong, which could lead to the whole setup catching fire because heat will continue to be generated in the wires until they are dangerously hot. Of course, you may be lucky, and this may never occur, but it is still very strongly recommended that you use fuses in your solar panel system.

Ideally, you should have fuses in three locations: between your battery bank and the inverter, between the charge controller and your battery bank, and between the solar panels and the charge controller. Having the "weak points" in these spots will ensure that no major components are likely to get damaged if something goes wrong with the system; This could save you a lot of money, making your home safer.

So, how do you choose the correct fuses? You need the right size: an incorrectly sized fuse will either fail to blow when something goes wrong (and therefore won't serve any purpose), or will blow constantly even when nothing is wrong (which is extremely frustrating).

You will need different fuses for the three different locations; I will explain how to size each one below.

The fuse between the battery bank and the inverter:

This is often the simplest fuse size to figure out because your inverter will state what size is needed in its manual, and some inverters already have fuses or breakers built into them – in which case you should not need to add another. Before installing an inverter, check whether it comes with an inbuilt fuse or if you need to install one manually.

The fuse between the charge controller and the battery bank:

Figuring out what size fuse is needed between your charge controller and your battery bank should also be very simple once you know the amperage of your charge controller. If you have a 20 amp charge controller, you should need a 20 amp fuse. There is no need to do a calculation here; just match the amperage and work correctly.

The fuse between the solar panels and the charge controller:

This is probably the trickiest of all the fuses in your system to make sense of, so be careful. Firstly, you need to look at how you have connected your panels (parallel, series, or series/parallel), as this makes a big difference to what kind of fuse is needed.

For parallel connected solar panels, the amperage of the panels adds up, but the voltage remains the same. In this case, you will need to add together the amperage for each panel and then add an extra 25% safety margin (per industry rules). This will give you the fuse size. If you have five panels producing 10 volts and 10 amps each, your total output would be 10 volts and 50 amps. Multiplying this by the safety margin of 1.25 equals 62.5 amps. You should always round up, not down, so a 70 amp fuse would be suitable.

For a series connection, the voltage is added up, but the amperage stays the same each time – which is why you need a very different calculation. To use the same example, if you have five panels producing 10 volts and 10 amps, your total output would be 50 volts and

10 amps. Again, take the amperage and multiply it by the industry safety factor of 25%. This would be 10 amps x 1.25. You should get 12.5, which translates into needing a 15 amp fuse (the nearest equivalent).

According to your specific setup, don't neglect to do these calculations properly. It might look slightly complicated, but it should not take you long, and as you can see, it makes a big difference to the kind of fuse that you will end up using. If you don't fuse this connection properly, a short circuit could destroy your panels and your charge controller, which would be very expensive to replace. It is a good idea to check instruction manuals for advice on fusing and look online to see whether recommendations have been updated since the time of writing.

Summary

In this chapter, we've covered:

- The differences between cables and wires, and how to choose cables that are correctly sized for your system
- How to ground your system, both for stationary homes and mobile homes, and how to reduce the lightning risks
- The purposes of inverters and charge controllers and how to select the correct ones
- The fuses that you need and the various points of the system that will benefit from being fused correctly

Hopefully, you now feel that you have all the information required to calculate which components you need to create a functioning, efficient, and safe system.

In the next chapter, we will bring together the information contained in the previous chapters and unlock the steps for actually building a solar system. We'll look at the various setups that are workable and practical for RVs, boats, and small homes, and then we'll uncover the available connection methods. Hence, you know how to turn this theory into a functional system that will give you power wherever you are in the world.

6

Build Your Own Solar System

"I have no doubt that we will be successful in harnessing the sun's energy. If sun-beams were weapons of war, we would have had solar energy centuries ago."

-George Porter

You're probably already aware that every solar panel system – especially the DIY ones – is slightly different from the others, even if most of the components remain the same. It's vital to set up solar panels in a way that suits the environment they are operating in, and that means adapting the standards to make them work for you.

Now that we have explored in detail all the different major components of setting up a solar panel system, it's time to look at actually setting one up. There is no point in knowing what kind of inverter and fuses you need if you don't know how to mount the panels and set the system up, so in this chapter, that's what we are going to start covering.

We're going to explore the various situations in which you may be mounting panels. Although all the components are likely to be pretty similar whether you are creating your solar panel setup on an RV, a cabin, a boat, or somewhere else, the mounting options and methods will certainly change. At this point, therefore, I'm going to start breaking it down, so you know how to mount panels effectively regardless of the setup you have.

These are the steps you'll be following once you have calculated the size of the system you need and chosen the components, ensuring you know what you fit. Before you purchase anything, you should build a map of your system and check that everything works. You may find that while you wanted five panels, only four will fit on your roof – and this will change the calculations for every other aspect of your system too. Measuring up is a key part of building any solar system, whether on a boat or a mansion.

Remember to calculate for weight and physical size and check that your roof (or other fitting areas) is strong enough to hold the panels. Also, mark where you will need to drill holes for cables or fans and store the battery bank. You might find it helps to create a scaled model of your home and fit the components into it. This will help you to avoid any nasty surprises later.

Once you're sure everything fits as planned, you can start buying items. You don't have to have every component purchased and ready to go before you start setting the system up, but you should have a strong sense of the dimensions, cable lengths, and weight so that you know what you can fit where.

Mounting Solar Panels On An RV

Step One: Measure Up. As mentioned, you will start by checking that all your components fit. It is best to begin by measuring the roof, as this will let you know how many panels you have space for. Try to avoid mixing and matching solar panels of different sizes, and make sure you take into account vents and aerials, as these will need to be worked around.

Step Two: Consider Key Questions. A few of the crucial elements you need to cover are:

- Will I fix the solar panels permanently, or do I want removable panels?
- Do I want to wire the panels in series or parallel?
- Do I need roof space for anything else, or can I dedicate all areas to solar panels?
- What tools do I need, and do I need to buy or borrow any?
- How am I going to get access from inside the RV?

Step Three: Purchase Your Components. Ideally, you want to have as many necessary components as possible before you start. This will let you layout a skeleton design and check that everything is compatible and working before you start fixing parts of the system together. Any errors can be corrected, and you can ensure you're satisfied with the layout and compatibility before you start fitting the system. This will also allow you to return any components that are not compatible and have been purchased in error and replace them if necessary.

Step Four: Assess Inevitable Damage. When installing solar panels, you will inevitably do some damage to your RV unless you have not yet kitted it out. If you are building the whole system from scratch, you should fit solar panels before you fit insulation and linings because then you can fit these around your cables. However, if you are retrofitting solar panels (as many people will be doing), you will need to assess how you can minimize the damage and cost up any repairs that need to be done after you have finished the fitting.

Step Five: Assemble Components And Purchase Extras. As well as all of the components discussed in the previous chapters, you will need some other bits and pieces for fitting everything together. You should have:

- Solar panels
- A solar charge controller
- A battery bank
- Solar mounting brackets (for fitting the panels to the roof without drilling holes in it)
- MC4 connectors (for extending solar cables safely)
- Solar cables (for carrying the current from solar panel to charge converter)
- A solar panel gland (for sealing the hole around the cables that run from the panels into the RV)
- Fuse holders and fuses
- Battery cut off switches (so you can isolate the battery if necessary)
- Battery terminal eyes (for connecting the solar panel cable to the battery)
- Heat shrink (for joining bare wires)

Step Six: Test Your Equipment. Before you spend time putting everything together, it's a good idea to test that everything you have bought is in working order so you can return any faulty units without having to spend hours undoing your work; This can make a huge difference if you are unlucky enough to end up with something faulty.

Step Seven: Install Your Battery. Start by installing your battery, isolator switches, and fuse holders. Your battery should be fitting in a secure area and firmly fixed down so that there is no risk of it moving or falling while you are travelling or in the event of an accident. You should attach it to the hull of the RV, rather than any movable internal components, and then make sure that you ground it promptly.

Next, fit the isolator switches and the fuse holders, but do not put the fuses in place yet. Test that everything is secure. Flip all isolator switches to the "off" position.

Step Eight: Fit The Solar Panels. It is best to do as much work as possible from ground level, but you will undoubtedly need to access the roof for this step. If possible, use cardboard templates to mark where your panels will fit and where the mounts should be attached, as this is easier than working with the panels directly and reduces the risk of damaging them.

Cables should be installed to be accessed when the panels are in place, especially when mounting fixed panels. You don't want to have to remove everything to change a cable.

Test each of your solar panels works well by placing them in the sun and using a multimeter; this is important to do before mounting them, as it could save you a lot of work if one of the panels is faulty.

Once you have done this, attach the mounts to your solar panels using the instruction manual. Usually, you will be using Z brackets, which will be fitted to pre-existing holes in the panel's frame using the supplied bolts.

Some people also use VHB tape and butyl tape on the bottom of the Z brackets to increase adherence to the roof.

This gives a better attachment because it adds thickness to the screw hole, and the butyl tape also waterproofs the hole that has been made, reducing the risk of rust and water buildup. You may want to fit the panels without this tape, to begin with, to test that they fit well, and then add the tape once you are satisfied with the positioning.

Note that your brackets need to be mounted with maximum contact with the surface below, so work around any ridges or lumps on your RV roof. Don't put mounts in positions that reduce the contact, or the mounts may come off, and the panels will fall.

Once you are ready, lift the panels to the roof and make sure that the cables are pulled free so they don't get trapped underneath. Use a power drill to drive the self-tapping screws into the roof and check that each is secure. Your panels should be fitted tightly, with no wobbliness. You can add a further coat of sealant over the screws if you like.

Next, mark the holes for the cables, and then drill them. Fit the cable glands, prime and paint the hole edges to seal them. The cables will be added later.

Fit your solar panels to the mounts and check that they have firmly bonded in position. It is best to have at least two people for this job to pass tools and equipment up onto the roof while the other works.

Step Nine: Wire Up Your Panels. You may find that it helps to draw yourself a diagram to show how the panels should be wired before you start. Your panels will usually have a meter of positive and negative cable fitted to them, ready to use. If you need to extend this, make sure you use the correct connectors of a suitable voltage.

Attach the gland collars to the cables and double-check that all of your connections are correct and secure. Use the multimeter to ensure everything is working correctly, and then feed the cables through the cable gland and get the collars in position. Tidy up all of the wirings so that nothing is loose or trailing.

Step Ten: Install The Charge Controller And Inverter. This will be done inside the RV, and again, the charge controller and the inverter must both be securely fixed to a solid wall.

Use the manufacturer's directions to wire up the controller and the inverter, as the directions may vary from unit to unit. Note that you may not need an inverter in an RV, as your RV's battery may already have one of these.

Finally, add your fuses, turn the isolator switches to "on," and test the system. If there are any issues, immediately cut the switch to the battery again, take out the fuses, and start inspecting the system until you can locate the issue. Once you have done so, rectify it and test again. Always test your system before a long trip to ensure nothing has come loose or been damaged.

Mounting Solar Panels On A Boat

Some of the early steps for mounting solar panels on a boat will overlap with those for mounting on an RV – so check out the full instructions in the above section if you need more information. A few aspects mentioned there may not apply to boats, but most will.

Step One: Measure Up. As with mounting panels on an RV, you first need to measure up, but in this case, you need to first think about where you will be positioning the panels. This will depend heavily on the kind of boat that you have. Many people will mount their panels on the roof of the boat as this overcomes issues with shading and maximizes space, but there are some situations in which this may not be suitable.

If you have a sailboat, you might want to look at mounting the panels on the cockpit dodger, although you will usually need flexible panels to achieve this. Some people mount a panel on the stern rail, while others may even mount them on the deck.

Of course, there are some disadvantages to mounting the panels on your deck; you will encounter more shade, and you need to buy expensive, robust solar panels that will tolerate constant foot traffic. You also need to think about allowing for a little airflow beneath the panels.

Once you have decided which space is the most suitable for adding solar panels, make sure that you measure it accurately, taking into account any bars, poles, or other interruptions that will eat into the space available for the panels. You should also pay attention to the curve because you must deal with this when mounting the solar panels.

Step Two: Consider Key Questions. See the RV section for some of the most important questions.

Step Three: Purchase Your Components. The components will be similar to those of other systems, but you should always look for marine-suitable options. Your solar equipment will be perpetually exposed to dampness and possibly splashing, as well as salt (if you ever set sail on the ocean), and that means you need to ensure everything will hold up properly. Do not use ordinary wire; you will need tinned marine-grade, or the wire will likely lose its conductivity after a few months.

Step Four: Assess Inevitable Damage.

Step Five: Assemble Components And Purchase Extras.

Step Six: Test Your Equipment.

Step Seven: Mount Your Panels. There are many ways to mount solar panels on a boat, and it will depend a bit on the solar panels you want to use. If you intend to go for a simple setup, you may find that mounting the panels on the boat's roof is the best option – and this will be similar to mounting them on an RV.

Again, it's a good idea to use cardboard templates to see how the panels will fit, and this will also help you to determine whether the curve of the boat is going to cause issues. Any interruptions, like aerials, will be easy to spot if you lay the full solar panel system out in cardboard before adding the real panels.

Remember that if the solar panels will charge your boat's battery, they will need to be connected to it, often involving drilling through the deck. You will still need a charge controller.

Again, you can use Z brackets or mounts that come with your solar panel if applicable. You will need to ensure that they are suitable for the surface you plan to attach them to. If the surface is curved, you may have to purchase mounts specifically designed to mount curves. Using mounts intended for straight surfaces will result in poor adhesion between the panels and the boat, which could cause an accident.

Again, thoroughly seal holes with waterproof sealants, and make sure that the cable hole is fitted with a gland to prevent water from getting into the boat.

If you would rather not mount fixed solar panels on the roof of your boat, consider any of the following options:

- Purchasing marine solar panels with zips can be sewn to any fabric components of the boat (e.g. roofing). This keeps the panels out of the way and makes mounting them relatively easy. Remove the roof's fabric, measure up the panels, and sew them into place. They should be stretched taut once the fabric is reinstalled, but this is a great way to get panels out of the way and ensure they get plenty of sunlight.
- Mounting solar panels on a frame near the back of the boat. You will need to purchase a strong metal frame for your panels and ensure that this is very securely attached to

the back of the boat. All cables must be protected from splashing.

- Mounting solar panels using Velcro. This method may sound unsafe, but Velcro's proper strength is viable for mounting flexible solar panels. You must maximize the security and always build in a margin for error when considering the strength of the Velcro, but this is another great way to attach flexible solar panels to fabric or another curved surface. Many boats are not flat, so this may prove preferable to mounting on a frame or using Z brackets. Velcro also makes the panels easy to remove or replace when necessary.

- Mounting with a strong adhesive. Many adhesives suitable for use on boats should be sufficient to hold flexible solar panels in place, although you should be aware that some airflow is needed beneath the panels. If you are going to stick them down, ensure there is a little sealant or something in the corners to lift the panels just slightly off the surface that they are stuck to. You should check on the adhesive frequently to ensure it has not become brittle. Replace it if it is showing signs of wear.

Any of these mounting methods should be suitable for use on a boat. It is always a good idea to test and then stress test your solar panels once they are in place to ensure that they will not come loose on a proper boating expedition. Try them out in rougher weather, and then check the adhesion when you next dock. If it is pulling away in any areas, look for alternatives. Many forms of sealant and tape will hold flexible solar panels in place on a boat.

Step Eight: Wire Up Remaining Components. Once your panels are in place, wire them up according to the manufacturer's instructions (and the RV guide above if necessary). You will still need a charge controller, but again, you may not need a battery inverter if you already have one on your boat.

Mounting Solar Panels On A Cabin

Mounting solar panels to a fixed, unmoving structure such as a cabin (or another form of tiny home) is often the best option because you don't need to deal with movement, dampness, salt, etc. However, you still need to set your system up carefully to ensure your panels are mounted securely and withstand strong winds, lightning, and general wear and tear. You also need to think about positioning; getting the panels angled to make the most of the sun is key because your building does not move.

Again, some of the steps will remain the same or be similar to the other two mounting situations.

Step One: Measure Up. You will need to get up onto the roof of your cabin to measure it accurately. Take into account chimneys, aerials, etc.

Step Two: Consider Key Questions. See the RV section for some of the most important questions.

Step Three: Purchase Your Components. The components will be similar to those of the other two systems, but you will need to purchase a battery inverter because your cabin is unlikely to have one of these pre-installed. Make sure you add this to the list.

Step Four: Assess Inevitable Damage. You may be able to access the roof of your cabin without damaging anything, but if the cabin is insulated, you need to think about how to avoid or repair damage to the insulation. If you can, wire up your solar panels before you insulate.

Step Five: Assemble Components And Purchase Extras. Note that you may need to hire scaffolding to install solar panels on a two-story tiny home safely.

Step Six: Test Your Equipment.

Step Seven: Mount Your Panels. Because you are working with a fixed and (usually) more generous space than with an RV or boat, you may find that you have more mounting options. You are also less likely to encounter ridges or curves, although you might still have to deal with chimneys and aerials.

You can pick from various mounting options (I will cover some of them in the following section), but many people use bracket and rail systems. If you have a tiled roof, be aware that you will need to remove the tiles in places to attach the brackets to the rafters.

You will then be attaching a rail to the brackets, which will often run along the length of the roof. If you are only installing one or two panels, it may not cover the whole roof, but it will need to protrude a little beyond the panels so that it supports them fully, even if it contracts in cold weather.

Next, you should bolt the specially designed clips to the edges of the panels, attaching the panel securely to the rail. Make sure that each panel is secure before moving on to the next, and remember that it's best to have a minimum of two people for this sort of installation, particularly if your cabin is more than one story high.

The cables behind each panel will be attached to the neighboring panels and then fed through a hole in the roof to the interior space, where your charge controller will usually be positioned. The advantage of the bracket and rail system is that it is very easy to remove the panels if they get damaged or need replacing, and it's also fairly easy to extend it if/

when you want to increase your solar power network.

Ensure that any holes are sealed with a waterproof sealant, and all tiles are replaced.

A similar method can be used for a wooden roof, but note that wood can be a trickier material to work with as it is sometimes brittle and at risk of cracking. More fire concerns are associated with using solar panels on wooden roofs, but this should be safe if installed correctly.

Step Eight: Wire Up Inside. Once the panels are in place and secure, you can connect the wires to two DC isolators and then, to the charge controller and inverter. According to the manufacturer's instructions, these should be wired up and fixed firmly to a wall in an accessible but out-of-the-way spot. You will only need to get to your inverter if something goes wrong or requires maintenance.

Connection Methods For Mounting Solar Panels

As you have already noticed, there are many different ways solar panels can be mounted. I have explored quite a few above to offer you as many options as possible, but here are some of the commonest methods you might want to try. Because there are so many different circumstances in which solar panels can be installed, it's a good idea to understand as many mounting systems as possible so that you can choose the one that is the most suitable for your setup.

Above Roof For Tile/Slate Roofs: This is often inexpensive if your tiny home has a tile or slate roof, and it is also efficient because it allows for airflow (which helps keep the panels cool); This is the method described above, in which tiles are removed to allow brackets and rails to be attached to the roof. The panels are then clamped to the rails, and the tiles are put back. This method is great for traditional housing on pitched rooftops.

In Roof Solar Panels: This system is usually only suitable if you are redoing the roof from scratch; if you are, it is possible to build the panels directly into the roof; This has some cost savings because it reduces the amount of roofing material that you will need. However, it does not allow the panels to cool as efficiently, and it may mean you struggle when the panels need replacing unless you can get some with identical dimensions.

Solar PV Roofs: You can turn your entire roof into a giant solar panel if you purchase panels that have been designed for this. These are flat and can look attractive, but you will probably only find them useful if you build a cabin or tiny home from scratch. They are unlikely to work well on boats or RVs, as the roofs tend to be part of the vehicle's fabric already. You can also buy tiles/slates that will allow you to tile your roof with solar panels.

Z Brackets: If you want just to install a few panels, you may find that the rail system is overkill, and in that case, you could consider using Z Brackets. These are often suitable for boats, RVs, and tiny homes, and they can be effortless to fit. However, they will need the holes to be sealed, or they may compromise your roof.

Adhesive/Velcro: In some situations, Velcro and/or a strong adhesive will be sufficient for attaching small panels. This is usually only the case for systems that are lower down, as, on a house, solar panels will experience significantly more uplift (where the wind rushes under the panel and attempts to lift it away from the roof). It is not advisable to glue down solar panels (huge ones) to the roof of a house; you should mount them properly with metal brackets. If you use adhesive or Velcro, you need to stress test the system and ensure it is sufficiently strong, even in poor weather, and keep your panels securely attached.

Standing Seam For Metal Roofs: This generally involves clamping a U-clamp onto the raised seam and then attaching solar racking to it to mount the panels on. The advantage of this is that there is no need to drill into the roof. If you have a corrugated metal roof, you can similarly avoid much drilling by installing specially designed brackets over the corrugations.

Summary

In this chapter, we've covered:

- A simple method for attaching solar panels to your RV roof
- The possible methods for attaching solar panels to your boat
- The commonest method for attaching solar panels to a standard rooftop of a cabin or tiny home
- Depending on your circumstances, some other attachment methods may prove viable in certain situations.

In the next chapter, I will look at some of the issues that you may encounter as you swap to off-grid solar power and how you can overcome these problems. It isn't always straightforward to make the switch, and you're bound to find you run into the odd hiccup along the way – but hopefully, I can talk you around or through some of these to make the experience the best it can be.

7

The Challenges Of Solar Power

"It's really kind of cool to have solar panels on your roof."

-Bill Gates

Solar power might be one of the "cool kid" things to do, and there are certainly very major benefits that you are probably aware of – but it is not without its faults, especially when you are building your system from scratch. In this chapter, I will run through some of the challenges you may encounter and how you can troubleshoot these issues to optimize your system.

Technical faults with solar panels are surprisingly rare if installed correctly, but many people experience both major and minor issues with their panels. Quick resolutions – or prevention – should get you back up and running as soon as possible, ensuring you get the most from your panels.

Nobody wants to be without their solar panels. Still, those who depend upon them in an off-grid setup are hit even harder by issues, so it's important to spend a bit of time familiarizing yourself with what can go wrong and how to avoid it or fix it swiftly.

Issue One: Animal Invasions

A surprising but common issue is animals taking up residence in your solar panel setup. This usually occurs in solar panel setups on fixed abodes, not mobile ones, but it is not unheard of for animals to nest among solar panels even when they have only been in place for a short period. This is particularly true if you have parked in an area with a lot of wildlife accustomed to human presence.

The commonest creature to find making a home for itself among your solar panels is birds. Because solar panels need to be slightly spaced out to allow heat dissipation, birds often build nests between the panels, where a narrow channel is perfect for nesting in. While this might sound cute, it can cause quite a few issues, and it isn't something that you should encourage.

Firstly, it often creates a lot of noise, especially if the birds successfully hatch and rear chicks. In a tiny home, you may sleep close to the roof, and this can be very frustrating if it prevents you from getting proper rest. Since many birds take weeks to hatch and fledge, it's also not a short term issue.

Furthermore, the nest and/or the birds could cause damage to the panels, especially if they climb on them or try to get underneath them. They may scratch the panels and get them dirty, which will reduce their efficiency, especially over a long time.

Additionally, if you are in a mobile home, you may not want to disturb the birds when the time comes to move again, and this presents a moral dilemma that is best avoided if possible. You don't want to be stuck on a campsite for longer than planned because you have a nest full of baby birds on your roof, and you feel responsible for their well-being.

Birds aren't the only issue, either. Other animals such as rodents could also use the panels for nesting, presenting even more serious problems. They might damage the wiring or chew their way into your home – both of which need to be avoided if possible. Squirrels and rats are unwelcome in most houses because they can be so destructive and may spread disease, so it's important to take action to protect your panels, your home, and your health.

The solution: Fortunately, there are a few things that you can do to prevent this. Installing coiled wire or mesh between the panels or blocking off access to the channels with plastic strips should stop the birds from building nests there and prevent access for all but the most determined rodents. Some rodents may still chew their way into the space if they can smell food or are desperate, but the wire, in particular, should deter them.

If you end up with animals among your solar panels, it's a good idea to call a company to deal with them. This may not be an urgent issue, as most animals are unlikely to do severe damage in a short time, but you should still get professional help to remove them if possible. Acting promptly, especially for birds, may help the wildlife out because they will put less energy into building nests and laying eggs if they are removed quickly, rather than being allowed to start on a home before being disturbed.

If you have nesting birds on your roof, make sure you look into the legalities of moving them. Many species are protected by law, so prevention is much better than cure in this scenario.

Issue Two: The Solar Inverter

According to Which, more than one in ten solar panel owners experience issues with their inverters.[viii] Of course, this is a UK stat, but it's likely to apply similarly in the United States, and it highlights just how tricky this particular bit of equipment can be to make the most of.

Unfortunately, the solar inverter is also crucial for keeping your system operating correctly. Without it, you won't be able to use your solar panels for anything but direct current. Quite a few things can go wrong with a solar inverter, but it's important to note that some solar inverters don't last very well.

Because most solar panels have such long lifespans (20+ years), many people automatically assume that a solar inverter will do the same – but in fact, most solar inverters only manage between 5-15 years. That is a pretty significant difference.

A high-quality solar inverter should last for longer than a cheap one, but even so, it is unlikely that an inverter will last for as long as a solar panel will. Although inverters can be expensive to replace, you should recognize this likely cost and prepare for it. Check what warranty the manufacturer offers before purchasing anything, and always make sure that it isn't still covered before you purchase a new unit. It's a good idea to set funds aside for replacing your inverter.

If your inverter is still working but is displaying an error message, refer to the manual for guidance on what's wrong and how to fix it. You should check the fuses and ensure that breakers are not getting tripped. If they are, you will need to start testing various parts of the system to try and detect any faults that may have developed.

The solution: If your inverter needs replacing, you will have to buy a new one and wire it in. It is worth investing in a good inverter despite the upfront costs because this increases its chances of lasting well.

However, if your inverter displays an error, you will need to check the manual for information about what is going wrong. If the fuses keep blowing or other errors occur, make sure you test the system or get an engineer to inspect the system and diagnose the fault. Although this will cost you, it could also save you a lot of time, because it won't always be easy to tell what's going wrong.

Issue Three: Corroded Wiring

Like all parts of your system, the wiring is subject to failure. You should regularly check on your wiring, especially outside the home, because this is more likely to corrode. It's essential to look out for loose connections when you do this general maintenance check, too. Try to do this every few months, or more frequently if you live in a very wet environment.

If you live on a boat, make sure that you increase your wiring checks' frequency and build this into your general "boat maintenance" routine. Any exposed wiring will corrode much more quickly than in a dry environment with constantly damp air.

Any corrosion issues should be dealt with promptly, as they could break your system, cause fire hazards, and reduce the conductivity. This decreases the efficiency of the solar panel, meaning that you are generating less energy overall, even if the panels are still working. A lot of corrosion could have a significant impact on the system.

The solution: Make sure that wires are sealed in a waterproof casing. This is particularly important for wires outside of the home, but it should be done for all wiring. If you live on a boat, you need to be even more careful to look out for corrosion, both on wires and contacts. This will ensure that you can fix issues promptly and keep your solar panels at maximum efficiency. It is also important for maintaining safety.

Promptly replace any wires that have corroded, and turn the system off until you have done so, especially if the corrosion is bad. While it is unlikely to cause safety issues, it's still better not to use corroded wiring.

Issue Four: Corroded Solar Panels

Solar panels can get corroded, too, although this will usually only occur if the panel gets damaged in some way. If something falls onto a panel, breaking the seal, water can start to seep in and corrode the components inside.

As with other corrosion, this can reduce the efficiency and may, in some cases, be dangerous. It is, unfortunately, also very difficult to fix.

The solution: This problem can usually be solved by replacing the solar panel. If you notice that your solar panels have been damaged by a falling branch or something similar, it is important to do a thorough inspection and take action if you find any sign of damage. If you have an off-grid system, you may depend on a constant flow of power, and a corroded panel could leave you in a difficult situation.

Some people claim that you can repair solar panels by sealing the crack, but this is not likely to work very well in most instances and will still result in reduced performance. A PV solar panel needs to be completely sealed to operate efficiently, so be cautious of attempting this. Most sealants will turn foggy or discolor in the sunlight that solar panels are constantly exposed to, which will reduce the panel's effectiveness over time.

If you are going to try to repair a solar panel, make sure you get the inside of it as dry as possible before sealing over the crack with your chosen material. This will reduce the risk of corrosion, but if it has already begun, it may not solve the problem.

A broken panel will need to be replaced. You may be able to patch it up temporarily, but at-home repairs are not likely to work for long. At present, there is no dedicated material for mending a damaged solar panel – especially once it has begun to rust internally.

Issue Five: Dirty Solar Panels

This might not sound like a very serious problem, but it can be a surprisingly big issue. Dirt and debris getting built up on the panel can dramatically reduce how much sunlight hits the solar cells, and this will reduce how much energy they generate for you every day.

If you live somewhere near a tree and the leaves blow onto the panel, or there is a lot of air pollution, or birds commonly perch on the panels, you may find that they quite quickly accumulate a film of dirt and leaves. A little dirt should not noticeably affect your panels, but if a panel gets very dirty (for example, from bird droppings or leaf litter), you will need to address this issue.

Similarly, if you are operating a boat with solar panels and are frequently out at sea, the panels will likely collect a misting of salt over a few months. This will also decrease the efficiency and reduce the amount of electricity your panels produce each day.

The solution: Cleaning the solar panels is usually fairly straightforward, although it can be more challenging to do safely if you have a two-story home. You may need to hire a company or at least some scaffolding to get the panels clean successfully.

Otherwise, simply get to the same height as the panels and clean them using soap, water, and a soft cloth. Do not use harsh chemicals or heavily abrasive materials on your panels, as you may scratch them or damage their coating; soap and water should do the trick in most cases. Use an eco-friendly soap if possible to reduce the risk of damage to the environment.

If you are struggling to remove dried-on bird droppings or something similar, try leaving a wet cloth on the mess to help it soften, and then have another go at cleaning it later. I've found that being allowed to "soak" in this way helps to loosen almost all the dirt that might get onto solar panels.

Regularly cleaning your solar panels should make them easier to clean, whereas if you allow a thick coat of dirt to build upon them, they are likely to prove more challenging. It's a good idea to clean them with soap and water at least once a year, or more often if you live in a heavily polluted area. Remove debris such as leaf litter with a long brush as necessary.

Issue Six: Cracked Solar Panels

Sometimes, your solar panels will develop cracks after they have been installed. Interestingly, this is often due to micro-cracks, which would have been present before you installed the panels but are not visible. These tend to occur during transportation, so choose a reputable shipping company for transporting your panels to you – or consider collecting them in person if you can use them so that you can minimize the risk of knocks occurring. Solar panels are unfortunately quite delicate, and it's effortless for them to get damaged in transit.

You may occasionally be able to see these cracks if you inspect the panels very closely before installation, but unfortunately, they are usually invisible. As time passes, they are likely to grow larger, and eventually, they will start to impact your solar panels' ability to generate power. When they are tiny, the impact will be exceedingly small, but as they get bigger, you might start to notice a drop in the efficiency of your panels.

It is somewhat unusual for panels to get damaged once installed as they are, in general, safe from sharp impacts that could harm them. However, falling branches, a thrown stone, balls, and other flying objects might cause a crack that was not there before installation.

The solution: Unfortunately, there is not much you can do about this sort of thing. You will simply have to replace the panel. The one upside to this is that the impact from most cracks will not be huge, so you do not need to rush to replace a panel before you can afford it.

Issue Seven: Hot Spots

I mentioned earlier how heat can be problematic for solar panels and losing efficiency when kept in warm environments. That's why hot spots are another important thing to look out for when it comes to maintaining your solar panels properly. A hot spot is an area on a solar panel overloaded. It becomes much warmer than the other parts of the panel while operating.

There are a variety of causes of hot spots, but you must do your best to mitigate all of them, both when installing and when maintaining your solar panels. Hot spots could reduce the lifespan of a solar panel and may also reduce its performance day today. They can cause short circuits and damage and need to be prevented or fixed if they occur.

Some of the common causes for hot spots include connections that have been badly soldered, debris buildup in areas of the panel, or structural defects. Partial shading can also be a problem to watch out for.

The solution: Sometimes, you will need a professional to work out that a hot spot even exists, but there are a few things that you can do yourself to reduce the risk of them occurring and fix them quickly if they do appear. The first of these is to make sure that you have soldered all connections thoroughly. Routinely check on connections and ensure that all are still firmly attached.

Secondly, keep your panels clean and free from debris, and where possible, remove items that shade the panels. This may not always be viable, but if not, consider repositioning a panel that gets heavy shade in one area consistently. This will help ensure that all solar cells within the panel generate electricity and spread evenly throughout the panel.

If you have fixed a hot spot, but the panel is still not performing as it should, you may need to consider replacing it. Hot spots can do severe damage to solar panels, and once this has happened, there is little that you can do to solve the issue.

Issue Eight: Incorrectly Estimating The Amount Of Power Needed

This is a much bigger issue if you operate in an off-grid setup because it matters how much power you generate. If you have the grid's security behind you, it might be annoying not to generate sufficient power from your solar panels. Still, it is unlikely to have a considerable impact on your daily life – although you will have higher power bills as a result.

However, if you are operating off the grid, you have no backup if you need more power than you are generating. You are entirely dependent on your equipment and what it can create, and if you end up draining your batteries, you could find yourself without heat, light, and your cell phone at a very inopportune moment. If you are a long way from civilization, this becomes even more of an issue.

This is a common problem for people who rush into creating a solar setup experience, and it's usually a result of not factoring in all the equipment you will be using. If you don't count your fridge, laptop, air conditioning, or other major power drains, you may find your system is seriously under-equipped to meet your needs.

The solution: Fortunately, there are a couple of things that you can do about this problem, and these are best done in advance before you set the system up. It is sometimes possible to rectify issues with underpowered systems later, but it's much better to plan first, even if you have calculated your power consumption accurately.

Before you decide what you need for your solar panel system, take some time to think about and list all of the equipment you use. You may find that it helps to do this over a few days or even weeks, writing down every electric device you utilize in that timespan. Think about different times of the year, too. *Do you have a plug-in heater for the winter? Will you have air conditioning running in the summer?* Get input from family or friends, and list everything that you can.

Once you have this list, add up all the power consumption and a safety margin. This covers devices you haven't thought of, instances in which you may use more power, etc. If a friend wants to charge their cell phone at your house, you don't want to find this throws your whole calculation out, so create a good safety margin of 25% or more.

Given your space and budget, this should give you a good idea of how much power you need to generate and how viable this is.

Secondly, think about making your system scalable. Wherever possible, purchase components that will allow you to upgrade and expand when necessary. Many solar systems are modular, meaning that you can add extra batteries, panels, etc., as you need to in the future. If you build a system with scaling it up in mind, you could save yourself considerable costs if you need to expand later.

Remember, it is always better to have a little more than a little less. You don't want to end up fumbling around in the dark in the middle of winter because you have miscalculated, and there are likely to be a few things you have not thought of during your calculation. Over-build and ensure there is scope to expand, and your system will hold up well.

Issue Nine: PID

You may have come across the term Potential Induced Degradation while looking at information about solar panels. This is an issue that can occur over the lifetime of your solar panel system.

Although you will have earthed your solar panels, you can run into this issue if there is a mismatch between your earthing and the amount of voltage generated by the solar panels. You may encounter some partial voltage discharge in the main circuit when this occurs.

This can lead to a loss in performance, and it can also damage the lifespan of your solar panels – obviously something that owners want to avoid. In some cases, the stray currents will damage your solar panels so much that you see a power loss as high as 30%. This will have a massive impact on your system.

It is worth noting that this issue is even more likely to occur in systems that are not earthed, so it provides another good incentive for properly earthing your solar system. It is both safer and protects your equipment.

Heat and humidity can also cause PID, and it is widespread, although not every solar module will encounter this issue. PID is not something that you will be able to detect visually, and it's quite a big issue for many solar systems. Because unavoidable environmental factors can cause it, it's challenging to prevent it.

The solution: In some cases, PID can be reduced if you can ground the negative DC pole in your inverter. Not all inverters allow for this, and you may need to get a specialist to do it, but it is one option for reducing or negating PID.

Another solution is to buy an "anti-PID box." This will need to be built into your system between the strings and the inverter, and it reverses the effects of PID (although if the effects have been long term, the damage will remain).

Alternatively, if you wish to prevent PID from occurring at all, you may wish to purchase solar panels that have been specifically designed to minimize the risk. These are available but are likely to cost more. Some frameless PV modules are at less risk of PID, but they cost extra and are heavier than standard panels.

High-quality panels are more likely to resist PID, so if you can budget for a more expensive panel, you may find it worth doing so. It is also worth discussing the PID resistance with the manufacturers and asking how their panels fare and what they do about this. Unfortunately, PID is a pretty complicated issue, and as yet, there are no simple solutions – although improvements are being made.

Summary

In this chapter, we've covered:
- Some of the foremost problems that solar power systems suffer from over their lifespans
- Why this option may be worse if you depend on an off-grid system rather than being connected to the grid
- What you can do to prevent or solve these issues when they occur, so your system runs smoothly as much as possible

Conclusion

"We are star stuff harvesting sunlight."

-Carl Sagan

In this book, I've covered the foundations of how solar power works and how solar panels harvest energy from sunlight and convert it into electricity for our homes. I've talked about the differences between off-grid and on-grid solar setups, how to build a simple off-grid solar power system, and what the phases of installation will include.

We then looked in a bit more detail at the differences between power and energy to create a foundation from which to work through the rest of the book. Following that, we moved on to the basics of solar power and then delved into the equipment you will need and how to select the correct components to set up an efficient and functional solar power system.

I talked about the different kinds of batteries and how to choose the correct one depending on your setup and requirements. This section covered the differences between lithium-ion batteries, flooded lead-acid batteries, sealed lead-acid batteries, and nickel-cadmium batteries, suitable for various situations. With a little information about the environmental impact and the advantages and drawbacks of each, this has hopefully helped you establish which you could use in your solar setup.

We moved on to one of the most imperative sections next – selecting the correct kind of solar panel. Here, I offered information about the pros and cons of each and also took a brief look at the environmental impact of manufacturing the panels. I compared monocrystalline, polycrystalline, and thin-film solar panels and briefly discussed the situations in which each one might be the preferable choice. All of these have viable applications, even though thin-film is lagging in terms of its efficiency ratings.

After that, we delved into some of the other major components of a solar-powered system and how to choose cables, inverters, and controllers that are suitable for your system. This chapter also covered fuses and offered information on grounding a system to maximize its safety and limit the risk of lightning damage.

Following this, I talked about the various situations in which a person might be mounting solar panels on their roof and covered detailed instructions for mounting solar panels on RVs, boats, and cabins/tiny homes. I also looked at some of the things that you should do before installing them, such as measuring your space correctly and testing all the components of the system.

In the final chapter, we looked at some of the pitfalls that solar panel owners might experience, and I discussed how you could resolve these or even totally avoid them. Hopefully, this will give you a better experience with your solar panels, both now and for years to come, maximizing the efficiency of your system. By keeping your panels clean, looking out for damage, and replacing components when they wear out or run into issues, you can ensure that you are generating enough power to keep your off-grid home functioning fully.

This book should have given you everything you need to set up a solar panel system that is efficient and safe and maintain it in the future. Every one of these systems is different. The more unique and unusual your off-grid setup is, the more complicated you might find the installation process – but the principles offered here should apply to almost every situation.

Hopefully, they will guide you through the process and answer most – or all – of your questions about solar power.

Solar energy is an astounding resource.

Many people are astonished by how long it has taken humanity to start utilizing the power that this unique technology gives us access to. Instead of depending upon a renewable, free source that is available across the globe, we have focused upon non-renewable, unclean energy sources that have to be transported thousands of miles and are not available to anyone who isn't connected to the main system. This has left people tied to civilization or sacrificing the necessities of modern life – but fortunately, that's all changing, and solar power is becoming mainstream.

Getting off the grid is enormously freeing, will save you money, and is a step in the right direction for tackling climate change. It is probably one of the biggest things that individuals can do to help the planet and decrease their carbon footprints.

Solar power allows you to reduce your dependency on big energy companies and non-renewable resources, cuts your costs, and frees you to travel anywhere you want to go, so there's no reason to wait. It's also a valuable backup if you are off adventuring, even if you don't plan to use much electricity. Having a solar-powered system set up could save your life in a tight spot.

If you're ready to get started, I'd recommend you sit down and make a list of the applianc-es you use so you can begin calculating how much power you would need a solar system to generate and what sort of setup you would like to create.

Now that you have all the information you need, there's no reason to wait because solar panels are better than they have ever been, and most of the world is moving in this direc-tion.

Let's bring the ingenuity of humankind to light and create our power from nothing but the sun!

SURVIVAL MEDICAL HANDBOOK:

BOOK 4

A Complete Beginners Guide to Prepare for Any Emergency When You Are Off Grid | Includes First Aid and Natural Remedies

BY

BRADLEY STONE

Introduction

"Wherever the art of Medicine is loved, there is also a love of Humanity."

-Hippocrates

The ancient words of Hippocrates raise something fundamental to the human condition. If we love and care for ourselves as a species, we must practice medicine. We need to know how to mend injuries and heal illnesses to perpetuate our species. If we love humans, we must also love the practices that ensure survival. You can take this to a much smaller level if you prefer: *if I love my companions, I want to know how to fix something wrong to preserve their well-being or possibly even their lives.* Knowing what to do when an emergency arises could make the difference between life and death – especially in a situation where outside help is not close at hand.

Did you know that around 120 to 140 people die in National Parks every year?[ix]

That's pretty low considering how many visitors the National Parks get, but it's still something to take seriously. People at National Parks tend to be camping or even just hiking, rather than living off the grid, and this figure alone indicates just how dangerous being out and about, some distance from other people and the safety of society, can be. You need to be prepared if you're going to walk away from the net of security that our social living offers.

Going off the grid is a unique and incomparable life experience. It takes you out of the hustle of daily life, makes you self-sufficient, pushes you to take a new perspective, and changes how you operate. It can be a life-altering thing to do and may work wonders for stress problems and mental health issues – but it comes with a serious caveat. At times, you will be a long way from help, and you will need to know how to handle issues when they arise.

If that makes you apprehensive, you aren't alone, and you are reasonable. Apprehension means that you recognize some of the dangers you are likely to face in choosing to be somewhere challenging for emergency services to reach. Apprehension means you're more likely to be prepared for emergencies and better able to handle them. Apprehension means that you recognize your limitations and take steps to overcome them.

Most people today are not self-sufficient enough in healthcare issues for the simple reason that we rarely need to be. We have excellent doctors and hospitals to take care of everything from broken bones to infections and diseases. We don't need to learn how to patch ourselves up, treat burns, stitch wounds, or handle food poisoning because we have highly competent, specially trained people who can do it for us in modern society.

However, when you're off the grid, you may be many miles from help, stuck on your own or with an injured second party. If you don't know what to do, the outcome can be devastating. It is crucial to educate yourself, take first aid courses, recognize the signs of major health complications, and know how to treat injuries. Often, this will be a stop-gap until you can seek proper medical care, but the stop-gap could mean the difference between life and death. Take it seriously and protect yourself and others you are with by learning what to do when the worst happens, and someone is injured or ill. This is the only responsible way to approach spending significant periods off the grid, and it's as crucial as other safety precautions that you might take.

I take this subject seriously because I know just how critical it can be. A childhood friend of mine lost her mother when a camping trip went wrong, and they were too far to get help for a bad asthma attack. It was a devastating tragedy that changed the trajectory of her life. With more preparation and understanding, things could have been different. I hope that this book will make it different for some of its readers, empowering them to take control and protect themselves and their companions when they do not have access to emergency services.

This book will teach you how to prepare for medical care off the grid. It's not a substitute for proper medical care from a doctor or other trained professional. It is intended to help you prepare yourself for accidents, deal with dangerous situations, and detect when an illness requires proper medical intervention. My goal is to help you make your off-grid world – where you do not have access to a doctor or emergency services – safer and build your confidence and competence when dealing with emergencies and minor injuries that can be treated at home. Don't use this to replace proper medical care, and always seek help from professionals as soon as this becomes a viable option, especially if the injuries are severe.

An injured or sick person would always be taken directly to a hospital or a medical practitioner in an ideal world. However, if you are going to spend time in the wilds, away from society, you need to face the reality that you will not have these resources at your fingertips, and non-ideal solutions must be turned to. Having a good foundation to work from, awareness of the dangers you may face, and information about how to treat common injuries and diseases should help you and your companions stay safe when you're not able to call on professionals.

It's a good idea to take some first aid courses in conjunction with reading this book so that you can learn more about the proper techniques and get guidance from professionals before you go off the grid. You will learn a lot from practicing firsthand, asking questions of medical experts, and observing techniques being demonstrated. You can then use this book to better understand medical care in general. Refer to it when you need reminders, reassurance, or assistance on any of the areas covered – or not covered – by the training that you have undertaken.

We're going to look at the entire gamut of illnesses and injuries that you and your companions might encounter while traveling off the grid so that you are prepared for as many situations as possible.

The topics will cover what supplies you should carry and how to use them. Some of the top techniques you should learn before going off the grid are common health issues at play, dealing with their symptoms, and handling minor emergencies that might occur, such as toothaches, nosebleeds, sprains, constipation, etc. and infections. Afterward, we will move on to major emergencies such as electrocution, heatstroke, poisoning, severed fingers, burns, broken bones, shock, and pregnancy. Finally, we will touch on the natural remedies you may wish to stock in your first aid kit, how to make your hand sanitizer, and some other natural healing recipes.

My goal is to make you as prepared as possible so that when an emergency arises, you have the tools to stay level-headed and deal with it to the best of your ability. An off-grid emergency is never something you want to handle, but the fundamental reality is that these things happen, and you can either be prepared and do your best or be unprepared and powerless. It is imperative to take responsibility for yourself and your companions' health and safety and learn the tenets of how to deal with emergencies when you are off the grid.

We're going to start by looking at how you should begin preparing to go off the grid, what supplies you will need, where you should keep these supplies, and how to get organized. We'll also touch on designating responsibility, recognizing your dependents, and undertaking relevant training for the situation you are going into.

1
Preparing To Go Off-Grid

"Medicine heals doubt as well as diseases."

-Karl Marx

Understanding What First Aid Is Before You Go Off The Grid

Before looking at anything else, it is worth getting to grips with what first aid is.

First aid is generally defined as assistance given immediately upon detection of an injury or illness. It aims to prevent loss of life, reduce the risk of the condition getting worse, or – ideally –restore the body to health. First aid is often followed up by proper medical care, but as the name suggests, it is the first help when a problem arises.

When you're at home in a typical setting, first responders usually provide first aid for anything serious. However, most people have applied first aid to themselves and others in some situations. For example, if you have ever stuck a band-aid on your child's knee, you have performed first aid. Your goal is to reduce the risk of the injury getting worse and give it a chance to heal without dirt getting into the wound.

Of course, performing first aid in an off-grid situation can be relatively more severe. You may find yourself splinting broken bones, dealing with major trauma to eyes or other crucial organs, dealing with choking or performing CPR.

Nevertheless, it's essential to be clear about your goal with your medical intervention. You are ultimately trying to prevent the condition from getting worse and allowing the body to recover if it can. First aid is not about long-term treatment; it is just about halting the issue as much as possible so that the body can try to recover or the person can be transported to a medical facility.

Being clear on this is important. Your first aid training does not mean you can stay off the grid and ignore major injuries or illnesses. You may need to return to society if something happens, although some minor injuries can be left to heal alone if they are given the correct treatment. Recognize this before you set out on your venture, and keep it in mind if ever a situation occurs. It's better to seek proper treatment when in doubt than to patch it up and hope for the best.

Explain First Aid To Your Companions

Depending on who you are traveling with, you need to make sure that they recognize this definition and have a clear understanding of first aid's purpose; This is probably more important if you are traveling with adults than with children.

Make health and safety everyone's responsibility while traveling. Having one person trained in first aid is a good start, but if something happens and nobody else has the relevant training, the party is not safe. You need to ensure that at least two people in a group can perform basic first aid.

Preferably, every group member will have at least some understanding of dealing with injuries; This reduces the risk if someone gets separated and injured when the rest of the party isn't available to help.

It's also crucial to ensure everyone knows where the first aid kit is, everyone can access it, and at least most people know how to use some of the items. Although it's tempting to designate one group member as your "doctor," and some people are only too happy to assume this vital role, this isn't a safe or responsible approach. If everyone can take care of each other, you are much more likely to overcome problems when they arise.

Before leaving, every group member should be clear about this, even older children.

Young children may not be able to administer first aid, but it is still worth ensuring that they know where the first aid kit is kept and how they can access it (although be safe about keeping medications out of the reach of very young children).

Having everyone on board with the first aid discussion is a great way to start your trip out with safety at the forefront of everyone's minds.

Get The First Aid Kit Ready

Once you have started talking about safety, getting the first aid kit ready is the next priority. The contents of the kit will vary according to where you are going and who you are traveling with, so do not just buy a ready-made kit. Think about every party member and their needs. Take any allergies into account and do not buy medication that people cannot use. Think hard about any existing conditions that could make your group members more vulnerable.

You should prepare a kit with input from all of your group members. Every individual should carry the bare essentials, such as band-aids, pain relief, alcohol wipes, and antihistamines, but create an overall larger kit.

We will cover what to put in the larger kit shortly, but it's a good idea to sit and take stock of your kit before every trip you make (or on a schedule if you are in a constantly off-grid situation – perhaps once a month). Think about what you have used, what needs replacing, and what might be going out of date.

Being organized about your first aid and always having a kit ready is crucial when you don't have access to emergency services. Stock up on supplies regularly and always note when you have used something or are getting low on it.

You may also want to consider making up some smaller kits as well as your main ones. These might be distributed among your group members to be stored in personal bags or carried with you when you're away from your off-grid living setup. For example, if you are hiking regularly, it's wise to have a small first aid kit available with the basics, just in case.

Medical Supplies And What To Carry

So, what should a kit contain? Although the kits will vary, almost all kits should include items intended for treating:

- Wounds
- Burns
- Allergies
- Infections
- Illnesses
- Pain

Kits should also contain extras relating to prescription medication if anyone in your group takes it; This means if you get stuck somewhere, they will have more leeway before running out of medication. Many doctors will fill additional prescriptions if you are traveling.

Wounds:

- Sterile gauze dressings in a variety of sizes
- Band-aids
- Distilled water
- Safety pins
- Bandages
- Scissors
- Bandage scissors (these are curved so you can more easily cut bandages when they are in place against the patient's skin)
- Tweezers
- Sterile dressings for eyes
- Eyewash
- Chemical ice bags
- Duct tape (this can be used to close wounds in an extreme emergency, although it is not suitable for everyday medical use)
- Butterfly sutures
- Splints
- A sling
- Sutures
- Sterile needles

Burns:

- Lavender oil
- Aloe vera gel
- Sunblock
- Burn creams
- Burn dressings

Allergies:

- Cream to relieve rashes
- Cream to relieve bites and stings
- Anti-allergy medication (even if you do not think anyone in your group suffers from allergies, carry an antihistamine cream of some description; allergies can kill people fast and with little warning)
- An EpiPen or Epinephrine (crucial if anyone has a known allergy)

Infections:

- Antibiotic cream (if you can get it)
- Antiseptic (e.g., Isopropyl Alcohol, Peroxide)
- Alcohol-free wipes
- Disposable gloves

Illnesses:

- Over-the-counter medicines for any existing conditions (e.g., if someone needs cream to treat conditions such as athlete's foot, this should be contained in your first aid kit)
- A digital thermometer
- A cold compress

Pain:

- Pain relief (make sure you have some that are suitable for children if there are any children in your party)
- Aspirin (this can be used as pain relief but is also helpful if someone has a heart attack)
- It is also a good idea to include the following items:
- Cotton swabs
- Cotton balls
- A flashlight
- Matches
- Medical cups
- Soap
- A syringe
- A CPR face shield with a high-efficiency particulate air (HEPA) filter
- Clean, absorbent cloths
- Some clean spoons
- A survival blanket
- An emergency dental kit (this can be purchased as a set kit)
- A manual and some basic first aid instructions for using the equipment and performing first aid techniques
- A cellphone that has a charged battery so you can contact emergency services

This might seem like an extensive list, but it covers most of the basics you are likely to need. You may feel that some items are unnecessary, and there are very likely to be things you want to add based on the location you are going to. Build your kit with care, and remember that it is much better to be overstocked than to risk running out of something.

Always carry enough supplies for every individual and assume the worst. Most items in a first aid kit can be kept long without needing replacement, although you should make sure medication is within date. Once you have built your basic kit, it should last you for years (unless an emergency arises). Restock it before every trip and make sure nothing has expired.

Store The First Aid Kit In A Suitable Place

It's imperative to think about where you will stow the first aid kit when off the grid, making it easier to move around if you use tents or RVs. Still, whatever situation you're in, you need to ensure that your first aid kit is accessible and everyone knows where it is stored.

You also need to make sure that it is out of reach of young children, especially if it contains medication or sharp tools, but within reach of older children who may need to access the kit. Furthermore, the kit should be protected from both damp and temperature extremes, so it is a good idea to keep it in an insulated, sealed box if you are sleeping in tents.

If you sleep in a tent, but your vehicle is easily accessible, it is often best to keep the first aid kit in your vehicle. It will be kept drier and warmer, and it is easier to prevent it from getting lost. Tents can end up cluttered and messy, especially where children are involved, and you do not want to be searching for a first aid kit under piles of clothing and bedding because someone has moved it and there's an emergency.

Have a dedicated, clearly marked box only used for the first aid items. This can be placed in a cupboard, glove compartment, or any other storage spot available, but it should always be kept in a dedicated place. Put it back after you have used it, as soon as possible to increase the chances of people quickly locating it in an emergency.

You may wish to put some silica gel packets inside your first aid kit to absorb any moisture. Although most medical supplies are sealed to keep them sterile, this is an extra precaution that is easy to take and will help to ensure that your stores last well.

If you need to relocate the first aid kit at any point, inform everyone, including children, that it has been moved. You should also consider putting a sticker in the old place or somewhere else in your vehicle that lists the new location, allowing people to grab it quickly even if they have forgotten about the change or don't know where the kit is stored.

How To Disinfect Medical Supplies

There will be times when you need sterile medical supplies that are not inherently sterile.

When you take a sealed gauze out of its packaging, it should be sterile, but your tools – scissors, tweezers, needles – need to be sterilized by you before and after every use. Identify these tools and remember to sterilize them before you start dealing with an injury.

Tools that have not been sterilized can be dangerous. They will introduce infection into the wound and potentially even into the bloodstream, which could cause severe illness. Infections can kill a person in just a few days; ergo, disinfecting medical supplies will be crucial.

You should note that clean tools are not the same as sterile tools. A clean tool is free from dirt and surface residue, whereas a sterile tool is completely free from microbes. Sterile tools massively reduce the risk of infection, whereas clean tools only mitigate it to a degree.

In most hospital settings, tools are sterilized using modern equipment to ensure they are free from bacteria. However, you will not have access to these tools in your off-grid environment, which means that you need to learn how to sterilize your tools safely and reliably yourself.

There are various safe methods for sterilizing tools when you don't have access to machinery; I'll run through each of them, and you can choose which method(s) seem most applicable to your situation.

Method One: Soaking In Bleach

You can soak your instruments in bleach for up to 30 minutes to sterilize them, but you must remove them at this point. If you continue soaking them past the 30-minute mark, there is a risk of rust occurring.

Once the tool is sterile, remove it from the bleach solution and rinse it with sterile water. Do not rinse it with normal water, or the sterilization will be undone.

If you don't have bleach, isopropyl alcohol will also serve the same purpose. Again, soak the tools for 30 minutes to ensure that they are indeed sterilized.

Method Two: Boil The Instruments

Place your tools in water that is gently bubbling and simmer them for 30 minutes to ensure that the bacteria is killed; This is a generally reliable method, although not 100% effective. It may be the easiest to achieve in an off-grid situation, assuming you have access to heat and water but no alcohol or bleach.

You should sterilize tools in their "open" position if they have one (such as scissors), as this ensures that the sterilization is effective. Closed instruments may not be truly sterilized.

Method Three: Sterilize In The Oven

If you have access to an oven, wrap your tools in aluminum foil and place them in the cold oven. Heat the oven to 400 degrees F, and then allow the instruments to bake for 30 minutes. Make sure you protect your hands while removing them.

This method is preferable in that it should not cause rusting over the tools, but many off-grid situations will not have access to an oven, so you may find that it isn't a feasible option.

You might be concerned that none of these methods lends themselves to swift sterilization. There is rarely a need to sterilize tools so urgently that you cannot leave time to sterilize them properly. Sterilization is crucial, especially when dealing with open wounds because introducing bacteria and microorganisms to the bloodstream could be fatal in some cases. Do not skip over this step; sterilize tools before you use them.

Determining Responsibility And Length Of Responsibility

This is particularly important if you are traveling with a group of adults. You should discuss what first aid responsibilities there are and who will be responsible for what. I mentioned earlier that you shouldn't have a single "first aider" for the trip peradventure something happens to them, but it is a good idea to list the responsibilities and work out who to delegate them to. It keeps things organized, prevents work from being done twice, and ensures nothing gets missed.

For example, one of the responsibilities might be to check the medical kit is adequately stocked once per month. You might give this responsibility to one group member for the trip or share it among group members. Have a schedule drawn up, set reminders, and ensure everyone knows what they should be doing and when, which reduces the risk of errors and ensures that tasks are done.

You might designate one person to be in charge of ensuring medication is not expired or picking up supplies when in town. Another person's responsibility might be to assess the kit and update stock lists. A third's might involve running through the basics of first aid techniques once a month so that everyone stays up to date on how to do these things.

It's also a good idea to spread responsibilities around, so one person is not overwhelmed, which is a common risk in big groups. It's easier to note so-and-so handles the first aid kit, but doing this has two issues. Firstly, it puts a lot of pressure on one person, who may not like this. You can't trust that they will speak up if it gets too much, or they would rather not do it.

Secondly, it means you are dependent on that person. If they stop doing it, don't take it seriously, or make mistakes, the whole group will suffer as a result. It is much better to spread responsibility and regularly rotate who is doing what. This brings in oversight, ensures tasks are being completed, and reduces pressure and monotony, leading to mistakes.

Encourage discussion among the group members about responsibilities and ask people to be upfront if they have issues. If one group member is slacking, the others should raise it and ask what's going on. It's important not to be confrontational but to find out why that person isn't doing their share and how you can support them in doing it next time.

It may not seem worth spreading responsibility around small family units, but discussing duty and scheduling is still a good idea. *Which parent is in charge of ensuring the first aid kit is stocked? Who deals with handing out medications? If a child in the group needs regular medication, who is providing that and ensuring it is taken as it should be? Who is a dependent, and who is a caregiver?* Think about older children, and communicate with them about what they can and should do if an emergency arises when an adult isn't immediately available.

Having a conversation about these things massively reduces the risk of errors and makes it much easier to keep first aid straightforward and to operate smoothly.

Identifying Likely Scenarios

Part of the problem with emergencies is that they are, almost invariably, unexpected. You don't know what you need to prepare for, which means it's pretty impossible to anticipate. However, that doesn't mean you should blindly head off the grid without taking the time to think first.

Take some time to consider the situation you are entering and the terrain and challenges you are likely to encounter. If you are staying near water, think about handling any swimming incidents and keeping each other safe on or near the water. If you are going to be in hilly terrain, think about dealing with falls, sprains, and broken bones. If you are getting close to wildlife, find out what creatures you might encounter, how they might be dangerous, and how you can counteract that danger or deal with stings, bites, or major injuries.

Think about the risks associated with hot and cold weather, lack of power, food storage, water safety, and everything else that may come up when you are away from civilization.

Let's look at some examples.

You are staying near a river with two children under ten. You have had discussions about water safety, and both children can swim and are aware of the dangers of currents. Despite these precautions, you should still:

- Learn how to perform CPR
- Learn the common signs of drowning (because many people mistakenly believe that the over-dramatized film version of drowning is what true drowning looks like)
- Learn how to treat hypothermia
- Learn how to treat hyperventilating

You may decide that other first-aid preparation is also necessary, but this will cover many basics when you are around water. Consider also determining whether you are likely to encounter dangerous creatures and how these can be dealt with.

Alternatively, imagine that you are hiking with a group of other adults. You have agreed on safety procedures such as not going off alone and carrying basic medical supplies. You might also:

- Get some practice splinting a broken bone
- Learn how to treat hypothermia
- Carry emergency supplies for heatstroke
- Do some reading about insect or snake bites and learn how to identify common insects for that area, including what reactions their bites can cause and how they can be treated

You can perform a similar risk analysis for any situation you are going into. Think about the common dangers, the injuries that result from these dangers, and how you can address and deal with these injuries.

It may help do this with other adults and even older children in your group. If everyone can recognize and assess dangers before going to an area, there is a reduced risk of accidents occurring in the first place. There is also a much higher chance of the accident being dealt with correctly if it cannot be averted, but everyone has a clear idea of how to respond.

You should have a written risk analysis and the protocol following an injury. The more scenarios you can plan for, the more likely you are to:

- Have the relevant supplies to deal with the injury
- Know how to deal with the injury (e.g., having CPR training)
- Stay calm in the face of the injury
- Successfully treat the injury

These things will make your first air more effective and reduce the risks you face. Be proactive and constantly analyze the potential issues you may address, particularly when you move to a new area and new risks need to be factored into your behavior and first aid kit.

What Training Should You Undertake Before You Leave?

The kinds of training that you should take will depend, to some degree, on where you are going and what you are likely to be doing. It's always good to do more than you need, rather than less – the training may come in handy later, even if it is unlikely to affect this particular trip.

You should consider doing:

- Wilderness first aid: this should be a top consideration for anyone going off the grid. It explicitly handles how to help someone in an emergency where professional assistance may be slow to arrive.
- Emergency first aid: this will center on life-threatening injuries and generally addresses breathing issues, circulatory issues, etc. It's possible to do this course for both children and adults.
- Basic first aid: this will cover the standards, such as applying bandages, dressing wounds, treating minor injuries, etc. It will also often deal with head injuries, spinal injuries, medical emergencies, and poisoning.
- Marine first aid is likely to be helpful if you are working near or in water, where you need to recognize the symptoms of drowning quickly and reliably and deal with the outcome.
- Emergency child care first aid: if you are traveling with children, it's crucial to familiarize yourself with the different approaches needed to provide first aid to them. Common issues like child choking, wound care, etc., will be covered.
- Standard child care first aid: this will cover similar to the above, but emphasizes less on emergencies. It will also touch on child illnesses, head injuries, safety awareness, wound care, etc.
- Mental health first aid: this may not seem like a priority, but in an off-grid situation where nobody else is available to help, you may find yourself coping with panic attacks, suicidal thoughts, substance abuse, anxiety, and more. Learning how to handle these things is crucial and very often overlooked.
- Pet first aid: if you are traveling with animals, bear in mind that you may be a long way from the nearest emergency vet, and animals can suffer from accidents and illnesses just as quickly as people can. This kind of course usually covers illnesses, pet CPR, injuries, etc.

You may not need to do all of these, and indeed, this number of courses could be prohibitively expensive. However, it is worth bearing in mind that they all exist and assessing which are the most likely to be useful in your situation. If you cannot afford to do courses in everything you would like to cover, consider learning about each relevant section online and talking to others in your group about them.

If you are traveling with other adults and it's not feasible to have everyone trained in every area, consider diversifying so that everyone brings something new to the party. It is a good idea for everyone to understand the basics, but you may then be able to train each other or increase the number of situations that your group is equipped to cover. Ideally, individuals all want to be competent in as many areas as possible, but where this isn't feasible, spread skills among your group and teach each other where you can.

Remember that there are many free resources online and if you can't afford to attend courses in person, watching videos, reading books, and sharing skills is the next best option.

Summary

In this chapter, we've covered:

- What first aid involves and what the purpose of first aid is
- How to talk about this with your companions and make sure that everyone is on the same page before you set out on a journey together
- How to prepare your first aid kit and work out what to carry with you, with a comprehensive list for creating a basic first aid kit that you can build on
- Where to keep your first aid kit and how to store it
- Tips for disinfecting and sterilizing tools
- Information on how to delegate responsibility
- Suggestions for how to identify and prepare for likely scenarios that you may face off the grid
- What kinds of training you may wish to undertake before you set out on your journey, and how to diversify the overall skills available within your group

In the following chapter, we will look at some top first aid techniques, including CPR, mouth to mouth and mouth to nose; the recovery position; and the Heimlich maneuver. We'll also look at accurately taking a pulse and creating splints and slings to support injuries properly. Finally, we'll look at wound closure, exploring when wounds need to be closed and when they should be left open, bandages and gauze, and the basics of sutures and staples.

2
Useful Techniques To Learn

"The aim of medicine is to prevent disease and prolong life; the ideal of medicine is to eliminate the need of a physician."

-William J. Mayo

In this chapter, we will start looking at some of the practical applications of first aid and some of the basic techniques that you may benefit from knowing how to perform. It's an excellent idea to get some hands-on experience with these techniques and read about them; this will help you ensure that you are doing it right and improve your ability to perform the technique.

Remember that you will often be providing first aid in a stressful situation, and it is crucial not to panic. Although you will need to act promptly, take enough time to gather yourself and ensure that you are doing things right. Don't just launch into a technique with half an idea of how it is done unless the emergency is so dire that you think any action is better than nothing, and the patient is at risk of losing their life if you don't do something.

If possible, practice with your group members and give each other feedback on these techniques. If you can practice with a medical professional, too, take this opportunity. The more confident you are in your abilities to perform a technique, the more likely you are to do it well under pressure and not to panic and forget everything.

Even if you become very confident with these techniques, you may still find it beneficial to have a few basic, printed instruction sheets (preferably with pictures) stored in your first aid box. This can bolster your confidence when the real emergency arises or may help someone not trained in first aid perform the maneuver if they don't have guidance from an expert. There are plenty of graphics online for performing such maneuvers; use some simple ones and place them in your first aid kit.

Now, let's look at how to perform some first aid!

How To Perform CPR

Before we start, it is vital to note that CPR is to be used during a breathing or cardiac emergency, and it is among the more intricate first aid maneuvers to perform. It can damage the person's ribs and should only be used when necessary.

Suppose a situation is dire enough to need CPR. In that case, you should also look for emergency services to the patient as soon as possible, even if it may be challenging.

The first advised step of CPR is always to call 9-1-1 or get someone else to do this. If you are not currently somewhere that emergency services can reach you, you should still get in touch with them, as CPR is often required consistently until an ambulance arrives.

CPR For Adults

The advice varies depending on whether you have undertaken formal CPR training or not. If you are not familiar with CPR, it is always better to attempt it than do nothing, but you may wish to stick to chest compressions. We will provide the complete method below.

Before performing CPR, check that the area is safe and see whether the person is conscious. Tap or shake the patient's shoulder and loudly ask if they are okay. If the person does not respond, begin CPR.

1. Roll the patient onto their back on a firm surface and ensure that the airway is unobstructed.
2. Begin the C-A-B approach. This stands for Compressions, Airway, Breathing. Compressions are intended to restore blood flow, and this is where you should begin.
3. Kneel next to the patient's shoulders and place the heel of one hand over the person's chest, between their breasts.
4. Place your other hand on top of the first hand and then lean so that your elbows are straight and your shoulders are directly above your hands.
5. Press down hard, compressing the chest to at least 2 inches down, but not further than 2.4 inches. Use your body weight to press, rather than just your arms.
6. Allow the chest to spring back, and then push down hard again. You should aim to push at a rate between 100 and 120 compressions per minute; this is surprisingly fast. It is a good idea to practice this to find the rhythm.
7. Continue doing this until help arrives. If you are trained in CPR, you can move on to the following steps, Airway and Breathing. If not, stick with compressions only.

8. Airway: start by opening the airway once you have performed 30 compressions. You should do this by placing your palm on the person's forehead to tip their head back and then gently lifting their chin with your hand. This method will be demonstrated in first aid training. It opens the airway and ensures that the person can breathe.

9. Breathing: you can breathe for the other person if you have been trained how. We will cover mouth to mouth and mouth to nose in the following section. This should ideally be done using an appropriate CPR filter but can be done without in emergencies.

CPR For Children Between 1 and 12 Years Old

It is crucial to understand that CPR for children is similar but not the same process. When tilting the child's head back, be careful not to go too far, as children have more delicate airways than adults do.

You could seriously injure a child, especially a young child, if you use the full force of your body weight to administer compressions, so be careful. The chest should be compressed to about 1.5 inches to 2 inches (generally 2, but less for young children), and you will not need as much force to achieve this. Some CPR professionals will recommend just using one hand rather than two.

This advice applies to children up to 12 or those that weigh less than 121 pounds.[x]

CPR For Babies Under 1 Year

If you are traveling with an infant, it is advisable to take a special CPR course. Babies are considerably more delicate than adults or even young children, and there is an increased risk of doing damage by performing CPR.

Start by checking that the baby is unresponsive by tapping the soles of its feet and shouting nearby (not directly in its ear). If it is not breathing, tilt the infant's head a short way back to look like it is sniffing the air. Next, place two fingers in the center of its chest and begin compressions to about an inch and a half deep. Do not put too much force on the baby's chest.

It should be noted that performing CPR takes priority over calling emergency services for babies and children, especially if you are far from help. Both children and babies have higher resilience and a greater chance of survival if CPR is begun immediately, so don't hesitate before you start. If someone else is available, have them call the emergency service line. If not, contact them when able.

How To Perform Mouth To Mouth, Mouth To Nose

It is essential to have proper training before performing the mouth-to-mouth or mouth-to-nose aspect of CPR, as there is a greater risk of doing damage if you are untrained in this area. If you cannot afford training, stick to doing compressions in the event of an emergency, and do not risk mouth to mouth, especially with a child or baby, which is likely to be more vulnerable.

However, if you have had the training and are simply rusty or would like a written reference, you will find the steps below.

The same method is used for mouth to nose, but it is better to do mouth to mouth unless the individual's mouth has been injured. If possible, use a specifically designed filter for this part of CPR.

Mouth To Mouth For Adults

1. Open the airway using the head-tilt, chin-lift method after performing 30 compressions.
2. Pinch the patient's nostrils shut if you are performing mouth to mouth. Cover the patient's mouth with yours, sealing your lips together to prevent any air from escaping.
3. Give one rescue breath, lasting for one second, and watch to see if the patient's chest rises as you do so. If it does, give a second breath, lasting one second.
4. If the chest does not rise, repeat the maneuver to open the airway and give the second breath. Do not give a third breath.
5. Resume chest compressions.

A complete cycle is considered 30 compressions followed by 2 rescue breaths. Keep cycling until help arrives or the patient begins to move. If the patient moves before help arrives, you should still ensure that they are seen by medical professionals as soon as possible. Keep them lying still and stay with them.

It is important not to breathe too hard or too often. Stick to 2 one-second breaths per cycle.

Mouth To Mouth For Children

The same method applies, but you must be particularly gentle with children. Their airways are more fragile, and you need to ensure that the head is not tipped back too far. Breathe gently and keep cycling breaths with compressions. You should still do 30 compressions for every 2 rescue breaths.

Mouth To Mouth For Babies

Again, the same method applies, but a baby will require even more care. Tilt the head only a little way, and be very gentle when providing the rescue breaths. Simply puff up your cheeks and blow into the child's mouth, rather than breathing with the full force of your lungs.

Keep the rate of compressions the same: 2 breaths for every 30 compressions.

How To Put Someone Into The Recovery Position

Learning how to put someone into a recovery position is a crucial aspect of first aid, and it is one of the first things you should look at. A person who is unconscious but breathing and not in a life-threatening situation should be placed in recovery. This ensures that the airway is kept clear and open, so there's no risk of fluid or vomit choking the individual.

Note that the recovery position should never be used if there is a risk that the person has a spinal injury. If you suspect you are dealing with a spinal injury, do not move the person, but if you need to open the airway, put your hands on either side of the head to support it and gently lift the jaw. Do not jolt or reposition the neck. People with spinal injuries should not be moved except by emergency services. If this has occurred while you are far from help, keep the patient warm and stay with them, but do not attempt to move them or allow them to move.

Follow the below steps to put someone in the recovery position:

1. Check that the area is secure and there are no immediate threats to safety.
2. Roll the person onto their back on a flat surface and kneel beside them.
3. Take the arm nearest to you and extend it out away from their body until it is at a right angle. Their palm should be left facing upward.
4. Lean across them and take their other arm. Guide it across their body and place the back of that hand against the cheek closest to you, and hold it there with one of your hands. Their arm will be resting across their chest. If it is their right arm, their hand should be touching the left cheek, and vice versa.
5. Use your free hand to take the person's knee on the far side of their body and draw this up to a right angle.
6. Gently tug on the bent knee so that the person rolls over onto their side. Their bent arm will now support their head so that it doesn't flop, and the extended arm will prevent them from rolling further. Check that the bent leg remains at a right angle to the body to offer more stability.

7. Gently tip the person's head back slightly and lift the chin to open the airway. Check there are no obstructions and that the person is still breathing.
8. Remain with the person until you can deal with whatever has caused them to pass out. You may need to call for help from other members of your group or inform emergency services. Ensure that the person stays warm and do not leave them unattended.

How To Perform The Heimlich Maneuver

Choking is a danger that people face everywhere, so it's one you'll need to account for no matter where you are going off the grid. It is also where a quick reaction and a correctly performed maneuver can mean the difference between life and death. There is rarely time to call emergency services or even another person (although if multiple people are on hand to help, someone should contact emergency services while others assist the patient). Choking is a particular hazard for young children, who often put small objects in their mouths, but anyone can choke. You should learn the signs of choking before you travel. These include:

- Lips and nails turning blue
- Flushed skin turning pale or blue
- Squeaky noises when attempting to breathe
- Scrabbling at the throat
- Inability to speak
- Passing out

If you are dealing with an adult, encourage them to keep coughing if they can do so. This may dislodge the object. If not, you should perform the five-and-five maneuver, an updated version of the Heimlich maneuver, including other steps.

It can be done as follows:

1. Get the patient standing up and step behind them.
2. Lean the patient forward and wrap your arm around their chest. The upper body should be parallel with the ground.
3. Strike the heel of your hand against the patient's back between their shoulder blades five times.
4. Place your arms around the patient's waist and make a fist with one of your hands, the thumb resting against the patient's navel. Take the fist in your other hand and push it both inward and upward against the patient's abdomen, as though trying to lift the patient off the ground. Do this five times sharply.
5. Repeat steps 3 and 4 until the blockage is dislodged and the patient can breathe again.

If you are not familiar with the back thrusts, it is possible to just perform the Heimlich maneuver. However, the two methods used together may prove more effective.

If your patient cannot stand alone, straddle their waist and follow the abovementioned method.

Heimlich For Yourself

If you are choking and unable to get help, you can employ a similar technique:

1. Place a fist above your navel.
2. Grip your fist with the other hand and bend over a hard surface like a chair.
3. Shove your fist inward and upward sharply.

Heimlich For Pregnant Women

There's a much greater risk of harming a pregnant woman using the usual method, so instead:

1. Place your hands higher up, at the base of the breastbone, rather than the navel.
2. Perform the same abdominal thrusts described above. Be cautious of the woman's stomach.
3. Repeat until the blockage is dislodged.

Heimlich For Children

You can use the same method given above for children old enough to stand but kneel behind them. Most people recommend using abdominal thrusts only for children as there is less risk of damaging internal organs.

Heimlich For Babies

Follow the below method when dealing with a baby choking:

1. Sit down, rest your forearm on your thigh, and rest the infant across it face down. Support the head and neck with one hand, and lower the head below the infant's body.
2. Gently but firmly strike the infant's back five times using the heel of your hand. Be careful not to strike the infant's head.
3. Turn the infant over to face up but keep the head lower than the body. Press two fingers against the infant's breastbone and compress it five times to about 1.5 inches in quick

succession. Let the chest rise in between each compression.

4. Keep repeating until the blockage is dislodged.

In all cases, if you are not successful in dislodging the blockage or if the person loses consciousness, you should move on to CPR until emergency help can reach you.

How To Take Somebody's Pulse

Taking a person's pulse is suitable in many medical situations, and it is a skill that you should practice. The rate of someone's pulse will help you to determine how well that person's heart is working. Changes to the pulse can indicate a range of issues, although it's important to note that a pulse also naturally varies according to the person's rate of exercise.

There are two ways to measure a person's pulse: you can put your fingers on their wrist or neck.

Measuring On The Wrist

1. Hold the person's arm up straight and face their palm upward.
2. Put your first and second finger on the wrist, near the base of the patient's thumb.
3. Use a clock that will count the seconds to determine how many beats you can feel in one minute (you can count 30 seconds and multiply by 2 if this is easier).

Measuring On The Neck

1. Put your first and second finger on the side of the neck, just next to the windpipe (the soft hollow area)
2. Again use a clock that will count the seconds to count how many beats you can feel per minute.

If you cannot find someone's pulse, move your fingers around and press a little harder. It is hard to detect a pulse in some people. Most adults have a resting heart rate of 60 to 100 beats in a minute, although this varies depending on several factors, including medication, stress, age, fitness, etc.

It's a good idea to measure the resting heart rate of your various group members so that you know what their pulse rate should be and whether it is normal. Keep a log of this in your first aid kit, and discuss any abnormalities that you expect to see (e.g., if someone has a heart condition or takes medication that would alter their pulse) so that everyone is aware of this.

An irregular pulse can signify many different things, but knowing how to measure it is the first step. Be aware that a person's pulse is likely to be made less regular and significantly faster when they exercise.

Making Supportive Splints And Slings

There will be times when you need to support an injury, and creating a splint or sling correctly can make a big difference to the injured party. Splints and slings are intended to stabilize injuries, support the limb, and reduce the risk of further injury. You may often need both together, although sometimes an injury will only call for one or the other.

Often, these will be followed up with proper medical care when possible. For example, you may splint a broken arm until the patient can be got to a hospital, but you shouldn't neglect to take them to a hospital afterward, even if their pain levels are tolerable. Without x-rays and assessment by a trained medical professional, it's impossible to know if the bones are straight and in an excellent position to heal. It's also impossible to know if you are dealing with a break, a fracture, or just a bad sprain. Make sure you attend a hospital as soon as is feasible, no matter how good your splints and slings are.

How To Make A Splint

Splints are usually intended to stabilize broken bones and help with severe sprains. Their purpose is to immobilize the joint to reduce movement and provide support. You can splint many parts of the body, but commonly, you will be splinting a wrist, arm, ankle, or another joint to stop it from moving.

You can often find the materials needed for a splint in the environment, but you should also have equipment in your first aid kit. You will need:

- A strong stick
- A plank
- A towel
- A newspaper

You will usually attempt to immobilize the injury by splinting from above it to below. For example, an injured wrist can be splinted by running a stick from the elbow to the hand; the stick immobilizes the wrist and prevents the injury from being jostled.

Let's look at how to make a splint. Before you start, it's worth noting that you should not attempt to realign the injury if it looks crooked; you may cause grave damage by moving broken bones around. A hospital will set an injury later; all you aim to do is immobilize it to reduce the risk of further damage and minimize the pain. You should follow the steps below:

1. Deal with any bleeding. A splint should not be applied over a bleeding wound, as it is not intended to be sterile, prevent bleeding, or soak up blood. Put pressure on the wound until the blood stops, and apply disinfectant and gauze if necessary.
2. Pad the injury. You can do this using cotton balls, bandages, cloth, or even a towel or newspaper if necessary.
3. Place the splint in position. It should run from an uninjured joint to another uninjured joint if possible. You can splint the forearm by getting a longer stick than the forearm and splinting from the wrist to the elbow. Some joints are tougher to splint than others but do your best to immobilize the injury.
4. Tie or tape the splint in place. Do not put ties or tape around the injury site; apply them at the uninjured spots to provide support. Ties should be firm, so the splint is held close to the body, but not enough to risk cutting off circulation.
5. Keep watching for reduced circulation. As an injury swells, it is easy for a splint to become too tight. If any areas become pale, tinged with blue, or notably swollen, loosen the ties. A faint pulse is a further sign that the knots are too tight. Similarly, if the patient says it is painful, try loosening them slightly.
6. Encourage the injured person to lie down or sit down while the shock passes, especially if they feel faint. Elevate the legs slightly and tilt their head below the level of their heart if possible. Wait until they feel better before you try to move them, or there is a risk of them passing out.

Keep checking on the splint regularly until a doctor has assessed the person. If it becomes tight, loosen it to avoid circulatory issues.

Dealing With Wounds

You may find yourself dealing directly with open wounds at times, so you need to know how to handle them. Of course, wounds can vary massively in severity and how they are dealt with, so let's explore what kinds of wounds you might have to handle, the equipment you might need, and the approach to take.

1.   Minor Wounds

Minor wounds is a term that generally covers small gashes, shallow scratches, and general scrapes and bruises. Most minor wounds do not need a lot of intervention as they will heal independently.

Your first step will generally be to clean the wound. If possible, immerse the injury in warm, soapy water, but don't put soap directly on the cut. Use a soft cloth to rub away any dirt and allow any stubborn dirt to soak away. If necessary, sterile tweezers can remove fragments of dirt that remain.

Once the injury is clean, assess whether it needs to be covered or left open. There are advantages to both.

An uncovered wound will often heal more quickly because it will stay dry. Many minor wounds can be left open, but they should be covered if they are in an area that is likely to get rubbed (by tools, by clothes, etc.) or if the injured person is working in a dirty environment.

A covered wound will heal more slowly but will be protected and kept clean. You can often cover an injury with gauze and medical tape or even just a band-aid which should be changed regularly to ensure it is clean. If the wound is wet when you change the bandage, allow it to dry a little before cleaning it and applying a new dressing. This reduces the risk of infection.

Once the wound has begun to heal, remove the bandage to speed up the healing process.

In terms of treating pain, most minor wounds will not require you to administer painkillers, but over-the-counter ones can be taken if the injured person is uncomfortable. Analgesics such as aspirin and ibuprofen can reduce inflammation, so use these when necessary.

2. Major Wounds

Major wounds are much more severe injuries, and you will often need to combine your in-the-moment first aid with a trip to a hospital later to ensure that the injury heals correctly. However, knowing what to do in the heat of the moment is still crucial. Let's look at the steps for handling major wounds.

Step One: Identify The Kind Of Bleeding

You should quickly check what kind of bleeding is occurring, as this will help you determine how major the injury is. Arterial bleeding from a damaged artery will usually be fast and bright red. It will come in spurts in time with the person's pulse. This kind of bleeding needs to be addressed quickly, as it may be severe.

Venous bleeding occurs when a vein is punctured and is notably slower. The blood is usually darker and flows consistently rather than in spurts. Again, you need to act quickly, even if the blood doesn't seem to be flowing fast.

Capillary bleeding, the last kind, is minor and comes from the surface skin (e.g., a grazed knee). It will be bright red but only appear in small amounts, and it isn't threatening.

Step Two: Applying Pressure

In most cases, you need to stem the bleeding before doing anything else. Bleeding helps to flush dirt out of a wound, but a lot of bleeding can be dangerous, and you can't patch a wound that is bleeding heavily.

You need to stop the bleeding by applying a clean, absorbent pad. A scrap of cloth, some tissue, or some gauze will work for this, but don't use anything dirty. Place the cloth against the wound, and then apply gentle pressure to it, even if this is painful for the injured person.

If the blood continues and soaks through the cloth, simply add another piece of absorbent, clean material and keep applying pressure until the blood stops. If practical, lifting the injury site above the level of the patient's heart will also reduce the bleeding. Don't be tempted to release the pressure to check if the injury is still bleeding until at least a few minutes of pressure have been applied, giving the blood time to clot.

Bleeding should stop in ten to fifteen minutes for most wounds. It is likely to be severe if it doesn't, and you should plan for a hospital trip when possible. Keep applying pressure until the bleeding stops.

Step Three: Closing The Wound

Next, you will need to clean and close the wound. Do not close a wound that has not been cleaned, as this invites infection. Always ensure wounds have been thoroughly cleaned and all dirt has been removed. Use sterile tweezers if you cannot get the dirt out by washing. Make sure you clean your own hands regularly throughout the procedure. Pat the wound dry (do not rub) once you are ready to close it.

How you close the wound will depend on the supplies you have on hand and the kind of injury you are dealing with. Your options include:

- Gauze and tape
- Glue

- Butterfly bandages
- Sutures
- Staples

Most wounds will be closed using gauze and bandages, but you may need to use stitches if the wound is deeper or longer than 0.5 inches, if it's gaping open, or if any fatty tissue, muscle, or bone has been exposed. Cuts on the face, hands, or genitals are more likely to need stitches, as do cuts on a joint.

In these instances, you can also use staples, but note that you cannot use a paper stapler to heal an injury; you will need the proper equipment. We will look at all of these methods below.

3. Using Gauze And Tape For Wound Closure

Gauze is suitable for many wounds because it can be cut to size. However, it will not hold the skin closed, so it may not work for gaping wounds.

To apply gauze and tape to a wound, you will usually cut some clean gauze to a size that is a bit bigger than the wound. The gauze cushions the wound and prevents the tape from sticking to it and doing more damage. Place it over the wound, making sure the injury is fully covered, and then tear off strips of medical tape and use them to hold the gauze in place.

The gauze should be taped firmly but not tightly over the wound. The tape should not be pulling on the patient's skin but should form a close bond against it. Once this has been done, check that the patient can move without the tape pulling free.

4. Using Glue For Wound Closure

You may wish to use skin glue (which is **not** the same as ordinary glue). It is suitable for wounds less than 2 inches long and not deep. Glue isn't ideal if the edges cannot be pulled together easily. In general, glue is better for minor wounds.

It is a good idea to avoid touching the glue for 24 hours after it has been applied and keep it dry. It should peel off in around 5-10 days. Avoid working in dirty environments if skin glue has been applied, and don't use any lotions, band-aids, etc., on the glued area.

5. Using Butterfly Bandages For Wound Closure

If you don't feel that gauze or glue will work, look at applying a butterfly bandage instead. This involves using adhesive strips to pull a wound closed, and it should only be used on shallow wounds that are less than 0.5 inches long. You will be using strips of medical tape to pull the wound shut, with about 1/8th of an inch between each strip. Butterfly stitch usually involves several pieces of tape crossing the injury, with other elements at right-angles to hold the tape in place.

You can find images online that will show you how to perform butterfly stitching, and you can practice this with members of your group if you are unsure.

6. Using Sutures For Wound Closure

If you are going to be applying sutures, you need a sterile environment, and you should give the patient some pain relief. Sterilize all tools before using them. If possible, use a proper suturing kit, as regular needles are not designed for this. Note that you should only apply sutures if you can't see a doctor within 12-24 hours, as they can be dangerous if incorrectly used and may leave a nasty scar even in best-case scenarios.

- A suture kit should contain:
- A needle driver
- Tissue forceps
- Scissors
- A sterile needle
- Thread

There are many techniques for suturing wounds, and it is an excellent idea to get training on suturing if you expect to need it, so you have hands-on experience. If possible, get the patient to a medical facility for proper stitches, but otherwise, here is a simple method for sutures:

1. Clean the wound and your hands, make sure that all equipment has been sterilized, and then put on clean disposable gloves.
2. Grab the needle with the needle driver, and check that the needle clamp has locked into place. Get the threads ready.
3. Apply the tissue forceps to expose the part of the wound you will work on. Get the edges of the wound as close to being in line as possible.
4. Angle the needle at 90 degrees, a little to the right of the wound, so that it is against uninjured flesh.

5. Push the needle to just above the layer of fat, but not deeper. Twist your hand clockwise to bring the needle out on the other side of the wound. It should be directly across from the entry point.

6. When the needle is free, unlock the driver, attach it to the tip of the needle, and pull until you have about 2 inches of thread left at the entry point, on the side of the wound you started on. You should now have a piece of thread embedded beneath the skin.

7. Release the needle, and then use your left hand to wrap the thread on the left side of the needle around the tip of the needle holder three times. Go clockwise.

4. Open the needle holder a short way and pick up the 2 inches of thread on the right-hand side of the wound.

5. Use your left hand to pull on the long piece of thread, sliding it off the needle holder which will create a "first throw," an overhand knot with two loops in it. Gently tighten it to pull the edges of the wound together, but not so much that they pucker or overlap. You want the knot to be lying flat at the edge of the wound, not touching the injury site.

6. Use your left hand to wrap the long end of the thread around the needle holder clockwise. Again, open the needle holder to grab the short end of the thread, and use your left hand to pull the long end off the needle driver and create a "second throw." Gently tighten as before.

7. Repeat the above step for a third time, creating a "third throw," but this time, wrap the suture counter-clockwise, not clockwise, which will prevent any risk of the knot slipping.

8. Cut the thread, move a quarter of an inch further down the wound, and repeat this process. Continue until the wound is closed. All knots should be on the same side of the wound.

This is known as a simple interrupted suture, and it's the most basic method, although there are many others. Stitches should almost always be covered in an antibiotic ointment and gauze, and both should be reapplied daily.

Non-dissolving stitches can be cut out once the wound has healed, which usually takes a week for head or neck injuries, and up to two weeks for other injuries, depending on the severity.

7.   Using Staples For Wound Closure

Staples again should only be considered if medical help is more than one or two days away. They are suitable for wounds on the scalp, torso, legs, and arms. Such wounds must have straight edges.

Sutures are generally better, but staples often treat head injuries. If possible, apply anesthetic or provide painkillers before starting, or the patient may go into shock.

1. Line up the edges of the wound and place the stapler against the surface of the skin. Put the center marker over the center of the wound.
2. Gently squeeze the stapler handle so that a staple is applied.
3. Move a little less than 0.5 inches from the first staple, and apply another. Keep working until the wound is closed.

Staples should almost always be covered in an antibiotic ointment and gauze, both reapplied daily. Where possible, pass staple removal to a trained professional. Stapler removal tools can also be used.

Summary

In this chapter, we've covered:

- How to perform CPR for adults, children, and infants, including the basics of mouth to mouth resuscitation
- How to put someone in the recovery position
- How to perform the Heimlich maneuver and the five-and-five method
- How to take a pulse
- How to make splints and slings
- How to handle minor and major wounds, and the different closure techniques that can be used

In the following chapter, we will be looking at medical conditions and how you should prepare for these before traveling. We'll cover things like allergies, asthma, seizures, diabetes, and anemia, so you know what supplies you need and what training you should take if anyone in your party suffers from these issues.

3

Preexisting, Chronic, And Permanent Medical Conditions

"Therefore, in medicine, we ought to know the causes of sickness and health."

-Ibn Sina (Avicenna)

Being prepared is vital when it comes to emergencies. You cannot prepare for many because they are so unexpected. Still, when it comes to preexisting and permanent health conditions, preparation is both possible and crucial – and it's your best friend in these scenarios. Let's look at some of the foremost issues that you might need to be prepared for and ensure that you are as well equipped as possible to handle them.

Heart Attacks And Chest Pain

A heart attack is an instance in which the immediatec care, without medical help, can be crucial. This is particularly true if you are off the grid and far from assistance. Immediate care can change how much muscle dies, which has a massive impact on short-term and long-term outcomes.

Heart attack symptoms include:

- Chest pains or discomfort (the commonest symptom)
- Shortness of breath
- Nausea/vomiting
- Lethargy/exhaustion
- Cold sweats
- Faintness
- Pain in one or both arms, the back, neck, stomach, jaw, or shoulders

In general, chest pain/discomfort will be experienced by both men and women, but the other symptoms are more commonly found among women.

If someone has a heart attack, you should call emergency services as soon as possible.

Give them an aspirin to chew on, as this will reduce the risk of blood clotting.

Suppose the person has a history of heart attacks and has been prescribed nitroglycerin in the past. In that case, you should ensure availability in the first aid kit and administer this according to instructions. However, do not give nitroglycerin if it hasn't been prescribed by a doctor, as it could be harmful.

If the person falls unconscious, begin CPR. Continue CPR until the person regains consciousness or help arrives. If you cannot contact emergency services, treat the heart attack as best you can, and prioritize getting the person to a hospital when this becomes possible. The extent of the damage will need to be analyzed and care provided, which will be done in a medical facility.

Strokes

Strokes also depend upon very swift responses – every second counts when a person has a stroke. Call emergency services as soon as possible because treatment will be undertaken in a hospital setting. The longer a stroke goes untreated, the more dangerous it can be, so do not wait, even if you are a long way from help. Many stroke treatments must be given within hours of the stroke occurring but prioritise getting in touch even if it takes longer than this for emergency services to reach you.

However, there are other things that you can do to help with a stroke when you are a long way from help. Let's look at how to spot a stroke and then move on to treatment. The best way to remember the symptoms of a stroke is the acronym FAST, which stands for:

* Face: is the face numb or drooping?
* Arms: can the patient raise both arms above their head equally, or is one weaker than the other?
* Speech: can the patient talk clearly, or are they slurring their words?
* Time: call for help promptly

Other symptoms can include:

* Headaches
* Dizziness

- Lightheadedness
- Tingling, weakness, numbness on one side of the body
- Loss of bowel or bladder control
- Blurred vision, particularly in one eye
- Loss of consciousness
- Loss of balance

Note that these symptoms can disappear in only a matter of minutes. You should not ignore them just because they resolve themselves; the patient still needs to see a doctor.

Next, what should you do if you think someone has had a stroke? Firstly, do not give the person food, drink, or aspirin, as these could be dangerous for certain types of strokes (and you won't be able to tell which is which by looking).

Put the patient in a comfortable position, lying on one side with their head slightly raised incase they throw up. Talk to them calmly and reassuringly, and keep them warm. Avoid moving them, especially if they are experiencing weakness. If possible, note the time the symptoms started, as this can help doctors determine the proper course of treatment.

If the patient stops breathing, perform CPR until the patient regains consciousness or help arrives.

Seizures

Seizures are also serious emergencies, and you should know if anyone in your group is predisposed to seizures. Talk to them about the condition, any triggers, and what to do to help, as advice may vary between different people. Many seizures do not constitute an emergency, but you still need to know how to react, protect the patient, and when you need emergency services.

There are two main kinds of seizures: focal onset seizures and generalized seizures.

Focal onset seizures start in one part of the brain, and the patient may experience involuntary movement/twitching. As the seizure progresses, the patient is likely to zone out and become unaware, and they will not remember anything afterward.

Generalized seizures start in multiple parts of the brain, and the patient will usually be unaware when they are occurring. These are the more common kinds of seizures and encompass several well-known ones, including tonic-clonic seizures and grand mal seizures. These tend to be more dramatic, frightening, and more serious.

Often, they will follow approximately this pattern:

- The patient becomes unresponsive to external stimuli and sometimes will collapse.
- Their muscles clench for a few seconds (tonic phase)
- They start to jerk convulsively for seconds or even minutes (clonic phase)
- They regain consciousness but may be disorientated or confused for a while

What you need to do depends on the situation and the severity of the seizure, which is why it's a good idea to talk to any party members that suffer from seizures. Make sure everyone in the group knows how to respond. Usually, you will need to:

- Time the seizure's length from start to finish
- Roll the person onto their side if possible (this keeps the airway clear)
- Keep everyone out of the way
- Keep hard or sharp objects far from the patient

Don't try to put anything in the patient's mouth, and don't try to hold onto them. Allow them to thrash and make the area safe as far as possible.

If a seizure lasts for more than 5 minutes, call emergency services as it is becoming dangerous, and there is little else that you can do. Seizure activity should be discussed with a doctor when this becomes feasible.

Severe Allergic Reaction/Anaphylaxis

Like seizures, allergies should be discussed before the trip begins, and procedures agreed upon. Known allergens, as far as possible, should not be kept in the off-grid setting or should be kept in sealed, clearly labeled containers to reduce the risk of an allergic reaction occurring. If a person is allergic to certain animal stings, e.g., wasps, avoid situations that are more likely to be encountered. Make sure allergy information is shared widely, and everyone knows how to recognize an allergic reaction and what to do if one occurs.

The symptoms of a severe allergic reaction usually include:

- Swelling (of the tongue or other body parts)
- Pallid skin
- Floppiness
- Abdominal pain
- Vomiting
- Persistent, wheezing cough
- Difficulty breathing/noisy breathing

- Tightness of the throat or swollen throat
- Difficulty talking
- Dizziness
- Collapse

If a member of your group is having a severe allergic reaction, you should

1. Lie them down flat on their back.
2. Give them an adrenaline injector (make sure that your first aid kit contains at least one of these if anyone in the group has an allergy).
3. Call emergency services as soon as possible.
4. Give further adrenaline if symptoms are not improving within 5 minutes.

If the patient also has asthma, you should provide them with their inhaler, but only after the adrenaline injector. The asthma reliever puffer may be offered once the adrenaline has been given.

If a patient has a severe allergic reaction, but the adrenaline solves the issue, it is still good to see a doctor following the incident when this becomes possible. The adrenaline injector must also be replaced as soon as possible to avoid a situation in which adrenaline is not available during an allergic reaction.

Ensure that everyone in the group understands how to use an adrenaline injector and knows where this is kept.

Asthma

Similarly, anyone in the group who suffers from asthma should discuss this with other members and clarify their standard approach to attacks, how severe their asthma usually is, and what approach they would like others to take. Prompt this discussion if the person does not initiate it themselves; it's critical to have everyone on the same page about dealing with an attack.

Asthma usually comes with the following symptoms:

- Coughing and wheezing
- Difficulty breathing (this may be minor or major, but could increase in severity if the attack gets worse)
- Difficulty talking clearly
- Difficulty standing or walking
- Skin tugging at the base of the neck or between the ribs

In very severe cases, asthma may also result in:

- Lips turning blue
- Confusion
- Exhaustion
- Inability to speak more than a word or two in one breath
- Collapsing
- Little relief is given by the inhaler
- Gasping

If you see symptoms from either of these categories occurring, you need to act quickly, so let's look at what you should do.

1. Get the person to sit upright and loosen any constrictive clothing.
2. Talk to them calmly and reassuringly, as panic will worsen the symptoms. It is easy to panic when faced with an asthma attack, but the calmer you can be, the better the patient will handle the attack.
3. Give the patient 4 puffs from their inhaler. You can do this with or without a spacer (step 4 and step 5), but using a spacer is preferable.
4. To use a spacer, remove the cap and shake the inhaler thoroughly. Insert the inhaler into the spacer, get the patient to breathe out as much as possible, and place their mouth around the spacer's mouthpiece, sealing it. Press the inhaler once so that one puff is put into the spacer. Get the patient to breathe in slowly through their mouth and then hold their breath for 10 seconds. Repeat this 4 times so that they have inhaled 4 puffs.
5. If you don't have a spacer available, 4 puffs from the inhaler will do instead. Remove the cap and shake well, and then get the person to breathe out completely and seal their lips around the mouthpiece. Get them to breathe in slowly and press down once. They should breathe in for up to 7 seconds and then hold their breath for 10 seconds. Wait for about 1 minute before giving the next puff, and apply 4 puffs total.
6. Wait for 4 minutes to see if the breathing situation has improved. If not, give another 4 puffs.
7. If there is still no improvement, give 4-8 puffs every 20 minutes until you get emergency help. If help does not come within 4 hours, lower the dose to give 4-8 puffs when needed every 1-4 hours.
8. Do not leave the person alone or let them fall asleep. A bad asthma attack can change symptoms, and even the cessation of wheezing does not mean they can be left unattended. When possible, they should visit an emergency room to be assessed and receive treatment for the attack.
9. In some cases, the patient may need to stay in hospital following a bad attack, so do

not leave them unattended or neglect to get medical aid when you can.

If the patient has been given different advice on using their inhaler, make sure that this supersedes the advice offered here; This is the standard procedure, but recommendations might vary.

A few early warning signals may (but will not always) precede an attack, so look out for these. You might see:

- Frequent cough at night
- Runny nose, congestion, sore throat
- Grumpiness, tiredness, moodiness
- Weakness or breathlessness when doing light exercise
- Shortness of breath

Be aware of these warning signs and prepared to step in if an attack should occur. Make sure everyone in the team is familiar with how to use an inhaler and that the first aid kit is stocked with a spare inhaler and any that the asthmatic party (or parties) has available.

Heart Palpitations

Heart palpitations can be alarming for anyone who suffers from them and other people close to the patient. Not all heart palpitations signify something serious, but it's still important to know how to handle them when you are far from help and can't access a doctor.

Consistent heart palpitations should prompt you to seek proper medical care when able, as they could be a sign of a health problem, and they may get worse. However, when you are off the grid, there are a few techniques that the patient can employ to reduce the risk of heart palpitations.

Heart palpitations can be caused by:

- Caffeine
- Anemia
- Dehydration
- Nicotine
- Alcohol
- Low levels of potassium or sugar in the blood
- Exercise
- Low levels of carbon dioxide or oxygen in the blood
- Some kinds of medicine (e.g., cough medicine)

- Fever
- Blood loss
- Stress, panic, anxiety

If you see these symptoms, there are a few things that you can do to mitigate them. Many of these are long-term strategies, not an overnight cure.

One: Drink Plenty

Sometimes, dehydration causes heart palpitations, so the patient should drink sufficient amounts of water throughout the day, particularly for patients who notice dark yellow urine; This is because dehydration thickens your blood, making it harder for it to move through your veins, which can increase the rate of your pulse and may cause palpitations.

Two: Regulating Stress

Techniques such as deep breathing, yoga, and meditation may reduce the appearance of heart palpitations at times. Patients should keep their stress levels low, get enough sleep, and avoid stressful situations if they suffer from heart problems.

Exercise may also help regulate stress, but it's a good idea for patients to consult with their doctor before taking up a regular exercise routine, especially if they are out of shape.

Three: Avoid Certain Foods

Heart palpitations are often associated with spicy and rich foods, so it is best to avoid these where possible. Consider also cutting out caffeine, alcohol, and cigarettes.

Four: Breathe Deeply

Sometimes, deep breathing can help to regulate the heartbeat. It will encourage the body to relax. You can also try the Valsalva maneuver, which involves pinching your nose shut and trying to blow air through the sealed nose. Do not blow hard. Try these techniques for at least several minutes.

Five: Splash Your Face With Cold Water

Sometimes, splashing the face with cold water is sufficient to stimulate a nerve that manages your heart rate. This is known as the vagus nerve, and stimulation can be done at home, but it's worth discussing it with a doctor before you try this. A cold shower or an ice pack on the face for about 20 seconds may have the same result.

If a person is suffering from severe palpitations or showing other symptoms, try to get them to a hospital. It is not easy to diagnose the cause of heart palpitations, and it may not be possible to treat them without proper medical equipment anyway.

Hyperglycemia

Hyperglycemia is a condition that affects people who have diabetes, and if treatment is not administered when it occurs, it can lead to grave complications. If there are any diabetics in your party, you should discuss this before traveling. They should make you aware of the symptoms and the treatments and how they handle this.

Early signs include increased thirst, headaches, fatigue, blurry vision, and frequent urination. However, many people will only notice this issue later, when toxic acids have started to build up in the patient's urine and blood. At this stage, symptoms often include:

- Weakness
- Confusion
- Abdominal pain
- Breathing difficulty
- Vomiting
- Nausea
- Dry mouth
- Breath that smells fruity

Sometimes, hyperglycemia can lead to a coma, and in the long term, it can damage many vital organs in the body, including the heart, eyes, kidneys, and nerves. Hyperglycemia will often result from the patient taking too little medication, overeating, exercising unusually, or going through emotional or physical stress. In most cases, hyperglycemia develops slowly and may not require first aid (but it definitely needs to be treated, so arrange to visit a doctor or hospital when possible).

You should treat hyperglycemia by:

1. Giving the patient a small amount of sugar (although hyperglycemia means that there is too much sugar in the blood, the body isn't accessing it effectively, and a small amount more will not hurt. It will rule out the issue of having too little sugar).
2. Reassure the patient and calmly speak to them. They will usually begin to recover.
3. If the condition does not improve or the person falls unconscious, you will need to contact emergency services.

In most cases, prevention will be better than cure for hyperglycemia, so the patient should follow their doctor's diet and exercise.

Hypoglycemia

Hypoglycemia occurs when the patient's insulin level gets too high for the amount of sugar that the patient has in their blood at the time. If the patient misses a meal or snack, throws up, takes too much medication, or exercises more than usual, it could lead to hyperglycemia. The brain will struggle to operate because the patient will not have enough sugar, leading to insulin shock.

In general, most diabetic emergencies are caused by hypoglycemia, and you should familiarize yourself with the symptoms and the steps for treating it. Hypoglycemia may result in:

- Seizures
- Cool skin
- Sweatiness
- Lack of responsiveness
- Irritability, aggression, or confusion
- Pallor
- Slurred speech, difficulty walking, and other apparently drunken behavior
- Panting
- Looking unwell
- Feeling unwell

Take any of these symptoms seriously and encourage the patient to take action or help them to do so. Because hypoglycemia can cause confusion, it is essential to step in, as, in some instances, the patient may not realize that they are ill or how to deal with it. You can help someone by:

1. Encourage them to sit down.
2. Give them a sugary drink or glucose sweets.
3. Wait until they feel a little better, and then provide other high-sugar foods, such as jelly sandwiches, to keep their blood sugar levels up.
4. Wait to see if they improve. If they do not improve within 10 minutes or they get worse, call emergency services. A severe attack can be fatal if treatment isn't received. Severe hypoglycemia may be treated using intravenous glucose or glucagon injections, and these are not things that you will have access to off the grid

Note that even if the patient improves rapidly, they should still get checked over by a doctor as soon as they can. Insulin will still be active in the bloodstream, and patients need to get their levels assessed to check they are returning to normal. This is particularly true at night, as the patient's blood sugar levels will drop while asleep, and they may fall unconscious.

When treating both hyperglycemia and hypoglycemia, it's vital to choose fast-acting carbohydrate snacks to start. Fruit juice, honey, and sweet candy are good options. Stock some candy in your first aid box if you are traveling with a diabetic, and ensure that this is not used except for medicinal purposes. Avoid foods with protein or fat.

You should also encourage the patient to measure their blood sugar levels if they can do so. If these remain under 70 mg/dL 15 minutes after they have eaten the candy, get them to eat another 15-20 grams of fast-acting carbs. Continue doing this until the blood sugar level rises above 70 mg/dL.

Hypertension

Many people in today's world suffer from hypertension, and there are multiple possible causes. A few triggers for hypertension include lack of physical activity, stress, and a salty diet.

Many people with hypertension will also be on medication from their doctors to solve the problem, but some will not know in advance and can suffer from hypertension when you are far from help. Therefore, it is crucial to understand how to address this issue and recognize it when it occurs.

You may be suffering from hypertension if you get:

- A sudden, severe headache
- Fatigue
- Breathing difficulty
- Chest pains
- Vision problems
- Heart palpitations
- Confusion

If a member of your group starts displaying these symptoms and you cannot get them to a hospital, there are quite a few things that you should do. It's important to note that hypertension can occur with no symptoms, so make sure you know if any of your group members are at risk of this before traveling together.

Let's explore how to combat hypertension.

Stay Calm

Like many medical situations, calmness on the patient and the person delivering first aid can make a big difference. Encourage the patient to take a deep breath, hold it, and release it. Repeat this until their breathing is regulated and calm, which should help to reduce blood pressure.

Eat Dark Chocolate

A piece of dark chocolate will encourage the patient's body to release the endorphins they need to calm down. Keep a small block of dark chocolate in the first aid kit for emergencies.

Provide Blood Pressure Medication If Possible

If a member of your group is at risk of hypertension, they should discuss this with their doctor before going off the grid. The doctor may prescribe some medication, which should be taken as instructed to reduce the patient's blood pressure.

Avoid Stress

Stress is known to elevate blood pressure, and the more a patient is stressed, the higher their blood pressure is likely to be. Often, high blood pressure results from many contributing factors, so reducing each of these factors will help. Encourage the patient to avoid stressful situations and take a more laid-back approach to life. This may involve techniques such as meditation, deep breathing, or possibly adult coloring books; these will all aid relaxation.

Reduce Salt Intake

Eating a lot of salt increases blood pressure for some individuals because it causes the body to retain fluids. Ideally, you shouldn't eat much more than half a teaspoon of salt per day.

The patient should aim to stop adding salt to their foods and use spices or herbs for flavoring instead. Where possible, opting for low-sodium foods may also be a beneficial approach to take.

Exercise

It is likely no surprise that exercising is a significant aspect of reducing hypertension, and it's recommended to do between 30 and 60 minutes of exercise per day if possible. However, patients should speak to their doctor about this first to develop a safe exercise routine.

Exercise could involve swimming, jogging, hiking, or just walking. You don't need access to a gym or fancy sporting equipment to get into shape. Try to make sure at least some of the exercise is challenging, but do anything that feels good.

Cut Out Alcohol And Cigarettes

Both alcohol and cigarettes may contribute to hypertension, and patients should cut back or entirely give these things up.

Cigarettes raise blood pressure when they are smoked. This often only lasts for a few minutes per cigarette, but heavy smokers will find that their blood pressure level can stay high for hours after a cigarette. Entirely cutting out cigarettes is a great way to control blood pressure.

Similarly, alcohol can be dangerous if drunk in more than very moderate quantities. A small glass of wine will not be harmful, but consuming large amounts of alcohol can be. It may also reduce the effectiveness of medication intended to combat high blood pressure.

In general, men can drink two alcoholic drinks per day, but women should only drink one. Exercising control of alcohol and cigarettes can considerably impact the patient's blood pressure.

Drink Chamomile Tea

Chamomile tea is often heralded as a calming substance, and you may find it is beneficial to someone suffering from hypertension. Brew a cup of this tea, sit the patient down, and talk to them while they get calm.

If the person used cigarettes as part of their calm-down routine, help them trial other options, so they don't feel powerless and out of control.

Diabetes

We've covered first aid diabetic emergencies in hyperglycemia and hypoglycemia above. Still, it's also worth learning what you can about this health condition, as it is prevalent nowadays, and you are likely to encounter someone who has it at some point.

Type 2 diabetes is a disease that means the body either does not produce enough insulin or cannot effectively use the insulin it produces, which can cause elevated blood sugar levels.

Type 2 diabetes is generally managed by using an insulin pump and monitoring blood sugar levels using a glucometer so patients can regulate what they eat according to their current sugar levels.

People with type 2 diabetes often need to ensure that they eat regular, controlled portions and exercise in regular, controlled ways. This must be considered if you often plan activities or if your off-grid situation requires physical labor at times (e.g. gathering wood, taking down/putting up tents, farming, carrying grocery bags, etc.).

Talk to the patient about how they manage their diabetes and support them.

Many people who have diabetes need to check their blood sugar levels regularly. You may not need to be involved with this, but it's worth understanding the process. They also need to regulate their meals carefully, which needs to be understood and respected if your group has shared cooking duties. Not meeting their food needs can be dangerous.

Thyroid Issues

Hypothyroidism occurs when the patient's thyroid gland is underactive and not producing sufficient hormones to keep the body running normally. This can lead to many symptoms, including:

- Depression
- Fatigue
- Abnormal menstrual cycles
- Increased cholesterol
- Dry skin
- Constipation
- Difficulty losing weight
- Decreased libido
- Swollen legs

- Irritability
- Cramps, aches, and pains
- Sleepiness
- Slow heartbeat
- Sensitivity to cold

Hyperthyroidism can also be an issue, with a thyroid that is over-producing hormones. It can cause:

- Increased appetite
- Anxiety or irritation
- Heart palpitations
- Rapid heartbeat
- Weight loss
- Difficulty sleeping
- Sensitivity to heat
- Trembling
- Fatigue
- Sweating

Usually, a person suffering from either of these conditions will have medication that they can take to keep themselves functioning. However, you should recognize the signs and symptoms and familiarize yourself with the medicine they take.

Some supplements can improve thyroid health, such as vitamin B and probiotics, but it is good for the patient to talk to their doctor before making dietary changes.

Anemia

Finally, anemia is a condition that involves having a deficient number of red blood cells. A patient with anemia will have low hemoglobin levels, making it more difficult for oxygen to travel around their body. It can lead to fatigue and shortness of breath because the different parts of the body won't be given the correct supply of oxygen.

It is a common condition, and many women suffer from it due to their periods. There are numerous kinds of anemia, which can be very mild or more severe. Symptoms often include a fast heartbeat, headaches, dizziness, cold extremities, weakness, joint pain, and pale skin.

Anemia has many different causes, and the treatment will vary. The patient needs the type of anemia to be diagnosed by a doctor before a course of treatment can be chosen. The below options for treating anemia at home should be checked with a doctor first if possible:

- Eating more green vegetables to boost the amount of iron in the blood.
- Eating sesame seeds to boost iron intake.
- Increasing the intake of vitamin C, as this is crucial to helping your body absorb iron.

If the patient feels faint, get them to lie down and raise their legs above their head until the dizziness passes. They can then take an iron supplement, preferably with a glass of orange juice to boost their vitamin C levels.

Be aware if anyone in your party suffers from anemia, and talk to them about handling it, which increases the chances of addressing it appropriately if it gets out of control.

Summary

In this chapter, we've covered advice on what the following conditions result in, and how you should be prepared to deal with them if an emergency should arise:

- Heart attacks
- Seizures
- Severe allergic reactions
- Asthma
- Heart palpitations
- Hyperglycemia
- Hypoglycemia
- Hypertension
- Diabetes
- Thyroid issues
- Anemia

The following chapter will address minor emergencies that you might encounter while off the grid. We're going to look at dental issues, eye trauma, insect bites and stings, sprains, and a whole lot more so you know how to address minor issues promptly and efficiently and prevent them from escalating.

4

Mild Emergencies

"Emergency preparedness is a team sport."

-Eric Whitaker

A mild emergency might not seem like something you need to be overly concerned with preparing for, but that isn't the case at all. "Mild" doesn't mean unimportant in this context.

A mild emergency can be intense and painful. Instead, "mild" simply refers to emergencies that are not (usually) life-threatening. However, you still need to know how to handle them.

In this chapter, we will cover all sorts of issues that you may encounter that are usually relatively minor but which can develop into something major if you do not know how to deal with the problem. You should find everything you need here, from teeth problems to fainting to infections.

Dental Problems

So many things can go wrong with a person's teeth that we now have dedicated doctors assigned purely to their care and treatment – dentists. However, when you're off the grid, you need to be your own dentist to a degree, and it's essential not to overlook oral issues because they can be exceptionally painful and miserable if not treated. Being prepared is crucial.

There are a lot of dental issues that can arise, so let's look at them below.

Dental Hygiene

Ensure that everyone in your party understands good dental hygiene, as this can go a long way to combating dental issues. Each member should have a toothbrush with a few spares and toothpaste. Flossing is also essential.

Teeth should be brushed twice a day, and flossing should be completed once to prevent issues, including gum disease, rotten teeth, and more. Encourage good dental hygiene as much as possible.

Tooth Decay

Tooth decay will occur quickly if the teeth are not properly maintained. Bacteria will soon build up inside the person's mouth and permanently damage the teeth, leaving tiny holes that infection can get into.

This may be immensely painful and can happen without the person knowing until the infection sets in. The decay will continue if not treated.

Survival Dental Kit

You should have a dedicated dental kit to use off the grid and know how to use it.

This kit ought to contain:

- Headlamp
- Sterile cotton balls
- Dental picks
- Gauze
- Toothache drops
- Clove oil
- Temporary fillings
- Mixing bowls
- Sterile gauze pads
- Sanitizing wipes
- Dental floss
- Painkillers
- Dental wax
- Extraction forceps
- Surgical gloves
- Tweezers
- Dental mirror
- 2 spatulas

Make sure that you have enough supplies in your kit to treat multiple dental emergencies, especially if you plan to be off the grid for some time.

Toothache

Toothaches can be minor or major, but they are close to debilitating at their worst. They can cause headaches and sleep problems, and they will not resolve themselves. The nerves inside the pulp of the tooth are among the most sensitive in the entire body, so toothache has the potential to be worse than almost any other pain.

Toothache is usually caused by tooth decay, a broken tooth, infected gums, a damaged filling, an abscess, tooth removal, or tooth eruption (new teeth coming through). It may be accompanied by throbbing and swelling and the infection draining.

You may be able to treat toothaches with warm salt water, clove oil, cold compresses, and pain medication, but the cause of the issue will also need to be addressed. Some causes, such as tooth removal or tooth eruption, may solve themselves as the skin heals, while others will need treatment.

Fillings

Many adults have fillings, and if a filling comes loose while you are off the grid, this will expose the tooth to re-infection and damage. You will need to learn how to temporarily fill a tooth using the instructions in your kit or by watching videos online. The aim is not to create a perfect filling but to temporarily patch the hole until a dentist can be seen.

Abscesses

Mouth abscesses are extremely painful and occur because of infection. An abscess may look like a pimple. Do not pop it. The patient should brush and floss as much as they can until they visit a dentist. Salt water rinses, clove oil, cold compresses, and garlic can all help deal with an abscesses if visible. Rub or rinse them onto the infection, and see a dentist when possible.

If the infection goes down, the patient should continue using salt to sterilize their mouth and minimize the chance of the infection growing again.

Broken Teeth

Broken teeth can sometimes be repaired. Current advice is to find the broken fragment and store it in milk until it can be reattached. If you have dental cement in your first aid kit, you should use this. The patient should then see a dentist when possible.

Loose Teeth

Good dental hygiene is necessary if a tooth is loose but still attached. Brushing and flossing, gargling with salt water, avoiding sweet drinks or using a straw will all help. Loose teeth can be caused by poor dental hygiene, osteoporosis, injuries, plaque, and more.

In some cases, medication may be prescribed to deal with loose teeth, but it is best to get professional guidance as soon as possible. In the meantime, avoid touching the tooth, brushing it hard, or putting any stress on it.

Knocked-Out Tooth

If a baby tooth has come out, leave it out. If an adult tooth has come out, current advice is to clean it (no more than 10 seconds under cold running water), place it back in the socket if possible, bite on a clean handkerchief, and see a dentist. If the tooth cannot be replaced, put it in milk. The tooth must not be allowed to dry out.

Teeth need to be repositioned in the mouth within 30 minutes if possible. If an emergency dentist cannot be reached within this time, you may be able to splint the tooth yourself, attaching it to the surrounding fixed teeth, but this is far from ideal. The tooth may reattach itself within a couple of months. As soon as it is feasible to see a dentist, do so.

Tooth Removal

Don't remove a tooth unless it's necessary. It has exposed nerves if it is constantly hurting, loose, and/or broken. If you think it's likely that you will need to attempt tooth removal, it's a good idea to get an experienced dentist to show you how before you travel, if possible.

You will likely need two forceps (one upper universal and one lower universal), an elevator to loosen the tooth, and a probe.

If possible, you should use a local anesthetic (check the patient is not allergic) or provide painkillers. Explain everything you are doing to the patient and know when they are likely to feel pressure.

Make sure you have good working light.

To remove a lower tooth, you will push it down and pull it up, so position your patient on a low stool. To remove an upper tooth, you will push it up and pull down, placing your patient on a high seat.

Make sure your hands and tools are sterile, and use clean gauze to stem the blood. You may need to hold a cold compress to the face to reduce swelling.

Note that you should only remove teeth if you have some experience and as a very last resort. Otherwise, leave the tooth in place and prioritize visiting a dentist.

Bites And Stings

Bites and stings are another major hazard of living off the grid, and it's imperative to take some time to learn about the bites and stings of the creatures you might encounter. Learn how to identify them, keep appropriate treatments in your first aid kit, and ensure you know how to administer them.

The first thing you should do is remove any debris in the wound, whether this is a stinger or hairs (e.g. from a caterpillar). If there is a tick, remove this by using a pair of tweezers without squashing the tick or pulling its head off. When the wound is clear, wash the area with soapy water.

Next, get a cold compress or an instant ice pack, and place it against the injury. Hold it on for 10 minutes or more to bring the swelling down. Elevate the affected area if possible, and don't let the patient scratch at it.

Don't add vinegar or bicarbonate of soda, as this isn't likely to help. Over-the-counter pain-killers can be taken, along with over-the-counter cream for insect bites or antihistamines.

Choking

Choking is a risk wherever you are, so learn the common symptoms and how to perform the Heimlich maneuver and the five-and-five maneuver This is something that every adult party member should do.

Eye Trauma

Eye injuries are alarming and need conscientious treatment to reduce the risk of further injury. Get the patient resting comfortably and tell them not to try moving their eyes or head. Ideally, they should keep their eyes closed to reduce the risk of movement and further injury.

Next, cover the eye with a clean eye pad. Do not attempt to remove any debris from the eye, but pad around the socket to reduce pressure. The person then needs to be taken to a hospital as soon as possible.

Nosebleeds

Nosebleeds can be minor or severe, and they are common. It's valuable to know how to handle them. Get the patient to sit up straight and lean forward a little way to reduce blood pressure in the nasal veins and prevent swallowing the blood.

Get the patient to blow their nose gently and then spray a nasal decongestant if available. They should then pinch their nostrils shut and breathe through their mouth for 10-15 minutes. They can do this for a further 15 minutes if the bleeding continues. Emergency care may be needed if the bleeding lasts for more than 30 minutes.

If the nosebleed results from an injury and there is a risk that the nose is broken, you should try to get the patient to emergency care if possible. Applying ice and cold compresses will help reduce the swelling and pain if you cannot get the patient to a hospital straight away.

After a nosebleed, the patient should avoid bending down or blowing their nose for a few hours.

Fainting

Fainting has a variety of causes that may require the patient to get checked over by a doctor, but knowing what to do at the moment is crucial. Fainting can cause the patient's pulse to slow down temporarily and is often caused by reduced blood flow to the brain. Fainting will usually cause a person to fall to the ground and may also be characterized by sweating, cold skin, pallor, and a slow pulse.

You should respond by getting the patient to lie down as soon as possible to reduce the risk of further injuries. Next, check whether they were injured (if they fell when they fainted). Treat any injuries that you find.

Kneel beside the patient and raise their legs. Place their ankles on your shoulders, as this will encourage blood to flow back to the brain.

If possible, increase the amount of fresh air available and prevent bystanders from crowding around. Allow the patient to rest for a few minutes, and then ask if they feel ready to sit up. If they do, ensure that they move slowly and lie them back down if the faintness recurs. If it doesn't, get them to sit quietly for a while to reduce the risk of a second fall and wait. Ensure there are people ready to catch them when they stand up, and keep an eye on them for the rest of the day.

If the person passes out and remains unresponsive, call emergency services and check that the patient's airway is clear. If they stop breathing, perform CPR.

Headaches

Most headaches can be treated by drinking water, taking painkillers, and possibly lying down in a dark, quiet space. Placing a cool, damp cloth on the forehead can further alleviate pain.

Many headaches are either tension headaches or migraine headaches. Tension headaches will not cause nausea and are not usually worsened by activity. Migraine headaches can cause nausea and sensitivity to movement and may also cause other symptoms, such as loss of vision on one side, numbness, tiredness, etc. Migraines may not be helped by standard painkillers but should pass eventually.

If headaches recur regularly, follow a head injury, are extremely bad, or cannot be solved with medication, it's worth seeking medical advice.

Foreign Objects In The Nose Or Ear

If something gets stuck somewhere, the apparent course of action is to remove it, but this can sometimes do more harm than good. Let's explore how to deal with objects getting lodged where they shouldn't.

Nose

Close the unaffected nostril and gently blow out of the nose to try and dislodge the object. Don't poke at an object with cotton swabs or tools or try to inhale the object. Try to breathe through the mouth until the object has been removed. If the object can be seen, gently try to get it out with tweezers, but only if the risk of further injury is low.

If the object cannot be easily removed, seek medical care.

Ear

If the object is visible, try to use tweezers to remove it. Don't poke at it with other tools, as these may push it further in. Grip one edge with the tweezers and gently tug.

Alternatively, tilt the head to one side so gravity pulls the object downward and may dislodge it.

An insect can be removed by pouring warm mineral oil into the ear in some instances but shouldn't be used for any other objects. Tilt the head so that the afflicted ear faces up and tip a little mineral oil in. Don't do this if the eardrum may be perforated or if there are ear tubes in place.

Seek medical assistance if you cannot remove the object or if the ear is bleeding or painful.

Fever

Fevers are a common symptom of many illnesses, so it's essential to know how to treat them. They are the body's attempt at protecting itself, but they can occasionally be dangerous themselves. A fever is a reading over 100 degrees F (taken orally). Usually, the treatment just involves relieving discomfort and promoting rest.

Treat a fever by:

- Encouraging the patient to drink water
- Using a lightweight blanket for chills
- Providing ibuprofen or Tylenol (consult with a doctor first for children under 6 months old)
- Encouraging the patient to rest as much as possible

For babies, you should get medical care as soon as possible. For older children, teenagers, and adults, it's usually okay to wait for a fever out unless the patient has trouble breathing or swallowing, is vomiting a lot, has chest pain or a severe headache, is suffering dehydration, or has a fever but no sweating. If these symptoms arise, consult with a doctor over the phone, or take the patient to the hospital.

Don't try to lower a fever artificially. Cold baths and rubbing alcohol should be avoided. Lightly sponging the forehead with lukewarm water is okay.

Sunburn

Prevention is notably better than cure when it comes to sunburn, so make sure you have sun lotion suitable for all party members. However, it is easy for sunburn to happen even when careful, especially if you spend a lot of time outdoors. You can further minimize the risks by ensuring that everyone has lightweight, long-sleeved shirts, appropriate hats, and gauzy scarves that they can use to deflect the sun's rays when necessary.

If a sunburn occurs, you should start by cooling the skin, either with a cool bath or a damp towel. Next, apply an aloe vera lotion or gel or something similar to soothe the inflammation. Encourage the patient to drink water to rehydrate themselves.

Pain relievers can be taken, and the patient should avoid further sun exposure. Covering up is one of the best ways to reduce the risk of sunburn, especially if the patient frequently forgets to apply sun lotion.

Avoid breaking blisters. The area should be cleaned with gentle soap and water when they break and then covered with gauze. Keep the site clean and make sure it is healing well. If a rash begins, contact a doctor for advice.

Gastroenteritis

Gastroenteritis is usually not too serious, although it can be unpleasant. It's usually caused by consuming contaminated food or water but can occasionally be a side effect of medication, or a result of eating an allergen. It can last for up to ten days and has the following symptoms:

- Stomach cramps
- Chills
- Fatigue
- Headaches
- General aches
- Diarrhea
- Nausea
- Vomiting
- Low-grade fever (up to 100.8 degrees F)

It's not usually dangerous save for vulnerable people and can often be prevented by good hand-washing routines. It can be passed from person to person or transferred on surfaces, foods, and water. If a member of the party has it, make sure to implement strict washing routines, avoid sources of water that you don't know the safety of, and regularly sanitize kitchen areas.

You can help a patient with gastroenteritis by getting them to drink lots of water to avoid dehydration, which is the most dangerous element of this complaint. The patient can take over-the-counter medications for the symptoms and rest as much as possible. They should avoid eating for a while if they feel sick and then choose bland foods that are easy to digest.

If the symptoms get worse or blood appears in the patient's vomit or diarrhea, the person should see a doctor.

Sprains

Sprains are a common injury and can be very painful, even though they are not usually serious. They occur when two ligaments are torn or stretched, and they will often result in a warm, swollen, red area that is difficult to move.

Fortunately, sprains are easy to treat through rest. You should encourage the patient to avoid moving the joint much for 48 hours. Wrap an ice pack in a towel and apply it to the swelling for up to 20 minutes, but no longer; This can be done up to 8 times per day, but make sure you give the skin a break from the cold between each application.

If necessary, a compression bandage can support the injured area for a few days. Painkillers can be taken to ease discomfort.

It is crucial to verify that a sprain is not more serious, so make sure the patient goes for an x-ray if they are still in pain after a week, feel numb or tingling sensations, if the limb looks misshapen, or if there are any signs of infection.

Hyperventilation

Hyperventilation means that the balance of breathing is upset, and the person is exhaling more than they are inhaling. They will quickly run out of carbon dioxide, and this will cause the blood vessels that connect to the brain to narrow.

In severe cases, hyperventilation can lead to the patient passing out. It's usually a response to stress or a phobia but can occasionally be connected with depression or anger.

If someone in your party is hyperventilating, encourage them to purse their lips as they breathe to help slow the breathing down. They may also find it helps to breathe into their cupped hands or a paper bag. They should try to take belly breaths, not shallow chest breaths, and they may find that it helps to hold their breath for a few seconds.

Other options include breathing through one nostril and then the other in a pattern or walking briskly and breathing through the nose. All of these things may help to calm an attack.

In the long term, stress reduction and relaxation techniques effectively combat hyperventilation. Encourage the patient to exercise, meditate, and follow up with a doctor if they still have serious problems.

Constipation

An uncomfortable condition which can have many different causes, but it is relatively treatable. A patient who is suffering from constipation should be encouraged to:

- Drink at least 8 glasses of water per day
- Try a little coffee, as this can help with bowel movements (but a lot will cause dehydration)
- Limit high-fat foods
- Exercise regularly
- Eat more fiber
- Massage the abdomen

Some medications cause constipation, but it may also be down to lifestyle choices. It's better not to treat it with laxatives if other options are available, so try the above. Soft fruit is often helpful, and many people turn to prunes and pears to keep their digestive systems moving.

Food Poisoning

Food poisoning can be serious and is unfortunately easy to contract when living off the grid, especially if you don't have access to a fridge or other cold storage. Bacteria such as E. coli and salmonella can quickly spread within food that isn't stored below 40 degrees F or food that hasn't been cooked well enough.

The symptoms of food poisoning include:

- Diarrhea
- Vomiting
- Nausea
- Stomach cramps
- A fever

The patient may also suffer from headaches, dehydration, dizziness, aching muscles, etc. Some foods are considered higher risk than others, such as unpasteurized milk, raw eggs, raw/improperly cooked meat, seafood, and fresh produce. Not washing food prep equipment well in between ingredients can also be a problem. For example, if you put raw meat on a chopping board and then use the same board to prep salad, you are at risk of food poisoning.

Cases are more common in the summer when the heat will make food spoil in as little as an hour. A good cleaning and proper food storage can massively reduce the risk of food poisoning.

There isn't much you can do to treat food poisoning, but it will usually resolve itself. The patient should rest lots and sip water to reduce the risk of dehydration. They may not wish to eat much for a few days but must drink. When ready to eat again, they can have bland foods with no alcohol, fizzy drinks, or caffeine. The patient should not take anti-diarrhea or anti-nausea medication.

You will rarely need help from professionals for food poisoning unless it comes from eating wild mushrooms or seafood. Call emergency services if the symptoms are not improving after 3 days or if the patient is suffering from extreme pain, bloody diarrhea, a fever, pro-longed vomiting, or dehydration. Be aware of the more vulnerable groups (e.g. pregnant women, children, the elderly), and get professional help sooner if the patient is in one of these categories.

Dehydration And Diarrhea

Diarrhea is a symptom of many illnesses and complaints, and on its own, it is uncomfort-able and unpleasant, particularly in off-grid situations where washing facilities may be limited. However, it brings a much more dangerous issue: dehydration.

Mild dehydration can be treated using first aid techniques. For major dehydration, you should aim to get the patient to a medical facility as soon as possible, as this can be life-threatening. For mild dehydration, try the following:

- Encourage the patient to drink water or other liquids (preferably not caffeine-based). It's best to avoid full-strength fruit juice and other soft drinks, but some liquid is better than none. Get the patient to take small sips.
- Offer an oral rehydration solution if you have any available. These contain liquid, salts, and minerals, replenishing what the body losses due to diarrhea.

Drinking more will not increase diarrhea, so the patient should not be concerned about this. The patient should also eat if they can, replacing lost nutrients. Avoid fatty foods, and opt for fiber-rich ones instead. Foods high in electrolytes, protein, pectin, and potassium will all help.

Skin Rashes

If a member of your party has a skin rash, take some time to try and identify it and check whether it is an allergic reaction and whether it poses any risk of anaphylaxis. If it does, treat it as an allergic reaction and act accordingly.

If the rash is the result of touching a poisonous plant or insect, use the following steps:

- Clean the rash with soap and warm water for 10+ minutes, using a soft cloth.
- Take a cool bath if possible, and add oatmeal if available, as this is soothing.
- Apply an anti-itching lotion up to four times per day.
- Wash clothes thoroughly in hot water to remove any remnants of the irritant.

The patient should see a doctor if the rash spreads to sensitive areas, shows signs of pus, or becomes more irritated/itchy. Don't cover up or allow the rash to be rubbed or scratched.

Infections

Cuts and scratches, even minor ones, can get infected, and it's vital to know how to handle an infection. In some cases, minor infections can be treated without antibiotics, but it is good to have some in your first aid kit to deal with more major infections.

A wound is infected if it:

- Becomes more painful than when it was inflicted initially
- Swells
- Turns red and hot at the edges
- Oozes yellow pus
- Becomes itchy

The infection will be localized to begin with but will spread. It can get deep into the tissues and cause sepsis if it is not treated. This medical emergency requires hospitalization: it has many different symptoms but usually involves a high fever, mottled or pale skin, fast breathing, sleepiness, and abnormally cold skin. If you think a patient has developed sepsis, they must be taken to a hospital as soon as possible.

More minor infections can be treated as follows:

1. Wash the injury site well.
2. Soak the injury in water as hot as the patient can tolerate (without burning their skin). Repeat this step multiple times throughout the day. The patient will likely find that it

relieves itching and tension in the wound and makes it more comfortable.

You can then do any of the following:

- Apply over-the-counter antibiotic creams.
- Apply diluted (using a carrier oil) tea tree oil to the site.
- Apply honey to the site.

These will hopefully address the infection. Keep a close eye on it, and if you see a red line traveling away from the injury, get medical help. It is a sign of lymphangitis, which can be severe.

Summary

In this chapter, we've covered the causes, prevention, and common at-home treatments for the following issues:

- Dental problems of all kinds
- Bites and stings
- Choking
- Eye trauma
- Nosebleeds
- Fainting
- Headaches
- Foreign objects in the nose/ear
- Fever
- Sunburn
- Gastroenteritis
- Sprains
- Hyperventilation
- Constipation
- Food poisoning
- Dehydration and diarrhea
- Skin rashes
- Infections

In the following chapter, we will start looking at how to handle major emergencies and what you should do when you can't immediately get help for them. Being well-equipped in these situations could be crucial to survival.

5

Major Emergencies

"To appropriately respond to an emergency requires a very clear mind, to cooly analyze what the observations are and how to fix it."

-Buzz Aldrin

In this chapter, we're going to start looking at some of the more significant emergencies you might face while off the grid. It's important to remember that where possible, you should contact emergency services or transport the patient to a hospital personally; do this as soon as you can, even if it will take time. Many of these problems cannot be treated at home and will need emergency care; the information below is intended to help address the immediate care and increase the patient's chances of recovery.

Shock

Shock can be life-threatening because it prevents the vital organs in the body from getting enough oxygen. The symptoms of shock include:

- Gasping
- Nausea/vomiting
- Weak pulse
- Gray-blue skin
- Sweating
- Restlessness/aggression
- Unresponsiveness

Shock is usually caused by severe bleeding, loss of bodily fluids, spinal injury, severe allergic reaction, or heart issues.

Start by treating the cause of the injury if possible (stem bleeding, etc.). Lie the patient down and lift their legs to increase blood flow to the vital organs. Loosen tight clothing, and cover them with a blanket. Reassure the patient, stay with them, and make sure they stay responsive. Begin CPR if they stop breathing and wait for help to arrive. The patient should not eat or drink anything.

Smoke Inhalation

Smoke inhalation needs to be treated seriously, as it can kill. Its symptoms include:

- Chest pains
- Confusion
- Fainting
- Blue/gray skin
- Hoarse breathing/speech
- Headaches
- Shortness of breath
- Coughing

Patients with heart or lung conditions are more in danger of death from smoke inhalation. Try to remove the patient from the area with the smoke if possible, and get them somewhere with fresh air. Check that they are breathing, and perform CPR if not. If you have an inhaler available and the patient is breathing, use the inhaler.

Burns

Burns are a risk in almost every off-grid setting, especially if you use open fires, gas cookers, etc. Follow these steps if a burn occurs:

- Stop the burning process by removing the person from the area, dousing the flames, or smothering them.
- Remove anything touching the burnt skin (but don't pull it away if it has stuck).
- Cool the area using cool or lukewarm water, which should be done for 20 minutes. Don't put ice, cold water, or greasy substances on the burn.
- Keep the person warm using a blanket, especially if you are cooling a large area.
- Cover the burn with plastic wrap in a single layer (do not wrap the limb/burnt area).
- Give the patient pain relief.

The patient should then go to a hospital unless the burns are minor. Electrical burns and chemical burns should prompt an immediate hospital visit.

Cuts And Wounds

Most cuts and wounds will require pressure and bandaging to stop the blood flow. Refer to the section on Dealing With Wounds in Chapter Two for more information on identifying the different kinds of wounds and what kind of dressings should be applied. You will also find information about stitching and staples there.

The basic approach for sealing a wound is:

1. Remove the patient from danger if necessary.
2. Apply pressure using a clean, absorbent pad. Press the cloth against the wound, and add a second absorbent cloth if it soaks through. Keep doing this until the bleeding stops.
3. If possible, lift the injury site to reduce the bleeding and keep applying pressure for at least a few minutes to allow the blood to clot.
4. If the bleeding doesn't stop within fifteen minutes, arrange to get the person to a hospital.
5. Once the bleeding stops (if the patient isn't hospitalized), clean the wound with warm water and remove all dirt and debris. Pat the wound dry.
6. Close the wound using gauze, glue (minor wounds), butterfly bandages (minor wounds), sutures, or staples. The latter two should only be used if help is more than 12-24 hours away, as they can be dangerous if misapplied.
7. Keep regularly inspecting the wound for signs of infection and to make sure it is healing. Get the patient to emergency care when possible unless the wound is minor.

Severed Finger/Toe

The faster emergency care can be sought in this situation, the better, as severing or partial serving may affect the functioning of the hand/foot in the long term. In the short term, the injury should be dealt with as follows:

1. Rinse the injury gently with clean water or a saline solution.
2. Cover the injury with sterile gauze.
3. Elevate the injury above the head if possible to reduce swelling and bleeding.
4. Put gentle pressure on the injury to slow the bleeding.

You should not attempt to remove jewelry.

If the digit has been totally severed, find the missing part and:

1. Rinse it with clean water or a saline solution.

2. Cover it with damp gauze.
3. Put it in a clean bag (waterproofed), and then put that bag in another clean bag, and place them on ice. Take it to the emergency room.

If you are dealing with more than one amputation, put the digits in separate bags. Don't get the digits wet, but keep them as cool as you can without directly resting them on ice.

You will likely also need to deal with shock if this situation arises. While waiting for the ambulance, get the person to lie down and keep them warm.

Head Injuries

Head injuries can be severe and may result in spinal or neck injuries. If someone in your party has injured their head, you will need to call for help and assess the injury. You should look for:

- Confusion
- Headache
- Dizziness/nausea
- Loss of responsiveness
- Scalp wounds
- Loss of memory

To treat a head injury, get the patient to lie down with their feet elevated and then follow the below steps:

1. Place a towel-wrapped ice pack against the injury to reduce swelling. Keep it there for up to 20 minutes.
2. Assess the patient's alertness level, determining how responsive they are and how confused they are.
3. Treat any wounds by applying clean gauze and gentle pressure.

If the patient is drowsy, vomiting, or confused, they need to see a doctor as soon as possible. If they appear clear and coherent, continue to monitor them and do not leave them unattended for several hours at least. It is best to get all head injuries assessed at a hospital if possible, as internal damage may have been done even if the injury looks minor. If this isn't feasible, keep monitoring the patient for any changes over the next few hours and days.

Concussion

A natural result of some head injuries, concussions are a common type of brain injury. A concussion involves a short-term loss of mental functionality. The symptoms include:

- A brief loss of consciousness following the injury
- Confusion, delayed answers to questions, blank expression
- Short periods of memory loss
- Short-term blurry vision or visual disturbances

You cannot diagnose a concussion off the grid, and a patient that shows these symptoms will need emergency care. In the meantime:

1. Get the patient to lie down with their feet elevated.
2. Apply a cold compress (wrapped ice or a cold, wet towel) to the injury for around 20 minutes. This should be done every two to four hours. Never place ice directly on the injury; it must be wrapped first.
3. Offer painkillers, but do not give the patient non-steroidal anti-inflammatory ones (e.g. aspirin, ibuprofen), as these may cause bleeding.
4. Allow the patient to rest but ensure that someone is with them for the first 48 hours after an injury (if they cannot be taken to the hospital at this time).
5. Don't let the patient do anything strenuous until they have been assessed and cleared by a doctor.

Poisoning

Poisoning is the result of inhaling, swallowing or touching certain substances. The party members most likely to be vulnerable to poisoning are children, who are both more likely to consume things they shouldn't, and more susceptible to harm because they are smaller. However, both adults and children can be poisoned, particularly if you take up foraging while off the grid. Always use reliable resources if you are going to forage for food, and never eat something that you cannot identify with 100 percent certainty.

Poisoning symptoms can vary but generally include at least some of the below:

- Vomiting
- Drowsiness
- Confusion
- Burns, swelling, or redness around the mouth
- Breathing difficulties

You should try to identify what has caused the poisoning and keep a sample of the plant, food, or other substance. If it was a packaged product, keep the packaging. Call emergency services, and follow the advice below.

For ingested poison:

1. Remove as much of the poisonous substance from the person's mouth as possible (if it is still there). The person may rinse and spit, but do not let them swallow any of the water they rinse with.
2. If applicable, read the packaging and follow any instructions related to poisoning.
3. If the person is dizzy or drowsy, place them in the recovery position. If they vomit, make sure their airway is clear.
4. Begin CPR if the patient stops breathing.

For inhaled poison:

1. Move the person into fresh air as soon as possible, away from the poisonous substance.
2. Place them in the recovery position and make sure the airway is clear.
3. Begin CPR if the patient stops breathing.

For poison on the skin:

1. Remove contaminated clothing (use gloves to avoid getting poison on your skin).
2. Rinse the skin for up to 20 minutes with lukewarm water.
3. Place them in the recovery position and make sure the airway is clear.
4. Begin CPR if the patient stops breathing.

For poison in the eye:

1. Flush the eye using lukewarm or cool water for 20 minutes or until emergency services arrive.
2. Get the patient to keep their eyes closed after this time while waiting for assistance.

If you believe your child has swallowed a button battery, prioritize going to the hospital even if they seem fine. These batteries can cause internal burning in a concise space of time. Doctors will locate the battery and determine what action to take.

To reduce the risk of poisoning, keep medical supplies out of reach of young children. All medication should be kept in the original packaging so that it is not mixed up, and anything decanted into another bottle must be very clearly marked and labeled. Avoid decanting wherever possible as information about side effects and drug conflicts may be lost.

Heatstroke

Heatstroke can be life-threatening. It may cause damage to vital organs, including the brain. Anyone who works in the heat or is exposed to hot weather for too long can suffer from heatstroke.

The common symptoms of heatstroke include:

- Headaches
- Fainting
- Flushed skin
- Rapid breathing
- Rapid pulse
- Confusion, slurred speech, agitation
- Vomiting
- Nausea
- Heavy sweating or hot skin
- Fever higher than 104 degrees F

You should take action by calling emergency services and immediately seeking ways to cool the person down. You may be able to do this by sitting them in a cold bath, spraying them with a hose, getting them into a cool shower, or sponging them with a wet, cold cloth. Ice packs can be placed in areas with lots of blood flow, including the armpits, the neck, and the groin.

You can also fan the person while misting them with cold water or wet a sheet and cover the person with it. The faster you can cool the person down, the more you will reduce the risk of damage to their brain and other vital organs.

If the person can drink, give them some cool water to help them rehydrate. Avoid caffeine, sugar, or alcohol. Icy drinks may cause cramping and should be avoided too.

Be prepared to perform CPR if necessary.

Get the patient to a hospital when possible, even if the danger has passed, so that the damage can be assessed.

Hypothermia And Frostbite

On the opposite end of the scale, hypothermia and frostbite are serious risks if you are working in a cold environment, especially with inadequate gear. It is always good to have a supply of warm clothing and survival blankets available when traveling in winter, even if it rarely gets freezing. If your power supply goes down and you do not have access to wood, these could save your life.

Knowing how to treat hypothermia and frostbite is also crucial. We will cover hypothermia first.

Hypothermia

Hypothermia can prevent the patient from thinking clearly, which makes it particularly dangerous, as they may not realize they are getting too cold. All party members should be aware of the risks and the symptoms of hypothermia before working in a cold environment.

Common symptoms of hypothermia include:

- Shivering
- Fumbling
- Confusion
- Exhaustion
- Slurring speech
- Memory loss

You should treat hypothermia as fast as possible. If you suspect someone has hypothermia, get them into a sheltered place and take their temperature. If it is below 95 degrees F, try to call emergency services. Next, follow these steps:

1. Remove the person's clothes if they are wet.
2. Focus on warming up the central parts of the person's body. The chest, groin, neck, and head are the best places to focus on. You can do this by using heat pads, electric blankets, or even skin-to-skin contact.
3. Provide a warm, non-alcoholic drink if the person is conscious and can drink it safely.
4. Keep the person dry and wrap them in a warm blanket. Include their head, as a lot of heat is lost through the head.
5. If the person falls unconscious and stops breathing, perform CPR. You should keep doing this even if the patient does not respond and seems dead. A patient can be resuscitated when emergency services arrive. Keep warming the person up as you perform CPR.
6. If the person wakes up again, keep them warm and do not leave them unattended. They need to be assessed by medical professionals when possible.

Frostbite

Frostbite is an injury caused by exposure to extreme cold. It can cause permanent damage and even amputation. Its symptoms include:

- Loss of color in the affected area
- Loss of feeling in the affected area
- Skin that feels waxy or firm

Frostbite usually affects the toes, fingers, cheeks, chin, nose, and ears. You should treat frostbite in the following way:

1. Get the person to a warm room/shelter. If the frostbite is in the toes/feet, don't let the person walk if this can be avoided, increasing the risk of permanent damage.
2. Put the frostbitten area in warm water. Never use hot water. It should feel comfortable to unaffected body parts. If you don't have warm water, use body heat. Frostbitten fingers can be tucked into a warm armpit or cradled in warm hands.
3. Avoid using heat packs, stoves, lamps, or other extreme heat sources. Because the area is numb, there is a high risk of burning.
4. Keep warming the digits until feeling returns to them. When possible, get the patient checked by professionals.

Note: you should not rub or massage frostbitten digits. This will not help and can cause damage. Do not rub snow onto these areas either, as this will make them colder.

Fractures

A fracture can be challenging to diagnose without being able to take an x-ray, but if you see any of the following symptoms, a fracture is quite likely:

- Difficulty moving the limb
- A grating noise
- The sense that the bones are rubbing together
- A limb that appears bent, twisted, or short
- Deformity
- Swelling or bruising
- Signs of shock
- An open wound with the bone sticking out (also known as an "open fracture")

You should treat fractures in the following way:

1. Cover any open wounds in sterile, absorbent cloths and put pressure around the wound

rather than over the break. When the bleeding stops, secure a clean dressing over it.

2. Get the patient to sit quietly and keep still while splinting the injury. Remember, the purpose of splinting is to immobilize the joint (refer to Making Supportive Splints And Slings in Chapter Two).

3. Pad the injury and place the splint in position, making sure that it runs from one uninjured joint to another if possible. Tape the splint in place, being careful not to cut off the circulation.

4. Get the person to lie down, especially if they are shocked or dizzy. Allow them to stay there while the shock passes. The person can take pain relief and use ice to reduce the swelling.

5. Keep monitoring the injury. It may be necessary to loosen the ties if the limb swells. If the fracture is on the arm, creating a sling may make the patient more comfortable and further help to immobilize the injury.

When possible, a fracture should be assessed by a doctor. This is not as much of an emergency as life-threatening injuries, but it should still be prioritised. If the bones are not in the correct position, the injury will heal poorly and may cause long-term pain. X-rays, setting, and a proper cast may be needed.

Broken Bones

A broken bone should be treated the same way as a fractured bone, as they are much the same thing. Follow the above steps to immobilize the injury and get the patient to a hospital when this becomes possible.

Electrocution

If you think a member of your party is in contact with a live piece of equipment, do not touch them, or the electricity may transfer to you. Turn off the power source, or separate it from the person using an insulating material (e.g. wood) or by using rope to pull their limb away.

When you are sure contact has been broken, perform CPR if the patient has passed out and stopped breathing. Avoid moving them unless it is necessary for safety. Even if the patient seems okay, you should not leave them unattended. Call for help and keep the patient warm.

You can also cover any burns with sterile gauze, but little other first-aid help can be given at the scene.

Drowning

Be aware that drowning does not usually involve screaming and splashing. It happens quietly and quickly, with the person dipping below and above the surface a few times, often silently. Implement safety procedures whenever your group is near water and assign someone to watch for anyone struggling. Avoid swimming in adverse conditions.

If you pull someone from the water, you should:

1. Check whether the person is breathing. Tilt their head back and feel for breaths, and if you can't detect any, do the following:
2. Have someone call for help, and then begin CPR. You can refer back to Chapter Two, How To Perform CPR. You should be delivering 30 chest compressions at a rate of about 100-120 per minute.
3. If the person does not respond, tilt their head back and seal your mouth over theirs. Gently pinch their nose and blow into their mouth. Repeat this twice to deliver 2 rescue breaths. Begin a cycle of 30 compressions to 2 breaths until the patient responds or help arrives. If you are not confident delivering rescue breaths, do chest compressions only.
4. If you are treating a child or infant, start with 2 rescue breaths, and give compressions at a rate of about 100 per minute. Continue until the child begins breathing or help arrives.

Natural Disasters

If you are preparing for a natural disaster while living off the grid, there are a few things that you should consider. Firstly, determine whether you will face droughts, lightning storms, hurricanes, floods, etc. Make a plan for each emergency, and discuss it with the group to know their activities and responsibilities.

If a known disaster is approaching, move to a suitable, government-provided shelter. Make sure all party members have a phone. If you plan to stay at your off-grid location instead, stock up on supplies well in advance if you cannot access civilization for longer than expected.

Every member of your group should have an emergency bag that they can grab with the basics in it. This should contain some water, non-perishable food, and medical supplies.

Ensure that all group members are involved in planning for emergencies, including children. Set a safe rendezvous that everyone can access, and discuss a backup plan. The key is preparation.

Pregnancy

Dealing with pregnancy in the group can be particularly challenging when living off the grid. You will need to be particularly vigilant about problems, and it is wise to ensure that you are never more than a few hours from help at the most, in case you need medical intervention.

A pregnant woman should take on less strenuous work, particularly bending and lifting, as the pregnancy progresses. They should also be more vigilant about food poisoning, contaminated water, and staying safe from temperature extremes. They should make sure they are still following up on regular appointments to check that everything is going smoothly, even if this means making long journeys to the nearest city.

If the woman intends to give birth off the grid, this requires a whole new level of preparation and careful consideration before the decision is taken.

Summary

In this chapter, we've covered how you can deal with:

- Shock
- Smoke inhalation
- Burns
- Cuts and wounds
- Severed finger or toe
- Head injuries
- Concussion
- Poisoning
- Heatstroke
- Hypothermia and frostbite
- Fractures
- Broken bones
- Electrocution
- Drowning
- Natural Disasters
- Pregnancy

In the following final chapter, we will look at natural herbal remedies that you can turn to. Many of these have been used for centuries, and while you shouldn't use them to replace modern medicine, they can offer a helping hand in many situations. These remedies are a crucial part of off-grid living for many, and it's essential to familiarize yourself with them. We'll also look at how to store them and make some that you may need.

6
Natural Remedies For Emergencies

"Herbalism was the grounding of flower power. Nature woke us up."

-David Hoffman

Modern medicine has done an indescribable amount of good for the world and its people and should never be underestimated. Its power is extraordinary. However, there is also power in the past remedies, and these are at risk of being forgotten by many. If you want to get in touch with the earth in an off-grid situation, you may wish to turn to natural remedies as a means of healing yourself and others.

Natural remedies are potent and valuable, and you certainly shouldn't leave them out of your first aid kit or practices if you want to use them. On the other hand, it is critical not to depend too heavily on them or use them when other medicines work better. A harmony between modern medicine and historic remedies will serve you well; use whichever is most suited to your current situation.

Essential Oils

In general, essential oils should not be applied directly to your skin. They are highly concentrated, and while they are usually safe, they can cause adverse reactions. Use a carrier oil. Essential oils should not be ingested, although clove oil can be used for toothaches (there is minimal swallowing here).

It's important to note that there is currently little scientific proof regarding the benefits and effectiveness of the oils. Most information here is based on anecdotal evidence and the history of their use rather than clinical trials.

However, many people find that essential oils have value, and I use them personally in day-to-day life. Many are effective – sometimes even more effective than the modern alternative – and would encourage people to supplement their medical kit with them.

Essential oils that are useful in your medical kit include:

- Lavender oil: this is good for first-degree burns, and it's anti-inflammatory, anti-bacterial, anti-fungal, anti-viral, and may help with pain relief. It is also very calming and may assist in restful sleep.
- Tea tree: this is strongly anti-septic, fights infections, and can soothe respiratory issues if added to a diffuser. It's also used to fight fungal infections and insect bites.
- Chamomile: this is a natural painkiller and anti-inflammatory, and it may help to soothe rashes, stings, and bites.
- Peppermint: this is excellent for treating sore muscles. Some people recommend it for soothing stomach aches and nausea, but it is better not to ingest it (although some claim to be food-safe; use these if consumption is intended). Inhaling it may help to soothe nausea.
- Clove: this is predominantly used for treating toothache but can also be diluted with a carrier oil and rubbed on the skin to treat warts and ringworm.
- Eucalyptus: this is a powerful decongestant when put in a diffuser, and it also serves as an insect repellent. When used with a carrier oil, it can be massaged into sore muscles.
- Sandalwood: this can help to improve focus and reduce nervousness.
- Citronella: this can be used to repel bugs for a couple of hours but has short-lived effects.
- Orange: smelling this may reduce anxiety, but do not put it on the skin when working sunlight.

Herbal Teas

Herbal teas are also great for adding to your first aid kit; they provide a wonderful pick-me-up on cold days and can cure minor ills. Teas to try include:

- Peppermint tea: this is used to treat stomach upsets, nausea, and indigestion. It may also ease some of the symptoms of irritable bowel syndrome. Mint is sometimes used for other pain relief, so placing a cooled tea bag on a bruise may help to ease the swelling. Some people find it can also help with toothache.
- Chamomile tea: this tea is often used to treat sleep problems and may have anti-bacterial and anti-inflammatory properties. It might also be able to reduce premenstrual symptoms.
- Lemon verbena tea: this can give you a boost in fighting off colds and fevers. It may also help with weight loss.
- Rosehip tea: this is thought to fight inflammation, protect against heart disease, and

boost the immune system – and some people even say that it can make you look younger!

- Ginger tea: this is another effective anti-nausea drink, and it may even be able to treat stomach ulcers and constipation. It is suitable for motion sickness and can relieve period pain.

Storing Natural Remedies In First Aid Kits

You need to ensure that your natural remedies are appropriately kept inside the first aid kit. That means checking storage recommendations, padding bottles, and protecting them from breakages. Most herbal medicines should be kept cool and dry, like non-herbal options.

Dry herbs should last for about 12 months if stored correctly, and tea bags may come with a use-by date. Essential oils generally last for at least two years, sometimes upward of a decade, although their potency may decrease as they age.

Ensure that any breakable natural remedies (e.g. essential oils in glass) are wrapped in fabric or another cushioning substance, especially when traveling. Store your first aid kit somewhere away from direct light and heat (not close to a cooker or fire), and make sure it stays dry. This should be enough to protect most herbal remedies.

Regularly check the dates of your herbal remedies. Although many will last for a long time and may be okay to use past their "use-by" date, it is still important to keep replenishing your stock and discard remedies that are very out of date. Many herbs will lose strength as they age, and you may find that it is better to use them up and replace them with new supplies when you can.

Certain items will be better stored in their plant form. For example, if you wish to use aloe vera gel for sunburns, you can just grow an aloe vera plant (if this is compatible with your off-grid setup). The gel will always be available to you since you can just snap off a stem when you need it. Some other natural remedies can be stored in their neat form, such as honey (mix this with other ingredients when you want it), garlic, coconut oil, and so on. These can be kept in a suitable cupboard rather than the first aid kit since they serve a dual purpose and will take up space and/or turn moldy in the kit.

Recipes For First Aid Material

There are a few different remedies that you may wish to mix when someone in your party is unwell. Let's look at some of the top options below.

Honey And Garlic For Sore Throats And Coughs

If someone is struggling with a sore throat or persistent cough, a honey and garlic mixture can be perfect. The quantities are not enormously important, so you can alter them to suit your patient's tastes, but use the recipe below as a guide:

- 0.5 cup of honey
- 2 bulbs of peeled garlic (about 12 cloves)
- A sterile jar

Once your jar is sterile, add the peeled garlic cloves. You can rough the edges up a little with a knife or fork if you want to speed up the infusion process. Pour the honey over the top, and then allow it to steep.

It will take several days, so it's a good idea to make this in advance. It should keep for a month or two, possibly longer, especially in the fridge.

The patient can then take a spoonful of honey as cough syrup and may wish to eat a garlic clove or two per day. Both of these ingredients will help to fight bacterial infections.

This remedy shouldn't be used for children under 1 and a half, who should not be given honey.

Chili Relief For Sore Muscles

Chili can create heat when applied to the skin, which is an excellent way to make a natural heat rub. You will need:

- 1 cup of coconut oil
- 3 tablespoons of cayenne pepper

Mix the two ingredients in a small pan and heat gently until the oil has melted. Stir for five minutes, and then pour into a bowl and allow to cool. This can be massaged onto the affected area. Do not use it on the face or near the eyes, and avoid touching sensitive skin after application. Check that it does not cause a skin reaction before use.

Relieve Sunburn

If you don't have an aloe vera-based sunburn lotion, you can use the plant directly. Snap a stem off, slice away the outer skin, and mash the gel into a paste. Test first on a small area of the skin to check it doesn't further the irritation, and then rub it into the rest of the burn. It has a cooling, rehydrating effect.

Repel The Bugs

You can make an effective, all-natural bug repellent by combining many essential oils with a carrier oil and spraying them on your skin. This disguises your scent and makes you smell unpleasant to most biting insects, including mosquitoes, midges, and biting flies.

Citronella is a particularly effective means of deterring biting insects, but you can also use lavender, eucalyptus, clove, or a combination of them all. Don't apply these oils directly to your skin, and avoid spraying them on your face.

Olbas Inhaler For Earache/Congestion

If your patient has a bad cold and a lot of congestion, it's well-known that steam can help, so that may be a good idea if a hot shower is available. However, if that isn't possible or needs something more, a steam inhaler may help.

You will need:

- Olbas oil
- A heatproof bowl
- Some boiling water
- A large towel

Set the bowl on a stable surface and have your patient sit so that they can lean over it. Add boiling water to the bowl and one or two drops of Olbas oil (not more; it will be uncomfortable if made too strong).

Your patient should then lean over the bowl. Drape the towel over the head to touch the table on all sides, trapping the steam. They can then close their eyes and breathe as deeply as feels comfortable.

They may wish to take the towel off for a break now and again to cool down.

If the process is uncomfortable, they should stop. However, this often helps relieve congestion and should help them breathe more easily.

Poison Ivy Reliever

If someone has accidentally walked through or fallen into a patch of poison ivy, they may be suffering. First, they should wash thoroughly to remove any traces of the plant from their skin.

- Next, mix up some poison ivy reliever. You will need:

- 3 drops of lavender oil
- 2 drops of peppermint oil
- 3 drops of tea tree oil
- 2 tablespoons of apple cider vinegar
- 2 tablespoons of distilled water
- ½ teaspoon of salt

Stir well until all ingredients are combined, and the salt has dissolved. Use a clean rag to apply the mixture to the rash, and store the mixture in the fridge until the next application. Stir well every time you need it.

Disinfectant And Hand Sanitizers

You should depend upon soap and water in most circumstances, but when you're off the grid, hand sanitizer might sometimes be the best you can do – and it's certainly better than nothing. You can purchase hand sanitizer from a store, but it's also pretty easy to make your own. There are a few different options, and below you will find two recipes.

Alcohol-based Hand Sanitizer

You will need:

- 3 tablespoons of high proof grain alcohol (190 proof): this will dry the skin, but strong alcohol is the most reliable way to kill germs, so this is the kind of hand sanitizer that you should be using in most emergencies, where you need to know your hands are clean before treating wounds.
- 4 drops of orange oil
- 5 drops of tea tree oil
- Distilled water
- A suitable bottle (ideally a spray bottle)

Mix all the ingredients except the distilled water thoroughly and be careful about your measurements.

Tip them into your spray bottle, and fill the bottle to ¾ with distilled water. Put the lid on, and shake thoroughly to combine. Shake again before use for around 30 seconds to ensure all the ingredients are combined. To use, spray thoroughly over your hands, and then rub them together until the liquid dries.

Remember, this isn't an alternative to washing your hands, and it should only be used when you need it.

Aloe Vera-based Hand Sanitizer

This hand sanitizer is gentler on the hands, but be aware that it does not contain alcohol, and its disinfectant properties will not be as strong. This should be used for general cleaning, but it's best to use an alcohol-based sanitizer in an emergency.

You will need:

- 4 drops of lavender oil
- 4 drops of tea tree oil
- 8 drops of marjoram oil
- 4 drops of lemon oil
- 8 fl oz of pure aloe vera gel
- 1 teaspoon of melted coconut oil
- A suitable bottle

Stir all the ingredients together thoroughly and make sure they are well combined before adding them to the bottle. It is a good idea to shake the bottle before use.

Alternatives To First Aid Kit Material

If you don't have access to all the modern supplies you need or want to lean more heavily on natural medications, there are a few other things you can stock in your first aid kit. Most of these are not suitable for significant injuries but may help make small cuts and minor complaints less painful and encourage swift healing.

Bruises

Arnica is well-known for its ability to fight bruising and muscle aches. It is usually used as a cream, rubbed onto (unbroken) skin. Do not consume the cream or use it for more than a few days at a time. Arnica tablets can be purchased but tend to be too diluted to have limited usefulness.

Witch hazel is another good option for swelling and may be safer to apply if the skin has broken in any areas. It can be purchased as a cream (often including other ingredients such as tea tree) and is very soothing. It's great to have on hand for minor cuts and bruises. It is also thought to have anti-bacterial properties.

Cuts

For mild cuts that have been adequately cleaned, applying coconut oil to the wound may help stave off infection. It has anti-bacterial and anti-inflammatory properties and can help to seal the wound.

Itches/Rashes

Once you have determined the cause of the rash and washed the skin thoroughly with mild soap and water, there are various soothing treatments that you can apply. Different ones may work for different people, so consider:

- An oat bath. Oats are moisturizing and will rehydrate the skin, relieving discomfort. Oats are a great way to get rid of itchiness.
- Calamine lotion. This has a soothing, cooling effect and has been used for years.
- Cool packs, which can be soothing and rehydrate the skin

Some people recommend aloe vera, but there is little evidence to show this helps with itchiness (except for sunburn), and some people find it makes it worse. Apple cider vinegar may be worth trying, as its anti-fungal and anti-bacterial properties will sometimes help, but it can again exacerbate a problem because of its acidity.

Toothaches

Clove oil has been mentioned as a cure for toothaches because it is one of the few effective remedies. Always keep some of this in your medical kit. It's best applied by adding some to a cotton ball or tissue and then lightly biting on this with the affected tooth. It will numb the nerves. You can also use whole cloves, although they have a strong flavor.

Alternatively, try a peppermint tea bag. Biting gently on a warm peppermint tea bag can bring relief if you have a tooth abscess (although you still need to see a dentist urgently). The peppermint has a numbing effect that will ease the pain, and the warmth should help combat the infection. Don't bite down on a boiling hot tea bag, however.

Saltwater rinses may help, too. Salt is a natural disinfectant and can combat mild infections, especially in an area it can access. Rinsing the mouth with salty water can reduce the risk of infection occurring or help combat one that has started.

Headaches

The first approach to a headache is to identify a clear cause (hunger, dehydration, lack of sleep, etc.) and then address that directly. If not, or if this hasn't helped, natural remedies may assist. Try the below:

Essential oils, such as lavender or peppermint, may help. Add them to a diffuser, or use a carrier oil and rub them onto the temples. Some people find lavender unpleasant when they have a headache, while others find it immediately soothing. Lavender is thought to be particularly effective for relieving migraine pain.

Ginger tea is also thought to help relieve some kinds of headaches. You may also find chamomile, lavender, or peppermint helpful.

In some cases, caffeinated beverages may ease a headache, as they can relax the blood vessels, reducing tension and increasing circulation. However, be cautious about using caffeine as this can cause headaches in some people.

Indigestion

If a party member is suffering from indigestion, you can try a few natural cures. However, be aware that what work's for one person may not work for another. Approach natural remedies with caution and listen to your patient's experience before deciding whether to continue treatment.

Apple cider vinegar is one such recipe with great results for some people. A teaspoon mixed into a glass of water may reduce acid reflux.

Bananas may also help, as they are bland and low-acid. The vitamins may stop spasms, but so far, nobody knows whether these fruits prevent acid reflux.

Chewing on liquorice root may help, according to some sources. This has been used for centuries to treat stomach complaints, and it is thought that it may increase the mucous in the esophagus, protecting it from stomach acids. Licorice tea is an alternative. However, be aware that licorice can interfere with some medications, so a doctor should be consulted before a patient takes licorice regularly.

Summary

In this chapter, we've covered many of the natural options for treating minor health complaints and some remedies that you can make yourself at home, including:

- Essential oils
- Herbal teas
- Storing natural remedies in first aid kits
- Recipes for first aid material
- Disinfectant and hand sanitizers
- Alternatives to first aid kit material

Conclusion

"To keep the body in good health is a duty... otherwise, we shall not be able to keep the mind strong and clear."

-BUDDHA

This book has sought to empower you to keep yourself and others safe when traveling off the grid, away from help. Nobody wants to think that they will have to deal with an emergency, but unfortunately, crises arise at the worst possible times, and if you aren't prepared, you may find that tragedy strikes your group. You owe it to yourself and others to learn how to handle a crisis and care for the human body.

Humans are amazingly resilient and yet also surprisingly fragile. Numerous complaints can strike a person down, and debilitating pain can stem from the most trivial causes. Knowing how to address illnesses and injuries effectively and tackle both the cause and symptoms is crucial for surviving off the grid. You will have to deal with diseases, wounds, broken bones, and the shock that can accompany these, and you'll need a cool head to do so effectively. There is no room to panic at such times.

We've covered all kinds of situations you might encounter, both minor and major. Whenever you are planning a trip, it's essential to spend some time in advance assessing the dangers you may face, the health conditions of your party members, and the equipment you are likely to need. Think about allergies, pre-existing diseases, the landscape you will be operating in, and the climate you face. Consider worst-case scenarios and how you can ensure that everyone will get through these alive, and how you can equip your party members to deal with disasters.

Remember that the burden of first aid and emergency planning should never fall on one person. All adults (and indeed, children as soon as they are old enough) should take responsibility and know how to deal with at least the basics of first aid. Don't be afraid to talk to children in the group about what to do if something goes wrong; you may not be there to help them, even if you plan to be. A child has a right to know how to address a situation correctly, and even young children can be taught the value and importance of basic first aid.

Make sure that you have plans in place for things like natural disasters, floods, and sudden changes in the weather. Your kit should always include items that will help you survive in extreme cold or extreme heat (depending on where you are located), even if you don't expect to deal with these extremes. Make sure that party members have access to the supplies they will need, and consider including information booklets, diagrams, and what-to-do sheets in the kit so that those who are less well-equipped can still deal with emergencies.

Restock your first aid kit regularly, and constantly reassess whether your approach to first aid is valid and working. It never hurts to run through the basics, especially when someone leaves or joins your group. Everyone should have standard protocols that they can follow and a good idea of any health conditions that others have (especially allergies) to work with these, not against them.

It's effortless to brush first aid under the mat and forget about it because we aren't forced to think about it – until the worst happens, and you're stuck without essential equipment or know-how because nobody planned adequately. When the emergency services are far away, this is not a situation that you want to be in. Don't let yourself or the people you travel with fall prey to inaction; be prepared and be equipped. You never know when you will need it.

You should now have a good understanding of the situations you might face and how to prepare yourself for them. This is best combined with hands-on training from professionals, so organize to take some first aid courses (with other group members if possible) as soon as you can. If this isn't feasible, at least practice the basics using online videos and resources alongside other members of your party. There is a wealth of information out there, and the more understanding you have, the more likely you are to stay calm and respond appropriately in an emergency.

It's time to get prepared because tomorrow may be too late when it comes to the health and safety of your off grid group.

PREPPER'S LONG TERM SURVIVAL BIBLE:

BOOK 5

The Essential Guide To Off Grid Survival | Includes Self Sufficient Food, Water & Shelter, Plus 3 More Life-Saving Strategies

BY

BRADLEY STONE

Introduction

"I can survive well enough on my own— if given the proper reading material."

-Sarah J Maas

Have you ever found yourself stuck in a difficult situation with no access to the societal safety net that many depend upon?

Being off the grid can seem idyllic until the point where something goes wrong, and you suddenly realize that you are a very long way from help and the comforts of the modern world. Whatever disaster may strike, you need to know that you are prepared for it.

Back in 2013, it was estimated that about 1.7 billion families globally lived off the grid without access to basic facilities. That number has only grown, especially given the increased availability of information on how to effectively live off the grid and the cost reduction of devices like solar panels. More and more people are looking to move off the grid, but if you count yourself among those people, you need to stop now and think very hard about being prepared.

Why?

Many people don't realize that an off-grid setup takes enormous work to be safe and comfortable. You will suddenly lose access to things that most of us take for granted – light, clean water, proper sewage treatment, readily available food and cooking facilities, electricity, and reliable heating. These are things that humans have surrounded themselves with, and for many, they are considered necessities. Going without them might seem easy on paper, but it can be a real challenge and even dangerous. You, therefore, need to empower yourself with an understanding of what you need, what you have, and how to access the necessities for life when something goes wrong.

You will depend on yourself and your group entirely when you are off the grid. You may be miles away from help, cut off by rural roads or bad weather, and if you cannot step up and hold your own against nature, you could end up in serious trouble.

I've spent a lot of time researching the off-grid world and have lived off the grid myself in the past. I was born on the grid, but my parents moved off it when I was a baby, so my early years were spent on a converted school bus with no running water, minimal space, and a tight-knit community of people living off the land. I know why it is essential to assess and plan for disasters in advance and how this can be done. I know how dangerous it could have been to be unprepared and under-equipped in that remote community setting. I am grateful that the people we shared our space with were resilient, knowledgeable, competent, and resourceful, and I want to make sure that you have this experience.

Even when we moved back onto the grid, my childhood was littered with blackouts, and the power could be off for days at a time. Learning how to deal with this situation, stock up on fuel, have candles at the ready, and prepare for the worst was crucial. It imbued me with a desire to ensure I am always equipped for emergencies, whether I can turn to societal structures for help.

That's what I want to share in this book. Anyone who steps off the grid needs to know that they can handle it – that they are on top of both standard living and potential disaster situations and will survive if the worst should happen. Whatever you find yourself grappling with, survival will come down to your skills, understanding, and ability to deal with the situation. This book is for anyone who wants to move away from the society we currently live in and test their survival skills, and it should serve as a guide for you in both normal life and disasters. I recommend familiarizing yourself thoroughly with its contents, adapting the concepts and ideas shared to fit your local situation, and taking the time to make plans for disasters.

With this book, you can prepare yourself for ordinary living and emergencies and increase your chances of survival. I will cover all the basics that you need to know and think about before you step into the off-grid world, so you know how to handle everything the world might throw at you.

We will look at finding food and water, locating, or constructing safe shelters, staying warm, and staying safe, especially when dealing with fires. I'm also going to explore the crucial tools you will need for off grid living to make sure that you are fully equipped and ready for anything. A survival kit is about just that – survival. When you are away from the safety of society, this is your responsibility, and you need to empower yourself to stay safe.

Many people go off the grid with companions, whether friends, family members, or young children. If you are off the grid alone, it's even more crucial that you take responsibility for your survival, but even with a group, you should still take charge of your safety. You never know when you will be cut off from other group members, and you shouldn't depend upon anyone else to have the answers that could mean the difference between life and death. Give yourself the confidence that comes with knowledge.

If you have children in your group, it's important to share what you can of this guide with them, as far as it is age-appropriate. While the adults will ideally be responsible for the safety of children, it's still a good idea to equip minors (especially those approaching the teenage years) with as many tools as possible to help them survive if something goes wrong. Discuss the topics shared in this book and encourage your children to know what to do if the worst should happen. If you aren't there to protect them, this could make a significant difference.

In the next chapter, we will start with one of the essential resources needed for life and one that is often in short supply when you are off the grid: safe water. We'll look at how to find water sources, check whether water is safe, and make it safe if it isn't clean. We'll also cover water storage and how to make a water map that is tailored to your local area. Keep reading to find out the basics!

1

How To Store And Purify Water

"Water is life, and clean water means health."

-AUDREY HEPBURN

This chapter will start with the essential resource you will need in your life off the grid: water.

Water is heavy to carry, hard to store, and impractical when it isn't being cleaned and piped in by a sewer company, so how do you handle this commodity when you are off the grid? We all know that it is hazardous to drink dirty water, to the point that it could kill you, but if you don't have clean water coming through your taps, you might not know where to start. Let's find out!

Finding Water Sources

There are numerous sources of water that you may be able to use, depending on your situation, surroundings, and the climate. These include:

- The sea
- Lakes
- Streams
- Rivers
- Puddles
- Rainwater
- Digging
- Harvesting plants

You may be able to use various sources, and they all have advantages and disadvantages. It's often good to have a backup water source for unexpected situations and emergencies, so make sure you think about all these options, especially if you are struggling with water. Some may be unavailable in your area but make sure you think about as many as possible, including more obscure sources such as harvesting plants. Don't dismiss a potential water source until you are sure it isn't available to you.

It's also worth categorizing water as stable vs unstable. For example, a large lake is unlikely to dry up in the summer months, but puddles and rainwater will, and streams may do. Depending on plants may not work at certain times of the year. Let's look at each of these sources in a little more detail.

It's important to note that these methods harvest water safely with minimal equipment. If you have access to water purification tablets or a filter water bottle, you will have more options about where you get your water from.

The Sea:

If you live near the sea, you may be frustrated about how difficult this water source is to use. Ocean water is too salty for human consumption; drinking it could make you vomit, and drinking a lot of it could kill you.

However, you can make seawater palatable with the correct setup. New technology is currently being developed that may make this easier, but for now, boiling seawater is one of the best ways to make it drinkable. You will need to trap the water vapor as it is boiled off the salt.

The easiest way to do this is to set a pan full of seawater over a heat source and then place a small vessel in the middle, with its rim above the level of the seawater. Put an inverted lid on the pan so that the lid's handle is directly above the vessel in the center.

The water will evaporate as it boils and then re-forms into condensation when it hits the lid. It will trickle to the handle, the lowest point, and drip down into the vessel below. The water that collects in this vessel will be safe to drink.

Lakes:

Lakes might seem like a more accessible water source, but there is a risk in drinking lake water that hasn't been filtered and cleaned. If you have a stationary off-grid setup, you may wish to invest in a filter system, plus chlorine or UV-based purification system that will kill the microorganisms in the water.

If you haven't got a permanent setup, boiling water will help make it safe. You need to make sure that the water reaches a rolling boil for at least five minutes to assure yourself that you have killed any harmful bacteria; This isn't a completely foolproof method, but it is usually safe.

Streams:

Like lake water, stream water may carry harmful bacterial strains and microorganisms. It should be boiled before consumption.

Rivers:

Again, make sure you boil the water for at least five minutes before consuming the water from a river. Be aware that this will not get rid of sediment, so if the river is turbulent, choose a calm area to take water from.

Puddles:

Although rainwater is usually clean and safe to drink, be cautious about puddles. Puddles can form anywhere and may contain all sorts of pollutants and contaminants. The rain will have disturbed the ground, meaning that these contaminants are more likely to be mixed in if it has just rained recently. Try to avoid drinking from puddles unless you have the means to clean and sterilize the water.

Rainwater:

Rainwater is generally clean and safe, so it's a great water source if you can harvest it. Almost any receptacle can collect rainwater, but make sure it is clean, so the rainwater doesn't get contaminated. Be aware that rainwater is an unstable water source, so it shouldn't be your main one unless you live somewhere with guaranteed regular rain.

Digging:

If you want to dig your well, you'll need to research the specific area you will be operating in and your handling conditions. However, if you wish to dig a hole to access water below the surface for an emergency, this can be done too.

You are more likely to find groundwater in low areas, so head downhill. Look for ground that feels damp or saturated, and then dig. How deep you need to dig will depend on the conditions, but once you have found water, let it settle out before boiling and drinking it. You must clean water that you dig from underground before it is safe for consumption.

Harvesting Plants:

Some plants are much easier to harvest water from than others, so start by identifying common ones in your area that looks promising. Next, decide whether you will cut the plant or collect water vapor from it.

If you will cut the plant, choose a plump section, and then squeeze this until you see water coming from it. Drip this into a container to examine it; clear water is likely to be okay, but milky or sticky water should not be drunk as it may be poisonous.

If you want to gather water via plant vapor, you need a clear plastic bag. Put this around some of the plant's leaves and seal it as well as possible. The water vapor from the plant's respiration will collect inside the bag over the next few hours, although in relatively small quantities. It should be safe to drink this water.

Indications Of Water Sources From Wildlife

If you are trying to find water while off the grid, one of the best things you can do is watch the local wildlife. Every living creature needs water, and while some will get theirs from sources that are too small for you to use, most will know the local water sources and regularly travel to them. You should look out for signs of this if you are struggling for water.

Following the footprints of animals is often a good start, especially if large mammals exist in the area (e.g., deer). Animals tend to have a much keener sense of smell than humans, so they may be able to smell water even if they don't know where it is. Use this by following animals or the signs of their activity to locate water, and remember that almost all animals will visit some water source to drink each day.

Of course, some animals will get their water from their diet, but in most cases, if you can track an animal for long enough, it will lead you to a water source that you might be able to use.

How to Determine Water Quality

If you come across a water source, one of the first things you will need to do is test whether the water is high enough quality to drink. Doing this properly requires equipment, and there are many things that you should look at, including the surroundings, checking the source of water (if possible), and making sure that it is running rather than standing water.

Running water is less likely to have harmful bacteria, and cold water is also likely to be safer because it prohibits algal growth. When you find a water source, you should check out the surrounding area. Firstly, make sure the water is far enough from a city or other urban area that it is unlikely to have been polluted by that area. Secondly, look for any potential contaminants, particularly above the site you are thinking of drinking from. Dead animals are often found near water, making it unsafe if they have died in contact with the water.

There is no sure test for water potability that you can practically set up in the wilds, but employ these three rules: it should be running, it should be cold, and it should be clear. It is usually fairly likely to be safe if it ticks all of these boxes, especially if you can purify or boil it. If the water has a bitter or brackish flavor, spit it out and find a different source.

Purifying Water – Boiling, Tablets, Filtering, Distillation, Chemicals

We have already raised the possibility of boiling water to make it safe, and this is a good option. Still, it may not always be possible for you, as you won't always access a heat source (especially in emergencies). You should therefore have some backup means of purifying water, including purification tablets, filtering systems, distillation methods, and chemicals.

Before we start exploring these methods, some are aimed at removing harmful bacteria and germs from the water, while others aim to remove the debris from the water. It's important to know which of these two methods you are employing because although there is some overlap, one does not stand-in for the other.

Boiling, purification tablets, and chemicals are usually about removing biological dangers, while filtration is usually about removing particles and other contaminants. Distillation may do both if you have the correct processes in place.

Boiling:

Boiling water is one of the most effective and straightforward ways to make it safe to drink. You do not need any special equipment, and this can be done over an open flame if you can start a fire but have no other heat source. As long as you have a heatproof container, you can boil water and allow it to cool, and it will usually be safe to drink.

Be aware, however, that boiling water will not remove sediment. Its job is to eliminate germs and bacteria that could make you sick; it will not get rid of grit and other particles in the water. If you want to get rid of other particles, you will need to filter the water before you boil it (which we will cover shortly).

Keep the water on a rolling boil for at least five minutes. It takes time to kill bacteria and germs, so you need to be patient. When the water has finished boiling, allow it to cool, and then it can be drunk (or use it hot to make tea, coffee, etc.). This method has been used for a long time to ensure that water is safe to drink, and it is an efficient, simple technique.

Purification Tablets:

These tablets are designed to kill germs in the water and make it safe to drink. It is good to have some water purification tablets in an emergency supply kit that you can grab if a disaster strikes or if something goes wrong with your off-grid setup. Have as many as you can feasibly store, especially if you are part of a large group and are a long way from civilization.

A water purification tablet works by releasing either chlorine or iodine or combining these two components into the water; This will quickly kill microorganisms in the water, making it safe to drink without needing other equipment (e.g., pans, heat source). In a disaster, they could save your life, and they are a staple of hikers and backpackers because they are small, convenient, and can work anywhere.

It is essential to know how to use them, so read the instructions on the packaging (this will vary between manufacturers). Find out how much water a single tablet can purify, and then make sure you have a way to measure this when you need to use the tablets; This might mean storing them with a dedicated vessel you already know the volume of.

Using the tablets with the wrong amount of water could be unsafe because it won't be effective if you dilute the tablet too heavily. On the other hand, if it is too concentrated, it will make the water taste odd and could be harmful to you. Get the quantities right for maximum safety.

Usually, you will need to drop a tablet into the water you wish to purify and then wait for some minutes after it has fully dissolved. It will give it time to neutralize the contaminants in the water and ensure that the liquid is safe to drink. Follow the manufacturer's guidelines, but a rough rule suggests 30 minutes is the safe amount of time.

Some water purifying tablets taste terrible, and you may need an iodine neutralizer to counteract this taste. Chlorine tablets can usually just be left open to the air for a while, and the chlorine will gradually evaporate off.

When choosing your water tablets, think about weight, efficacy, smell, taste, etc.

Filtering Systems:

Sometimes, you will need to filter the water to get rid of the contaminants in it and purify it. Remember that filtering does not necessarily remove biological hazards from the water, so you may still need to deal with bacteria before you drink the water. Filtering will help to remove any debris.

You can build your water filters, which we will cover shortly, or buy ready-made filters. They will help your water taste better but won't make contaminated water safe to drink.

Distillation:

We mentioned distillation to make saltwater potable; this method essentially means boiling the water until it evaporates, catching the steam, and condensing it into drinkable water. This method is one of the best ways to remove sediment and biological contaminants. It can also eliminate things like limescale, lead, and many microorganisms that might affect your drinking water.

That might sound great, but be aware that distillation is not a perfect solution and will not always give you ideal drinking water. Some contaminants have a lower boiling point than water and will be trapped, condensed, and poured straight back into your "clean" water supply. Benzene is one component that will boil before your water does, so it can't be removed through distillation.

Many commercial distillers will also contain a filter that will help trap these particles and prevent the water from being contaminated. Still, if you are making your version, you will need to be aware of the potential contaminants that could remain in the water.

Chemicals:

You might not like putting chemicals into the water you are about to drink, but this is essentially an extension of the water purification tablet idea. Small amounts of chemicals will be sufficient to kill off microorganisms and leave the water safe for you to consume.

If you have one available, it is better to use a commercial water purification tablet because there is more scope for something to go wrong if you measure and mix your chemicals. Still, if you are stuck and have no other means of purifying the water, there are a few things you can do.

Most household disinfectants will kill off the bacteria in water, just as they will on surfaces. Adding things like household bleach is an excellent way to purify water, but you need to know what percentage of sodium hypochlorite has been used. According to the CDC, most unscented bleach in the United States will use between 5 and 9 percent.

If that is the case with your bleach, you will be adding two drops of bleach to a quart (1 liter) of water using a dropper (if you have one). If you do not have a dropper, use 0.1 ml or the smallest amount. To purify a gallon of water, the CDC recommends adding 8 drops or ½ ml of bleach or just under 1/8th of a teaspoon. For 5 gallons, add 40 drops of bleach or 2 ½ ml or ½ teaspoon of bleach.

As you can see, the amount of bleach is minimal. You will need to stir the water thoroughly and then leave it to stand for a full 30 minutes before you drink it, giving the bleach time to evaporate off and leaving the water safe to drink.

Note that using bleach will not work against parasites in the water, so be aware of this. A filter may help get rid of the parasites, so create a filtration system or run the water through a fine-mesh such as a coffee filter.

Build Your Own Filter

Remember that filtration is about removing physical contaminants from the water, not bacteria or microorganisms. You should only use a water filter if you can decontaminate the water in other ways, too, because on its own, this method will not make the water safe to drink.

You should also remember that you should avoid muddy water or those full of debris. Try to choose water that will need minimal filtering because it is much more likely to be safe for you to consume. Of course, even with clean-looking water, filtering can still be a major plus that makes the water taste better and makes it safer.

Now, let's look at how to build your filter. There are quite a few options here, so you may be able to adapt this to fit your particular circumstances.

Fixed Water Filter:

If you are setting up an off-grid home and want a water filtering system, you can set up a fixed filtration system with relative ease, provided you have the suitable materials. A tried and tested method involves using a ceramic filter. For this, you will need:

- 1 spigot
- 1 ceramic filter cartridge
- 2 large buckets
- A 1/2" and a 3/8" drill bit

Your buckets must be food grade because you don't want any risk of chemicals leaching into the water you are trying to clean. You can use any size, but the larger the setup, the more water you can filter at once.

You can buy a ceramic water filter easily online. When you have all your equipment, you will need to drill a hole in the bottom of one bucket and a hole in the lid of the other. Slot your ceramic cartridge into the hole and then turn the bucket over and line the hole in the lid up with the cartridge's spout.

Next, put your lidless bucket on a stable surface and stand the lid, ceramic cartridge, and bucket on top of it. Put the lid on the top bucket, and you have a filtration system. You can add water to the top bucket, and it will gradually pour through the filter into the bottom bucket. Add a spigot to the bottom bucket, and you can get filtered water at any time. Be aware that this system isn't the fastest, but it is reliable, cheap, and used for years.

Emergency Water Filter:

If you're stuck in an emergency, you might be looking to make a mini, portable water filter from bits and pieces. You may not have everything you need to hand but aim for something like this:

- Gravel
- Coarse sand
- Fine sand
- A clean piece of cheesecloth
- 1 large plastic bottle
- 1 coffee filter (or fabric filter with a very fine weave)
- Charcoal
- A pair of scissors/a knife
- Something to put the filtered water in

Start by cutting the base off the plastic bottle. Clean it out and dry it, and then punch a small hole through the cap so water can trickle through. If you don't have a cap, cut the top off the bottle instead and poke holes through the base.

Next, stuff your clean cheesecloth, coffee filter, or other fabric filters into the bottle to cover this hole. The finer the mesh, the better it will work. If you have access to diatomaceous earth, add a layer of this next, followed by a layer of charcoal. If you don't have access to these things, don't worry. Pour in a layer of fine sand and then a layer of coarse sand. Next, add a second layer of fine sand, followed by a few inches of gravel.

Finally, cover the open end of the bottle with a fine cloth, and you can begin pouring water in. As it passes through the various layers, it will gradually leave behind sediment, bits of grit, and any other debris.

Remember, you will still need to disinfect this water to ensure safe to drink.

How To Store Water In Your Off-Grid Home

If you are looking for a way to store water alongside your off-grid home, you will probably need a nearby water source. It could be a lake, river, pond, or artificial well. Make sure you know how much water this can provide you with and whether it is likely to run dry during the summer.

Many people use rainwater for their off-grid homes, but this has the disadvantage of being unreliable and needing a lot of storage. Rain barrels can be a great option, especially if you grow your food and need a supply of non-sterile water. Still, they may not be ideal for storing water that you want to drink, as algae and bacteria will eventually start to collect in the barrels in most situations.

Ideally, you will want a central system to pump water into from many different sources and rely on throughout the year, which will be as close to your house as possible and will usually be fully contained, so there is no risk of contamination once pure water is in the system. It may be fed by rainwater, lake water, or water you collect from a ranch water station or other central water supply (although this requires a large vehicle and can cause a lot of wear and tear on that vehicle). You may use purification methods depending on the water you are harvesting, but this will need to be area-specific to ensure enough to keep the water sterile.

Another option is to invest in a well, but this can be expensive if you are far above the water table, so it may not be practical.

How To Store Water While You're In The Wilderness Away From Home

If you are operating in the wilderness, there probably isn't much you can do to store large amounts of water; it is hard to carry, and you may not have access to it. However, there are things you can do to collect water, and if you can, you can store this in clean plastic bottles. It's a good idea to keep these bottles in a bag or otherwise covered so that they don't get too much sunlight, as this will cause algae to grow in the water.

If you stay in one place for a while, the best way to store water will be in a large plastic container, covered to keep the sunlight off it. You can collect water by leaving out water-tight vessels to catch rainwater and dew and tip this into the container whenever you have collected enough. Similarly, covering plants with a plastic bag to collect water may help.

You may find that it is good to bury the water container if you are in a hot climate, as this will keep it cool even if there is limited shade. However, it can make it difficult to get water from the container when you need it. Depending on the ground, see if you can hollow out an area that allows you to slide it in and out easily. Keeping the water out of the sun will reduce the risk of bacteria growing and make it more refreshing to drink. If you cannot dig a hole, try to find a shady spot for the vessel so it doesn't get too hot.

Making A Water Map Of Your Region

Whenever you move to a new area, it is vital to start by scouting out local water sources – ideally, at least a few of them. You never know when a water source might suddenly become unusable because of contamination problems, droughts, or other issues, so it's crucial to be on top of where you can find more water if something goes wrong.

Making a water map that your entire group has access to is crucial. It can be used as part of your emergency planning; if something goes wrong and you have to evacuate your home, it's helpful to have a rendezvous point, and this should be located near some reliable source of water if possible.

When drawing up a water map, you can use a mixture of technology and physical exploration to locate local water sources. Use online satellite images to identify bodies of water, but make sure you also visit them in person to check how viable they may be and make sure the images are accurate. Remember to think about things like potential pollution, dead animals, etc. You can't guarantee that a source won't be contaminated later, but when making your map, it's something you should consider.

Think about things like the size of the water body and the time of year, too. If you find a small stream in the middle of winter, it may shrink away to nothing in the heat of summer. It's still worth marking on your map, but you should be looking for large bodies of water too.

Draw a map of the surrounding area, and mark the nearest water sources and the further-flung ones (these may be useful in an emergency). Write how long it takes to get to these sources and make any notes about them that you think may be useful later (e.g., needs filtering, may dry up, etc.).

If you stay in the same place for a long time, you can refine your water map with the changing seasons and additional notes. For example, you may mark seasonal water sources or note when specific sources are more viable than others. Make sure everyone uses the water map and agrees about what water is being used for. For example, you don't want anyone accidentally contaminating your drinking water by bathing in it or throwing out waste near it. Be careful and communicate well.

You should make a water map whenever you move to a new area and ensure it is available to everyone, including children. You may also want to supply individuals with personal copies of the water map to get themselves to a water source if an emergency arises.

Summary

In this chapter, we've covered:

- How to find water sources and what viable sources may be available in your area.
- How wildlife can help you locate nearby water sources.
- How to tell if water should be safe to consume, using the three rules of running, cold, and clear.
- The various methods used to purify water, and the difference between filtration and purification. We looked at boiling, using purification tablets, filtration systems, distillation, and chemicals that you can use in an emergency.
- A method for building a fixed filter and creating an emergency filter to deal with sediment and debris in water.
- How to store water in a fixed off-grid situation.
- How to store water in the wilderness.
- How to create and use a water map of your region.

In the following chapter, we will look at the next most important resource for living in the wilds: finding, preparing, and storing food that is safe for you to eat. We will cover the basics of foraging, trapping, fishing, and hunting. We will also look at insects that may provide food, discuss the reptiles, amphibians, and fungi you can look for, and cover seafood and eggs. We'll also look at plants you can eat and how to prepare and store food both in an off-grid home and while traveling in the wilderness.

2

How To Find And Store Food

"If more of us valued food and cheer and song above hoarded gold,
it would be a merrier world."

-J. R. R. Tolkien

Food, like water, is crucial to survival, and whether you are in an emergency or not, knowing how to find or catch food can be a major advantage. In everyday situations, foraging and hunting can reduce your food bill, cut down on your food miles, and help you stay in touch with the land you are living off. These skills could mean the difference between life and death in emergencies.

We will look at all aspects of finding food in the wild in this chapter, and then we'll briefly touch on how to cook and preserve foods, especially in situations where you don't have access to a fridge or freezer.

Where To Find Food: Foraging

Food is often abundant in the wild, and no matter where you look or what you want to eat, you will usually find foods readily available to you. However, you need to understand your local environment, what foods to look for, what seasons to look in, and what plants or animals to avoid.

Although I will aim to cover many of the basics here, I highly recommend getting a book or two that tells you about the foods available in the area you will be operating in because foods can vary so radically from place to place. At the very least, make sure you familiarize yourself with any dangerous plants that may be present in that area and talk to others in your group about how to avoid these. It is also a good idea to be aware of the animals that you may encounter (both when foraging and in everyday life) and how you can minimize the dangers that these may pose.

Always make sure you are safe when foraging, and don't venture too far from home, forage in dangerous areas, or approach dangerous animals to get food. For example, stealing honey from a beehive is unlikely to be a good idea in most cases and could get you into a dangerous situation. It is much better to look for plants or attempt to catch fish if you cannot easily hunt in your local area.

Never risk your life to get a meal; look for food elsewhere rather than taking a chance of getting injured which is particularly important if you are in an emergency where you have limited access to medical assistance if something goes wrong.

If you ever expect to end up in a situation where you are going to be foraging for food, whether for an emergency or day to day living, you may find it helpful to use a food pyramid that denotes the difficulty level of the food you are looking to collect. The one recommended by Primal Survivor looks like the below:

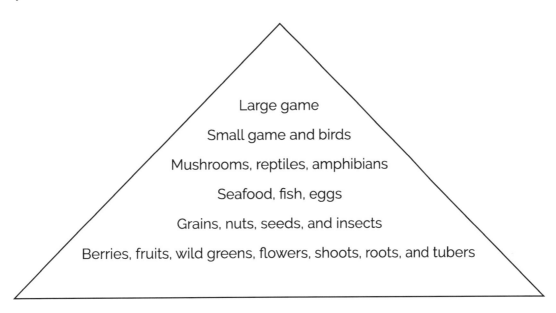

You may wish to create your version of this triangle based on your local environment and your particular skills, but it is a helpful starting point for many individuals. You shouldn't be hunting for a large game unless you have some training; this is unlikely to be a good way to gather food. Similarly, even trapping or hunting smaller animals can be challenging. Reptiles and amphibians represent the next difficulty level, along with mushrooms (because they are hard to identify and potentially dangerous if misidentified). Seafood will be a reasonably easy option if you can fish, alongside stealing eggs from birds' nests. Insects, nuts, grains, and seeds tend to be easy to gather, followed by the last group of flowers, plants, and fruits, which are the easiest of all.

This list may not apply strictly as it appears above; you might find that you have a ready source of safe fungi or that fish are almost impossible to catch and not worth your time, but it's a good idea to use this as a guide, especially if you are unfamiliar with the area. It should help you maximize your foraging efficiency and make it easy and reasonably safe to collect food.

Next, let's look at the various kinds of food gathering you might try, the pros and cons of each and how you should approach the activity. Some types of food gathering won't apply in some areas, so learn the ones that are most likely to be helpful to you.

Trapping, Hunting, And Fishing

Trapping, hunting, and fishing are activities that can take up a lot of time and may have some risks (especially when hunting dangerous animals), but they also offer high rewards because they yield food rich in protein and fat. You may wish to do some training courses in these subjects before you head off the grid; there are a lot of skills involved in all three types of meat-gathering activities.

Familiarize yourself with hunting, fishing, and trapping laws in the local area before you undertake any of these activities; this is crucial if you plan to depend upon these activities to supply you with food regularly.

Trapping:

There are multiple kinds of snares that you can use, and most can be set up with minimal materials. In general, you will only need sticks and a cord, and if you are a keen trapper, you should make sure you are always carrying some suitable cord with you. You should be able to find sticks when out and about.

You will also need some bait, although what kind you carry will depend on what sort of animal you are looking to trap. Peanut butter is a good option for rodents and many other fat-loving animals, but you can also carry small tins of fish if you don't mind a little extra weight. Try to opt for bait that can be kept almost indefinitely so you can make a trap kit without needing to change your bait constantly. Foodstuff that will easily fit in your pockets is the best.

It's essential to be aware that your scent will be on anything you have touched, and this is likely to frighten off any animal you are trying to trap. You can purchase a de-scenting spray or use powdered charcoal to get rid of this. Try to avoid getting your scent in the area around the trap too.

Traps you may wish to learn how to set include:

- Paiute Deadfall
- Figure 4 Deadfall
- Squirrel Pole Snare
- Rolling Snare
- Treadle Snare
- Peg Snare
- Grave's Motion Triggered Snare

Learn these and more before attempting to trap animals in the wild. The best traps kill the animal outright to reduce its suffering and the risk of escaping. Check your traps regularly to ensure that you utilize what they catch rather than losing food to other predators.

Hunting:

If you are going to hunt, make sure you can do so safely. You should know how to handle a gun with minimal risk to yourself and others, and you should be a good shot who practices regularly. If you are going to hunt with other group members, take precautions to keep each other safe and reduce the risk of accidents.

You should save hunting for big game animals rather than wasting your time on a small game that can be trapped using snares.

Fishing:

If you have access to them, fish can provide a precious food source. You can make a fishing rod with a strong sapling, some cord, and a hook, or a fishing spear with a strong pole and a handful of small nails or sharp bits of metal, so fishing equipment can be improvised relatively easily. Many online guides will show you how to make both tools, and hooks can be created from thorns, bones, or other shaped natural objects.

Fishing often requires time and patience, but it is a low energy activity that can be great in the right situation. Take some time to learn which fish to catch and how to catch them. Some fish can also be caught using your bare hands if you have the proper technique. You should also learn how to gut fish and prepare them for consumption.

We'll cover foraging for other kinds of seafood further down.

Edible Insects

Insects are incredibly nutritious and often reasonably easy to forage, depending on where you are. In some cases, you will be able to harvest large amounts of insects, although some insects do have stings, poison, or the ability to bite, which you will need to be aware of if you are going to harvest them.

Many insects are edible, and they are a valuable source of protein, but you need to make sure you are choosing the correct kinds of insects. Do not eat arachnids, millipedes, centipedes, ticks, or venomous insects. Some people do eat scorpions, but only after removing the tail. Be wary of any insects that are brightly coloured or insects that have stings or long hairs.

You should familiarize yourself with the specific species in your area, but in general, ants, crickets, termites, grasshoppers, snails, and slugs are often edible. Many beetles are also okay to eat, but some are toxic; you need to be more careful. Grubs, maggots, stinkbugs, woodlice, earthworms, aphids, earwigs, and some dragonflies are edible.

Do take the time to get to grips with what insects you can eat that might be found in your local area, familiarize yourself with poisonous and dangerous ones, and how to deal with them if you do encounter them.

You can find insects in all sorts of places, which is one of the reasons they are such a good source of food. Try turning over rocks, looking in crevices, peeling back tree bark, or even moving things around your home or camp – insects will be everywhere. It can be challenging to gather them in large quantities, although this depends on what you are looking for.

Reptiles, Amphibians, And Mushrooms

I've grouped these three because they represent a similar difficulty level in gathering them. Reptiles and amphibians may prove easier to hunt for than game or large animals, but they are still somewhat challenging, and mushrooms require a good level of expertise before they become a safe and viable food source. Let's explore all three in more detail.

Reptiles:

You may find reptiles reasonably challenging, as many can bite or sting. If the situation is desperate, you may be able to kill and eat certain kinds of snakes and lizards. However, you should be aware that this kind of meat can carry dangerous bacteria that could make you sick, and both snakes and lizards are good at defending themselves. Snakes often have venomous bites, and even lizards have sharp claws, and many have sharp teeth.

Most reptiles are fast-moving during the day but can be slow in the morning before they have warmed up in the sun. If you are going to hunt them, do so when the weather is cold, and they cannot move quickly.

Some people also hunt turtles, but due to the endangered nature of many of the turtle species, this is best avoided unless you are in a life-or-death situation, and you could face heavy penalties for harming a turtle. In general, hunting reptiles should be reserved for emergencies.

Amphibians:

You might already be on board with the idea of frogs' legs, and there are many other amphibians that you can hunt in the wild for food, although this should be done with a good understanding of local laws and regulations. You will also need to identify any poisonous species and avoid brightly coloured amphibians, which are likely to be toxic. Do not assume a frog is edible unless you can accurately identify it.

On the whole, amphibians are quite an endangered group, and many are protected. Avoid eating them except in difficult circumstances with limited other food options available. Catching amphibians can also be challenging, especially if you don't have a net. Frogs can jump long distances and may not be worth the time it takes to catch one. If you live near a lake, you may decide that frogs are a more viable food source, but be responsible about how many you catch and kill, and remember that frogs are an essential part of the ecosystem.

Mushrooms:

If you pick mushrooms, you need at least one reliable book that will help you identify them (and preferably more than one so you can cross-reference the information). You should look at where and what mushrooms are growing on and their appearance.

It's a good idea to cut mushrooms off rather than pulling them up, as this minimizes damage to the roots and encourages more mushrooms to grow. You should try to forage when the conditions are damp, as almost all fungi like heavy rains, especially following a dry spell. Most mushrooms will be found on decaying matter and burnt wood, so they tend to be easy to locate. Often, if the conditions are right, they will be available in large quantities.

Although they are a tempting food source, it is crucial to make sure you know what you are doing before you pick mushrooms because many kinds are toxic, and some will outright kill you if you consume them. Learn the most dangerous varieties that you are likely to see in the local area and use this information whenever you are foraging.

You should aim to eat mushrooms in fairly small amounts, too which reduces the risk posed by misidentifying one and makes foraging these plants safer.

Some distinctive edible mushrooms include oyster mushrooms, chicken of the woods, lobster mushrooms, lions mane mushrooms, and cauliflower mushrooms.

Seafood And Eggs

Both seafood and eggs are excellent sources of protein, and fish is a source of healthy oils. These foods are relatively easy to harvest safely, although you will need to make sure you are fishing for species worth catching – some fish are almost entirely bone. You should also be cautious about fishing in highly polluted areas. Also, water can be a source of other seafood, including clams, shrimps, mussels, seaweed/water plants, crabs, and more.

Seafood:

Water can provide you with many different kinds of foods, and it's a good idea to assess what might be available in your area, particularly if you have a body of saltwater nearby. Things like clams, crabs, and seaweed are great options. You aren't likely to be able to catch fish from the sea unless you have a boat, but this will depend on the setup, so don't dismiss the idea entirely.

If you are near freshwater, you may still be able to find shrimps and fish like trout, catfish, carp, and bass. Edible plants may also be a good option; familiarize yourself with the things you are likely to find in your state and area.

Eggs:

Eggs are also a great food source and can be easy to harvest if you can find them, although some birds make their nests very high up in trees. The eggs of almost all birds are edible, and many reptile and fish eggs are also acceptable for us to eat. Eggs are a balanced and rich food that may help if you are struggling to survive in the wild, although you should be wary of stealing too many, as this can have significant impact on the species involved. Bird eggs are often protected, so be aware of this and only turn to them for food in an emergency.

Bird eggs will need to be cooked to make them safe to eat. You can roast the eggs in a fire in their shells if you don't have a pan; gently make a hole in one end of the egg and then stab a stick to pierce the yolk and stop it from exploding. Next, put the egg in among the outer coals of your fire, wait for a few minutes, and rotate the egg. An egg the size of a chicken egg will take about 10 minutes in total, while smaller eggs will not take as long.

Fish eggs can also be cooked to kill bacteria, although some people eat them raw. It is harder to cook them on an open fire; ideally, you will need to fry them in a pan. You should also cook reptile eggs if you end up eating these, as they may contain salmonella and could make you very sick.

Nuts, Seeds, And Grains

Next on the list, nuts, seeds, and grains tend to be easier to forage, and many people pick these even if they don't live off the grid. If you live off the grid, you may choose to harvest them throughout the year to supplement your main diet, although the availability will fluctuate with the changing seasons. If you are going to forage for these out of choice rather than necessity, be mindful of other wildlife that may depend upon the food to get through the year, and don't take more than you need.

Nuts:

There are many nuts that you can forage for, and they are a rich source of fats, healthy oils, and other essential nutrients. Nuts are also convenient for carrying and storing, and they are found all over the United States, depending on the trees you have in the local area.

Nuts often have a hard shell, but this can usually be cracked off using a stone. Leave it intact until you are ready to eat the nut to make it last longer.

In some situations, you can eat nuts from a wide range of trees, including beechnuts, hickory nuts, pecans, pine nuts, chestnuts, and even acorns. Acorns in North America are edible, but some will have a bitter flavor as they contain a lot of tannins. These come from red oaks. White oaks produce sweeter acorns that are more palatable. The leaves of white oak trees have rounded lobes, while red oak trees have pointed lobes.

Always make sure you have identified a nut correctly before consuming it. Most nuts can be eaten raw, but some are more pleasant when cooked; you can roast them on the edge of a fire and enjoy the sweet crunchiness.

Seeds:

Seeds can be abundant, especially in the summer and fall months, when plants have flowered and are closing up for winter. Seeds are rich in calories, so they are a great way to fuel yourself in a difficult situation, but they will not be around for long because they are also popular with all kinds of wildlife.

If you want to eat the seeds of a plant, you need to be able to identify the plant as edible and know that its seeds are edible. In many cases, the seeds are toxic even if the rest of the plant is fine to eat. After all, plants don't want the hard work they put into producing the next generation to get chewed to pieces by a hungry animal.

Many seeds are perfectly safe, and some common ones include chickweed, rosehips, dock seeds, evening primrose seeds, and mallow. Avoid eating seeds from plants you know to be toxic, such as foxgloves.

Grains:

Grains are relatively easy to come by in many wild spaces and can be a great way to enhance your cooking if you are making flour or a cooked porridge. Wild rye is a good option for "breakfast mush," especially when cooked with hot milk. Barnyard grass is another plant to look for; its seeds will serve as a grain if you grind them into flour. Lamb's quarters and curly dock are further good options, although lamb's quarter (and flour made from it) must be cooked before consuming, as it isn't safe to eat raw.

Plants And Berries

Most people think of plants and berries when they are foraging, and this is the best place to start learning how to forage. Learn the common plants for your area, the plants to avoid and any berries that may be available to you.

Plants:

There are so many plants in the wild that we can eat. It's crucial to learn what to forage for and how to forage for it. Different plants will have different seasons, and they can be used for all kinds of things – food, drinks, and medicines. You may wish to buy a pocket guide to plants in your area to identify the many options reliably and quickly.

Plants to look out for include:

- Wild onions
- Dandelions
- Plantains
- Chickweed
- Clover flowers
- Wild asparagus
- Wild garlic
- Nettles
- Cleavers

- Wood sorrel
- Mullein
- Yarrow

These are just a handful of the common plants that you can forage. Make sure you look at things like habitat, season, and companion plants before picking anything, and use all your senses and an excellent guidebook to decide what is and is not safe to eat.

Berries:

Berries are a great food to forage for, and you can turn them into preserves and desserts and eat them raw. However, you must be careful, as many berries are poisonous. Unfortunately, there is no simple test for whether a berry is safe to eat or not; you will have to be able to identify it accurately and the plant it is growing on. Try tasting just one if you are really stuck and cannot identify berries. Spit it out and rinse your mouth if it tastes bitter or sour. Do not try this with poison ivy berries; these are round and white or green, and putting one in your mouth could kill you even if you spit it out.

Try to avoid eating berries that you cannot identify unless you are in a desperate situation. Here are some common berries you may be able to find in the wild that are safe to eat:

- Wild strawberries
- Blackberries
- Elderberries (when fully ripe)
- Huckleberries
- Mulberries
- Buffaloberries
- Gooseberries
- Cloudberries

Don't eat yew berries, ivy berries, pokeweed berries, mistletoe berries, or holly berries.

Cooking And Food Preservation At Home

There are many foods that you can preserve at home, and it's well worth learning about the different kinds of preservation and the foods you can preserve. Often, you will find an abundance of one type of food in the wild, but it will only be available for a short amount of time, and then it will disappear until the following year. It's therefore helpful to preserve the food for an extended season, but you need to know how to do this safely, and you may need some equipment to do it well.

You can try multiple kinds of food preservation, including canning, bottling, pickling, freezing, curing, fermenting, and drying. These will help foods last for longer, but which one you choose will depend on the kind of food you are preserving. For example, meats are often dried or cured, whereas many fruits can be canned or dried. Vegetables tend to be fermented or pickled, but there is some crossover between all of the different areas, and at times you may wish to use another method for preservation.

If you can cook in your off-grid setup, you will find that many more foods become available to you, as some foods require cooking before you can consume them. Even if you only have the tools to make a fire, it's worth knowing how to prepare and cook common foods from your area. Things like meat and eggs must be cooked, but some other plants are also toxic unless cooked. Cooking can also help preserve foods and make them last longer because it kills bacteria. Let's look at some of the options for keeping food fresh in more detail below.

Canning:

Canning involves boiling a food (usually fruit) to sterilize it and then sealing it in a sterile jar. The fruit will be covered in a hot liquid, and as the liquid cools and contracts, it pulls the lid of the jar down, creating a tight seal that will prevent bacteria from spreading into the food and keep it safe to consume.

Food canning is a relatively simple process once you know what you are doing, but having a canner makes the process much simpler and will increase the end product's safety. If you aren't careful, canned foods can contain the bacteria that will cause botulism, so it's crucial not to undertake this without a good idea of sterilising jars and safely handling the foods.

Pickling/Fermenting:

Pickling involves preserving food in vinegar, while fermenting usually involves using brine. These methods help the food last very well for years because the liquid is too salty or acidic for bacteria to spread. Pickled foods usually have an intense flavour and tend to be eaten in relatively small quantities. However, pickling is a great way to make savory foods last well and ensure that you can enjoy a variety of out-of-season vegetables throughout the year. Try pickling onions, beets, shallots, zucchini, gherkins, walnuts, garlic, cabbage, and more to keep them throughout the year.

Freezing:

Freezing and refrigeration are among the best methods for storing food, but they are often unavailable off the grid. You should be aware of this and make sure you use food up accordingly. Food stored above 40 degrees F (room temperature) will need to be used up much more quickly than food that can be chilled. If you are going to store things like meat, you will either need to cure it or dry it to ensure it stays safe at room temperature. However, you may be able to create cold storage that is safe for vegetables without needing power.

Many ancient civilizations used to bury food to keep it cool even in hot weather; the ground usually stays cold. You may not want to unearth your food every time you want to eat it. If you can dig a cellar beneath your off-grid setup, you will find that it is much easier to keep foods in the long term, and this method was used extensively before refrigeration became common. It will keep vegetables fresh for months, especially if it is also dark. However, this will not be an option if you are dealing with an emergency or moving around, but it is well worth considering for a fixed off-grid setup.

This is particularly true if you grow a lot of your vegetables because you will need some-where to put them – and underground is the best place. Vegetable growing usually in-volves the gluts of certain foods, so long-term storage is crucial, or you will waste a vast proportion of what you grow.

Curing:

Many types of meat can be cured; this involves drying the food out by adding salt to the surface to help preserve it (sugar or smoke may also be used). The salt pulls the moisture up out of the flesh, so it's a good option if you don't have access to a heat source, but it does require a lot of salt. It also leads to highly salty foods, which should be eaten in lim-ited quantities.

Drying:

Drying is sometimes known as dehydrating, and it's a good option if you have access to a heat source. You can dry meat, but you can also dry various vegetables and fruits to make them last better. Dried foods are easy to transport and often retain much of the flavor of the original food.

If you are going to do a lot of your food preservation, you should invest in some books that will describe the methods in detail, as it's crucial to make sure you get the process right, or the food may become unsafe to eat. If you aren't careful and you don't take the right approach, you will leave yourself at risk of food poisoning. Food preservation can be straightforward, but you must make sure you know what you are doing and working in a suitably clean environment.

Remember that preserved foods will not last indefinitely; the idea is to extend the shelf life of the food. Make sure you rotate your preserved foods to use up old foods first and put newly preserved foods to the back of your storage system.

Cooking And Food Preservation In The Wild

Cooking in the wild will often be limited to a fire, and preservation may be challenging. It is wise to carry the means of making a fire whenever you are out and about, as you may find that you need this both for warmth and for cooking.

Preserving food in the wild is going to be challenging. You won't be able to can, pickle, ferment or freeze foods in most circumstances, but you may be able to dry some foods in the sun. This method has been used for centuries and can help pull out the moisture that would otherwise make the foods rot. If you are in a hot enough environment, laying strips of meat, fish, or vegetables in the hot sunlight for a few hours may preserve it if done with care.

If you can make a fire, you may also be able to smoke certain foods, particularly meats. Be aware that this can take up to six hours (depending on the kind of meat you smoke), and it may be very difficult to do if you don't have the right equipment. Preserving food when you are out and about won't be easy, but you can carry pre-made foods with you, and there may sometimes be options to preserve food while in the wilderness.

Summary

In this chapter, we've covered:

- Where to find foods, and the different kinds of food gathering techniques that you might employ, including hunting, trapping, fishing, and foraging.
- The kinds of foods you might use, such as meat, game, plants, berries, nuts, seeds, fish, eggs, insects, and fungi.
- Some of the wild plants you should look out for as viable food sources.
- Cooking and food preservation in an off-grid fixed setup.
- Cooking and food preservation while on the go.

In the following chapter, we will look at how you can keep yourself warm when the conditions turn nasty, the kinds of gear you should carry for cold situations, and the importance of keeping warm. We will also cover building a fire and fire safety techniques that you should adopt when out in the wild.

3

Keeping Warm In Bad Conditions

"A spark can set a whole forest on fire. Just a spark. Save it."

-Charles Bukowski

One of the biggest dangers you can encounter when far from society is getting too cold. Many people face this danger, and it is one that you need to be both aware of and prepared for (unless you are in a rare part of the world that never experiences extreme cold). This can also be an issue in off-grid setups; many people are used to the luxury of central heating and forget the dangers that the cold can present even if you are in a shelter. Whether you are out in the wild or safe in your shelter, knowing how to keep yourself warm can be invaluable. It may help you to save energy (e.g. limited gas supply, firewood, etc.) and could save your life if your reserves are low.

Even if you don't expect to get stuck out overnight or you have a plan to keep your home warm, you should be prepared to survive the cold. If something goes wrong with your heating system, you want enough equipment to keep yourself alive, particularly overnight. Temperatures can drop massively when the sun sets – even if they are high during the day. We will look at the dangers of cold weather and what you can do to mitigate these. We will then move on to fire safety and how and where to build a fire.

Why Warmth Matters

The temperature at which you could get hypothermia varies depending on wind, chill and whether you are wet. This condition occurs when your body temperature drops to 95 degrees F or below. It's a dangerous condition that can cause confusion, tiredness, the inability to think or speak, pale skin, and blue lips. Hypothermia is a medical emergency, and it will usually be treated in a hospital. So it's clear that you desperately need to avoid this condition if you are a long way from help.

If you are ever operating in a cold environment, ensure that every group member recognizes the critical signs of hypothermia (pale skin, slurred speech, confusion) and knows what to do. The afflicted individual needs to be moved into a shelter as soon as possible, stripped of wet clothing, and warmed up.

If not dealt with, hypothermia can quickly kill a person and may lead to other severe conditions such as frostbite. It is crucial to take this seriously, even if you rarely experience bad weather. Have backup gear prepared for a major storm or power loss, and always carry the basics for keeping warm if you are venturing out into the wild – particularly alone. Even in a group, you should ensure that someone has the means to light a fire and provide some shelter that will keep you warm if you get lost, hurt, or otherwise cut off from your regular source of warmth.

Do not treat the cold lightly or assume that you won't ever have to deal with it because you have a stable, off-grid setup. You must have a backup plan and recognize how dangerous cold weather can be.

What Clothing To Choose

Clothing is your first line of defense against cold weather, and you should choose what you wear with consideration for the worst conditions you might face. Don't leave your home in the full sunlight and assume you will only need a t-shirt. Your clothing requirements will vary depending on where you are and what sort of weather you are likely to face, but think about the following:

- How much the item weighs (you don't want to be lugging a hugely heavy coat with you every time you go for a walk)
- How insulating the item is
- How waterproof the item is
- Whether the item can be layered with other items
- How hard-wearing the item is
- What material has been used to make it

You will need to think about the following categories:

- A hat: you lose most of your body heat through your head, so having a good hat will make a big difference in keeping you warm enough and staying cozy while out and about. You can also wear a hat if you are indoors at night; it will make an incredible difference to how warm you stay in bed. Indeed, this is why many people wear nightcaps; it is one of the best ways to keep warm overnight.

- Shoes: your shoes must be comfortable, waterproof, well-fitted, and warm. Any shoes that don't meet these criteria are unsuitable for any situation you will be out for an uncertain period. That might sound excessive, but getting wet or sore feet will massively hamper your survival ability. If you can't walk comfortably in your shoes, you will struggle to reach a suitable shelter, and if your feet are wet, you are far more likely to get chilled.

- Socks and underwear: your basic layers are essential; these are against your skin and will make a big difference to how much body heat you lose. You should choose wool for your socks, which will wick water away from your feet and keep them very warm. Synthetic may be best for your underwear, as it dries quickly and is usually comfortable. If you are going to be wearing long underwear, choose wool.

- Layers: the rest of your clothing should be made up of multiple layers. It may take some getting used to, as wearing many layers can initially feel uncomfortable, but you will adjust. Choose wicking fabrics to wear against your skin to pull away the moisture, and heavier, rougher fabrics outside. Layers are ideal because you can strip off if the weather warms up or put clothing back on when it cools down.

- Your jacket: a waterproof jacket is often the best final layer, and many technical fabrics today will allow moisture to pass from the inside of the fabric to the outside, but not the other way. It is worth investing in a high-quality outer coat at the very least, even if the rest of your wardrobe is predominantly made up of second-hand or cheap clothing.

It's a good idea to look at the material before you determine whether an item of clothing will be comfortable and cozy or not. Many "technical" fabrics have been developed to provide the best possible warmth and comfort, but even standard fabrics should be weighed up and considered with care.

Cotton is a staple of many wardrobes, but it isn't ideal for wearing against your skin, as it does not dry quickly. It is very absorbent, so it will cling to your sweat and atmospheric moisture, which may lead to chafing and discomfort. It can be breathy and comfortable when working around the home, but it isn't ideal for a survival situation.

Wool is a very popular fabric, and it has some fantastic qualities. It stays warm even when it is wet, but it also doesn't absorb moisture quickly, and it will wick dampness away from your body. This is one of the reasons that wool has been a popular sock fabric for a long time; it will keep your feet dry. Wool is easy to hand wash, and it is surprisingly breathable in hot weather, even though wool clothes are more insulated than cotton. If you can't afford modern technical fabrics or if you want to avoid them, wool is your best option. However, wool can be heavy, which may not be ideal if you need multiple layers.

On the whole, you should avoid clothing that has been made using rayon, viscose, lyocell, and Tencel, as these tend to be water-absorbent materials and therefore will not offer much insulation. Polyester and nylon are better options because they wick moisture and dry very quickly, and they are much lighter than wool.

Sleeping Bags

Having a good sleeping bag is crucial for off-grid survival – whether you are sleeping under the stars or tucked into a cabin somewhere. Unlike traditional duvets or blankets, a sleeping bag provides an enclosed bubble of warmth that will effectively trap your body heat. It insulates your body against the ground's chill, and it encases your head, which is very important. It will ensure that no air is lost in any direction, and it stays close to your body, which massively decreases the loss of heat. Your sleeping bag is one of the essential pieces of kit in dealing with the cold, and you should invest in a good one. You can always add blankets and other insulation later.

A down sleeping bag is often ideal if you are sure that you will be able to keep it dry. Inside a dry shelter, a down sleeping bag is perfect and will offer an excellent level of warmth. It is also light if you need to travel – but it will lose its insulation if it gets wet, and it is not a good idea for sleeping outdoors.

Synthetic sleeping bags are the other standard option. These tend to be heavier than down, and they may not be as warm, but they are much better at handling moisture. They will prove the better option if you sleep out in damp conditions.

As well as thinking about the material, there are several features you should look for in your ideal sleeping bag:

- Draft collar: this helps ensure that the sleeping bag fits snugly around your shoulders and prevents the loss of body heat.
- A hood: many sleeping bags have good hoods, which is the biggest feature of keeping warm. Remember, you lose a large percentage of your body heat through your head.
- Draft tubes: these cover the zipper and reduce the heat loss that otherwise occurs through it. They are crucial for cold weather.

You can supplement your sleeping bag with blankets and an insulated mat for all kinds of conditions – whether you are at home or in the wilds. An insulated mat will make the ground more comfortable to lie on and will prevent the soil from leaching the warmth from your body, so it's an integral part of keeping you cozy. Blankets can be layered up on top of you, and each will provide a bubble of warmth that is crucial to survival. Like clothing, creating multiple layers is far more effective at trapping heat than one thick layer.

If you are in an emergency, you should layer your clothes on top of the sleeping bag once you are inside it. This will keep you much warmer than continuing to wear them. You should also place blankets underneath you because the ground will constantly leach warmth away from your body. If you have access to cardboard or other insulating materials, put these under you, and stay dry if possible.

For those working in fixed off the grid setup, you might prefer to have blankets or a duvet on your bed, but it is still wise to have a sleeping bag available. If cold weather hits or you do not have a reliable heat source, this can make an enormous difference to how warm you can stay. Stow sleeping bags for each party member under the beds or in some other storage spot, even if you don't expect to need them in most circumstances. This could save your life.

Weather Radio

If you live off the grid, one of the essential tools in your kit is your weather radio – and it's worth mentioning here rather than in the chapter about tools because it is such a crucial defense against disasters. When you are off the grid, you will often find that you end up cut off from society and news, even if you attempt to remain engaged. That could be dangerous: weather can change abruptly with very little warning, and if you don't know that a natural disaster is about to strike, you cannot prepare for it.

You should have and use a weather radio. Check it before heading out on an excursion, but also pay attention to it regularly, especially if you live somewhere with frequent natural disasters. A weather radio will let you monitor both local news broadcasts and the national Emergency Alert System, so you know what's going on and how to deal with it. This will give you the information to figure out a survival strategy and implement it before the bad weather hits.

You might be wondering why you need a weather radio rather than a normal radio, and the answer is that it has a few key advantages. Firstly, most weather radios can be run from multiple power sources, so you can use yours no matter what power you've got – some can even be hand-cranked for true emergencies. Weather radios also tend to be more robust, and most have multiple functions and may even let you charge other devices from them. Some have a built-in flashlight, and many are small enough to be easily carried with you.

It's a good idea to look for a weather radio with the following features:

- Able to be charged by hand-cranking, you can use it even if all your other options have failed.

- Lightweight so you can easily transport it.
- USB port for charging smartphones and other emergency devices.
- A flashlight.
- Multiple weather station presets to tune in when you need to easily.
- Excellent reception quality, so you don't find yourself out of range.
- A glow in the dark edge somewhere on the radio so you can locate it.
- Multiple means of powering the battery (e.g. battery slots, solar power compatibility, etc.)
- Other useful display information, e.g. date, humidity, temperature.
- Good volume, so you can hear even in wild conditions.
- Autoscan to find available weather channels.
- Blinking red emergency light.

You may decide that you don't need all of these features, but most of them will be helpful in emergencies and could save your life. Ensure that your weather radio is always stored in the same place (if not traveling with you), so you can quickly grab it if an emergency strikes. Proper planning is key.

Building A Fire: Location

If you have ever spent any time off the grid, you will already be aware that being able to build a fire is probably one of the most crucial skills you can master. Fire gives you access to light, heat, cooked food, safety, and visibility. It may also help you defend yourself against wild animals or other people. Being able to build a fire has saved countless people's lives, and even if you aren't in danger of freezing, it can make your off-grid world massively safer and more comfortable. It lets you dry clothes, make a hot meal, clean water, sterilize equipment, and more.

However, fire has an obvious downside: it is hazardous when poorly handled. If you build a fire in the wrong place, you are liable to damage the environment, yourself, and others. Fire can spread incredibly quickly, and even modern technology isn't always enough to prevent vast wildfires from spreading – so fire always needs to be treated with respect.

Therefore, you must stop and think before you build a fire and choose your location with care; This is true whether you are out in the wild or close to your home – but if you're close to your home, you will probably want to build a proper fire pit, which we will cover in the next section. For now, let's look at how to choose a suitable location when you are in the wild.

You can't set a fire going just anywhere that seems appropriate. You need to identify a safe location, especially if the conditions are windy and the weather has been dry lately. Even if you think the chances of the fire spreading are low, you should be very cautious.

Ideally, your site needs to be sheltered from the wind. It is often best to build a fire in the lee of a rock, beneath a cliff, or even under a tree (provided the tree is tall enough not to be damaged by the flames or at risk of catching fire) to ensure that the wind cannot fan the sparks and spread the fire unexpectedly.

Next, you will need to clear the ground. You should remove all dry vegetation within about 10 feet of your fire site. It may seem like a large area to clear, but it is essential for safety reasons. Once you have cleared an area, scratch away the top surface of the soil to remove the top layer, and set this aside. You can throw it onto any flames that spread.

If you have rocks available, use these to build an edge around your makeshift fire pit; they will make it harder for the sparks to spread. They will also help to protect the flames from sudden gusts of wind.

Don't build your fire at the top of a hill, near a lot of dry grass, in a boggy area, or close to buildings of any sort. Try to make sure you have some non-flammable material available to put the fire out with when you've finished or if it starts to spread.

How To Make A Fire Pit

You can employ some of the above information if you are going to make a fire pit near your home, but you will be able to spend more time and take more care in building. Safety will be crucial, especially if your home is built of flammable materials and you regularly intend to use the fire pit. Ensure that you keep kindling and fuel a reasonable distance from the fire to reduce the risk of it spreading. Ensure the fire is adequately extinguished (which we will cover shortly) before leaving it unattended.

Start by identifying a site a decent distance away from your home. How far it needs to be will depend a little on the wind and other conditions, but make sure you are at least eight feet from the building – preferably further. You don't want any risk of the sparks spreading. The location should be as level as possible, making it easier to make the pit flat. You can level the ground using a shovel if necessary.

Next, make a large circle using an alternating pattern of large and small bricks. Make sure you level the ground further if any bricks do not sit flat against the ground. The more you can do to level this first layer, the easier it will be to create the rest of the pit.

Once you have your first layer, build another layer using alternating small and large bricks. Adjust your approach so that the large bricks overlap across small ones and vice versa, keeping the wall as even and symmetrical as possible. Build several layers up; this will protect your fire and keep the sparks from flying all over the place. It will also mean that you can suspend pots above it or smoke meats across it.

Next, get a hoe and clear the area around your fire pit as much as possible. You should aim to remove all dry plants and – as much as possible – leave only bare earth and rocks; This will reduce the flammability of the surrounding area and reduce the risk of the fire spreading. Take the time to do this properly, as it could mean the difference between a safe fire and an emergency.

If possible, you should then prepare the area with crushed stones, as this will prevent plants from growing back. It will also help keep the bricks in the right places and prevent the fire pit from washing away or falling apart as time passes. You can also tip some crushed stones in the bottom of the fire pit; this will help to ensure that the surface you will be placing your kindling on stays dry because it will help with the drainage.

You may also want to make a cover for your fire pit to keep it dry. A metal or thick wooden board will keep the inside of the pit from getting damp, making it easier to light fires.

Lighting A Fire

Next, let's look at how to light a fire in the wild. It is best to learn this skill from someone in person if possible, as you will pick up many useful tips and get a good visual idea of how to do it, but you can learn the theory here.

To make a fire, you will need a starter (dry grass, small dry twigs, etc.), a heat source (matches, a lighter), and fuel to keep it going (logs, coals). A fire needs oxygen to stay lit, so you need to make sure that you build the sticks into a pyramid that will allow the air to circulate. Alternatively, you can create a grid by stacking sticks from side to side. Place two sticks at one edge, two at the other edge, and then create the same pattern on top, going in the other direction. Keep stacking like this until you have several layers, allowing the flames to pull oxygen in underneath.

There are other ways of building a fire too. You can place one large log to the side and proper sticks up on it or make any other shape that works well for your situation. As long as there is airflow at the base of the fire, this should keep the fire going.

You need to use dry kindling for a fire, so make sure you have some of this available. If you need to dry fuel, you can set it beside the fire, but don't put wet fuel on the fire; it will smoke heavily and will not burn well. You risk putting your fire out if you add a lot of wet fuel.

There are a few different ways to light a fire if you don't have matches, a lighter, or another source of heat. These include:

- Steel and flint
- A magnifying glass
- A plastic bottle and sunlight
- A battery and steel wool

Depending on what you have available, you may be able to light a fire without a lighter. It's always a good idea to carry flint and steel or something similar when you are out and about, plus a small bundle of kindling.

Steel And Flint

Place a piece of tinder on top of the piece of flint, and hold these two in one hand. Take your steel striker in the other hand and strike it against the flint at a 30-degree angle. This should produce sparks, land on the tinder and make it smolder.

Magnifying Glass

You can hold it over the tinder if you have a magnifying glass, a pair of glasses, or anything else that will concentrate the sunlight. Even a mirror can be used to direct an intense beam. Put the tinder in the brightest part of the sunbeam and wait.

Plastic And Sunlight

If you have a plastic water bottle, you can again concentrate the beam of the sun onto the tinder. Use the top concave of the water bottle to reflect the light through the water and onto the tinder. You can also use a Ziploc bag with water in it. Hold it as steady as you can until the tinder ignites.

Battery And Steel Wool

A small bundle of steel wool and a battery will also light a fire. You'll need two AA batteries or one 9 volt battery. Tape the batteries into a series so that the current passes through them (if using several). Extend a piece of steel wool from the battery's positive end to the battery's negative end; the wool should then start to spark and ignite.

Safely Extinguishing A Fire

When you have finished with a fire, it is crucial to put it out properly to reduce the risk of the fire spreading once you have left the area. Even a fire that looks completely dead should not be left, especially if it was a large one; sparks and heat may remain in it for a long time. If the wind picks up, it can easily fan embers back into flames, which could spread fast.

The safest way to extinguish a campfire is to let it die down low and then pour water on it. If there is a lot of smoke and steam, wait a few minutes and then pour more water on it. Pour water on the boundaries around the fire pit, as this will make it harder for the fire to spread outside its boundary if the embers do get fanned.

Try spreading the wood and embers out, too; This will help them cool faster and reduce the risk of hot pockets remaining and reigniting the fire. Add more water until the embers stop hissing, and don't just pour the water onto the red embers.

If you have ashes that can easily be scooped onto the embers, this can help to smother them and put out any remaining flames.

If you don't have water to extinguish a fire safely, you should dig up some damp soil and stir it into the embers, burying any still hot. The wetter the soil, the more effectively it will put the fire out, although even dry soil should help cool the embers down and prevent the fire from reigniting.

Summary

In this chapter, we've covered:

- The dangers of getting too cold.
- How to choose the correct clothing for keeping warm in the wild, including material properties and the clothing that should be chosen.
- Sleeping bags and why they are important.
- What to look for in a weather radio.
- How to choose the right location for a fire in the wild.
- How to build a fire pit near a dwelling.
- How to light a fire.
- How to extinguish a fire safely.

In the following chapter, we will look at how you can find or make shelter when you are lost in the wild, so you don't find yourself exposed to the elements if something should go wrong.

4

Finding Or Making Shelter

"Every powerful storm will help us to make a stronger shelter."

-Mehmet Murat Ildan

In this chapter, we will look at why you need a shelter and what kinds of shelters you can build in different terrains and seasons. After that, we will look at some techniques for building good shelters, what materials you should use, and the location you might choose. We will also cover keeping cool when the weather is dangerously hot.

No matter the climate you live in, you are likely to need shelter from the elements if you are out and about. Even if temperatures are mild, you are likely to be left dealing with rain, sunshine, strong winds, and more. If you don't have any way to protect yourself and your belongings from the elements, you are unlikely to survive well in the wild, even if conditions aren't extreme.

If conditions are extreme, the need for shelter becomes urgent. Whether you are facing hot or cold weather or major precipitation, you must have a means to stay out of the worst weather, even if your shelter is makeshift and doesn't offer you complete protection.

Before you go out in the wilds, even if you don't plan on staying out, it's important to learn how to make a shelter and be aware of the resources that are likely to be at your disposal in the local environment. It will give you a much better chance of survival if something should go wrong while you are out there.

The Need For A Shelter In The Wilderness

You might be wondering if you need shelter, especially if you don't plan to stay out overnight for long periods or if your current environment is relatively temperate. However, you never know when the weather may turn or if something is going to go wrong, and if you are left without shelter, you could find yourself in serious trouble.

Having a shelter massively increases your chances of survival in harmful conditions. For example, suppose you are caught in a heavy rainstorm. You could quickly develop hypothermia even if the air temperature is not extremely cold because having wet clothes lowers your body temperature quickly. If you can't get under shelter and get dry, you may be in danger. The biggest threat you will face while out in the wild is loss of body heat, particularly at night when temperatures drop, and you are more likely to be inactive. A shelter is vital for reducing the loss of body heat.

A shelter also makes it possible to safely gather food and store your possessions. Some shelters could offer protection from animals or at least make it more difficult for animals to steal food. A shelter provides you with a spot to sleep at night and to carry resources to, and it may also make you more visible to rescue efforts. You can stack firewood inside to keep it dry or give damp wood a chance to dry out, and you will have far more ability to stay warm throughout the night.

For many people surviving in the wild, a shelter represents the ability to exert some control over the surrounding environment. It provides warmth, dryness, security, protection from the wind, and more. Don't underestimate the importance of a shelter, and prioritize learning how to build one if you spend any significant amount of time outdoors in remote places.

Before reading more on this subject, you should never light a fire inside your shelter, except if you are in danger of freezing. The risk of it setting fire to your shelter is much too high, and it makes causes a buildup of smoke that could be deadly. If you need a fire, it's much better to light it at a safe distance from your shelter and use it to dry clothes, heat rocks, warm a hot drink, or create warmth in other ways. Make this a firm rule at all times.

Different Types Of Shelters You Can Build Depending On The Terrain And The Season

The kind of shelter you need to build will be dependent on the weather you are dealing with and the resources you have. It is a good idea to familiarize yourself with the specifics of your situation thoroughly. In this section, I will cover as many different kinds of shelters as possible. You can then adapt these to suit your situation, what you have, and need. Various shelters you can build include:

- A lean-to shelter
- A platform shelter

- A snow cave (cold weather shelter)
- A leaf hut
- A debris shelter
- A tepee
- A ramada shelter (hot weather shelter)
- A pit shelter
- An igloo (cold weather shelter)
- A Quinzhee (cold weather shelter)
- A fallen tree shelter
- An A-frame shelter

Remember that you will need different shelters according to the terrain and the seasons. Stay dry and warm in the winter, as cold temperatures can be hazardous, and focus on airy shelters in the summer. Now, let's learn about these common shelters in more detail.

Lean-To

You have probably seen lean-to shelters plenty of times in movies and picture books, and they are an elementary kind of shelter that is easy to build with many different types of resources. A lean-to is usually used in areas with plenty of wood available, and it can provide shelter from rain, wind, snow, and cold. However, because the end is open, it isn't enormously warm.

Many people build a fire at the entrance to the lean-to to warm the inside and prevent heat from escaping from the shelter. Be careful if you will do this and make sure sparks cannot spread to your shelter.

Lean-to shelters are ideal because they are quick and easy to build. You can use any cliff face, large boulder, tree, or other structure to form the back wall of the lean-to and then lean wood up against it. This kind of shelter is flexible and can be made with almost anything, as long as you have access to poles. Lean-to shelters can be made warmer by insulating them and waterproofing the outside with moss, grass, or plastic.

Platform Shelter

A platform shelter can be useful if you are in a situation where staying at ground level is unsafe; This may be because of animals or insects that could bite, sting, or otherwise attack you, especially when sleeping. A platform shelter is designed to get you off the ground and out of harm's way.

Platform shelters won't be possible to build in all situations, and they tend to require more skill. What you build will have to be able to support your weight reliably, or you might fall. You need to have practiced building one of these shelters in advance because otherwise, you are unlikely to be able to build it well enough to be secure. You are also very likely to need tools to build a platform shelter safely, which you may not have available.

However, there are situations in which you will need to make a platform shelter, and you may find you have the resources to do it, depending on your environment, so it's worth having this kind of shelter in your database.

Snow Cave

If you are caught in snowy conditions, a snow cave is the easiest kind of shelter you can build, although you will need a suitable spade or shovel, or you will put yourself in danger of freezing when it takes to make one of these.

A snow cave is built into a snowdrift, and it is an excellent way to escape from the wind chill, hostile creatures, precipitation, and more. It will not be particularly warm, and it is possible to maintain the internal temperature at around 32 degrees F. This could keep you alive in freezing conditions. Your body heat will be crucial for keeping the cave warm.

Leaf Hut

A leaf hut will provide you with a warm, reasonably large, enclosed area, and it is easy to build if you can find the right natural resources (wooden poles, leaves, etc.). Leaf huts can be warm and dry because of the insulating layer of leaves, and they are a great option if you are going to stay in one place for a while.

Leaf huts often take some time to build because they require a lot of materials, and they will be impossible in many areas (e.g. if you are somewhere with few trees), but they will work well in some situations.

Leaf huts can be adapted to suit ongoing needs and may be suitable for larger groups. They are also warmer than a lean-to shelter because they are mainly enclosed beside the door to keep heat loss to a minimum.

Debris Shelter

A debris shelter is much simpler to make and requires fewer materials, although you will still need long poles to build one. There will be three poles necessary for this kind of shelter, and you'll need to gather up lots of leaf litter to cover the shelter with.

Debris shelters tend to be easy to create, but they can't be made in areas without leaves and strong sticks. You will require one of the poles to be taller than your head height.

Tepee

You have probably seen tepees on TV and in books, and they are often associated with foreign countries. A tepee is one of the few shelters initially designed to hold fire, with a central hole to let smoke vent from inside. However, you should be very cautious about building a fire inside one of these despite the design; it could still be unsafe.

Traditionally, tepees were made using wooden poles and animal skins, and they were designed to be easily transportable. You can take them down and assemble them quickly, but they are not enormously easy to build in the wilderness, and if you don't have any experience in doing so, they may not be the best shelter. A tepee may be impractical unless you have easy access to tarpaulins and wooden poles. However, they do have their uses, and if you have the materials, they are one of the few shelters you can take with you when you travel.

Ramada Shelter

A ramada shelter is used mainly for protection from the sun, as it has no walls; it is just an overhead shelter. It will not trap heat around you or reduce the wind or rain, but it will keep the sun off you. If you are in a hot area, this kind of shelter could be invaluable for survival.

Some ramada shelters do have one wall to increase the shade they provide, but most are open to improve air movement and keep the insides cool. If you want to include a wall, make sure you are not blocking the wind from entering the shelter because this will help keep the temperatures low.

Ramada shelters can be made from anything readily available, but they often incorporate a piece of fabric as the main overhead part. Other materials tend to be in short supply in arid regions, so you may not have access to wood or other plant matter with which to weave a shade.

Pit Shelter

A pit shelter can be ideal if you don't have a lot of materials, and it's an excellent way to hide if you don't want your shelter to be very obvious. This kind of shelter is usually semi-permanent because a lot of work goes into hollowing out the ground, and it won't be transportable. A pit shelter is a lot easier to make if you have a shovel, but it can be dug out by hand if necessary.

You still need natural resources to make the roof of a pit shelter. It will have a door for you to access the dugout through and should protect you from rain, sun, and other bad weather. Dugouts have some advantages: they are highly customizable, and it's easy to make storage space and seating arrangements. They are also an excellent way to get out of the wind almost entirely without building dense walls.

However, you may have issues with drainage, and it can be challenging to heat a pit shelter. If it rains a lot, you will need to make sure the water drains away from the parts of the pit shelter you use, or it will become impractical and uncomfortable.

It is sometimes safe to have a fire in a pit shelter, but you will need to make sure the shelter is extremely well ventilated to do this. If you are going to be stuck in the wild for a long time, a pit shelter is an excellent option.

Igloo

Unlike a snow cave, an igloo is built of snow blocks rather than carved into a snowdrift. It lets you choose where to put the igloo, but it does mean a lot more work.

Igloos tend to be relatively large and may be an excellent way to shelter a large group if the conditions are bad. They take a lot of work to build, and you must know how to build one to ensure that the dome is stable, or it could be an unsafe shelter. Only practiced, skilled survivalists should attempt to build igloos, although they are probably the best option for long-term sheltering in the snow.

Quinzhee

Quinzhees are like snow caves, but instead of simply using a snowdrift where you happen to find one, you will pile the snow up in a convenient area. It will then be hollowed out to create a cave, allowing you to get out of the wind.

It takes quite a long time and a lot of energy to make a quinzhee, so make sure you are up to the task. If you are already exhausted and cold, make a snow cave instead to have somewhere to retreat to, and think about building a more convenient shelter when you have rested and got warm.

Fallen Tree Shelter

If you find a fallen tree, this can be an excellent option for making a shelter for yourself. Fallen trees will provide you with a ready-made structure that you can work with, saving you enormous amounts of time. However, you should make sure that the tree is stable before you start using it to build a shelter, or you could be risking your safety.

Fallen trees can be used to create lean-to shelters, but you can also drape a tarp or a blanket over one if you have these materials available. Peg the four corners out with stones, and you've got a makeshift shelter with very little time needed.

A-Frame Shelter

An a-frame shelter is quick and easy to build and makes an excellent alternative to the lean-to if you cannot find a wall to build against. You will need a long, sturdy branch, plus shorter sticks, so this is best made in woodland. You can prop up both ends of the branch to make a level roof, or just prop up one end and make a shelter that narrows to the ground at one end.

This shelter can be reasonably warm and cozy, although it shares the lean-to's disadvantage of having open ends that heat can escape through. A-frame shelters can be made in varying sizes to suit the number of people you need to shelter or make room for provisions/gear.

Building A Shelter, The Materials You Should Use, And Picking A Location

Next, let's find out how to build the shelters mentioned above. You may need to adapt the instructions to suit your particular environment, but they should give you a good starting point. It is imperative to think about stability when building a shelter, especially when out in windy conditions. You don't want any risk of it collapsing on top of you!

Build your shelter somewhere with as much natural protection as possible, but don't position it right at the bottom of a slope, or you will find that it gets very wet as rainwater runs down the hill. The shelter of trees or boulders may be a good spot. If you are waiting for a rescue effort, choose somewhere more open so that you will be visible from the air. You should also think about how far away the nearest water source is and check you are a good distance away from animal burrows or dens.

It's good to practice building these shelters before you need them; This can be a fun activity with kids and make you far more confident and competent if you need to build one in an emergency. If possible, train with an expert because you will pick up on tips suited to your specific area, and you are also likely to learn a few extra tricks that will make your shelter-building efficient. In the meantime, however, here are some basic how-to guides for each kind of shelter.

Lean-To

Remember, a lean-to shelter is one single wall made up of multiple poles, supported by two vertical poles driven into the ground, with one pole set between them.

Start by cutting your two vertical poles to the right height – ideally higher than your head so you can stand within the shelter. Once you have these poles, decide how wide you want the shelter to be and drive them into the ground this far apart. Make sure they are stable before you move on to the next step.

Once the poles are in the ground, cut another pole so that it is long enough to be placed between them; this will rest on top of them and support your wall. Lash it in place with cord so it can't slip.

Next, cut multiple shorter poles, and lean these up against the pole you have fixed in place. Create a wall from these poles, pressing them into the earth or banking the earth up around them if necessary to reduce any risk of them slipping. This wall should face the wind to provide as much windbreak as possible.

Once your wall is stable and finished, you can cover it in mud, leaves, moss, or other debris to improve its waterproofing and windproofing. If you have blankets, a tarpaulin, or other materials, you can also use these.

Platform Shelter

Make sure you have sturdy enough materials to build a platform shelter before you start putting energy into this. Think about the platform you will lie on, the structure that will elevate it from the ground, and the roof. You also need to think about the height you need to achieve.

If you are just trying to stay away from wet ground and small predators like scorpions, snakes, or insects, you don't need to go more than 50 centimeters off the ground. However, to get safety from large predators, you will need to be a meter or more into the air. Even predators that can climb do not often hunt in trees, so this should provide enough height to keep you reasonably safe.

You will almost always be building in a tree for a tall shelter. Use thick, sturdy poles between the branches, and make sure everything you are using can easily hold your weight. Lash the poles into place against the tree branches so that they cannot slip or roll while in the shelter, and make sure it is wide enough that you are not likely to roll off while asleep. Consider putting some extra poles in as "sides" to stop you from falling.

Ideally, you will also want to construct a roof above you to provide further protection from predators and help the rain roll-off. If you are building your platform shelter close to the ground, a tall lean-to may work, but if you are high up in the tree, you will need to improvise as best you can using tree branches, tarpaulins, blankets, or any other material you have. It is important to use something lightweight so that if it comes loose and falls, it won't hurt you or knock your platform out of the tree.

Platform shelters are not easy to get right, so if you are likely to need one, make sure you practice with an expert first. An improperly built platform shelter is dangerous. You may wish to consider carrying a lightweight hammock with you as an alternative if you are going to a location where sleeping at ground level could be dangerous.

Snow Cave

To build a snow cave, identify a snowdrift in a sheltered area. Make sure there is no risk of avalanches. Next, walk back and forth over the snowdrift, compacting the snow and making it dense enough to dig under. Keep walking until you are satisfied you have pressed the snow down into a tight wall.

Next, take your shovel and dig an entrance into the wall, as low down as possible. You should then start digging upward. The sleeping area should be higher than the entrance; this is the best way to trap heat inside and prevent loss through the entrance.

Once you have hollowed out the inside of the snowdrift, make a few small holes for ventilation. Otherwise, you risk suffocating. Little heat will be lost through small holes, and they will ensure the air can flow in and out of the shelter.

Built yourself an insulating layer to sleep on using any material you have so you are not resting against the snow. A sleeping bag, insulating mat, blankets, cardboard, or clothing can be used to create this layer. Make it as thick as you can to minimize the loss of body heat to the snow underneath.

Leaf Hut

A leaf hut is usually made by cutting lots of large, long poles and forming most of a circle, with a gap left for the door. The poles can be driven into the ground, with the tops interlocking to give the hut structure.

To achieve this, start with three poles. Space the ends that touch the ground out to form the perimeter of the hut and pull the ends in the air together. The height will depend on how tall your poles are, but you should be able to sit comfortably inside. Lash the tops of the poles tightly together to stand up independently.

Once this has been done, you can cut the other poles to size and start spacing them between your three main struts to create a loose wall. The three main poles should support them, and you can interlock them so that they hold each other in place.

You can start using smaller, thinner branches to weave between the struts when you have a structure, working horizontally. You don't need to fill in too many gaps but adding these horizontal branches will make it easier to build up a layer of moss and leaves. When you have a good structure, collect up as much moss as you can, and use this to create an insulating layer all around the leaf hut. Next, add a layer of leaves. If you can't find moss, just use leaves. These will help to waterproof the structure, while the moss will insulate it.

The deeper you can make the moss and leaves, the warmer and drier your hut will be. It's worth gathering leaves from the surrounding area and adding to your insulation over several days, especially if you plan to stay in the hut for some time.

Debris Shelter

A debris shelter can be built with one long, straight pole and two Y-shaped sticks. The Y-shaped sticks will make the front end of the shelter in a /\ shape. The longer pole will be propped up on these two sticks at one end and run down to touch the ground on the other end. Drive the Y-shaped sticks deeply into the ground to be stable and interlock their ends with the other pole.

You can then use short sticks to create ribs along the long stick. Bank up some earth or use leaves, sticks, straw, or any other available debris to fill in between the ribs, creating a solid wall on either side.

Tepee

A tepee can be made in much the same way as a leaf hut, but it tends to be smaller, and you will not be using leaves to cover the shelter. Instead, you will need a tarpaulin, some tent material, blankets, canvas, or treated animal skins (if you want to be traditional).

Get a piece of canvas approximately 15 x 30 feet and a selection of long, sturdy poles. Ideally, you want about 12 poles. Next, use a sharp knife to cut a tepee pattern into your canvas; This is a semi-circle with two notches cut on either side, plus an extra tapered flap on either side of the centre to shape the door. You will also need to leave two additional rectangles of fabric on one side of the semi-circle, one before the notch and one between the notch and the door flaps. Cut a small "v" into the fabric's very center, and your cover is complete.

Next, use a natural rope to erect the frame, starting with a tripod and lashing the poles together with a clove hitch. These three poles can then be erected, and the remaining poles added. Tie the canvas tightly to your "lift" pole, roll it around the pole, lift it into place, and then unfurl the canvas and wrap it tightly around the structural poles until it is in position.

Ramada Shelter

Ideally, you should gather up four sturdy poles, although you can make this shelter with three in a pinch. You will also need branches, tarps, or other material for the roof part.

Drive the poles into the ground, far enough apart to easily lie down between them. If you have four poles, make a rectangle; if you only have three, make a triangle. Next, stretch your tarp or blankets between the poles, or cover them with branches or any other material that you can find. The idea is to create as much shade as possible overhead without reducing the airflow.

Don't depend on a ramada for overnight shelter in a hot place, as temperatures can drop very low overnight. You need a proper, insulated shelter if you stay out during the night. You may be able to incorporate this in your ramada by building a lean-to alongside it, but make sure you don't block too much airflow, or the ramada will get hot during the day.

Pit Shelter

A pit shelter is reasonably easy to make; simply dig out the ground to the size and shape you want. However, you should think carefully about the location and ensure that the soil will not collapse inward. If the soil is loose, use strong poles to reinforce it, or you are at risk of getting hurt. Don't dig too close to water, at the bottom of a hill, or anywhere you are likely to get flooded.

You may need to dig a drainage ditch to allow water to run out of your shelter. You also need to create a roof; This can be done using strong poles and leaves or moss, preferably with a plastic sheet for waterproofing. Make sure you leave an opening to easily get in and out of the shelter.

Inside the shelter, bank up some earth to sleep on so you aren't lying at the lowest point, likely wet. Insulate this with cardboard, blankets, leaves, or other available material.

Igloo

Remember that an igloo should only be built if you are in a situation that allows you to work with a big group and have tools and appropriate clothing. These shelters take a long time to build and require experience. You will only use snow that comes from inside the igloo to build the shelter; do not take snow from outside.

Outline the wall for your igloo, making sure it is less than 10 feet in diameter because it may be unstable otherwise. Once you have a defined area, compact the snow within it and begin cutting it out in blocks. Most blocks should be around 3 feet x 15 inches x 8 inches, although you can adjust this if necessary. Pack the snow down hard, and start assembling the blocks around the perimeter, fitting them tightly. When you have made the first layer, use your knife to cut a slope into the blocks to form the curve of the igloo.

When necessary, cut more snow blocks from inside your igloo and begin adding the second layer. You will need to start shaping the blocks as you narrow the circle of the dome. Work from the inside of the igloo, getting each row you make to gradually slope inward, working so that the blocks meet in a dome above your head.

Keep cutting blocks from inside the igloo, decreasing in size as you work inward, beveling the edges to ensure that the ceiling blocks fit well against the layer below and are at no risk of falling. The last blocks of the igloo are hard to fit, so work slowly and carefully until you get them into place.

Cut small crescent-shaped vents into the sides of the igloo to allow CO_2 to escape, and then cut the bottom blocks and clear yourself a pathway out of the igloo. You can stack more blocks around this to minimize heat loss and create a porch.

Don't try to build an igloo without practice; it may not be safe and could collapse on top of you.

Quinzhee

Quinzhees are much easier to build, so they should be your choice unless you spend a long time in a cold environment and know how to build an igloo. To build one, pile up some gear (e.g. backpacks) on a tarpaulin and then shovel snow on top in a thick layer.

Pack the snow down hard until it is two feet thick in every direction, and then get a good amount of sticks of at least twelve inches and push them into the snow mound. You ideally want at least 30 of these sticks, preferably more, as they are your guides for how far to dig the snow out from the inside.

Once this is done, burrow into the quinzhee from one side and pull the tarpaulin and gear out. Start excavating the snow until you reach the ends of the sticks.

It will leave you with 12 inches of snow for the dome of your quinzhee, ensuring it is strong enough to stay up. When you have finished, make a ventilation hole in the roof, and your quinzhee is finished.

Fallen Tree Shelter

If you have a tarpaulin, you can make a fallen tree shelter very easily. Make sure the tree is stable, and then spread the tarpaulin over it and pin it down at the sides using rocks. If you don't have a tarpaulin, you can use branches and saplings to create walls on either side of the tree, like lean-to shelters, and then use debris, leaves, and moss to pack the walls and improve their windproofing and waterproofing.

A-Frame Shelter

An a-frame shelter can be made by balancing a long pole between the branches of two trees. Ideally, you want branches that are at approximately the same height. If you can only find one tree, you can drive the other end of the pole into the ground to make a shelter that is low at one end, with a high entrance at the other.

If you can find two trees, put the pole between two branches and make sure it is stable. Next, cut branches to approximately the same length, ensuring they are long enough to lean from the ground to the pole. These will make the walls on either side of the shelter. Again, you can pad them with moss if you choose to. This shelter is similar to the lean-to but has two walls instead of one.

Keeping Cool

We've already touched on using a ramada shelter to stay cool, but there are other things you can do to keep yourself cool when the weather is hot. A shelter will be necessary to keep you out of the sun, avoid the risk of heat stroke, and keep provisions fresh – but what other techniques can you employ?

Soak your clothes. You should only do this if you have water to spare, but it's a good way to cool off if you need to stay active when the weather is hot.

Wear long sleeves; This might sound counter-intuitive when you want to strip down as little as possible, but long sleeves will protect you from the sun. The same goes for long pants and a hat if possible – although not a woolly one.

Work in the coolest parts of the day, the morning and the evening. When the sun is at its hottest, retreat to your shelter and stay cool.

Prioritize staying hydrated because this allows you to sweat, keeping you cool. Make sure you have a good supply of water and the means to collect and purify more if you are in a hot area.

If your water is too limited to soak your clothes, but you can spare a little, wet a headscarf and tie it around your neck or wrists. The blood supply is close to the surface here so that the cooling will be more effective.

Remember that the ground can be cool, so if you aren't in a desert, digging yourself a hollow in the shade may help you cool off. Mud can also protect you from the sun's heat and reduce the risk of sunburn.

Summary

In this chapter, we've covered:

- Why shelter is so important to have when in the wilderness.
- What kinds of shelters you can build, the terrains they are suitable for, and the weather you might face in different seasons.
- How to build the shelters and the kinds of materials you can use.
- Some tips for keeping cool.

In the following chapter, we will look at how to stay safe in your off-grid home, including how to defend yourself when in a permanent shelter and a temporary one. We will look at various defenses, including dogs, early warning systems, and structure hardening. We are also going to cover fire safety.

5

How To Stay Safe At Home

"Safety brings first aid to the uninjured."

-F. S. Hughes

Knowing how to look after your home and stay safe when in it is a crucial aspect of going off the grid. You may face different threats and hazards, and preparation will make a key difference. It's worth talking about safety precautions with your group before setting up your off-grid space and identifying likely threats that you might need to deal with.

Home Defense While at Your Off-Grid Home

You can't exactly call the police to come to your off-grid home (in most circumstances), which means home defense will be down to you. Whether your intruders are humans or animals, you need to have weapons available and a defense plan.

If you are trained and have a license, a firearm is generally a good idea for off-grid security, even if you only plan to use it against animals. You should also consider bear spray, loud alarms to frighten off beasts, and bright lights.

Not everyone can own or operate a gun, but you should also have some other weapons available, whether you can or not. A knife is a crucial tool for many kinds of off-grid survival, and it will serve you well in home defense. A knife allows you to deal with an attacker in a way that is less likely to be lethal, so it's a good option if you don't want to kill, but it may not be as effective against animals.

A strong metal rod can also be valuable if you need to defend yourself and may have other uses around your off-grid home.

Think too about other things that will keep your home safer and make it less appealing to approaching humans or animals. Things like motion-triggered lights are a major deterrent, as they alert the occupants to the intruder and will startle animals. Humans are more likely to leave as they know they are at risk of being detected.

You should assess the entry points of your home for weaknesses that might tempt an attack. If possible, windows should be made of toughened glass or have shutters that can be closed, and doors should be reinforced. How tough you can make your structure will depend upon what it has been built of, but as a bare minimum, make sure you can shut and lock all entry points, including windows. Even a weak lock is better than no lock.

A good alarm system is also a plus if you have access to power, although you can build a makeshift alarm system by hanging things like cans and wind chimes in common walkways. We'll cover these further in the section on early warning systems.

Always start your home defense planning by thinking about what intruders you might have to face and how they are likely to approach. Do not only prepare for humans – think about the animals you could encounter. If you keep food in your off-grid home, you may attract animals, including bears. You should have a warning system and a strategy for dealing with as many possible scenarios as possible.

Home Defense While Living in a Temporary Shelter Away From Your Off-Grid Home

It can be much harder to set up a good defense system when you are in a temporary shelter, because your shelter will provide minimal protection. A tent, tarpaulin, or even a lean-to or leaf hut will not offer much resistance against intruders of either the human or animal variety.

You will therefore be dependent on good planning and a weapon or two. If you are going to carry a gun – or indeed any other kind of weapon – you should ensure that you have enough training to use it safely. You don't want to hurt yourself or another party member while trying to defend yourself. Ensure that you have plenty of ammo, and always know where your weapon is, especially at night.

Even if your structure is of minimal defense, secure what you can before going to sleep. This might involve closing and tying shut a makeshift door, shutting a tent and locking the zippers together, or even just spreading dry twigs around your shelter so that you are more likely to be woken by an intruder approaching.

If you have a choice about where you are camping, it's a good idea to choose somewhere that is sheltered and not too close to water. Water often attracts predators, and although you want access, being too close may be unsafe. Being tucked out of sight, away from pathways, may help you stay safe from human intruders, so make sure your shelter is concealed. Consider adding sticks, leaves, moss, and other debris to the shelter you have built to keep it hidden.

If you will be staying in a temporary shelter for some time and you are concerned about intruders, there are other things that you can do to increase the defense of the area. For example, you might choose to dig a trench around the shelter if you have the tools and time.

Sometimes, you may find yourself in the wild with minimal resources and few ways to defend yourself. If this happens, consider making weapons from natural resources. You can sharpen sturdy sticks into weapons, longer branches into javelins, and use rocks as ammunition. It can be shaped into a makeshift knife if you can find flint. Stock up on stones and at least a few sharpened tools, even if you have to make them yourself because you have none to hand.

Ideally, however, you will carry weapons whenever you walk out in the wild, especially if you plan to stay away from your home overnight or longer.

Structure Hardening

You may have heard of structure hardening, which is often used to defend homes against natural disasters such as hurricanes. However, it can also help make an off-grid dwelling stronger and more intruder-resistant. Few of these methods will withstand determined attacks, but they can make you significantly safer. Let's explore some of the options.

You can use simple plywood to reinforce doors, providing a secondary layer that will make the wood much stronger and capable of withstanding an assault. Your doors should also have strong locks and solid frames to sit inside. If you are building your cabin yourself, make sure to use 3-inch screws and a large, long strike plate. You can also fasten a metal strip under the deadbolt to give it more strength and structure against a wooden frame.

Windows should also be hardened where possible. You can buy security film that will help protect the glass from shattering. You can also install metal bars across the windows as additional security. Growing spiky plants outside a window can provide a further deterrent for long-term protection.

Perimeter Defense

Making a perimeter defense is one of the best ways to secure an off-grid home, and it may help deter animals and people. In general, a perimeter defense will take the form of a fence, although you can also use plants, rocks, or other materials to make it more difficult to approach your dwelling.

You can build your perimeter defense using the natural resources you have to hand or buy fencing and erect it. Some people dig mounds into the earth to make it harder to approach their off-grid homes from certain angles.

You can also scatter things like holly leaves, old bramble, thistles, and other sharp, spiky materials in the vicinity. However, make sure you keep pathways clear to enter and exit your dwelling easily. While it may seem valuable to close off all routes, this could trap you near your home, which may not be very safe.

If you are short on spiky materials, you can simply create dead hedges from cut wood. This is easy to do; you just weave together old sticks, branches, and dead plants to form an impassable mesh. Even if someone or something does break through, they are likely to make a lot of noise, alerting you to their presence.

You should not create a perimeter defense designed to injure someone who is approaching. It is unsafe and illegal in many states, so doing so could get you into trouble with the law, especially if it hurts someone. Digging and concealing pits, creating tripwires, or otherwise rigging the environment to make it unsafe for someone approaching is dangerous and illegal and should be avoided. Booby traps are not the solution to keeping your home safe.

Early Warning Systems

An early warning system is also a great idea; it will alert you to animals or people coming near the house. Start by working out how far you want your early warning system to be from your home. You need to hear it when it sounds clear, but it should be far enough that you get a good amount of warning when someone is approaching. You may find that it helps to talk to other party members and agree upon a distance together.

Early warning systems usually rely on either audible or visual alerts, and these will give you a sense of which direction the intruder is approaching. They may involve triggering a light or an alarm, which will tell you that someone is coming. An audible system may be more effective if you need it to wake you up and might also be better for frightening off animals.

You might think that an early warning system isn't working for you, especially if you have limited or unreliable access to power off the grid – but actually, many systems will run reliably on battery power for long periods. LED motion lights, if bright enough, can easily deter both animals and people by startling them. If even that isn't an option, you can still create a basic early warning system by hanging up or balancing items that will make a noise when disturbed.

Many people use tin cans suspended on a wire, with the cans dangling at around head height (so the wire is not a hazard). Fill the cans with stones. Someone approaching the house will disturb the cans, creating a clattering noise that alerts you to their approach. Balancing rocks near pathways can also work, although this may make less noise and needs to be re-set each time disturbed.

Make sure your early warning system is tricky enough to trigger that it won't constantly be disturbed by the wind or by your own group members coming and going, or you may find that you stop responding to it as you should. Ideally, it should only be set off by someone unexpected approaching, although this may not be possible with some motion-triggered devices.

Traps And Funneling

As mentioned above, you need to be cautious about using traps to deter intruders because this puts you in an awkward position in terms of the law. It can also be hazardous to you and genuine visitors, especially after dark, so steer clear of setting up random traps around your home. However, don't dismiss the area entirely.

Funneling is a technique often used in hunting, and the idea is to push the prey into the right area so that it can be caught. Although you aren't treating intruders as prey, a similar principle applies here. Instead, you are trying to push them into open spaces where they are more likely to be spotted and less likely to hang around.

To set up this arrangement, you need to survey the area surrounding your home with care and assess the different spaces. *If you were trying to sneak around, where would you hide? What bushes, structures, and debris could provide shelter? What could you duck beneath?*

These spaces you want to push intruders away from, forcing them to stay on the pathway or in the open. You can funnel an intruder into open spaces by making the other spaces difficult to pass through. For example, piling up boxes or old tools in hideaways or along the edges of the paths makes intruders far less likely to stray into these areas. They are also more likely to make a noise and alert you if they attempt it.

Situational Awareness

Being aware of your surroundings is crucial for staying safe off the grid. You should always be alert to what's happening in your local vicinity and whether it presents any dangers to you or others.

You should practice being aware of your situation whenever you have an opportunity, particularly in a new area with potential unknown threats. For example, if you are somewhere where you might run into dangerous animals, you should be careful and look out for signs of what you might be dealing with.

Things like animal tracks, droppings, and damage to the local environment should help you establish what is likely to be in the local area. You might also pick up scents for certain creatures. If other people are in the area, you might find evidence of fires, dwellings, or debris (e.g., litter).

Developing situational awareness isn't easy, but you can do a few simple things to make a start, such as not listening to music while you are out and about and changing up your routine regularly so that you don't operate on autopilot.

Some people say that situational awareness involves perception, comprehension, and projection. Below is an example:

You are walking in a new area. You use your perception to assess the local environment and notice a pile of feathers under a bush. Your comprehension of the situation tells you that a predator must be nearby but that the bird was small and the only predators in this area hunt at night. You project that it is safe to keep walking, but you look for signs of fresh tracks and make sure that you have a weapon to hand.

Situational awareness is about taking in information, assessing the information, and acting accordingly. It could save your life if you make this your standard operating mode.

You should also work on this as a team effort, making sure you involve others in your group. Practice identifying common threat signs and discussing how you would resolve the dangers that could arise from them. This group exercise is a great way to improve collective and individual awareness.

Dogs

Having one or more dogs is a great way to keep yourself safe while in the wilderness, especially if you choose large canine companions. A dog's senses are far sharper than a person's, so your dog may alert you to danger before you detect it yourself. A dog is also a great deterrent against people and many other animals, and dogs are fiercely protective of their owners. They will alert you to someone approaching your home or danger out in the brush, and they are powerful fighters.

Many people operating off the grid choose to take a dog or several dogs with them for safety. A dog may also be able to assist you in:

- Detecting intruders
- Frightening intruders
- Avoiding nearby animals
- Hunting and finding food
- Alerting you to nearby danger
- Fighting off animals/intruders in extreme circumstances

Some people also use "Beware of dog" signs even if they don't have a dog – while this won't be effective against everyone, it may be enough to encourage some intruders to pause or choose another location.

Of course, having dogs does bring some additional responsibilities and advantages; you must feed, care for, and protect your animals just as they protect you. You will need a reliable source of food and water for them, the ability to keep them warm, and the ability to keep them safe. You must make sure you control the dog when something unexpected happens so it doesn't attack something dangerous and get hurt or escalate a situation you might otherwise be able to walk away from. Teach your dog faultless recall to get it away from other animals, or it may prove liability and an asset.

Nighttime Security

Nighttime security when you are off the grid can be challenging if you don't have electricity because you will usually operate in the dark. You should always have emergency lighting of some sort, even if it's just a flashlight that can be hand cranked.

If possible, use battery-powered motion sensor lights around your off-grid home, so you know that you will never be operating entirely in the dark; This can help you when you need to leave the house at night and deter intruders.

Practice a nighttime routine of locking doors and windows, just as you would in an ordinary home, and make sure you secure outside areas such as sheds and gates if necessary.

Fire Safety

It's crucial to be aware of the dangers posed by fire, especially at night. If your off-grid home depends upon fire for heating, it may be tempting to leave a fire burning all night, but this could be dangerous. It is always best to put fires out or leave them as very low flames, protected by proper fireguards, with no fuel nearby. Keep the area around a fire clear from flammable materials.

Ensure your property is fitted with smoke detectors and carbon monoxide alarms, and regularly check that these are working. You should also equip your home with a fire extinguisher, kept in an accessible spot.

Fire safety outside should also be taken seriously. Before leaving a fire unattended, put it out so that sparks cannot fly and catch on a nearby brush. Have water tanks available for putting out wayward fires; you can rig these up with a pump and a hose, so you have your fire-fighting kit. Tanks should be situated uphill where possible so that the pump is assisted by gravity.

Prevention is always better than cure, however. Use a good fire guard and keep the area surrounding a fire pit free from any flammables. Do not leave fires unattended, especially in windy weather. Make sure you have several buckets of non-flammable material such as soil or sand nearby to throw onto the flames if they do spread. These can be used in an emergency if there is no water available and should help you to put out any spreading fires.

Summary

In this chapter, we've covered:

- How to defend your off-grid home.
- How to defend a temporary off-grid shelter.
- How to harden your windows and doors.
- What a perimeter defense is.
- Early warning systems you can set up.
- The use of traps and funneling to protect your property.
- How to increase your situational awareness.
- The value of dogs and the disadvantages you should consider before getting one.
- Staying secure at night.
- How to keep fires safe when using them at night.

In the following chapter, we will look at the gear and tools you should consider getting before moving off the grid. A lot of survival is about having the right tools to stay alive, and although everyone's needs will vary, it's great to have a starting kit of gear that will help you hold your own against nature.

6

The Crucial Tools and Gear You Should Have

"By failing to prepare, you are preparing to fail."

-Benjamin Franklin

When you can't just drive down to the nearest store and pick up tools when you need them, you've got to think about what you will require in advance. It's always good to start by assessing the specifics of your environment to determine what you are likely to need. Still, in this chapter, I will cover some of the basic areas of tools that you should think about buying before you head off the grid for a long period.

Demolition Gear

You will need demolition gear – tools that can cut, hack, break, and prize for almost all aspects of surviving off the grid. You can't hunt, build shelters, or defend yourself without the relevant gear, so use the tools out there; there are some extremely clever and lightweight options, and many are multi-tools that will step up to a whole range of challenges.

At the very least, you should have several knives when you are in the wild. Strong knives let you cut, whittle, shape, and attack. They also let you prepare food, remove skins, cut up vegetables, gut fish, etc.

A saw can also be immensely useful and is often combined with multi-tools. A saw makes short work of any wood prep you need to do, whether clearing an area or gathering resources. Wood is one of the most useful resources you will have access to when you are off the grid, and if you can't cut it up, you can't use it.

An ax is similarly crucial because it lets you process wood much more quickly than a saw;

This will help you clear areas, cut down trees, and break firewood into kindling. If you are going to be lighting fires, an ax is a must-have tool; you will spend hours breaking wood down into usable parts if you don't have one. Axes are often large and unwieldy, but as part of a multi-tool, they are possible to carry and shouldn't be left out of your survival kit.

You may wish to buy these tools individually, but it's also good to have a multi-tool, as this will often come with other features and may be noticeably lighter. If you are going to buy a multi-tool, make sure that at least some of the blades are replaceable (e.g., the saw blade) to put a new blade in when yours gets blunt. Other blades, such as the ax, should be easy to sharpen.

Choose a high-quality multi-tool if you will get one and think about what other features may be useful in your given situation. A hammer is often extremely helpful, as are strong pliers, particularly if you plan to build structures while off the grid. A wrench is incorporated in many of these multi-tools and is also immensely useful for building and repairing. However, this does depend on the sort of survival you are going to be doing and what other equipment you are taking off the grid with you.

Tailor your demolition gear to the situations you are likely to encounter. An ice breaker could be handy if you are working in a cold environment, and a machete could be necessary if you are operating in a jungle.

As well as the bigger demolition tools, you should make sure you have a high-quality Swiss army knife with sharp blades. This sort of pocketknife can be carried with you every time you leave your home and will be useful for things like cutting traps, making emergency tools, defending yourself, opening cans, shaping wood, and more.

Cleaning Tools

Cleaning off the grid can be a major challenge, especially if you are short on water. You may sometimes need to get creative about keeping yourself, your clothing, and your gear in great condition, without a layer of dirt building up everywhere.

The most important thing to have is a bucket or two. That might sound basic, but when your water is limited and not available on tap, a bucket is the key piece of equipment for cleaning– yourself, your dishes, your clothes, and more.

A few buckets are best because you can split them by their job and minimize how frequently you must wash the buckets themselves (although you must keep them clean). You might dedicate a bucket to washing for yourself, another bucket for clothes washing and dishes, and a third for dirty jobs like cleaning garden tools, etc. You don't have to do this, but having at least two buckets can be beneficial, even if you just use one for soapy water and another for clean, rinsing water. Gray water can be put to other uses around the home, so don't waste it. Some people recommend keeping a strainer handy to filter any bits out of the water before using it on plants or using it for other washing purposes.

Buckets also have other uses, such as carrying fruit, storing dry goods, and hauling water. Try to get food grade buckets if you plan to store food or water in them, but you can use cheap or salvaged buckets to wash or make a composting toilet.

Next is a plunger, which is extremely useful for cleaning clothes. The plunger can be used alongside an old fashioned scrubbing board to agitate the water and free dirt from the clothing, and it's one of the best ways to save water when doing your laundry.

A good scrubbing brush is also crucial, and again, it may be worth having several so you can assign them to different levels of dirty work. For example, you might have a brush for dishes and another brush for outdoor work. Add dots of color to the handles to more easily establish what each one is for at a glance.

You should choose brushes that will last well and make sure that you don't store them in water; the wood will swell and split much more quickly, or the plastic may turn moldy. Instead, dry them well before putting them away.

Stock up on cleaning supplies, too; things like bleach may be crucial if you need to purify water in an emergency, and you should always have some available. Disinfectants and sterilizing liquids could be needed for cleaning wounds and stopping the spread of diseases, especially if somebody in your party gets sick with something contagious. Consider having white vinegar and alcohol gel in plentiful quantities.

Garden Tools

There are many tools that you will find useful if you are gardening off the grid. What you need will depend on the kind of gardening you wish to do, but let's look at a few basic tools. Many of these have uses besides just growing vegetables, so consider them even if you don't plan to grow your food.

You might need:

- A round-point shovel
- A garden fork
- A trowel

- A broom
- A mattock
- A hose
- Shears
- Gloves
- An adjustable ladder
- A rocket stove

Round-point Shovel

A shovel is probably the most important gardening tool you could have, and a round-pointed one tends to be the most versatile and useful. It is easier to get it into the ground than a shovel with a flat end, and you can use it to dig foundations, clear areas, remove unwanted plants, and create areas of bare soil for growing vegetables.

Choose a shovel with a good, sturdy handle to ensure it will last for years. Metal is often the most durable option, but it can be heavy, so choose wood if you would prefer something lighter.

Garden Fork

If you are dealing with hard ground, you will need a garden fork. This is far easier to drive into the ground than a shovel, and can help break up compacted earth. It is particularly useful for ground that has lots of roots or rocks. Again, choose one with sturdy metal prongs and a metal handle for the best durability.

If you are preparing the ground for planting vegetables, a fork is a great way to break the soil enough to plant seedlings.

Trowel

A trowel is important for planting seedlings and clearing small stretches of ground. It isn't the most essential of tools, but it is portable, which is also good if you're venturing into the wilds. Having a trowel will let you dig holes, uproot plants, and access a supply of soil for use in smothering fires or banking up ground. A trowel can easily be slung from your belt, and it's well worth having one around.

Broom

A broom has multiple uses, with sweeping being just one of them. It's great for clearing large stretches of ground, making pathways, cleaning up inside your home, and tidying up leaves. Brooms also work well for creating traps and clutter when you're making your home safe, as they tip easily and make a lot of noise when they fall. In a pinch, a broom can also be used as a weapon.

You don't need anything fancy from your broom, but having one with a wide area of bristles may help make short work of any sweeping you need to do.

Mattock

For tougher jobs outdoors, a mattock is a crucial bit of kit. Mattocks are ideal for building trenches, breaking up heavily compacted soil, and getting rid of tree stumps. If you expect to be clearing land, you will need a mattock, so make sure you choose one with a strong, sturdy, and preferably replaceable handle. Learn how to use one effectively before you start, as it can take a little practice to get the hang of swinging one.

Hose

A hose is ideal if you can set up a reliable water source. It will let you transport large amounts of water from one place to another without carrying them – and since water is heavy, this is an important ability. Choose a hose that is around 100 feet to stretch to any part of your off-grid home or garden, and make sure you get one that is suitable for all weathers, so it doesn't wear down too fast.

Shears

You might sometimes need to cut back and prune plants and trees, and shears will be necessary. The longer the handles, the more leverage you will have when cutting, but the heavier the tools will be. You may wish to get a pair with long handles and short handles for increased portability. The long ones will have the additional advantage of giving you more ability to reach overhead branches.

Gloves

Gloves are one of the absolute keys to any outdoor work; they protect your hand from the cold, insects, thorns, poisonous plants, accidental cuts from your tools, etc. Most people find leather gloves are the most protective and flexible, and they should also offer some warmth. A thick pair will protect you from all but the worst thorns and plants with good waterproofing.

Make sure that they fit you well; every party member should have a comfortable pair. Badly fitted gloves are liable to slip and come off, making it difficult to work safely.

Adjustable Ladder

A ladder has a great many uses in and around your home. It can be used to access the roof if you need to repair it and will give you the height to pick fruits from trees or cut them back where necessary.

Rocket Stove

A rocket stove is an immensely useful means of disposing of garden waste and creating heat simultaneously. Rocket stoves can be bought or made using bricks, and they burn very hot, allowing you to dispose of damp waste with minimal smoke. Some people even use rocket stoves for cooking.

Ensure you follow the fire safety guidance before adding a rocket stove to your garden and only use it when you are in attendance.

Fires And Fire Lighting

Having an outdoor fire pit is something to seriously consider when you are off the grid; This gives you the means to make heat and cook food outdoors –both practical and fun. You can choose from many fire pits or make your own, but make sure you clear a good area around the pit and practice the same fire safety discussed earlier. Do not leave lit flames unattended.

You should also get some gear together for lighting fires reliably, both at home and in the wilderness. You can make your fire-starter kits or buy ready-made ones if you choose. Always have some to spare, and make sure they are kept in a dry location.

A fire starting kit should usually contain:

- A lighter
- Steel wool
- Matches
- A pocket magnifier
- Tealights
- Twine
- A folding knife

- A waterproof bag
- A striker
- Cotton tinder tabs
- Magnesium capsules

This will give you a whole range of ways to make fire, both at home and in the wilds. Ensure that the kit stays bone dry at all times; you can keep your kits in waterproof sealed bags and add some silica gel packets if you choose to.

When you head off the grid, you should also take some dry wood with you if you will depend on fire (and really, even if you don't expect to depend on a fire). This will ensure that you have some supplies already and mean you don't need to focus on gathering more to survive immediately. Take enough supplies for a few days of fires.

Lighting

Light is one of the most important things to make sure you have access to when you are off the grid, and you should have various light sources with multiple different supplies so that you have at least one backup if something goes wrong. Ideally, you will have a hand-cranked flashlight so that if all other sources fail, you still have some light. You should also keep emergency candles stocked in a dry place inside your cabin, with some matches or a lighter.

In terms of tools, a headlamp is one of the most important because this frees up your hands for other work and ensures there is light wherever you are looking. You can buy some very bright headlamps that are chargeable via USB ports or ones with replaceable batteries, and you'll likely find that this is a crucial piece of equipment that you use any time you are out at night.

You should also have some regular flashlights available, preferably with a lantern mode to be used to light the inside of the home if necessary. Keep some backup flashlights with charged batteries in a designated area so that you can grab a spare if something goes wrong. Choose flashlights with a range of brightness, so you aren't wasting power unnecessarily if you only need a little illumination, but you can crank up the brightness when you need to. It may also prove useful to have an SOS flashing mode on your light.

Don't depend on the flashlight on your phone unless you need it; your phone has too many other valuable uses to waste the battery in this way.

Consider also having some lamps around your camp to turn them on if you need to work in certain areas at night. There are a great many options, but make sure you choose ones that are suitable for operating outdoors.

Protective Gear

We discussed some protective gear in terms of clothing in Chapter Three, but there's a lot more to consider for at-home use and when you're out in the wilds. Let's look at some of the top areas you may want to cover. These include:

- Eye protection
- Foot protection
- Head protection
- Hand protection

Eye Protection

Often, you'll be doing something that causes a risk of flying projectiles, and your eyes are probably your most vulnerable body part in many ways. You are likely to be facing the object, and you may even be leaning in to see it clearly – which puts your eyes in a vulnerable position.

Whether you are working in the garden, chopping wood, using welding tools, cutting trees, or walking through a sandstorm, eye protection is smart. You can choose how much protection you need, but at the very least, a pair of basic plastic goggles will help to ensure that you are not at risk of getting hurt.

If you are going to be doing any specialty work, like welding, make sure you have appropriate glasses to protect your eyes. Regular goggles won't cut it.

Foot Protection

If you don't have a good pair of work boots, you are also putting yourself at serious risk. A foot injury may be less long-term than an eye injury in many cases, but it can leave you unable to walk or fend for yourself, which could be dangerous when you are off the grid and a long way from help. You should therefore purchase a good pair of protective work boots.

The best work boots will be waterproof, well-fitted, and cushioned inside, so they are comfortable to wear for long hours at a time. You may want to get ones with steel caps built into the toes to maximize the protection if you are at risk of something falling on your feet, but you should be aware that this will make the boots stiffer and heavier, so they will not be as easy to walk in. However, cutting trees or walking in an area where rocks may shift could save you from serious injury.

You also want to ensure that your boots have excellent grips on their soles, particularly if you are frequently working in wet conditions. If you are somewhere with dangerous snakes, you may wish to invest in boots covering your ankles and calves, where snakes are most likely to bite. Be aware that these will be hotter and less comfortable, but they could save your life.

It's important to know your terrain when you choose your boots because if you'll be operating in snow, laces (generally the best fastener for boots) and weight will both become major issues. Choose your boots to suit your likely environment as much as you can.

Head Protection

You probably won't need head protection when you're not working near your off-grid home, but it's a must-have for any work involving overhead materials. If you are felling trees or even just cutting branches, you should have a good hard hat.

You should also wear a hard hat anytime you are working at a height – for example, on a roof. If you fall, it will protect your head from damage.

Hand Protection

We covered gloves earlier, but don't forget about them – and make sure that you have gloves that will protect your hands from the cold and knocks and bumps. Leather gloves alone may not be enough to keep your fingers warm if you're working outdoors in the winter, so make sure you have some insulated gloves.

Ideally, these will also be somewhat waterproof or thin enough to put under a waterproof pair and keep your hands cozy. Your gloves should also cover your wrists to minimize heat loss. They must be flexible enough so you can handle tools and grip things while wearing them.

Foldable Solar Panels

The ongoing challenge when you are off the grid is lack of power, which is something that so many modern gadgets depend upon so completely. There are lots of alternatives, but often, the best solution to a problem is to ensure that you have a power source, even if it is limited. You may not be able to have a full solar setup in your off-grid home, either for space reasons or budget reasons, but a foldable solar panel is certainly worth considering.

The great thing about these panels is that they are designed to be portable, so you can use yours when you are in your off-grid home or on the go. Foldable solar panels are a great safety kit to have around because they will let you charge devices in an emergency – so if your phone has run-flat or you need some heat, you can get at least a little power from the panel.

Foldable solar panels do have some drawbacks. They are easy to steal because they aren't mounted, so you need to be present when the panel is used. They also require you to set them up every time you want to use them, which is frustrating if you are used to a static system you can just plug into. Furthermore, they are more likely to be damaged if left out in wild weather.

However, a foldable solar panel is a valuable piece of equipment to carry. You should consider investing in one if you're going to spend any meaningful amount of time away from the grid and away from a fixed setup.

Other Tools

You should always make sure you have access to a few other tools while you're out and about. A first aid kit is such a must that it almost goes without saying but do make sure yours is well stocked before you set out on an excursion, and keep backup supplies at your base.

You should also consider getting a set of walkie talkies when you are out with a group. This can make it easier for everyone to track who is where without depending on cell phone signal and batteries. Walkie talkies might seem superfluous if you are used to using your phone, but they are a cheaper option with a much longer battery life, and they will let you save your phone's battery for more important things.

It's also a wise idea to have a good compass and to learn how to use it. When you move to a new area, use landmarks to orientate yourself with your base and make sure you know how to get back there from the surrounding area.

A survival blanket or jacket is a good thing to always have in your pocket; these fold down to very little and weigh almost nothing, but they can make the difference if you are stuck out in the elements. Have a couple of spare ones at your home, but keep one with you, even if you don't expect to be out overnight.

A map is also a must-have, especially when you are operating in an unfamiliar area. A compass will do you no good without a map, so make sure you always have one – don't just depend on a map on your phone. If the battery dies, you'll be lost. Keep a real paper map in your bag.

Some backup food is another good idea, even if you plan to be self-sufficient. You should always have a few weeks of dried food stored so that you can eat even if you get cut off from society, and things go wrong. You should store around 2000 calories for each person for every day of security that you want.

A solar charged power bank is also a smart thing to carry – these are often small enough to be clipped onto your belt or bag, so they can be charged while you walk, and they will reduce the risk of you ending up without power while you are away from your cabin.

Before leaving on an excursion, talk to your other group members about the gadgets you frequently use and determine whether there are any other must-have options specific to your situation. Purchase anything else you need to ensure that you are as prepared as possible.

Summary

In this chapter, we've covered:

- The right gear for demolition and breaking down raw materials.
- The tools you need to clean effectively.
- Garden tools you'll need for building a safe, productive environment.
- Fire pits, fire starters, and the importance of carrying some firewood when you go off the grid.
- Crucial lighting gear, and the different power sources.
- Protective gear, including hard hats and warm gloves.
- Foldable solar panels.

Conclusion

"I got my own back."

-Maya Angelou

You should now have a foundational understanding of what you need to survive in the wild. However, it is important to couple the information in this book with your assessment of the situation and the environment you will be operating in.

Think about things like the weather, the temperature, the changing seasons, and the dangers you will encounter. Draw up emergency plans, talk to your group, and spend some time with experienced survivors who know the land you will be operating in. Make sure you learn some practical skills, take some survival courses, and read about the subject. The more you learn, the higher your chances of survival are.

Whenever you are heading into a dangerous situation, think about the three biggest needs for survival: food, water, and shelter. If you don't have a plan for accessing these three things, you need to make one because you will not survive for long without them.

Whether you are operating from your off-grid home or out in the wild, think about how you can keep yourself and others in your group safe, what dangers you might face, and what resources you will need.

Remember that when you are in the wild, you are on your own, depending upon your knowledge and preparation – and there may not be anything else keeping you alive in such instances! You have a responsibility to yourself and to others to ensure that you are up to the challenge.

BACKYARD HOMESTEAD HANDBOOK:

——— BOOK 6 ———

The Ultimate Beginners Guide to Starting Your Own Self Sufficient Mini Farm in 7 Steps With Just a Quarter of An Acre

BRADLEY STONE

Introduction

"The greatest fine art of the future will be the making of a comfortable living from a small piece of land."

-Abraham Lincoln

Did you know that about a third of Americans grow food in their backyards?

According to the National Gardening Association, "35% of families in the United States grow their vegetables, fruit and other food at home."

That's a surprising figure, and I was taken aback when I saw it. One way or another, small-scale farming has been a part of my life for as long as I can remember. I recall picking fruits from our apple trees, gathering plums, testing the tomatoes for ripeness, and pulling faces at the salad crops. I also recall how few – if any – of the families I knew did this. Now, things are changing for the better, and many more Americans are finding joy in growing their own food.

There are so many reasons to grow your own food, and you are probably already familiar with most of them. Whether you're looking to reduce your food miles, cut your grocery budget, avoid pesticides, or just enhance your skills and chances of survival without the safety net provided by society, you might be interested in this topic – and if so, backyard homesteading is for you.

Before we plunge into the intricacies of this topic, let's spend a bit of time learning about the fundamentals of homesteads – starting with what a homestead is.

What is a homestead?

There are a few different ways to define a homestead, but at its most fundamental, a homestead means a house surrounded by land. This land is devoted to keeping animals and the growing of crops. The house is generally a farmhouse and is lived in by the family that owns the homestead, and there may be barns and farm buildings nearby.

You can create your own homestead with very little space; you just need enough land to grow crops and possibly keep a few animals (even small ones like chickens). In the US, certain dwellings are recognized as homesteads. These are treated differently from ordinary residences by US law; hence it's worth researching this subject if you wish to own a homestead and get your food from the land.

Who is backyard homesteading for?

You don't have to be a farmer or have generations of farmers behind you to become a backyard homesteader. Anyone who has a little space outdoors can launch into this kind of living.

Provided it has a bit of land, even an urban or suburban property can become a homestead. Your plot may be surrounded by concrete and tarmac, but with care, soil, and time, you can turn it into a growth paradise and enjoy the magic of growing plants. No matter what space you have, you can get a few things growing, even if you can't produce enough to be completely self-sufficient.

Backyard homesteading brings many advantages, which we will explore shortly, but before we do, take on board this lesson: **anyone can have a backyard homestead.** It doesn't matter if you think you are terrible with plants and have never grown a bean. It doesn't matter if you only have a few feet of space outside or just a kitchen windowsill. All that matters is that you are willing to learn and have a bit of time to invest in cultivating your plants. You don't need much else to create a thriving homestead in your backyard!

What are the pros?

Growing food at home brings a wealth of advantages that you will enjoy – almost too many to count. Let's look at some of the major ones.

Firstly, it is satisfying. Little else brings the same degree of joy and pleasure that serving up your homegrown vegetables to the table and watching them get devoured will create. Eggs from your chicken house, honey from your beehives, and – if you are particularly adventurous – meat from your animals can all go from backyard to table in almost no time. Every meal will bring you notably more satisfaction and connection.

Backyard homesteading makes your food mean something again.

Secondly, it's much better for the planet. You may already know that eating locally- produced and seasonal food is vital for reducing your global footprint, *but what could be more local than food from your own backyard?* Instead of shipping vegetables worldwide, you'll be stepping out of your door to pick them up. When you think about all the fuel and resources that go into picking, packing, chilling, transporting, washing, preparing, packaging, and displaying produce, you'll get an idea of just how much more sense it makes to grow your food this way!

Thirdly, if you're keen on healthy eating, this is one of the best ways to get fresh food. When crops are in season, you can literally pick them, wash them, and serve them immediately, so your food will be packed with nutrients and vitamins. Never mind soggy broccoli and limp lettuce – you can have your pick of the freshest vegetables, eggs, milk, and meat if you have the suitable animals!

Another attraction is the reduction in costs. Grocery shopping represents one of the most significant living expenses for many households, and fresh produce is a big part of this. You can shave a lot of dollars off your food bill by growing your vegetables and fruits, and you won't have to spend a fortune to eat well. If you produce your compost and save your seeds yearly, food grown in your garden costs only your time and occasionally a few dollars for equipment replacements.

Additionally, you have complete control over what goes into your food and how it's grown. If you are one of the millions of Americans concerned by pesticide use and the chemicals in your food – or what its packaging may be leaching – you will get a lot more peace of mind from growing your food. You can use whatever pest control methods you think will be beneficial and treat your food as you feel is safe.

The microbes are the final advantage of eating vegetables that you have grown in your garden. Some recent studies have drawn tentative links between the soil microorganisms and the microorganisms responsible for healthy guts. It is thought that the food you consume has a much more significant impact on your gut's microbiome than your genetics, so it makes sense to try to eat the right foods.

A lot more study is needed to help us properly understand how these microorganisms in the soil play in keeping humans healthy. However, they are likely essential in a world where so many people suffer from gastrointestinal issues, obesity, and other digestive problems; it is well worth exploring whether eating more freshly grown foods could make you healthier.

What are the cons?

Of course, creating a backyard homestead is not all positive – there are some drawbacks that you need to consider.

Firstly, it's a considerable investment of time, especially if you want to grow a lot of food. You will need to be out watering, weeding, and tending to your plants most days of the week. You'll have to harvest, wash, and process them. You'll need to plant seedlings, deal with pests and diseases, and find someone to look after your crops if you want to go on vacation. The rewards are high, but there is undoubtedly a lot of work in creating a back-yard homestead – so be aware of this before you start!

There is also a risk of injuries, although usually fairly minor ones. This is particularly high if you are out of shape, although gardening will improve your fitness levels. You may face back injuries, cuts, bruises, bites, and stings. Depending on where you are, insects, snakes, spiders, and other local creatures may present a natural hazard, especially if you have allergies.

Next, be aware that there will be an initial expense when setting up a garden in almost all situations. You will need to buy tools, seeds, compost, and more. These can add up fast, especially if you plan to build raised beds, chicken coops, animal enclosures, etc. You can start on a small scale but be aware that you will have to spend money on your garden, even if you take a frugal approach.

Another disadvantage is that you will lose some or all your outdoor space to crops. For most people, this drawback is minor, but it's worth thinking about, especially if you take pleasure in having flowers, a pool, or kiddie toys in your backyard. You may not have room for these anymore – although backyard homesteading can be flexible, and you don't have to dedicate the whole space to growing food if you don't want to!

Finally, there will be frustrations, especially for inexperienced gardeners. You should expect to lose whole crops at times to pests, diseases, fungus, or bad weather. As you gain gardening skills, your losses will be lower, but you will still have bad years and bad crops, which is just part of gardening. It can be disheartening, especially if you have put a lot of hours into a plant and lost it before enjoying the fruits of your labor.

Most people feel that the drawbacks here are worth the rewards you'll reap from gardening, but this calculation needs to be made by every individual. You know how much time you have, how much pleasure you get from this sort of thing, and how feasible it is in your space – so take all the pros and cons into account before you start sectioning off your yard into vegetable plots. If you aren't sure, consider starting on a small scale. You will probably soon find that you are hooked!

Why is having a backyard homestead important?

Some people feel that a backyard homestead is more than a hobby and a way to save money; It is a matter of security. A backyard homestead gives you the means to grow food for your family, a safety net that will protect you if a disaster strikes.

In terms of our planet's future, a backyard homestead is vital because it's widely recognized as something that many individuals can do to decrease their global footprint, strike back at harmful farming practices, and make the planet greener. More and more people are ripping out monoculture lawns and planting vegetables, which will have a massive impact worldwide.

In the first chapter, I will talk you through how to make a blueprint for your land and what you can do to maximize your crops even if your space is limited. Having a plan before you set your spade to the ground is crucial, so read on to find out how to get organized and make the most of your homestead!

1

Making A Blueprint For Your Land

"All you need is the plan, the road map, and the courage to press on to your destination."

-Earl Nightingale

Once you've decided that backyard homesteading is for you, you'll probably eagerly eye the space and wonder where to begin. You might already be envisaging where you're going to put things and thinking of rushing outdoors with a spade. Before you do, pause, and let's look at some plans.

In this chapter, I will walk you through the basics of how to plan your homestead and how to make sure your soil is good enough for planting in. Water conservation techniques to keep your vegetables refreshed even in the summer heat without watering them from the tap will be covered. We'll also cover the different compost options, what you can compost, and how to make hot compost, ideal for small spaces.

How To Plan Your ¼ Acre Homestead

When planning your homestead, the first thing to do is take a large piece of plain paper and draw a map of your home. It may help if you do this to scale, but even an approximate version will do. Draw your house and then draw the garden around it. Mark where the sun rises, and which bits of the area are the sunniest; crops tend to need a lot of sun to grow well!

Next, start thinking about what you want to include, and make a list by order of priority. Think about your staple foods, the ones that you eat most often. *Do you use onions? Potatoes? Bell peppers? Do you want eggs? Do you have enough space to consider keeping a goat?* Think about fruits, especially if you are in a warm climate (which many fruits prefer). Fruits are expensive to buy, short-seasoned, and often are shipped around the planet, so they are fantastic to grow in your garden if you can.

Once you have made your list of ideal things you would like to have, do a bit of research on each item, finding out how well it will grow in your area. Things like onions and potatoes will grow well in most climates, while peppers and tomatoes need much sunlight. Some vegetables need more space, while others are perpetually thirsty and need constant watering. You should also think about common pests and determine which plants are resistant to them.

You should look at:

- Light requirements
- Space requirements
- Water requirements
- Vulnerability to pests
- Vulnerability to diseases

Once you have a good idea of the plants you would like to grow, you can use these limitations to decide the most realistic and most likely to give you good yields. That done, start planning your space. Remember, you can always plant different things next year; you don't have to get this perfect each time!

You should usually start planning by deciding where to put your vegetable plots. These will need to be in the sunniest spots, so they should be placed first. Draw them onto your plan, deciding how many by thinking about how much time you have and how much food you want to grow. Remember to leave paths so you can harvest the crops.

 Sizes can be altered to suit your needs, but many vegetable beds are about 3 to 4 feet wide, so you can reach across them to pick plants. The length is up to you. Raised beds are an excellent way to cut back on digging work and make your soil healthier because the microorganisms won't be disturbed by the earth being turned.

Once you have your vegetable beds in place, think about the other things you might want. *For example, are you going to keep chickens?* If so, you will need a coop. You should also consider space for the storage of tools and think about where you can create a compost heap.

Once you have drawn up your plan with the major components of your garden, look at the white spaces that are left. Creating a homestead on a quarter of an acre means using all available space. Although you want to be able to move around unhindered in your garden, you also need to utilize as much as possible. You can fill in around the major parts of the garden with planters and smaller beds if you choose to.

Things like large flowerpots with fruit bushes (e.g. blueberries), a large bench for tool storage, or water butts should be slotted into any available room. Remember, however, that you will need to be able to walk easily between every area, and you may want to get tools like a wheelbarrow through.

You may also want to think about building a small pond on your homestead. That might seem like a waste of already limited space, but ponds are a great way to complete the ecosystem and will encourage both birds and amphibians to visit your homestead. These will help to pick off pests and keep your plants safe. Even a shallow pool will provide water throughout the summer and attract insects that will pollinate your plants.

Once you have drawn up your plan, take some time to walk around your yard and assess everything. Mark the different areas out with canes to help yourself visualize them – and don't forget to look at the sun's position at varying times of the day. *Will your vegetable beds get enough light? Does a tall tree shade them? Do they need to be moved to one side? Can you walk between them and the hypothetical water butts? Do you have space for a few more planters along the fence?*

If possible, get feedback from others on your plan, too. Having several pairs of eyes will help you to detect problems. Take a few days to think and assess before you start building the homestead, and don't try to do it all at once. Add a few things at a time and see whether you are happy with their functionality before slotting all the pieces into place. Don't be afraid to tweak and adjust the plan if something isn't working as well as you'd hoped. While planning is essential, a backyard homestead often evolves as it becomes a reality, and you get a better feel for what works and doesn't work. Be flexible and hone your layout.

Soil Improvement Techniques

Once you've started mapping out your mini homestead, you need to look at the soil. The soil is what you will grow your food in, and the quality matters. Many things can be wrong with soil, and a solution is needed for all of them. Let's look at a few techniques you might wish to use.

The first thing you will need is a soil testing kit; This will give you all the information you need about the kind of soil you are dealing with, and it is usually pretty inexpensive to purchase. You need to consider various elements, including the pH of the soil and the quantities of the macronutrients (nitrogen, phosphorus, potassium). These are usually the two largest determiners of soil quality. You also need to look at soil texture and determine whether you are dealing with sand, clay, or something in between.

Once you have determined your soil's needs, it's time to look at how you provide it. Below, you'll find 6 simple soil improvement techniques that you can do at home.

1: Add Compost

Compost is probably the best known and most accessible to apply soil amendment technique. You can make compost at home (we will discuss this shortly) or purchase it. Consider whether you want to grow organic vegetables before you start. Compost is one of the best ways to improve soil because it does everything – it adds nutrients, improves the soil structure, and aids water retention. Rich compost grows excellent crops, and you can never have enough of this material for your garden.

2: Add Manure

Despite how rich it is, you can't add fresh manure to your garden because it will burn your plants. Manure comes from animal waste (chicken, pig, cattle), and it's something you may have access to at home, or you may need to buy commercially, but either way, it needs to be aged before being applied to the ground. The different kinds of manures all offer several pros and cons.

- Sheep/goat manure is gentle on plants and easy to apply.
- Horse manure is readily available but often contains seeds from weeds.
- Chicken manure provides a great nitrogen fix but may burn if not sufficiently aged.
- Rabbit manure can be applied without aging but isn't the best option.
- Cow manure is all-purpose and doesn't burn too easily but is low in nitrogen.

If you buy manure, check what the animals have been fed before adding it, especially if you are creating an organic garden.

3: Try Natural Amendments

There are many natural amendments, including wood ash, lime, blood meal, and more. These things are used when you know what your soil lacks, and you want to correct one or two elements. Natural amendments can be used in the following ways:

- Low calcium – add lime
- Low nitrogen – add bone meal or legume crops
- Low magnesium – add Epsom salts
- Low phosphorus – add bone meal for a quick fix or rock phosphate for a longer one
- Low potassium – add wood ash

Soil amendments focus on correcting one deficiency, so they are most useful if you have used a testing kit and know something is missing.

4: Try Cover Crops

Cover crops are beneficial for rotating gardens and correcting the soil without much work or expense. However, they take up valuable space in your garden, so be aware of that before planting them. You can use cover crops to replace nutrients in the soil, keep beds clear from weeds, and boost soil organisms.

There are various cover crops, so choose ones that will correct your specific issues. For example, try something like Ryegrass if you need to break up hard soil. If you need to add nitrogen back into the ground, use legume crops.

5: Add Mulch

Mulch is applied to the top of the soil and allowed to break down slowly, and it is handy for trapping water in the ground. If you are working in a hot climate, mulch is a great way to reduce the amount of watering you need to do. Mulch can be made with a whole variety of things, but often straw or leaves are good options. Some people prefer to use wood chips. If organic matter can be laid on thickly and allowed to break down gradually, it will work as mulch.

6: Add Vermicompost

Vermicompost is an expensive commodity if you purchase it commercially, but you can make it home if you set up a wormery. Worm castings are ideal for soil and will boost the nutrients in the ground massively, giving you fantastic crops. You can also add composting worms directly to your soil, and they will help break it up and enrich it as long as they have sufficient food and suitable conditions. It is a great way to prepare an area with minimal extra work.

Water Conservation

Saving water will become a massive part of your life if you want to run a homestead. Even if finances aren't a problem when watering your crops, using a lot of water is not chiefly green, as processing tap water takes a lot of energy. You will want to minimize as much as possible – and fortunately, there are many ways in which you can do this. Let's cover some of the top options.

1: Save Gray Water

When you shower, clean out the fish tank, mop the floors, empty plant trays, or pour away cooking water, you're producing "gray water." Gray water is that which hasn't been contaminated with anything dangerous, and if you save this instead of tipping it back down the drain, it's ideal for use in the garden. For example, the water from your pasta pan or your bath can be saved, scooped up, and poured on your vegetables.

You might be amazed by how much gray water your household produces in a day, and the more you can save, the more you'll have for your garden. Do think about things like soap and chemicals, however. You don't want to be pouring harsh cleaning products on your vegetables, so make sure your gray water is food safe.

2: Use Water Butts

Rainwater is an invaluable resource, and your plants will grow much better when you use it than when you give them tap water because it contains trace nutrients and is free from chlorine and chemicals. You can set water butts anywhere you have space in your garden and use them to gather rainwater throughout the year. Make sure the butts are not a hazard to animals falling into them; they will need a lid and an input pipe.

3: Water At The Right Time

If you water your plants in the day's heat, the sun will burn the moisture off very quickly, stopping it from soaking into the soil. It is better to water when temperatures are cooler, so the maximum amount of water can go into the ground. That means morning or evening watering – but watering in the evening can encourage slugs and leaves your plant without anything to drink during the heat of the day, which can stress them out.

We prefer to water first thing in the morning in our household before the day gets hot. We're often out with a watering can as early as 6 a.m. on hot summer days, and it's a surprisingly satisfying and pleasant way to start the day. Your plants will then have plenty of water while they face the day's heat.

4: Let The Grass Grow

If you have a lawn, it can take a lot of water to keep it green all summer. You have two options here – either let it go brown (but water it enough so that it doesn't die) or allow it to grow a bit longer. Long grass will shade its roots and require a lot less watering. It should need less to drink if you cut it to about 2 inches long. Alternatively, consider replacing your lawn with a less thirsty garden.

5: Use Mulch

We have already discussed how mulch helps to trap water in the soil. It creates a dense layer that does not lose moisture quickly, and mulching around your plants is a great way to ensure that they have plenty to always drink. Lawn clippings will work for mulch, or you can buy straw. Circle each plant with a dense layer, and you will find them far more resistant to wilting.

Composting Types And Creation

There are four major kinds of compost – farmyard manure, green manure, standard compost, and vermicompost. All can be homemade if you have a bit of space and some organic matter, and all will benefit your garden. Let's find out a bit more about them.

Farmyard Manure

You won't be surprised to learn that farmyard manure is made using animal waste. It is rich in nutrients, but it needs to be aged so it does not burn the plants, and it should be mixed with compost to dilute its richness. If you keep any vegetarian animal, you can use its droppings to create manure.

Making manure at home isn't easy, although many backyard homesteaders do it successfully. You essentially need to gather the animal waste into a large pit and let it rot and decompose. After a few months, microorganisms will start to form and break the manure down, making it usable in your garden.

Green Manure

Green manure is created by growing certain crops (e.g. fenugreek, buckwheat, certain legumes) in a bed and then digging these into the soil after a set period; This could be a few months after sowing or even a couple of years. Green manures will stop any bare soil areas from getting taken over by weeds and provide a nitrogen fix to poor soil. Once the plant has been dug in, at least two weeks must pass before adding plants to the bed.

Standard Compost

Fortunately, this top method for creating organic matter yourself at home is relatively straightforward. You will need a space at least 4 feet by 4 feet or larger. You can create a rigid base or leave it directly on the soil. It will need sides and a back to contain the organic matter you add. Many people also add a front.

When this has been done, you can start throwing organic waste onto the heap, and it will gradually begin to attract worms and form microorganisms that will break this organic matter down and turn it into rich compost. You can add most things to a compost bin, although many people avoid meat, fish, bread, and dairy, as these can attract pests.

The most important thing to know about a backyard compost heap is that you will be adding two kinds of waste: greens and browns. Green ingredients are rich in nitrogen, while browns are rich in carbon. If you get too many greens, your heap will be sloppy, wet, and smelly, while too many browns will result in a dry, inactive pile.

Luckily, you don't need to be too precise about this, and an active heap will deal with all but the most extreme mixes. You want to aim for 50/50 of these two kinds of ingredients. Green ingredients include:

- Garden clippings
- Lawn clippings
- Food scraps
- Manure
- Weeds

Brown ingredients include:

- Straw
- Twigs
- Dry leaves
- Newspaper
- Cardboard
- Stalks
- Sawdust

As a rough rule of thumb, greens will be soft and squishy, and browns will be hard and dry. If you don't get the proper ratios, your compost bin will stop working correctly, but this is usually easy to fix. Composting is not fine art, and you don't need to spend hours getting it right. As long as you add greens and browns and stir it occasionally to increase the oxygen, it will usually operate with little other input, and you'll get fantastic compost for your garden!

Vermicompost

To make vermicompost at home, you'll need a wormery. You can buy one or make one from old plastic boxes. Many people keep their wormeries indoors to prevent drying out, freezing, or overheating, but you can keep one in a porch or garage. They don't smell much and are relatively easy to look after.

If you are making your wormery, get a 20-gallon storage container. Drill some holes in the base of your container and stand it on a tray, as it needs to drain liquid. Drill holes in the lid too. Next, shred some newspaper or cardboard, and fill the bin around 8 inches high. Add water so that it is wet but not dripping. The worms will live in this newspaper – it's their bedding.

Add some soil and then a good layer of food waste (worms will eat almost all soft foods except for citrus and onion family members). Add some compost worms (not earthworms) and let them do their thing! Within a few weeks, you should have rich black soil that you can use in your garden.

What Is Hot Composting And How To Do It

Hot composting is an excellent option if you want to process waste quickly; This might be because you need the compost fast or because your space is limited. You can buy hot composters, but they are expensive. With good sunlight and a bin at least 4 feet by 4 feet, you should be able to get even a regular compost heap to heat up.

Hot composting is done between 130- and 140-degrees F, and it occurs because the microbes in the soil are highly active. They are breaking down food quickly, which creates a lot of heat, which adds to the swift decomposition. The pile should feel uncomfortably hot to the touch.

You can encourage your compost bin to become hot by constantly turning and aerating the contents. Having plenty of oxygen activates the microbes. You also need to ensure that the heap stays damp, as they need moisture to survive. If you squeeze a handful of compost, it should be wet enough to exude some moisture drops but not so wet that it drips. Add cardboard if it is too wet, and water it if it is too dry.

With hot compost, you can have garden-ready compost in as little as three weeks. However, you'll need to be quite hands-on, constantly turning, aerating, and monitoring the pile so that the temperature stays high.

Summary

In this chapter, we've covered:

- How to plan your ¼ acre homestead, the key components, and filling in the gaps.

- Some top techniques for improving your soil and the amendments you can add once tested its conditions.
- Water-saving tricks that will let you minimize your water footprint.
- The various kinds of compost and how you can start making them at home.

In the following chapter, we will start looking at the vegetable garden – the heart of your homestead – in more detail. We'll cover all the different kinds of plants you might wish to grow, a couple of other growing systems, and the times and yields you might be able to expect. Keep reading, so you know how to build the essential parts of your backyard homestead and ensure it succeeds!

2

Your Vegetable Garden

"Go vegetable heavy. Reverse the psychology of your plate by making meat the side dish and vegetables the main course."

-Bobby Flay

Your vegetable plot is the heart and soul of your backyard homestead. It needs to take the spotlight metaphorically and literally – because it should be in the sunniest spot you have available. It is what will produce the majority of your meals, and it is the cornerstone of the homestead. Without a good vegetable garden, you can't even approach self-sufficiency.

There are so many things that make a vegetable plot essential. It's tricky to list them all, but you'll soon find that this is where you devote your hours and reap your rewards. Sowing, watering, feeding, tending to, weeding, harvesting, and clearing your crops are the biggest chores and often the biggest joys of your homestead. Your vegetables will make up the bulk of your food, even if you are a keen carnivore and love meats and dairy products.

Fill your plate with vegetables, and you will be happier, healthier, and wealthier. Before we begin, however, I want to remind you that everyone's gardens are different, and it will often take a bit of time for you to get to know yours. You will soon learn which crops flourish and which languish, but that will mean making the odd mistake, particularly in the early days. What works for some gardeners will not work for others. You will have a unique set of advantages but some unique challenges to handle.

As an example from my own life: we've got a fabulous backyard with a pond and some fruit trees, and we seem to be amazingly blessed in how few pests we face. I put this down to the ecosystem we have cultivated; we encourage birds, toads, ducks, etc. We create wild spaces and hideaways, and our pond houses more amphibians than you would believe! In payment, we get relatively few slugs, caterpillars, and other plant-munchers because we have all of these animals, plus ladybugs, spiders, frogs, thrushes, and other insect predators that keep everything in balance.

What we don't have is good soil. The ground is rich but made up of such dense clay you could craft with it. We work with it and love it, but what works for us won't work for others.

With that said, let's get started on creating your vegetable garden.

Growing Foods Sustainably

There are a lot of things to think about when you start growing your food, and before we do anything else, let's recognize that: there is no right and no wrong way to do this, and you are likely to keep honing your method as the years pass and your knowledge and needs grow and change. Try to view mistakes as learning opportunities and remember that you are teaching yourself a craft that humans have been working on for centuries. You aren't going to get it right overnight!

To grow sustainably, you need to take a scientific approach to your vegetable garden and cover the following areas.

Which Crops And How Many?

First, think about the crops that you would like to grow. Ideally, you will produce crops that you use in most of your meals because this will give you the best value and security. Use your grocery bills to get a sense of how much of any particular vegetable you use in a week and determine how many plants you might therefore need to supply each person with food. Remember, you can top up from the stores while getting to grips with this, and you don't have to become self-sufficient if you'd rather not.

Space And Yields

Next, look at your space and consider how realistic that plant is to grow in that space. Some plants provide much lower yields for their area, so avoid these if you haven't much room. Think about your conditions and what is likely to grow well – some plants will cope better with heavy rain and hail, while others (e.g. salad crops) will be battered and destroyed if not protected. High-calorie crops such as winter squash, sweetcorn, beans, potatoes, and grains are good ways to ensure your family members have full stomachs, and they can be supplemented with lower-calorie crops.

Growing Seasons

When you have settled on some crops you think you could grow, start thinking about the growing season of each plant. Often, you will want to choose a handful of varieties to extend the growing season. For example, having early, normal, and late cropping potatoes will maximize the time you can enjoy this vegetable. Not all kinds of vegetables are this flexible, but many are.

Succession Planting

When a crop has finished, you are going to have space. Working out how to maximize the efficiency of your vegetable beds so that you are planting a new crop as one season ends isn't the easiest thing in the world, but if you think of it a little like solving a puzzle, you might find you enjoy it more. You may wish to draw up some sample vegetable beds for each season or make graphs that show when the different crops start and finish. You can then slot them into place in the most efficient ways possible.

For example, if you have a potato crop that finishes in September and winter leeks that need to be planted in October, you can plan to put the leeks in after the potatoes have finished. You can then decide that that bed will be planted with beets after the leeks are pulled in March. It can take a while to get the hang of this succession planting, but it will make your vegetable beds far more productive.

Succession planting can also be done with the same crop, but in this case, it usually involves planting it in staggered sessions. You might sow some lettuce seedlings one week and some the next; This is to stagger your harvest so not all of the food will be ready simultaneously – otherwise, you'll have a lot of lettuce to get through!

Companion Planting

Companion planting is next on the list of things to consider. If you haven't ever done this, it's essential to spend some time looking into it once you have decided which plants you wish to grow – because some plants will give each other a boost, and others will grow to the detriment of their companions. Plants that need the same nutrients should be positioned far away so they don't compete, and the same goes for plants that attract similar pests.

Note that not all companion plants need to be edible. Sometimes, you will plant non-edibles among your vegetables to help fix nutrients in the soil, protect from pests, or attract specific pollinators. Which plants will work as companions depends on what you want to grow, but you may find the below information helpful.

- Mint: this can be grown alongside carrots, brassicas, tomatoes, or alliums to confuse pests.

- Garlic chives: these will drive away carrot root fly.
- Calendula: this will repel whitefly from tomatoes and attract aphids, taking their focus off your crops. It also feeds ladybugs and other predatory insects.
- Nasturtiums: edible in their own right; these can be planted as a sacrificial crop to take aphids away from your other plants.
- Lavender: the strong, sweet smell will deter aphids and attract pollinators
- Basil: this can be planted alongside tomatoes to deter thrips, armyworms, and horn-worms.
- Sunflowers: these don't repel pests, but they can provide support for other plants and offer shade.

There are many other companion plants that you may find useful, so spend some time researching the best "friends" for the crops you'd like to grow and the plants they aren't compatible with.

Food Storage

Think also about food storage. *How much space do you have, and how long can you keep the crop?* If you have access to a cellar, many crops can be stored for longer. If you only have a small freezer, short-life crops such as peas, zucchinis, and cucumbers may not be worth growing. We will cover food storage tips later, but don't grow vast amounts of any kind of food without at least considering how you will store the crop when it is ready.

That might sound like quite a lot of information to take in and think about – but again, you don't need to get all these right immediately. Try some things and see what works. Your homestead will grow with you, and your knowledge and understanding will increase. It serves to help you think about all the different aspects of selecting the right plants and growing them sustainably, so you can hone your approach over the years and get the maximum benefits from your land.

Vegetables

Vegetables will probably be the mainstay of your garden, but where do you start? If you're feeling overwhelmed by the above list and want an easy run of it the first few years, that's fine. Let's cover some of the easiest and best crops you can try while grips with the basics.

Although it is somewhat area dependent, some no-fail crops almost always yield. These include:

- Garlic
- Zucchinis

- Green beans
- Radishes
- Snap peas
- Swiss chard
- Kale
- Lettuce
- Beets
- Strawberries
- Bush tomatoes (slightly more challenging but the best if you want a tomato crop)
- Potatoes

That isn't to say these crops involve no work, have no pests, and never suffer from diseases. Even a no-fail crop will fail sometimes. You have to water them, tend to them, and protect them from predators – but these are the best crops to try when you just want to go. They are also crops that are generally easy to use in the home, and many households will enjoy them.

Remember that you don't have to create colossal vegetable plots with massive numbers of crops straight away. It's better not to. Depending on how much time you can commit and how much confidence you have (and how much risk you want to take), having one or two trial vegetable beds for the first couple of years is critical before expansion. Even a tiny planter may surprise you in how much food it can produce, and you are much less likely to get overwhelmed if you take it a few steps at a time.

As you become more confident and start establishing habits, you will need to start thinking about crop rotations, especially if you are working in a small space. Constantly growing the same plant in the same spot might seem convenient, but it is not a good idea. The soil will quickly become depleted of the nutrients that the plant uses most, and there's also a risk of diseases being harbored in the soil.

When you reach this stage of planning your vegetable beds in the long term, you may want to start using graph paper and tracing paper to create plans for your beds year after year. You can overlay the crops you will rotate and create a schedule that will let you maximize and ensure that your soil gets rested and replenished before you add more seedlings.

However, if you want to start simply, do so! There will be time to learn and improve later. You might never start if you try to do too much initially because it can be overwhelming to think about all these different elements. Grow with your garden, rather than trying to know everything before you begin.

Fruit And Nut Plants

Fruits are great to grow in your backyard. Many fruits are expensive, have big footprints, and come wrapped in plastic. Growing your own can be surprisingly easy! Nuts are not necessarily as straightforward, but there are a few you can add to a backyard homestead to make the most of it. Having nut trees is a great way to provide shade and shelter for birds and other creatures and make your homestead feel complete. So, let's take a look at these two crop categories.

Fruits

Depending on your space, there are many fruits you can grow in your backyard. Consider:

- Strawberries: are among the easiest and best crops to grow but are vulnerable to slugs.
- Raspberries: will fruit year after year with minimal work.
- Blueberries: need ericaceous compost, so they are best grown in containers. Choose 3 varieties with different fruiting seasons for the most efficient pollination and a prolonged harvest.
- Apples: choose cooking apples or regular apples to enjoy this delicious, hardy fruit. Apples have an enormous range of uses and keep better than most other fruits.
- Currants: are great for sauces and desserts and easy to freeze.
- Grapes: check your USDA zone before choosing grapes and grow them under cover if necessary. There are different varieties for eating and making wine, so choose with care.
- Cherries: a cherry tree is another major asset, but it will need plenty of water, and you'll have to beat the birds to the fruits.
- Plums: plum trees are perfect if you like making jams or bottling the fruits.
- Melons: if you live somewhere hot, melons are fantastic to grow, and they can be put in containers or vegetable beds. They need a lot of space and water, so they're best for experienced homesteaders.

Fruits are an essential part of a homestead; they bring sugar to your backyard garden and help supply desserts, jams, and some savory dishes. Most fruits take up a relatively small amount of space, and their flavor is extraordinary – especially compared with fruits that are picked unripe and shipped for thousands of miles. You'll never want to eat store-bought strawberries again!

Nuts

Nuts will require you to plant trees, so they may not be feasible if you're short on space – but it's still worth looking at them. Nut trees are ideal if you've got a bit of room and want some shade. You might want to try:

Sweet chestnut trees: are self-fertile, so you'll only need one; however, they can get enormous.

Walnut trees: again, a big tree, walnuts will produce better nuts if they can cross-pollinate, but they offer delicious and highly nutritious food.

Hazelnuts: if you want an easy tree, hazelnuts are probably the best, as they can be kept small. However, you will need at least two, so be aware of that before planting.

Herbs And Spices

Your garden can also provide you with some amazing herbs and spices, and these can often be planted among your vegetables to provide companion benefits and save on space. You might want to consider:

- Basil
- Mint
- Oregano
- Rosemary
- Lemon balm
- Parsley
- Dill
- Cilantro
- Cumin
- Mustard
- Fennel
- Garlic
- Bay
- Ginger
- Lavender

These plants have culinary uses, and many also have medicinal uses. Think about which ones you use most commonly in your cooking and which will grow well in your climate. Most herbs and spices like well-draining soil and heat are essential to check.

Growing Grains

Before starting this section, it's worth acknowledging that grains are not a mainstay of many backyard homesteads. They might be a staple in the kitchen, but they aren't a great option if you have limited space and want to maximize your yields. To get a decent amount of food from grains, you need space.

However, it is still worth looking at the grains you could grow if you are dedicated. Popular grain crops include:

- Wheat
- Barley
- Rye
- Oats
- Corn
- Amaranth

Grains have many advantages because you can use them to create bread, pasta, beer, oatmeal, and more, but most homesteaders find that the yield isn't worth the effort. Corn is probably the best because it only takes up a moderate amount of space and gives you a relatively high-calorie yield. You can make cornbread and cornflour, and you'll have something to feed to livestock, but you won't get as much value from the ground as if you grow vegetables.

Most other grains are hard to grow and need significantly more space. Amaranth is easy but has low yields. It also offers edible leaves, so you're at least getting a double crop, but it isn't a particularly exciting or tasty option.

Hydroponic And Aquaponic Systems

Hydroponic and aquaponic systems are becoming increasingly popular for backyard homesteaders. They can be immensely efficient if set up correctly. You get a lot more control over your plant's environment and the ability to save water for some water-intensive crops, such as salads. They can produce incredible yields in very little space, and you don't have to spend hours struggling with poor soil.

Unfortunately, the drawback is the cost, as these systems are expensive. You need many more materials to set up a hydroponic system, which means more investment upfront. However, if you have some funds, it's worth exploring these systems, so let's learn more about them.

Hydroponic Systems

Hydroponic plants are grown in soilless containers full of nutrient-rich water that provides the plant with all the food it needs. There are quite a few advantages. One of the biggest is that water is not lost into the soil but is kept as part of a closed-loop system. Ergo, you don't need to give the crops nearly as much overall, which is massively important if you have a limited water supply.

Other advantages include that you can more easily protect this system from pests and accurately control what nutrients your plants get and when. It's much easier to ensure a plant receives what it needs than when dealing with a traditional growing system.

Aquaponic Systems

Aquaponic systems are similar, but they also involve fish. The waste from the fish provides nutrients to the plants, and the fish themselves are a source of food for the homesteader – so this is a great way to increase your range of food without dramatically increasing the amount of space needed.

This kind of farming has gone on for years in China, where flooded rice paddies have fish swimming in them. When the fields are drained, rice and fish can be harvested simultaneously, thus providing the mainstay diet for many people. This ingenious farming is critical to making the most of your space.

However, aquaponic systems require a lot more management because you need to remove the waste from the system to prevent it from poisoning the fish. You also need to feed the fish, keep them healthy, and look after the plants. Setting up a viable aquaponics system can be pricey and requires a lot of learning – but it can be done if you have the time and the money, and it's an efficient way of getting two kinds of foods from one space.

Growing Time And Yields

It is essential to look at your crops' growing time and yields; This is key to determining whether the crop is a good use of your space or not. The longer a crop takes to grow, the higher its yield must be worthwhile.

Knowing how long vegetables will take to harvest is crucial if you want to do any succession planting or crop rotations because it will significantly impact these things. Different crops mature in different periods and vary somewhat depending on the conditions. You can create a plan for your beds if you know how long, on average, your crop will take to turn from a seed into a vegetable that is ready to pick.

If you want to grow lots of different crops in a reasonably small space, you may wish to choose fast-growing crops that you can harvest very soon. If you want high yields, you might be more focused on slow but productive plants. Some people opt for something in between or a mixture of the two. For example, you might grow lettuce alongside pumpkins and enjoy several lettuce crops before your pumpkins have even begun to swell. Some crops can be harvested again and again and will keep producing, while others have a one-off harvest season.

You might find it helpful to have a list like the below:

- Radishes: about 25 days to harvest.
- Carrots: about 50 days to harvest.
- Dwarf green beans: about 60 days to harvest.
- Spinach: about 30 days to harvest.
- Salads: about 20 days to harvest.
- Peas: about 65 days to harvest.

Once you have assessed the timing for a crop, you will need to think about how much food it will give you; This can be more complicated because it depends on the conditions and the variety you have chosen, but many plants will come with their yield estimates. A thorough assessment will help you calculate how many plants you'll need to supply all of your family with that vegetable for a specific period.

It is important to record how much of that vegetable you eat in a particular period. If you have four family members who consume 10 carrots per week and plan to eat carrots for about half the year, you need to multiply 10 by 4 to get 40 carrots per week. Next, multiply by 25 to get half of the year, and you've got 1000 carrots being consumed. That means planting at least 1000 carrot seedlings since each head only produces one carrot. Bear in mind that some may not produce at all.

That might seem like a lot but remember that you don't have to aim for complete self-sufficiency, and you can grow more varied crops if you prefer. Remember that you don't need to plant all these carrots at once. You need to stagger the planting sessions, so you don't get overwhelmed by carrots all at once and then have nothing for the rest of the season.

It helps keep track of the yields you get from certain plants to know how many to grow. Even plants with a yield estimate should be tracked to see how well they do in your soil. *How many zucchinis do you get from one plant? How many potatoes?* Find out, and you can fine-tune your growing habits.

Summary

In this chapter, we've covered:

- How to grow food sustainably, including information on companion planting, growing seasons, and which crops to select.
- Which vegetables are best for most beginners.
- Ideas of fruits and nuts to grow.
- Ideas of herbs and spices to grow.
- Grains you can try.
- Aquaponic and hydroponic systems.
- Growing times and yields.

In the following chapter, we will look at how to raise chickens and what advantages these offer to your backyard homestead. There's quite a bit to find out before you add these birds to your plan, so keep reading to learn more!

3
How To Bring Up Chickens

"Every unwanted animal ends up on my farm: alpacas and horses and dogs and cats and chickens and ducks and parrots and fish and guinea pigs."

-Salma Hayek

You might be wondering whether you should add chickens to your backyard homestead or if this is a bad idea. To be clear: I've raised chickens many times, and I love them. I also recognize that they require work and commitment. They are living animals. They need your time. They will get sick, they will need mucking out, and they will need looking after.

That said, chickens also bring enormous pleasure, especially if you are an animal lover. Watching them scrap around, coo over delicious treats, and sunbathe is highly satisfying. There's also a rare feeling of joy when you collect your first eggs from the hen house – that magic of peeking inside a dark, cozy nest box to see if some treasure is awaiting you. If you let your hens raise babies, you'll get further joy in watching the little chicks. Of course, before we get too sentimental about it, chickens are usually there to provide us with food.

You might keep chickens just for their eggs or as a source of meat, but either way, they can be an excellent part of your homestead, bringing protein and variety to your diet. Eggs are a crucial ingredient for many foods (baking a cake without eggs is tricky!), and chicken is a staple meat in many households. Additionally, chickens will give you excellent manure for your garden. However, be aware that they can also be destructive and will dig up and peck plants, so you may need to fence them out of certain areas.

Before we go any further on this subject, make sure that you have checked the zoning laws for your area and that they allow you to keep chickens. You may need a permit, you may have to comply with specific regulations, or you may not be able to keep them at all. You might also want to talk to any neighbors who could be disturbed by the noise.

Which Chickens And How Many?

It's essential to have enough chickens to supply your egg needs, or you'll find yourself running to the store to fill in the gaps. If you don't eat a lot of eggs, you will obviously need fewer birds, but bear in mind that it's better to have an excess than a dearth, and you can always sell or swap extra eggs (more on that in Chapter 7). There will also be periods when your chickens don't lay, and you may occasionally lose a bird to illness or predators.

If you are going to raise chickens for eggs, choose hybrid breeds that have been specifically bred to maximize their egg-laying capacity. You will generally want 2 birds per household member, plus an extra bird or 2 for baking/other cooking needs, which should be plenty.

Think about the breed and the space, too. Some hybrids are happier in small amounts of space, but many need to be ranging and exploring to be satisfied. You might think it doesn't matter too much, but happy birds will produce more eggs and be more resistant to diseases. Also, they will find food for themselves while foraging (although you must still provide food), which will enrich their eggs and make them particularly tasty.

You should also consider your environment. Chickens prefer mild climates, but some chickens are better at coping with heat or cold than others. Choose accordingly.

So, which breeds are great for egg-laying? If you live in a mild climate, you have choices. Some good options include:

- Black Australorp
- Speckled Sussex
- Rhode Island Red
- Wyandotte
- Leghorn
- Dominique
- Welsummer
- Cochin
- Orpington
- Marans
- Brahma

These are all particularly prolific layers and also hardy birds. They will do well in your homestead. If you're in a hot climate, consider:

- Barred rock

- Araucana
- Black Minorca
- Rhode Island Red

If you're in a cold climate, you could get:

- Australorp
- New Hampshire Red
- Barred Rock
- Orpington

The breeds that fare best in cold weather will usually have smaller combs, which is the area vulnerable to frostbite. They may also have fluffy legs. Check that the breed you choose will be able to survive and thrive in your climate because otherwise, you may lose your flock or at least have unhappy chickens.

Another vital factor to consider is the chicken's predisposition to broodiness and whether you plan to raise chicks. Broodiness can be an asset if you do, but if you don't, it's a flaw. Broody chickens will stop laying and stay in the nest box and may prevent other chickens from going into it to lay. They may also be aggressive and unhappy when removed from the box.

However, if you want babies, these characteristics become key because they make your hen a dedicated mother. Decide whether you will raise chicks, and then choose your breeds accordingly.

It's also worth noting that although you can start with a few chickens and enlarge your flock later, this isn't easy to do. Chickens can be enormously territorial, and once they have an established group and pecking order, they will not welcome additions. You should never try to add a single chicken to your flock – if you want to increase the numbers, add pairs as a minimum; This will reduce the risks of the addition being made an outcast and minimize squabbling.

Chickens can be very aggressive and surprisingly damaging when they single a member of the flock out, so try to avoid adding chickens where you can, and if you need to increase the flock size, only do so in pairs or greater numbers.

In addition, consider whether or not to get a rooster. If you plan to breed your hens, you will need one, but they can be noisy and problematic, especially as young male chicks grow up. It's easy to end up with too many roosters, and they are challenging to rehome (although they can be used for meat). However, they will defend your hens from predators, so they do offer advantages. You may wish to consider borrowing a rooster or purchasing fertile eggs rather than owning one.

Hatching Eggs And Early Care

Raising your birds from eggs is a fabulous way to establish a bond with them, and it's a must-have set of skills if you are going to let your chickens breed. If you've got adult chickens, they will often do the work themselves, but you should understand how this works to assist or even take over if necessary. There's plenty that can go wrong when it comes to raising chickens.

Hatching Eggs

If you're going to hatch your chickens from eggs, you'll need an incubator, and this is an instrumental piece of equipment. If you're letting adult birds raise the chicks, too, you can put sickly or unhatched eggs in them to boost their chances.

So, assuming you are hatching the eggs without input from adult chickens, how do you do it? Firstly, let's start with the fact that it takes 21 days for eggs to hatch, give or take a day or two on either side. Usually, this is a very exact measurement, and hatching will be exactly 3 weeks after you start incubating the eggs.

You should choose clean and undamaged eggs to incubate and ensure they are a standard size. Avoid eggs that are big, small, misshapen, or cracked. Don't wash the eggs; instead, place them in the incubator immediately after being laid (and at most, within 1 week). Keep them at room temperature in the meantime and turn them daily so that the yolk stays in the center.

When you've gathered the eggs, you wish to incubate, turn these to around 100 degrees F for a forced-air incubator or up to 102 degrees F for a still-air incubator. Still-air incubators need to be opened at least 4 times each day to let oxygen get at the eggs. Place the eggs inside with the large end slightly tilted up; this is where the chick's head will be.

Use a hygrometer and a thermometer to keep track of the conditions in your incubator. The humidity should be between 28 and 50 percent for the first 18 days and between 65 and 75 percent for the remaining days.

You will also need to turn the eggs at least 3 times per day. You may find that it helps to use a marker to put a dot on one side of each egg and a line on the other, making it easier to see when you have successfully turned all of them. You need to keep turning them for the first 14 days, preferably 18 days. Opt for an uneven number of turns, so the chick doesn't repeatedly spend the overnight period (usually the longest between turns) in the same position. After day 18, lock your incubator down, stop moving the eggs, and avoid opening the incubator.

You will often get somewhere between a 55 and 95 percent hatch rate from eggs, although the rate of shipped eggs tends to be low.

Early Care

Congratulation on your hatchlings! You should allow them to dry off before moving them to a brooder. Give them a shallow dish of fresh water, and after day 2, provide as much food as they will eat. Ensure the chicks cannot drown in the water bowl by adding clean pebbles or marbles or keeping it very shallow.

The brooder needs to be kept warm, starting at about 90 degrees F for week 1. Decrease this by around 5 degrees each week as the chicks begin to grow feathers. If the chicks begin to pant, provide cooler areas, whereas they need more warmth if they huddle under the light.

You'll need a chick crumb in terms of food, and you'll need to keep the food area clean. After a couple of weeks, you can start letting them explore outside briefly in a safe pen. Keep a close eye on them, as they are completely helpless at this stage. Don't put them out if it's cold.

Even as your chickens grow and mature, they still need protection from the cold and careful monitoring for early diseases. They won't reach adulthood until they are about 16 weeks old, so make sure you have the space for them and the time to commit to looking after them. Baby chicks are vulnerable to many problems, so you need to devote time and energy to their early care. Assume that it will be at least 60 days before they will be independent of you.

Putting Chicks In A Coop

When the chicks are around 6 weeks old, you can move them out to the coop with the adults, as long as you don't live in a very chilly climate. You should take them out in the brooder or a box, open it and allow them to explore at their own pace. Ensure they find the food and water quickly.

You may want to confine them to just one part of the coop initially. Check that the chicks have shade, shelter, water, food, and enrichment. They should also have a way to retreat from the hens, although these are unlikely to bother them. Keep an eye on things for a few days to ensure no issues occur.

General Care, Feeding, Housing, And Maintenance

What about the general care that your chickens will need? It isn't excessive, but you need to put time and energy into keeping your birds healthy.

General Care

Before getting chickens, spend some time reading about them. While they are generally hardy birds, they can become prey to many problems and diseases. Mites and other pests may attack them, they can get worms, they can get viral and bacterial infections, and they can get injured. They don't have a fantastic sense of self-preservation (*I'm looking at you, chicken that decided to eat a strip of silicon*), and they are vulnerable to most predators.

The more reading you can do on the details of keeping chickens, the more success you are likely to have with your flock. Learn about common diseases and issues that your birds may face, and find out common treatments to restore them to health.

Feeding

Your chickens might be free-ranging, but you still need to supply feed each day before they fill up on treats. Don't let your birds loose in the yard until they have eaten a good amount of their standard feed because this will ensure that they are getting a balanced and nutritious diet. They also need grit, which can be provided in oyster shells or crushed eggshells; This helps them get enough calcium to form strong shells. It should be always available to them.

If you're going to let your chickens range, look at the hazards they might encounter before letting them out. Chickens are curious creatures, and as mentioned, they don't necessarily understand what they should and shouldn't eat. I've even heard of chickens eating laundry soap. You need to minimize the risks and fence off unsuitable parts of your garden before you let them out.

Check local laws first if you want to give your birds kitchen scraps. Some places prohibit this. Even if your area doesn't, make sure that you keep these to small quantities, and always check that something is suitable before letting the chickens have it.

Housing

You'll already be aware that chickens need a coop, and you should provide one even if you have a barn or something that they can head into. A coop gives the chickens a place to roost, which they require. A coop can be as fancy or basic as you like, but make sure it is secure from whatever predators your chickens might face. If your chickens are going to free-range, you won't be able to protect them during the day, but you can do so at night.

Most wild animals can consume or attack chickens, but coyotes, foxes, wolves, bears, badgers, ferrets, stoats, weasels, and rats are the everyday offenders, and your chicken coop should defend against as many as possible.

You can build your coop or buy one to suit a whole range of budgets, but it should have:

- A nest box (or multiple boxes, especially if you have many hens or broody-prone breeds; a good rule of thumb is one box per 3 hens).
- A feeder and drinker area (although these can be in a covered area outside the coop if necessary).
- Enough roosting perches for all birds to perch, plus extra space.
- The space for you to clean it out easily.
- Enough strength and insulation to protect your chickens from predators and inclement weather.
- Chickens will also benefit from a covered dust bath, although this doesn't have to be in the coop. They love bathing in dry soil, which helps keep their feathers free from mites and dirt.

If you will build your coop, make sure you have the skills to create something sturdy. A nice-to-have feature is a stable door to open the top half to lean in and refill feeders/drinkers without letting the chickens out. Automatic door closers are also appealing, so you don't have to get up early to let the chickens out of the coop.

If your chickens aren't going to range in your yard, remember that they will need space to scratch, sunbathe, and explore. They will also need regular mucking out in this space and the coop itself. A dirty coop will quickly cause disease and stress. Putting removable trays in the house below the perches is a great way to make cleanup easy.

Maintenance

There are a few recurring chores you'll need to do once your chickens have settled in. Cleaning out is probably the biggest; your chicken house should be mucked out regularly to keep it clean and safe for them. Change the straw in the nest box, clean and refresh water and food bowls, and check for any wear and tear on the house. Some people do this daily, while others go weekly. As long as the house is clean, that's all that matters.

Other maintenance chores will include administering worm treatments and getting booster vaccines.

Gathering Eggs

This activity should be done daily (although if you go on vacation, it's unlikely to matter if it isn't done for a few days). It would be best to allow the laying chicken to leave the nest box before taking the egg unless you're having problems with egg-eating. Most chickens will lay about 6 days per week, so eggs will always be collected.

You don't need to wash the eggs, which may make them more vulnerable to bacteria. Date them and place them in your refrigerator (some people prefer to store them in a cool spot on the counter). Make sure you use eggs up within a month, preferably within 2 weeks.

If the eggs are dirty, you can spot clean them or give them a quick scrub with cold water. Let them air dry, and then use those eggs up more quickly.

Chickens As Meat

Raising chickens for meat will often incorporate many of the same tactics, but you will probably choose different birds. It may be harder to work out how many birds you need because it depends on how much chicken you eat but let's look at some estimates.

For example, if you use one chicken per meal for your family and eat chickens once per week, you need to know how quickly your next batch will be mature enough to eat.

Broiler chickens mature much faster than others and can be ready in as little as 7 weeks. Others will take about 18 weeks. Assuming it takes 18 weeks, you will need 18 birds to be sustainable – because you'll be harvesting one each week, so it will take 18 weeks to get through your flock, by which time the new chickens should be ready to harvest.

It will probably not work this neatly in reality, but this may help you to start sussing out how many birds you need, and how frequently you will be starting a new cycle of chickens. You will often have more than 18 birds (since batches will mature simultaneously, and you'll only harvest a little at a time), so make sure you have enough space for them.

Some of the best meat chickens include:

- Broilers
- Cornish Cross
- Jersey Giant
- Freedom Rangers
- Bresse
- Brahma

If you are going to raise your chickens for meat, you will need to think about the whole process – it isn't as simple as just putting the eggs in the incubator and getting meat on your table. You're going to have to provide space, food, and shelter, and you're also going to have to think about butchering the birds. *How do you turn them into meat?*

You may be able to find a local service that will do this for you. If you wish to do it at home, you will need to look into humane methods and best sanitary practices to minimize the risk of problems. Make sure you are familiar with any laws and do be considerate of your neighbors when undertaking this practice. Many will not feel comfortable with it, so you'll need to plan accordingly.

Many people kill chickens by covering their heads with cones to prevent stress. You will then cut the chicken's head off using a very sharp knife; This minimizes suffering. Catch the blood in a bucket to make cleanup more manageable, and then it's time to scald and pluck the chicken. You should submerge it in 150 degrees F water for about 7 seconds, making it easier to pluck.

Pluck the chicken and set the feathers aside (they have many uses), and then you'll need to gut the chicken; This can be tricky if you've never done it before, so ideally, get someone experienced to show you the method. The steps are below:

1. Cut off the wing tips and the feet (at the knee break joints) using a deboning knife.
2. Cut open the bottom of the chicken and, working slowly and carefully to minimize mess, remove the intestines.
3. Remove the rest of the organs, including the lungs (this is quite tricky).
4. Clean the chicken using fresh water.
5. Soak the chicken in cold water to further remove any blood and debris.
6. Finish cleaning off any remnants with a good scrub, and then the chicken can be portioned up or left whole.

The meat also needs to be stored safely, so make sure you have room for it in your freezer or fridge. It's certainly possible to raise chickens for meat on a homestead – just make sure you tick all of these boxes before you start!

Summary

In this chapter, we've covered:

- The various breeds of chickens and how many you are likely to need.
- How to hatch eggs and care for the chicks.
- Moving chickens into a coop.

- How to house, feed, and care for chickens, plus some general maintenance tasks.
- How to collect and store eggs.
- How to deal with meat chickens, including a simple method for butchering them.

The following chapter will look at the other animals you might welcome to your homestead, especially if you've got the space. These can provide a variety of great food sources, so let's start exploring your options.

4

Other Farm Animals For Bigger Homesteads

"Farming looks mighty easy when your plow is a pencil, and you're a thousand miles from the corn field."

-Dwight D. Eisenhower

We're now getting into the more unusual and adventurous parts of backyard homesteading, but there's enormous value to this. The range of foods that you can use and tap into if you're prepared to put in the time and work, and embrace a learning curve, is extraordinary. I would advise getting to grips with the basics first and not trying to keep all of these animals before you've mastered the other parts of this book. I'd also advise against getting them all, even if you have the space.

Build up your homestead slowly. It takes time to make something great and sustainable, and if you try to do too many things at once, you'll get burned out and fail. Farming is hard work, and there's no getting around that. You will have to put in a lot of hours – and if you start too many projects at once, there simply won't be enough hours to keep them all running. That means it's essential not to get carried away but to take a calm approach to your farming and choose the foods you keep with care.

Remember that as well as being a source of food, animals are complete, feeling beings. You need to be able to look after them for their sake and your own, as few will produce good food if they are kept in terrible conditions. If you're interested in keeping some of the more complex animals, you may wish to spend a bit of time volunteering on a farm so you can gain an understanding of how to look after these creatures. There is nothing like hands-on experience! You should also make sure that you know a good vet before you take on any large farm animal, so you can call an expert when things go awry.

So, which animals might you want to start keeping on your farm? There are many options, but the most popular ones include: bees, which will provide you with honey, wax, and pollinate your plants; goats, which will provide you with milk and, by extension, cheese and butter, as well as potentially meat; pigs, which will give you meat; and cows, which will supply dairy products, and meat. Apart from bees, all of these animals will also provide you with manure for your garden.

Bear in mind that if you plan to use these animals as a source of meat, it may be best to partner with a farmer when it comes to butchering time. The method described in the previous chapter for chickens will not work with larger animals, and you must make sure that you dispatch the creatures humanely. That usually means methods that cannot be applied on a homestead. I'm not going to talk about harvesting meat from these animals, but it is a possibility if you want to explore it with the options available in your local area.

Keeping Bees

There's much more to keeping bees than just putting up some bee boxes in your yard and waiting for the honey to pour in – but you probably already know that. You may not know that beekeeping can be a surprisingly challenging thing to do. It's also a wonderful thing to do because it supports bee populations, increases pollination, and adds more insects to our planet, which we desperately need. Anyone can benefit from keeping bees.

We're going to cover some basics, which you may want to supplement with courses or local experience – a lot of beekeepers will let you tag along, help them out, and learn on the job if you want to. We'll look at:

- What you need
- How to set up a beehive
- How to order bees
- How to feed your hive
- How to identify problems
- How to harvest honey

What you need

So, starting with the basics, what equipment will you need to keep bees? Firstly and most obviously, a beehive will be crucial; This protects your bees from the elements and predators and allows them to start storing food. You will often find that buying a kit with boxes, frames, and foundations is the best way to get a good setup.

Of course, you will also need the bees. You can buy honey bees online or choose a local supplier with a good reputation. It is best to buy locally, as the bees will be accustomed to your climate and the available plants.

Next, you'll need protective gear. You have probably seen this many times, but it consists of a bee suit (often one-piece but sometimes pants and a jacket), gloves, and a veil. The bee suit will help protect you if the bees get angry, although many people simply wear thick, long-sleeved clothing.

You will also need some tools, including a hive tool, a scraper, an uncapping scratcher, and a honey extractor. A hive tool looks like a crowbar, and it is used to break up the boxes when they get stuck together. The scraper will help to deal with wax and propolis build-up, and the uncapping scratcher will uncap the comb so you can get at the honey. As the name suggests, the honey extractor will pull honey from the hive so you can store it. Make sure it is large enough for the number of hives you get.

How to set up a beehive

Setting up a beehive depends on which system you use – Langstroth or top-bar. Langstroth is the commonest and involves having the bees in boxes that are somewhat like drawers. They can be pulled out to access the hive, while the top bar holds the hives horizontally and is harvested from the top.

Your kit should come with instructions that will help you set up correctly, but make sure you place it on flat, stable ground, in an area with shelter from the wind (e.g. bushes). Ideally, it should be put somewhere with early morning sun. If you live in a warm climate, ensure that the hive gets shade in the latter part of the day, but full sun is fine in cooler temperatures.

Elevate the hive so moisture can't creep in at the base, and set up a water source nearby so the bees can drink. Put the bees' entrance facing away from the path, so they are less disturbed, and make sure you can easily access the hive. If necessary, consider protecting it from predators such as bears and skunks.

How to order bees

If you are going to keep bees, I'd strongly advise contacting local organizations or other keepers, as having a network is a great idea, and you'll get access to a wealth of knowledge this way; This is the best way to get bees, too.

However, choose a reputable seller if you want to order bees online. You can request a nucleus hive, a small but established colony that usually contains a queen, some comb, some honey, drones, and baby bees. This choice will get your colony off to a quick and strong start. Ensure you choose a good seller to reduce the risks of ending up with a weak or diseased colony.

Alternatively, you can buy "package bees." These packages usually have a queen, some workers, and a feeder that contains sugar syrup. The queen will be shipped inside a special cage with the workers, who will gradually acclimatize to her. They can then be added to the hive and will start to build a colony, although this is a slower method.

How to feed your hive

You'll need to feed your bees at certain times of the year, and knowing how and when is critical. You are not likely to need to feed them if they have abundant natural food, so your bees can fend for themselves when the flowers are in bloom. However, they will benefit from being fed during winter or other low seasons. Choose a bee feeder suitable for the type of beehive you have chosen.

If you have honey reserves to spare, this is the best food you can give to your bees, but you shouldn't give them commercially purchased honey, as this could contain contamination that would be harmful to the hive. You may want to set aside some "emergency" honey for your bees. You can also use sugar syrup or dry sugar, but these are not such good options.

You may also want to buy or make some pollen patties, as these provide bees with protein. They need it when they are rearing broods in spring and fattening up in the fall. However, don't feed them pollen in the fall, as your bees might decide that means they should rear babies just before winter starts – which you don't want them to do.

Avoid feeding bees year-round, as they should forage. Sugar syrup is not nutritious enough to sustain them long-term and should be avoided except when necessary.

How to identify problems

Unfortunately, quite a lot of things can go wrong with a hive. Bees are vulnerable to infections and diseases, especially if other bees attack their hive. Fungus and ants can also be issues. Parasites, mites, beetles, lice, moths, cockroaches, earwigs, and even mice may attack your hive.

It's good to read about common problems before you set up your hive and get your bees.

Learn what healthy larvae look like, and familiarize yourself with some of the common pests that could attack your hive and how to deal with these.

Again, being in touch with local, experienced beekeepers is one of the best ways to learn about the problems your bees may face because there are so many. If you ever see mites or other tiny insects in the hive, your bees could be under attack. Adult bees acting oddly, trembling, or struggling with mite infestations are also worrying signs.

How to harvest honey

There are a few different methods for harvesting honey, and you'll need to wear protective clothing for this job. You may want to use a smoker to drive the bees down in the hive, although not all beekeepers do this.

Next, you will need to lift out a full-frame (it will have been sealed with beeswax). Use a hot knife to cut the wax away and set it aside for candle-making, wax wrap-making, or other uses. Grab your honey extractor to pull the liquid honey out of the frame without damaging the frame. Once the honey has all been gathered, replace the frame in the hive.

Remember to leave your bees with plenty of honey to eat, especially in winter. Responsible harvesting is key to ensuring that your hive survives and being a good beekeeper!

Keeping Goats

Goats are probably the easiest thing to keep on a homestead, especially where space is limited. They provide excellent milk, and they can also be a source of fiber, keep other animals company, and clear areas for you. Many people get very attached to their goats as they tend to have quirky and endearing personalities – so goats may prove a valuable addition to your homestead. However, bear in mind that goats don't particularly like being solitary, and you should always keep multiple goats if you can.

Let's look at:

- What you need
- How to care for a goat
- How to milk a goat
- How to harvest fiber from a goat
- Other considerations

What you need

You don't need a lot of fancy equipment to keep goats, although they prefer to be fed from a manger, as they dislike dirty food that has been on the ground and may reject it. Your goats will need a warm, weatherproof stall or barn that they can head into at night, and this should have a minimum of 20 square feet per goat. They should be able to go into this at any time, and it should be easy to clean.

It would help if you also had some excellent fences. Goats are notorious for their escapology, and this reputation is well deserved. They are incredibly clever, they have strong teeth that can bite through various materials, and they love to get into places they shouldn't. You cannot keep goats unless you have a well-fenced property – particularly if your neighbors would object to finding a goat in their garden.

Beyond that, goats need food, 30 square feet (each) of outdoor space, and little else. They are browsers, but you must still provide the right food to keep them healthy. You will also probably need some hoof trimmers, syringes and needles, and general first aid items like bandages (this is good for all animals).

How to care for a goat

You will mostly be caring for a goat by providing food, fresh water, and mucking out services.

Let's start with food. Your goats will spend a lot of time browsing when they can, so be aware that they will want to sample your trees and bushes. They aren't grazers, so they probably won't eat much of your lawn. They should be given a constant supply of grass-based hay and additional proteins such as alfalfa if they are in milk. Other grains can be given instead, but barley, oats, and corn are not as nutritious.

Goats may also benefit from a mineral block, and if your local soils are poor, this becomes particularly important. You can also give your goats baking soda to boost their intake of minerals, plus a salt block.

Fresh water should always be available to the goats, and you should check that it is every day. If the weather is cold, make sure the water gets defrosted.

How frequently they need mucking out depends on how many goats you have, how much time they spend outdoors, how ample the indoor space is and keeping the shelter clean and tidy. Dirty living conditions will make your goat vulnerable to pests and diseases.

How to milk a goat

You may want a milking stand to make milking easier, which will elevate the goat so you can sit rather than crouch, and it's easy to clean and sanitize. However, it isn't crucial. You should spend time handling your goats even when you aren't milking them, ensuring that they get used to you; This will make them easier to bring to the milking stand. Having a good routine and – believe it or not – being cheerful can also make the process smoother.

It takes a little practice to learn how to milk, and you might want to learn from a local farmer if you can. Place a bucket under the goat's udders and then put your hands on its teats and bring your forefingers and thumbs together – gently pinching the udder. Minimize pulling, and keep going until the milk stops flowing. When it does, gently press the udder a few times in quick succession with the palm of your hand, and return to milking, therefore, releasing more milk.

Goats vary in how easy they are to milk, so get help from someone more experienced if you have problems. The more you handle your goats and treat them kindly, the easier milking should be. Goats also have different preferences on how they like to be milked, so getting to know your goat will help.

How to harvest fiber from a goat

How you harvest fiber from your goat will depend on the breed, and only some breeds are good for fiber. Fiber goats tend to be more delicate and need greater care.

You may be able to harvest fibers as the goats naturally shed them, which will usually happen in the spring, depending on the climate. Usually, you will need to use a comb once the shedding starts or shear the goats. Shearing is something that you should have taught to you by an expert, as it is quite a skill.

There are many kinds of fiber goats, including Angoras, Nigoras, Licheng Daqing, and others. A lot of the fibers produced from goats are considered highly desirable, and this is a great way to boost your annual income if you have the time and energy to look after them.

Other considerations

There are a few more things to think about before getting a goat. One is that goats are surprisingly loud creatures, and this can be multiplied if you have a herd of them – so be aware of that and think of your neighbors before adopting.

Secondly, they can be pretty destructive. Since they are browsers, they love to sample a whole range of plants, and they will happily help themselves to all the things you are trying to grow for yourself and your family. They get rid of weeds effectively but be aware that if you can't keep your goats penned into specific areas (which is a challenge!), they will devastate your vegetables.

Keeping Pigs

Many pig owners love their pigs – and what's not to love about these beautiful animals? Of course, if you are keeping them for meat, you may not want to get too attached, but it's still important to know how to care for them to be happy and comfortable throughout their lives. Let's be clear that pigs aren't enormously easy animals to raise, and they aren't for the beginner homesteader. You also need a reasonable amount of space, and pigs, like goats, are good at escaping. Again, consider neighbors and local laws before getting pigs.

Also, don't think pigs will be garbage disposal for your food waste. Pigs have traditionally been fed on table scraps, but they don't make for a suitable diet and could cause disease. You should spend some time calculating your costs before taking on pigs because they need a lot of food, which can be expensive!

So what do pigs need? You have to provide space, shelter, good fencing, hay, straw, food, fresh water and regular cleaning. Let's break it down a bit.

Space

First, decide how many pigs you are thinking of keeping. They aren't the most space-intensive animal, but they are large and cramped pigs will be miserable. At the minimum, you'll need 20 square feet per pig, and if you choose the minimum amount of space, you'll be doing a lot of cleaning. I'd recommend being as generous as possible on the space; this will keep the pigs happier, although they may get skittish if they have lots of space and rarely get handled.

Shelter

Ideally, your pigs should be given a barn that they can pop in and out of as it suits them. This provides shelter from both the sun and the rain. An outdoor pig hutch will work, too long as it is large enough for them. Pigs must have a dry spot to sleep in, so don't try to keep your pigs outdoors. Even foraging and free-ranging pigs will require a barn.

Good Fencing

You might be surprised by how strong a pig is, and that's not great news for your fencing. You will need to build very sturdy enclosures with rigid panels. Some people use electric fencing, but this involves some training, as pigs will generally walk into fencing rather than away from it.

If your pigs do get out, use food to lure them back, rather than trying to herd them. You can get a pig to go almost anywhere for food!

Fodder

You will need to give your pigs a constant supply of hay, straw, and commercial feed to provide them with a balanced diet and keep them healthy. Even foraging pigs need to supplement their feed to ensure they get enough to eat.

You need to think about space for the food and the pigs. Straw and hay need to be kept dry and can require machinery to move if it is in large quantities. Make sure you're taking this into account.

Finally, ensure your pigs always have access to clean water. Troughs need to be cleaned regularly, and they need to be heavy enough that the pigs cannot tip them over. Alternatively, consider getting automatic waterers that supply the pigs with water via nipples. This water should stay cleaner and may prove less work.

Keeping Cows

Cows are probably the most challenging animals you might keep on your homestead. They also aren't necessarily cost-effective, especially if you raise them for milk only rather than for meat. You may not be able to sell your milk, depending on local regulations, as it won't be pasteurized. The best breed will also depend on where you live, so research local conditions and recommendations.

There is a lot to know about raising cows, so you may want to get some specific books, but I'll cover a few basics here.

Space

If you're just looking for the cow to provide you with milk, a single cow will often be enough, but even one needs enough space to get sufficient food and stay healthy. It's also worth noting that cows are not naturally solitary animals, and they will not be happy if they are kept alone. A herd will need significant amounts of space.

Cattle need more space than many farm animals; about 1 acre per cow will be necessary. That will put them out of reach for many backyard homesteaders. This land also needs to be suitable pasture so that the cows can graze. However, grass-fed beef is certainly popular because it is thought to be healthier, so if you have enough space, cows may offer profits if raised for meat.

Shelter

Like all animals, cows will need a clean, dry, windproof shelter where they can retreat to. Usually, cows are kept in large barns. You'll need to be able to muck the barn out easily, and it should be reasonably warm and comfortable. If you will be milking the cows, you may want to do this in a separate barn to keep the environment sterile.

If you live in an area with snowy weather, the barn should be enclosed, but an open barn may be suitable if temperatures never drop below freezing.

Good Fencing

Your fields will need to be fenced. Cows that wander freely could be a danger to themselves and others, and you need to keep them in. Make sure you've got suitable fencing in place before you purchase your cows, and remember that this will need to be maintained regularly, especially if your cows are keen to escape.

Fodder

Cows may spend the majority of their lives grazing, but they also need feeding, especially in the winter. You need to make sure the grass is healthy and at its optimum richness if you want good milk and meat – poor quality grass will not produce suitable consumables.

You will often need to supplement a cow's diet with grain and good hay, especially for dairy cows, which put a lot of energy into milk production. Cows also use roughage to keep themselves warm, so it's going to be particularly important to feed your cattle regularly in the winter, so they don't get chilled. Again, think about the space requirements of storing a reliable food supply. Clean, fresh water is always also a must.

Summary

In this chapter, we've covered:

- Looking after bees, how to feed bees, and how to harvest honey.
- How to keep goats, milking, and fiber collection.

- Keeping pigs and their top requirements.
- Keeping cows and how much space they need.

In the following chapter, we will look at food storage and how you can use both modern and traditional methods to ensure your food lasts for as long as possible. We'll touch on some top preservation techniques so you can fully enjoy your harvests and make sure your hard work doesn't go to waste.

5

Making Your Food Last

"You don't need a silver fork to eat good food."

-Paul Prudhomme

One of the major challenges that almost all backyard homesteaders face is how to store the food once they have successfully grown it. It is a problem that humans have dealt with since we started growing food, which fortunately does mean that there are numerous options – especially in today's world.

It is pretty much the nature of farming that you will get gluts of crops all at once. Some crops are particularly notorious for this, and you can sometimes mitigate it with staggered planting. Still, you will always be dealing with surpluses at times and lacking in that very same crop at other times. That means you need to learn about storing foods effectively to make them last as long as possible.

There are many different options, especially today, so let's learn about some.

Canning Foods

Canning is an age-old method for preserving your food, and it's ideal for fruits in particular. Things like plums are perfect for preserving, and this will make sure you can enjoy the fruits throughout the year.

There are three major kinds of safe canning methods, and it's important to follow one of these. Improperly canned foods could carry the bacteria that causes botulism, so take sterilization and the proper method seriously.

Once canned, foods should be placed somewhere cool and dark. Aim to use them up within a year.

Boiling Water Bath

The boiling water bath is one of the easiest ways for most people who want to get into canning. It involves heating the jars in boiling water to seal them and completely kill off the bacteria.

You can do this with foods high enough in acid to prevent the growth of the botulism bacteria. This kind of canning is usually used for fruits and pickled vegetables.

You should start by washing your jars with hot, soapy water, rinsing them and putting them to one side. Next, place the rack in the bottom of the canner and half fill it with warm water. Fill the jars with hot water, and then use jar lifters to put them into the canner (jar lifters are pretty essential; without them, you're going to burn yourself or break the jars).

Cover the jars with more water until they are submerged by at least an inch, and turn the heat up to medium.

Prepare the food that you are going to be canning, and then lift a jar out of the water, drain it, and fill it with the food. You need to leave about ½ inch of space at the top (consult your recipe for the exact amount) and then wipe the neck of the jar with a clean, damp cloth and put the lid on. Do not tighten yet.

Lift the jar back into the warm water and do the same for the other jars until you have used up all the food. Next, put your lid on the canner and bring the water to a high boil, following your recipe for time guidance. When enough time has passed, turn the ring off, remove the lid, and after 5 minutes, lift the jars out and place them on a cutting board.

Allow them to cool until you hear the "pop" that indicates the seal has pulled in, taking hours or as little as 30 minutes. Tighten the lids if necessary. After 6 hours have passed, check whether any lids will still flex. If they will, they haven't sealed properly and need to be stored in the fridge and used up quickly.

Pressure Canning

If you want to preserve low-acid foods, a pressure canner is your only option. If the pH of the food is higher than 4.6, you will need to use pressure canning to be safe. The pressurized steam will create a temperature of 240 degrees F, which should destroy the bacterial spores and keep the food safe from spoilage.

Before starting, wash and sterilize your jars and prepare the food ready to go into them. Next, add 3 inches of water to the base of the pressure canner, and then place the racks in the base. Fill your jars with food, lift them onto the racks, and put the lids in place. Leave the vent port off the canner, turn the heat up to the highest setting, and heat until you see steam coming out of the vent port. Wait for 10 minutes, put a weight on the vent port, and allow the canner to reach the designated pressure.

Once it has reached this pressure, begin timing it and make sure the canner stays at a steady pressure. If the pressure drops, increase the heat, and if it rises, decrease it. If it drops too low, pause your timer; it needs enough time at the proper heat to be safe to store.

When the time stated in the recipe has passed, turn the heat off and allow the pressure gauge to come back to 0 (or wait 45 minutes if you're using a dial gauge, following the manufacturer's directions).

Finally, remove the jars, set them on a cooling rack, and leave them undisturbed for 24 hours. Check that all the lids have been sealed before storing, and don't store jars with lids that flex.

Steam Canning

A slightly less common option, steam canning, may appeal to you; This is again not intended for foods with a pH value above 4.6. Steam canning has often been considered unsafe, but a 2015 study at the University of Wisconsin confirmed that steam canning is safe when done correctly.

To start steam canning, place an appropriate amount of water in the base of the steam canner (according to the manual); This is usually around 3 quarts. Next, put the perforated cover on and bring it to a low boil.

Wash and rinse your jars, and then prep your food and pack it while hot into the jars. Set the full jars back in the base to stay warm while packing the others. Allow the last jar a couple of minutes to warm, and then put the dome on top of the base over the next 5 minutes; gradually increase the temperature until a 10 inch column of steam can be seen coming from the holes at the base. You may also be able to use a temperature dial.

Once the steam has started, begin timing, referring to your recipe. Make sure the canner keeps steaming, and pause the timer if it slows down.

When the time is up, turn off the heat, wait for 3 minutes, and lift the dome away. Be careful you don't burn yourself on the resulting steam. Leave the jars to cool and seal, and then check they are sealed and store them in a cool, dark place.

Before using a steam canner, check that the recipe you plan to use is appropriate. Be wary if it steams for less than 45 minutes; this may not be enough to make it safe.

Drying Foods

There are many ways to dry food at home, and this is another technique that has been used for generations to make food last longer. All kinds of foods can be dried, which is one of the best ways to preserve food close to its original form. Dried fruit may not be as delicious and tempting as fresh, but it hasn't had its flavor changed to preserve it.

Drying food makes it difficult for mold and bacteria to grow, and it's an effective technique. Dried food is also easy to eat, so if you're outdoors a lot during the day, it makes a good option for a healthy snack. Lots of foods can be dehydrated, including:

- Meat
- Fish
- Many vegetables
- Most fruits

Be aware that dried foods won't last forever, and you should aim to use them up within a year at the most. The more water remains in the food, the faster it will need using. Always check that the food looks okay before you consume it. Chewier foods, like meat and to-matoes, need to be used up more quickly than those you dehydrate into hard chips (e.g. banana chips). Even so, this is an enormously versatile option for making food last!

So, what methods of drying are there? You can get a proper dehydrator dedicated to doing this job, and this may be the best option if you plan to dry a lot of foods, as it tends to be energy efficient. However, it isn't your only choice.

You can dry food in the sun, microwave, oven, and air some foods. You need to make sure that the method you choose is safe, particularly if you plan to dry meats, because otherwise, you could make yourself very sick and waste a lot of food. Let's break all these methods down.

Using a dehydrator

Dehydrators are fast and often the most effective method for drying food, but they come with the drawback of being another gadget to buy and store. However, they can produce superior dried foods and be pretty energy efficient, so they are ideal if you're going to pre-serve a lot of your foods by drying them.

Before adding food to your dehydrator, prepare it. Fruits should be washed and patted dry, with pits/stones removed. All food pieces should be approximately the same size, making it easy to dry them effectively without some pieces becoming tough. You need to dehydrate foods thoroughly if you want to store them at room temperature for extended periods, so make sure you follow a recipe if you aren't sure how long a food will need.

Don't overcrowd the dehydrator trays or foods that won't dry properly, and make sure all foods are clean before you put them in. Your dehydrator does not cook the food so that it won't remove any bacteria.

Using the sun

Sun-drying is probably the oldest drying method out there, and it is perfectly effective if you do it correctly. This method is great because it doesn't cost energy, and it's all-natural. However, you need to be in a pretty hot place for this to work – think temperatures over 100 degrees F. In a colder climate, it simply isn't going to work, and you could end up with moldy food.

However, if you want to give this a go and you are in the right area, you'll need to wash and slice your food into thin slices, space it out on a tray, and place it in the direct sunlight. If you put it outside, rather than on a windowsill, make sure you throw a light cloth over it to avoid insects landing on the food.

It can take days for foods to dry like this. Turning them occasionally may help. Keep them in the sun until they turn leathery and wrinkly, and then bring them inside to store. Do not let them get rained during the drying process!

Using an oven

An oven is a popular option for households that don't have a dehydrator. You might be surprised to learn that you can use it in this way, but on its lowest setting, an oven can work on drying out foods and make them safe to store.

As before, wash and pat dry fruits and vegetables, and then slice them. Thin slices will help speed up the drying process, and as ovens take a lot longer than dehydrators, this is important. ¼ inch slices should work.

Spread the slices out on a sheet pan and put them in the oven for around 7 hours, checking on them occasionally. If that seems too long, you can slightly increase your oven's temperature, but be aware that there is a risk of making foods crispy and cooked rather than dried.

Using a microwave

Your microwave is a good option if you want just to dehydrate small amounts of food, and the oven is too slow. Start this by washing the rotating plate in the microwave so it is suitable for putting foods on, and then prepare the food you wish to dry. Again, go for thin slices so that they can dry effectively.

Spread the fruit across the microwave plate and then switch the microwave to defrost, set the timer for 30 minutes and put the plate inside. Do NOT forget to put it on defrost and then walk away for 30 minutes as this could be a major fire risk. It is best to remain nearby while your food is in the microwave so you can intervene if something goes wrong.

After 30 minutes, turn the fruit pieces over (don't burn yourself) and decide whether they need longer. Some foods have more moisture than others and require up to 45 minutes, while others will only take about 30.

Move the fruits to a cooling rack and allow them to cool, and you're done!

Using the air

Some kinds of foods, especially herbs, can be dried by simply hanging them up and max-imizing the airflow around the food. It takes some time to dry like this, so it is only suitable for foods that can be safely stored at room temperature for an extended period.

A whole range of foods can be air-dried, including:

- Herbs
- Peppers
- Chillies
- Nuts
- Mushrooms
- Some fruits (e.g. apples) in the right conditions

You need to make sure that the room is not humid or damp, or the food will not dry prop-erly. If the air is too moist, the food is likely to mold. Having a good air flow is also import-ant for reducing the risk of mold, so don't leave the food in an enclosed space, even if it's warm.

The easiest way to air dry food is to tie it in small bunches, binding strings around the stems to hold it together. Don't use big bunches, or the central stems will not dry out no matter how long you leave them.

You may wish to lift the bunches down every day and rearrange the stems to improve the drying, but this has the disadvantage of being more labor-intensive.

When first air-drying a food, it's best to do a small batch, especially if you aren't sure whether it will work. Herbs can reliably be dried like this as long as the conditions aren't humid, but experiment before trying it with other options.

Freezing Foods

Of course, freezing is one of the most effective methods that we currently have of food preservation, and it's also one of the easiest. You can toss almost all foods in your freezer and take them out months or even years later – and they will still be fine to eat. Sometimes, their texture will have lost some quality, but they will remain safe, even if stored for a long time.

This is like magic for the backyard homesteader who needs to store food, and it's a device our ancestors would have loved, but of course, it does require power. Having a freezer can be expensive, and you need to make sure you are getting the maximum use from it to justify this cost; This is particularly true if you depend on your energy sources (e.g. solar panels).

Freezing is a lot faster than many of the other storage methods, and if you have a chest freezer, you can store large amounts of food; This works particularly well if you have multiple containers of one kind of food because you can stack them, so you create one stack of carrots, one of the zucchinis, one of processed meat, etc. If you want to freeze many different kinds of foods, chest freezers can be annoying because you end up with foods getting buried underneath other foods.

Upright freezers can be more convenient for storing many different kinds of foods, as the drawers keep everything organized and accessible. They are not as energy-efficient because they lose more cold air when the door is opened, but both are good options if you haven't got time for home canning or drying (or even if you have but want other storage options).

You can freeze all kinds of things from your garden. Almost all vegetables will freeze well, although they may not taste quite as great as when they were fresh. A few foods that do not do well in the freezer include:

- Raw cabbages
- Lettuce

- Celery
- Cucumbers
- Radishes
- Potatoes
- Eggs
- Custard
- Melons
- Mayonnaise
- Soft cheeses

Fruits generally do not freeze very well, as they have a high water content, which means the freezing process ruins them. Avoid freezing high water content foods, incredibly raw, as a rule of thumb. Things like cabbages and potatoes can be frozen once cooked, but their texture may not be as good.

Of course, one of the biggest advantages of the freezer is that you can cook your vegetables into healthy, nutritious meals or freeze them ready to go into meals. If you have a massive crop of leeks, for example, you can either make some great leek and potato soups and freeze them or cook the leeks and freeze them in portions. You can then simply add a portion of frozen leeks to whatever meal you're cooking throughout the year, and this will let you keep the crop long after the plant has finished and any fresh version would have rotted.

If you want to preserve the crop as close as possible to its normal form, consider learning about flash freezing; This may be preferable to cooking certain vegetables before you store them.

Many people consider a freezer the ultimate option for food storage because it represents convenience and will save you time – but let's not forget about the other options. You don't have to pick just one storage method; you can use as many as you like to maximize the lifespan of your hard-won food.

Other Storage Tips

So, what other storage tips are there? A few other methods are worth learning about, and a top option is a root cellar. Not every homestead will be able to make one of these. Still, if you can, it's an ideal way to store vegetables, particularly things like onions, garlic, beets, cabbages, carrots, parsnips, turnips, and potatoes. Apples also do well in a root cellar, which is great if you have an apple tree and want to preserve the crop for as long as possible.

A root cellar works by providing cold, slightly damp storage – a little like a fridge that doesn't need any power; They are dug into the ground and take advantage of the insulation this offers against hot days and dry weather. With a good root cellar, you can store some vegetables for months. Note that it does need some ventilation, or there's a risk of the food going off. If you are building a root cellar, you might decide to add a piece of piping from the outside at the top of the cellar to the inside at ground level. This will help with ventilation and create microclimates – allowing you to store cold-loving vegetables at the chilly floor level and vegetables that prefer a warmer environment near the top.

You don't have to do much (if any) preparation before storing the vegetables, as most will keep better if they are left with the soil on them and stored unwashed. However, you do need to check on the foods fairly often, using up or removing any that are starting to degrade so that they don't contaminate the others. Some foods can last for around a year if you turn them regularly and remove any companions that are going bad.

To make the most of a root cellar, you will need to check exactly what conditions are preferred for the fruits or vegetables that you wish to store. For example, apples like high humidity levels of around 90 percent or more and prefer to be kept at 30 or 40 degrees. By contrast, a winter squash prefers humidity levels between 50 and 70 percent, and a temperature of around 50 degrees.

You can also make miniature versions of the root cellar (or versions specifically tailored to the different foods) with boxes of damp sand or even with plastic totes filled with peat moss. If your crop likes a lot of moisture, this is an ideal solution.

Of course, this is not the only other storage option. If you want to preserve your fruits and vegetables in other forms, jams, jellies, chutneys, pickles, and fermented foods are all excellent things to try. These involve adding a preservative of some sort, such as sugar, vinegar, or salt. These are used in concentrations that kill bacteria and microorganisms, making the food safe to eat for longer.

Summary

In this chapter, we've covered:

- Some of the top methods for practical food preservation and why food preservation matters.
- Canning and the best 3 methods for canning at home.
- Drying and the various methods you can use to dry foods, including a dehydrator, your oven, or just a dry, warm room that they can be hung up in.

- Freezing foods, the different kinds of freezers available, and why freezing is often a preferred method.
- Other preservation methods that you may wish to use, including making jams or jellies, or fermenting the vegetable.

In the following chapter, we will explore what illnesses your plants may get and the pests and problems you may run into with some of the common crops. This will help you as you start to utilize your new vegetable plot and let you know which issues to guard for!

6
Pests, Problems, Plant Illnesses

"It's difficult to think anything but pleasant thoughts while eating a homegrown tomato."

-Lewis Grizzard

Lewis Grizzard may be very right about the pleasures associated with eating homegrown food, but there is a long way between seed packet and plate, and many things can go wrong between the two. Gardeners are constantly learning, and you can never know it all – but knowing the basics should make your first harvesting year significantly more enjoyable and may also help you save crops from destruction by diseases, predators, or other issues.

Of course, it's always a good idea to read up on the specific plants you plan to grow and the diseases that are common in your area. Still, in this chapter, I'm going to cover some of the basics of farming for your food – including the pests and issues that you should look out for, and what to do about them when you see them. Hopefully, you'll find yourself well-armed to take on vegetable growing with the information provided here!

However, it's important to remember before you start that you are almost bound to run into some issues while gardening – it's just the nature of the job. You will lose crops to pests, diseases, or lack of knowledge on your part. Sometimes, you'll lose them because of silly mistakes. We have all been there, and if you learn from it, it's not a waste of time. Don't expect perfection in your garden, or you are very likely to be disappointed.

It's also worth noting that I'm a big advocate for letting pests live where you can. Not all creatures need to be attacked with chemicals or traps. Think of your garden as a complete ecosystem; the more variety you can encourage, the better the balance. You might have a horde of aphids this week, but if you're also providing habitats for ladybugs, it will often sort itself out before long.

With all that said, there are times when you need to take action, so let's explore a few of the big issues that you might face.

Fungus Gnats

Fungus gnats can trouble almost any plant, and if you have houseplants, you have likely already seen them a few times inside your home. They tend to hang around soil and water sources, and they can be a pain to get rid of. They can also be enormously damaging to a plant if they aren't dealt with, and an infestation can multiply exceptionally quickly in the right conditions.

To be clear, the adult gnats that you'll see flying around are not responsible for killing your plants – the larvae are the problem. In theory, these only eat fungus in the soil, but if the population gets out of control and there isn't enough fungus, they will move on to the living tissue of your plant's roots.

This will kill seedlings and sometimes even adult plants if the infestation is bad enough. They can also spread the pathogens generally associated with damping-off disease (which we'll cover in more detail shortly). You will need to take action to kill the gnats quickly before their young overrun the soil and kill your plants.

You are most likely to be made aware of fungus gnats by adults drifting around the containers or near the plant's soil, but if your plant is looking limp and under-watered, it's possible that these little insects are damaging its roots.

Fungus gnats can be a nuisance to get rid of. Letting the soil dry out will leave your plant dry. Instead, try setting traps of apple cider vinegar and dish soap. Simply pour some vinegar into a shallow container and add a few drops of dish soap. The dish soap will kill the adults when they drink from it, breaking the life cycle. You will need to repeat this several times, as the larvae will soon hatch into adults and start laying eggs themselves. Keeping on top of the problem should stop the gnats from being able to breed and solve the issue.

You can also spray the plant's soil thoroughly with soap and water every few days for a week or two. This will kill the larvae as they emerge and prevent them from hatching into adults. The population should soon die off.

Earwigs

However you feel about creepy crawlies, you are probably aware that many of them are beneficial to your soil and plants, which is certainly true of earwigs. They are an important part of the ecosystem – in the right numbers. If their numbers get out of hand, they can be detrimental to your plant life. If you keep seeing earwigs, you may want to check what damage they do.

Most earwigs will only eat plant debris (as well as other insects, slugs, and snails), so they are great for cleaning up your garden. However, they can take this munching too far, particularly fond of most herbs. They also love strawberries and peaches and apricots and other fruits so that they can ruin these crops.

One great way to control earwig numbers is to introduce a natural predator. If you keep chickens or ducks, they will eat these insects by the beak full; they love them. Birds will also eat them, and this is an excellent way to work in harmony with nature.

If that isn't practical for you, consider adding some food-grade diatomaceous earth to the soil around your plants. Simply sprinkle it in a thick circle, and you'll find a few insects inside the circle. Diatomaceous earth is very sharp and slices the exoskeletons of insects open, making them vulnerable to drying out. Insects will therefore avoid it, and it's an effective repellent. However, be careful about using diatomaceous earth around flowering plants because it will hurt bees and other insects.

You can also remove earwigs by leaving some damp, rolled-up newspapers outside. The earwigs will crawl into them because they provide great habitat, and then you can relocate or kill them. If possible, feed them to birds, frogs, or other predators, but you can also drown them in soapy water if you choose to.

Blister Beetles

Blister beetles are another common pest not one you want on your homestead. They cannot bite or sting, but they can exude a toxic substance that will create blisters and sores on your skin. Don't pick up or crush blister beetles with bare hands. If you keep livestock and you have blister beetles, be cautious because ingesting these beetles can kill your livestock, found in grass and mow hay.

Blister beetles have narrow thoraxes with a black body and a bright redhead, so they are quite distinctive. They can be a problem if you're a beekeeper as they will hitch a ride into the hive and then feed on the larvae, but they are also unwelcome with other homesteaders, as they feed on plant leaves and eat the pollen, as well as drinking the nectar; This stops the plant from fruiting. Blister beetles can damage all kinds of crops. They love tomatoes, eggplants, melons, and potatoes, but they will go for other crops too.

If you're trying to get rid of blister beetles, diatomaceous earth is a good option, and you can again make rings around your plants so that the beetles cannot reach them. Some people also use a tool or stick to push the beetles off the plants and into soapy water. It's advisable to wear gloves while doing this, even if you don't plan to touch the beetle.

You should also eliminate any pigweed in your homestead, which is particularly attractive to the beetles. Alternatively, move all the pigweed to one area, and the beetles should relocate to that spot.

Flea Beetles

Generally, a small garden pest, there are many kinds of flea beetles, and the biggest is the spinach flea beetle, which can reach a quarter of an inch long. They come in a variety of colors, and some are even striped. You might see beetles that are gray, brown, or bronze, but mostly, you'll see specks on the plant leaves that disappear as you approach. They can jump an amazing distance, although they are not fleas.

Flea beetles usually come out of hibernation when the weather reaches 50 degrees F, and they will lay little white eggs around the base of the plants. These take a week to hatch, and then the larvae will feed on the plants' roots for 2 or 3 weeks. At this point, they turn into adults, lay more eggs, and keep spreading the infestation. The adults also attack the leaves, feeding on them and leaving many tiny round holes. They are particularly keen on seedlings and can do a lot of damage.

Furthermore, they will spread diseases like blight and wilt to your plants and make them stressed and vulnerable. It's a good idea to deal with flea beetles as soon as possible before they kill off your young plants. It's rare for these beetles to kill an adult, established plant, but this situation still needs to be addressed.

Fortunately, there are plenty of effective pest removal methods, and diatomaceous earth is again at the top of the list. If you dust it over and around your plants, the beetles and their larvae can't get at the food.

Alternatively, try neem oil; This messes up the insect's ability to produce eggs, preventing them from launching the next generation. You can simply wipe the plant's leaves with diluted neem oil or spray it on the insects, and it will coat their bodies and prevent them from breathing. You may want to test it on your plants first; neem oil is generally safe for plants, but it's always best to check. You can spray flea beetles with an insecticide soap if you prefer.

Attracting predatory insects such as wasps to your homestead by providing plenty of flowers and vegetation may help keep the numbers of flea beetles down and keep away other pest insects; This is the most hands-off solution.

Grasshoppers

Grasshoppers are a known plant pest, and they can appear in huge swarms that will strip your plants of leaves in very short spaces of time. They can kill whole plants this way, and they usually start to appear in late summer – just when the bulk of your crops are likely to be maturing.

These insects can be brown or green, depending on what they are eating and their growth stage. They will eat all kinds of plants with great appetite, and you need to take fast action, or you may lose whole crops.

Again, you can do a lot to dissuade grasshoppers. Keeping the grass short will help, giving them fewer places to hide and less to feed on. They like lush grass and may go elsewhere if you keep it short.

Dusting diatomaceous earth on plants you wish to protect will help kill the grasshoppers, and you should also encourage as many birds to your garden as possible, as these will eat lots of them. Putting out seeds, providing nest boxes and water, and making sure there are trees/bushes that they can use is a great way to draw birds in.

You can also use a garlic spray on your plants; this deters many kinds of pests. To create it, mix a tablespoon of dish soap with 2 cups of water, 2 tablespoons of red chili, and 2 cloves of pressed garlic. Give this a day to steep, and then spray it on your plants, making them distasteful to the insects.

Grasshoppers can be difficult to deal with, especially during long, hot summers, but these methods will hopefully help. Try using multiple forms of attack if the grasshoppers are persistent.

Moths

The cabbage moth caterpillar is a major problem if you want to grow cabbages. This moth lands on the cabbages and lays its eggs, which soon hatch into caterpillars – which eat your plants. A handful of caterpillars can wreak havoc on your cabbages. Of course, a few little nibble holes here and there won't do any harm, but if your cabbages are being seriously munched, you need to take action.

It isn't just cabbages, either. This moth will go for anything similar, such as kale, broccoli, Brussels sprouts, turnip greens, mustard greens, and collard greens. They will also attack other plants if none of these are available, although they will usually opt for the flowers, not the plant, in these cases.

Although the butterflies that lay these eggs are called cabbage moths, they are butterflies, and you may see them flitting around in the daytime. There's a similar kind of caterpillar called the cabbage looper, and this does come from a brown moth, and also eats cabbage leaves. Both can be dealt with similarly, and there are a few different options.

One is manual removal, and this is often surprisingly effective. The caterpillars are large enough to be picked off just using your hands, and you can then put them in a bowl and leave them out for the birds. Some may crawl off, but they are unlikely to make it back to your plants as long as you put them a good distance away.

You will need to check the plants at least once a week, and preferably more often. Check the undersides of the leaves for the little yellow eggs, and wipe them away if you find them. The caterpillars are well disguised because they are bright green, but you should be able to spot them if you look closely, and you can just pick them off.

You can also use row covers. This involves putting hoops vertically over your bed to bury half of the hoops in the bed, and the other halves arc above the vegetables. You then spread a fine mesh across the whole bed, and the vegetables inside will be protected; This stops the butterflies and moths from accessing them at all.

This is an effective way of protecting your plants completely, but it does require you to buy or make the covers and hoops. The covers will also protect your plants from birds and other pests, although they will keep out not all kinds of insects. When you want to harvest the plants, simply pull the cover back. It can be used year after year. Make sure you keep it in good condition and firmly tied down, however, because the net could pose a danger to birds and other animals if they get tangled in it.

The disadvantage of using row covers for some plants is that they cannot be pollinated. Cabbages don't need this, but be aware that if you want to cover things like squashes, you will need to hand pollinate them or remove the covers each day.

A third option involves choosing cabbage varieties that are not popular with these moths. Red and purple varieties don't attract them like green ones do because the caterpillars stand out and are vulnerable to predation on the leaves. It might also be because the red and purple cabbages contain anthocyanin antioxidants; This is great for people but mildly toxic to caterpillars – so the parents will usually avoid laying their eggs on the colorful varieties.

Slugs

The most commonly seen enemy of gardeners, slugs, are universally despised, and almost everyone has to deal with them occasionally. Slugs often go for young, tender plants, damaging them and possibly even killing them. They will eat almost anything, leaving the ribs of leaves and hollowed flesh on your vegetables and fruits. The more slugs you are likely to have, the damper your garden is.

It is worth learning about the different slugs because not all eat living plant matter. Leopard slugs, for example, hunt other slugs, so you don't want to remove those from your garden!

There are many ways to get rid of slugs. For example, beer traps are very popular. To create one, you simply pour cheap beer into a bowl, dig a little hole in the garden, and put the bowl in it. The slugs can then crawl into the bowl. They will try to drink the beer and will drown.

Alternatively, set some board traps. Lay some scrap wood or cardboard sheets face down in the garden overnight. Slugs will crawl onto the underside for shelter, and you can then remove and kill them the next day. It is best to remove them in the afternoon, as this is when they stop foraging and move into shady spots.

You can also use sand, wool, and other coarse substances to prevent slugs from going into certain areas, as they don't like crawling over rough surfaces. However, some of these lose their effectiveness when they get wet, and many people have mixed results with them. A better option is to attract as many predators to your garden as possible. Birds, chickens, ducks, toads, and frogs will all munch on slugs. The more predators you have, the fewer slugs you will have.

You can further make life difficult for slugs by reducing the cover around your vegetable beds. If slugs cannot hide in thick vegetation, they start to dry out. Remove old wood, cardboard, dead leaves, or other debris that the slugs might be sheltering beneath in the day's heat, and you should find fewer on your plants at night.

Damping Off Disease

When you first plant your seedlings, damping off is a fundamental issue to look out for and be aware of. It is a problem caused by several different kinds of fungi or similar organisms, resulting in your seedlings collapsing, even when they seemed healthy. It usually occurs when starting seedlings off indoors. Almost all seedlings can be affected by this problem.

Damping off usually occurs if you sow seedlings under glass or keep them in a humid environment with minimal air circulation. Thickly sowing seeds can also result in this problem. It's more common to see this issue in spring, when the weather is damper, but it can happen at any time.

You may either see seedlings failing to emerge or collapsing with a mass of white fungi around them. There is no way to treat damping off once it has happened, but you can reduce the risks in a few ways:

- Sow seedlings thinly
- Promote air circulation
- Don't overwater your seedlings
- Use clean pots
- Consider using commercial compost, which is unlikely to contain the organisms that cause this problem
- Use clean water, and ensure your rain barrels are properly covered to prevent contamination

These steps should all reduce the risk of your seedlings getting damping off. If it does happen, get rid of the seedlings, and start again with different containers and trays. There is no point in trying to save seedlings once this problem has set in.

Common Plant Problems

There are various other issues that you might face when you are a beginner gardener trying to grow your vegetables for the first time – so let's explore some.

Bolting plants

You may find that some crops, like lettuces, suddenly and unexpectedly produce a large flower head; This makes their leaves bitter and means the plant is about to die. It will usually happen at the end of the plant's life cycle but can occur earlier if it gets too hot.

Solution: plant cool-loving crops early to maximize their cropping season. Spinach, broccoli, and lettuce are the common problem crops, plus some other salads. Try to plant them in spaces where they will get some shade, even in the summer, or create artificial shade which may make them last better. Once they have bolted, remove the plants and replace them with something different.

Blossom end rot

This is where the end of the fruit, where the flower was, begins to rot and turn black. It's a common issue among peppers and tomatoes, and it usually occurs due to calcium deficiency.

However, before you start feeding the plant, consider that calcium deficiency is often due to improper watering, fluctuating soil moisture, or too much nitrogen in the soil. Periods of hot weather, followed by heavy rains, can often cause blossom end rot.

Solution: You may find that mulching the soil helps to keep the water levels more steady. Avoid over-fertilizing.

Black spots on plant leaves

Several potential causes for this, but the most likely is that your plant is getting too much fertilizer. It's easy to get too excited when feeding your plants, hoping to produce huge crops, but don't overdo it. While plants benefit from some food, too much is more damaging than too little in many cases. Overwatering can also cause black spots on the leaves.

Solution: Rinse the soil with fresh water and dry it out. Remove heavily damaged foliage so new growth can replace it.

Powdery mildew

It appears as a cloud of white dust on the leaves, this fungal infection attacks many plants, and things like zucchinis are particularly vulnerable to it. It will cause the foliage to rot and wilt and eventually kill the plant.

Solution: Improve the air circulation if possible, and remove affected leaves.

Yellow leaves

Numerous plants can suffer from yellow leaves, and it's a clear indication that something is wrong. Tomatoes seem to be particularly prone to it. If a few of the plant's lower leaves are a little yellow, it's unlikely to be anything to worry about, but if lots of the leaves are yellow, there's a problem somewhere. It is often a lack of potassium, or it may signify that your plant isn't getting enough light. Plants with yellow leaves will not grow well because they can't photosynthesize effectively.

Solution: *Get a soil test kit and check the nutrient levels in the soil. Are the plants missing an essential nutrient?* If so, add it in whatever form is convenient. If not, check whether your plants are getting enough light.

Seeds not germinating

A lot of gardeners run into this problem. It's frustrating to be thwarted so early in growing plants, and you might not be sure what's going wrong. Unfortunately, there are a lot of potential reasons for seeds not sprouting! Let's explore a few common ones.

REASON	SOLUTION
They haven't had long enough	Wait for another couple of weeks
It's too dry	Keep the soil damp all of the time, and don't let the seedlings dry out. If they have dried out, plant new seeds
It's too cold	Check what temperature the seeds need, and then sow them when they reliably have this temperature. Early sowing often leads to seeds not germinating
The seeds are old. Some seeds have a short shelf life, while others will last for longer. If you've had the seeds for several years or if they have got hot, damp, or exposed to strong sunlight, they won't grow	Purchase/gather/swap for new seeds
It's too wet (seeds will rot if they are perpetually flooded)	Clean the pots, plant new seeds, and water them less
The nutrient levels are too low	Start the seedlings in rich compost so they have all the nutrients they need to start building themselves up

Summary

In this chapter, we've covered:

- Various common garden pests, including earwigs, flea beetles, slugs, moths, and more, as well as some tips on how to deal with them naturally.
- Damping off disease and why you need to plant your seedlings in the right conditions to help them grow.
- Other common problems that plants can suffer from.

- The problems you may run into when planting seedlings and how to solve them.

In the next chapter, we will look at how to get profits from your garden and all the benefits associated with selling or bartering your products. You will have more from your garden than you need at times, so let's find out how you can utilize that to bring in money or produce that will help make up for gaps in your growth plan.

7
Produce Profits

"There are two spiritual dangers in not owning a farm. One is the danger of supposing that breakfast comes from the grocery, and the other that heat comes from the furnace."

-Aldo Leopold

In this chapter, we will start looking at how you can turn your produce into profits and make the most of the things you harvest, especially when you have a surplus. When you're creating your food at home (whether growing it, raising animals, or harvesting from things like bees), you will end up with an excess, which is invaluable.

Nobody can produce all the products at once from their land, and if you're only farming on a quarter of an acre, you will be missing things. You might be happy to live without those things, but if you can turn your produce into something more, you can still enjoy a wide range of healthy foods, even when your growing scope is limited.

As an example of this, think about people who swap crops with their neighbors, and have deals that they will grow X while the neighbor grows Y. Both sides benefit from the agreement because usually, growing a crop produces an oversupply, and it's better to swap this than to let it go to waste or have it underutilized.

Additionally, making the most of your surplus will top up your finances and provide a good income level if you do it efficiently. There is an enormous demand for homegrown food among people who can't grow it themselves, and you can make a surprising profit if you can market your crops. This money can support your household or pay for the upkeep of your homestead – because there are always ongoing costs in terms of tools, animal feed, seeds, fertilizer, soil testing kits, plant treatments, vet bills, and more.

Before we start, note that you should thoroughly familiarize yourself with any laws regarding the retailing of food in your area (and other states if you plan to sell online). You may need permits, inspections, and evidence that you comply with regulations. Because food safety standards are high, it's essential to check this before you start, or you could face grave legal issues. Do not operate without a permit or sell food that you can't legally sell, even if you know other people who do this. It's much better to set yourself up properly and follow the law.

So, let's start finding out how you can turn food into money (or more food).

Selling Jams

Jam might be one of the best foods when you first start selling produce. After all, jam keeps well, it is easy to make and divide into portions, and it's a fantastic way to use up fruit – especially fruit that doesn't look perfect but is still edible.

You can cut off any blemishes or bruises and use the rest of the fruit, reducing food waste and creating a product that will last for months. Even overripe fruit that is on the point of being wasted can be turned into jam.

Jams and jellies are widespread across the country, and homemade ones are often considered vastly preferable to commercial ones. Get some pretty jars, spend a few days in the kitchen, and have piles of jam that are perfect for both your home and for selling.

Some people sell their jams online via their websites, and if you are selling lots of other products as well, this is a great idea. You may also want to retail the product locally, either through a farmer's market or through independent grocery stores, as this is an excellent way to get your name out there.

Consider whether creating some social media around your jams might also help. You could showcase the jam-making process via videos or put up some amazing recipes – all of these things will allow customers to find you and start enjoying what you have to offer.

The one problem with jams is that they aren't particularly easy to ship since they are always stored in glass jars. You will need to think carefully about this process before you advertise jams for sale, or you may find that you're losing money on the mailing costs or getting a lot of wasted produce due to breakages. It may be best to stick to selling jam locally, rather than online if you're starting. You can expand later.

Selling Dried Fruits

Dried fruits are in high demand, with many people using them as an alternative to other snacks like chips or candy. They are also a great product to sell because they are light-weight, not particularly fragile, and tend to be quite expensive. You should consider selling dried fruits if you've got fruit to spare and want to enter a less crowded market than artisan jams.

If you're going to try this, do some research into whether anyone else local is doing it first so you don't create an overlap. Think about fruits that dry well, such as apricots, apples, mangoes, and plums.

You might also want to create dried fruit mixes, as these are often popular and can be a great way to make your product stand out from any competitors. Find out what mixes are desirable, and create a few varieties to tempt customers to try your options. Berries are particularly popular for mixes, and this can be a great way to use up things like raspberries, strawberries, and blueberries if you have a bumper crop.

Dried fruits are a luxury product, and they are easier to sell online than jams because they can be mailed in plastic or waxed paper rather than glass; shipping fees will be considerably lower, and there's little risk of breakages and loss.

The downside of making dried fruits is that it can be tricky to do correctly. If you leave too much moisture in the fruit, it will go moldy, resulting in sick customers and a lot of bad publicity. You may want to do a lot of testing yourself at home before selling dried fruit to consumers to ensure your process is sound and the food you're retailing is safe to eat.

Selling Meats

If you're going to be raising animals on your homestead, you should undoubtedly consider selling surplus meat. Meat is often expensive, so there's additional value in the harvest, and from an environmental and ethical perspective, it's imperative not to let it go to waste. Animals require a lot of resources to raise, and many people feel that they shouldn't die needlessly, so make sure you have calculated what meat you are going to use and what extra you might be able to sell.

You need to check and double-check about permits if you wish to sell meat. Because there is a much higher risk of food poisoning when meat products are involved, you will likely need regular inspections and have specific standards that you must meet. You may also need to prove that the animals are kept in particular conditions for labelling purposes (e.g. grass-fed, free-range, etc.).

Don't start selling meat to anyone until you have done these things, but don't write meat off as "too difficult." You may be able to make a deal with a local butcher or other business that will simplify the process and mean you are only handling the basics.

If you plan to sell meat, it is probably best to start with one kind of meat; This will let you get a bit of practice and understand the system and the regulations before you expand.

Chickens are probably the easiest meat you can raise, so they may be an excellent place to begin. Many farmers who raise chickens can make quite a bit of profit from them, but be aware that you'll need a reasonable amount of space if you want a big flock – especially if you plan to let them free range. The advantage, of course, is that free-range chicken costs more, so you will get a higher margin if you can meet the criteria.

You will need to find a means of storing the meat before selling it, which is another good reason to partner with a local butcher or similar business. Most will have a storage facility to handle the meat safely. You can't turn up at a local farmer's market with fresh pork cuts, so it's crucial to think about this.

Selling meat is one of the more complicated options for raising money from your homestead, but it is likely to make you a good amount of profit if you can do it successfully. If you are planning to raise animals anyway, do some research into the practicalities of selling the meat, and consider whether you have the space to expand your herd or flock to make some profit from them.

Selling Dairy

Like meat products, dairy products will require special permits and handling in line with regulations in most states (if not all). They present similar dangers regarding food poisoning, and you will need to make sure that you are ticking the health and safety boxes if you wish to sell things like cheese or milk. Pasteurization laws are an example of this, and if you want to sell "raw milk," you may only be able to do so in certain situations with the correct permits.

You will also face the same storage question as above. You may be able to display cheeses at a farmer's market if you live in a cool state, but in general, dairy products will also need to be retailed from a store with proper cooling facilities.

Don't ignore these stipulations, or you will put yourself at risk of legal trouble. Always find out whether you are allowed to sell something before doing it; food safety is taken seriously in the United States and should not be ignored by homesteaders, no matter how small your farm is.

Selling Herbs And Spices

For any beginner homesteader, herbs and spices are probably one of the easiest crops you can start utilizing for profit. Since herbs are generally easy to grow and preserve, they can be a great way to ease yourself into making money from your garden.

If you grow plants that you already preserve in the form of herbs and spices, it's not a big jump to start retailing these – either at farmer's markets or online. You will probably find that you have a surplus as soon as you begin preserving them since, in general, a little goes a long way – and many herbal plants are highly productive. Spices have several advantages, including that they keep well, compact, and lightweight.

Additionally, they are generally reasonably easy to process, dry, and store (although there are some exceptions, like saffron, which can be challenging). If you want to dry things like rosemary, oregano, basil, mint, and more, all you need is the plant and a low oven, plus some storage containers and a suitable spot to keep them in the dark. Furthermore, many herbs are easy to grow and do not attract pests, making them reasonably reliable crops to keep growing year after year.

Some spices also have very high margins, so if you have plants that grow particularly well in your garden, consider whether you could use these to start bringing in profits. There is a wide range of herbs and spices, and it's easy to sell them online and in person.

There is also a lot of demand for medicinal herbs, and if you're keen on growing things like bee balm, valerian, and echinacea, you might want to look into this market. However, be careful not to make any claims that aren't supported by science, and check if you are skirting any legal issues about how you advertise your products. There is a lot of misinformation online about medicinal herbs, and you want to make sure you steer clear of this at all times.

Selling Eggs

Selling eggs has been popular with homesteaders for as long as homesteads have existed. Because chickens can lay eggs erratically and the demands of your household are likely to fluctuate too, you may often find that you end up with an excess of eggs. Almost everyone needs eggs, and this is a fantastic way to start making money and ensuring that food doesn't go to waste.

Again, you should check out any laws regarding the sale of eggs in your state, but in general, eggs are easy to sell and extremely popular products. Although they are readily available in grocery stores, many people like eating eggs from local hens, especially if they also know those hens have a good life and are well looked after.

You should certainly consider utilizing egg sales if you have an excess. Another option is to put up an honesty box at the edge of your property and place excess eggs in this (make sure it is kept cool); This is a great way to share your produce with minimal work and will supply people local to you with fresh eggs whenever they want them.

However, you don't have to just sell eggs for eating – you can also sell fertilized eggs if you have a cockerel. You may wish to do this online to increase the scope of your audience; This is most likely to be successful if you have rare or in-demand breeds, but you can do it even with hybrids. You should check out any laws before you start and consider talking to breeders in the business to get any insider knowledge you may require, but overall, this is a great way to bump up your profits.

It also helps to avoid ending up with too many chicks if you've got a large flock. Having a cockerel is excellent because it will protect your hens, but it can be challenging to balance broody birds and keep your population under control. Selling fertile eggs may help.

Finally, some people also sell the chicks once they have hatched; This will significantly increase profit to reflect the extra work it involves. Still, you will need to research permits and licenses because handling livestock usually does require at least some regulatory oversight.

Selling Honey And Beeswax

Honey and beeswax are both enormously valuable products, especially in today's market, where more and more people are looking to move away from commercial sweeteners and use more natural options. Homemade, local honey is extremely popular right now, and if you end up with an excess of this product, it's definitely worth selling it to other households.

Of course, you need to make sure you aren't taking more than your bees can spare because otherwise, you'll be buying food for your hives. However, this is a great way to boost your income and ensure you have the funds to keep supporting your beehives. Many beekeepers do end up with more honey than they need for their households – since a little tends to go a long way – and therefore, this is a great option.

Honey also keeps well without refrigeration, which is another benefit of storing it to sell. You may find it challenging to retail online if you package it in glass, but otherwise, make sure you consider this.

There's a second product you get from beehives, which is beeswax. It has plenty of retail value. It is popularly used to make soap and candles, and you can either do this yourself or sell the raw product so that people can do it at home. In recent years, there has also been a big call for beeswax as wax wraps have become more popular. These are used for covering food and wrapping sandwiches as an eco and reusable alternative to plastic wrap, and many people are now making them at home. Beeswax is a crucial ingredient, and demand has dramatically increased.

You may have some uses for beeswax in your own home, but the chances are that you will have exhausted this product's usefulness to you (at least temporarily) after a while. At this point, it makes sense to sell it to others who will find it valuable because otherwise, it will just go to waste. Selling beeswax or the products used to create is a great way to make money from a product that has no other value to you.

Bartering Produce

Bartering is an excellent option for any backyard homesteader. You will likely find yourself doing this automatically if you spend any time dealing with other homesteaders because it helps everyone out. Bartering is a cornerstone of human survival and has long existed before we invented money and created fixed transactional values.

Being able to barter will increase the wealth of your farm tenfold because everything you can't use still has potential value as a swap. The things you have to exchange aren't just limited to produce but can also include labor, skills, animal loans for a specific task, space swaps, or other agreements. You might let your neighbor store equipment in half of your barn for a few months in exchange for some homemade butter or a couple of sacks of potatoes. They might offer to lend you their goat to clear a field and get some of your strawberry crops.

No matter how self-sufficient you manage to make your homestead, you will always bene-fit from trading and collaborating with neighbors. If selling doesn't appeal to you because of all the complexities it can involve (or just because you're busy!), don't just let things go to waste: swap them.

You can get very creative about bartering, too, and it improves the lives of everyone living on homesteads. Agreements on what to grow, seed swaps, plant exchanges, and assistance with harvesting all make life easier for everyone and creates a superb spirit of collaboration within the community.

Here are some ideas of ways that you can barter with your neighbors:

Exchange your favorite seeds for theirs; This increases the availability of varieties that thrive in your area and provides an insurance policy against loss if your crop suffers from a disaster one year.

Help with the harvest. Often, farmers help each other out when there's a large amount of a particular crop to be brought on, especially if this is time sensitive and there's a risk of waste otherwise. Even if you don't need help in return, you will reap the rewards for helping and may enjoy assistance in future years or other recognition from your work (e.g. a percentage of the crop).

Share working animals. Goats, horses, pigs, cows, and sheep all have functions around the farm by clearing fields or (for horses) pulling machinery, and being willing to share this is a great way to increase efficiency for everyone. Some people even rent their bees to help neighbors pollinate crops effectively.

Consider renting space. If you aren't using parts of your homestead, see if somebody else wants to use them. You might just be letting the ground go fallow for a year or two, in which case adding chickens to it could help enrich it. You might be waiting to plant crops in it later and not mind a neighbor housing their goat there for now. Be creative, especially where space is limited.

Swap skills. *Do you know how to sharpen tools, deal with a particularly stubborn weed, mend broken machinery, check over an injured animal, or something else that could be useful to the community?* Offer your skills around in exchange for assistance. Everyone has a different set of skills, and if these are shared, there's a huge opportunity to increase efficiency on the homestead.

Teach others – this has something in common with swapping skills but involves more long-term spreading of those skills. If there's something you find you are particularly good at, consider teaching others how to do it too. You can either monetize this by offering classes or bank up the goodwill and bartering value to cash in on later. Alternatively, identify an area you struggle with and get help from someone in the community to overcome that problem to become better farmers.

Bartering is often about creatively using the resources you have, and it's a delightful way to maximize what you get from your homestead without having to deal with money all the time. It enriches the community for everyone, and it's certainly something you should consider when you've got a surplus of anything. Swapping has an immense value that builds everyone up, and the art of bartering is one you should start to practice as you develop your other homesteading skills.

Summary

In this chapter, we've covered:

- How to sell jams.
- How to sell dried fruits.
- How to sell meat and dairy products and the complexities you might have to handle.
- How to sell herbs and spices.
- How to sell eggs, fertile eggs, and chicks.
- How to sell honey and beeswax, or beeswax products.
- Why bartering is so valuable and how you might use this to enrich your homestead and the whole homesteading community.

Conclusion

"Agriculture is the most healthful, most useful and most noble employment of man."

-George Washington

Backyard homesteading offers a wealth of advantages to the homesteader, including the opportunity to increase food security, be more eco-friendly, and the joy and satisfaction of growing your food. It challenges you to use new skills, solve problems, and get in touch with the history of humanity. It has enormous value to you and your family, and it also creates a deep sense of connection with the planet and with food, promoting healthier eating habits and a better sense of balance.

Agriculture is at the heart of so many things that we do, yet the vast majority of people have lost touch with it. There's a feeling of disconnection from the food that we cook and eat each day because we have no sense of value for that food anymore – we are not aware of or engaged with the work that goes into creating it. We lack the emotional attachment to the food we have grown ourselves. A funny sense of euphoria comes from laying a table and serving a meal from your garden and tended to by your hands.

Remember that a backyard homestead doesn't need to meet your every need, and you don't have to plunge in at the deep end straight away. You can start small. You can build just one vegetable bed, raise four chickens, or even try some lettuce leaves in containers. Build up slowly, and embrace the learning curve, because nobody gets farming right 100 percent of the time – even farmers. There will always be things that you can do better next time.

Most of all, take pleasure in your backyard homestead and feel pride in your achievements. Your homestead is yours, and this is your journey with food and nature. You should delight in the little things, like the strawberry plants that survived when they all died last year, your first tomatoes of the season, or the new batch of chicks that have just hatched. Take pleasure in brushing the goat or pulling up weeds, and praise yourself when the crops come to the table and you reap the rewards of all your work.

I hope you will enjoy your homesteading journey – and all the ups and downs – as much as my family and I have enjoyed ours. There is peace in working with the earth and growing food, and I hope you find it.

RAISING CHICKENS FOR BEGINNERS

BOOK 7

The Ultimate Beginner's Guide to Raising Organic Backyard Chickens For Eggs in 5 Steps

BY

BRADLEY STONE

Introduction

"Regard it as just as desirable to build a chicken house as to build a cathedral."

-Frank Lloyd Wright

Did you know that in the United States, around 300 eggs are eaten by each person yearly? That's not far off one egg every day for every individual, which shows how versatile and delicious eggs are. They have a role to play in all kinds of cooking, including things like spaghetti carbonara, baked goods, cakes, soufflé, desserts, and the classics, such as boiled eggs with soldiers or fried eggs on toast.

No matter your lifestyle, you probably eat eggs regularly unless you are a vegan. Even if you don't eat eggs on their own very often, you likely consume them in baked products frequently. The humble egg is often overlooked, but it plays a significant role in so much of our cooking world that it can be pretty hard to replace.

Of course, the egg consumption that we enjoy comes with its problems – that we need a lot of chickens to produce those eggs. In recent years, chicken welfare has come under the spotlight, and improvements have been made to adjust the living conditions of some very poorly treated birds. Still, many people are uneasy about purchasing commercial eggs because of factory farming. Even buying free-range eggs only alleviates this to a degree because you still have limited knowledge about the welfare and living conditions of the birds.

On the other hand, eggs are hard to give up, and they are highly nutritious. That leaves a lot of consumers feeling stuck and wondering whether they can produce eggs for themselves at home rather than depending on commercial eggs. Some people believe that raising chickens at home is a crazy dream; however, backyard poultry is growing in popularity. If you've got a bit of time on your hands and a keenness to learn, you could become an expert chicken farmer in very little time!

So, let's learn a bit more about it.

Should You Try Raising Chickens?

There are a few things that you should consider before you go out and purchase chickens.

One is how much time you have on your hands. Although chickens can be pretty easy to look after and don't generally need a considerable commitment, they are still an animal that you must care for. Food and water will need to be checked daily, and most people shut their chickens into a coop at night and let them out in the morning to keep them safe from predators; This can make it difficult to go on vacation unless you have someone who can take over.

You also need to consider things such as cleaning the chickens out and whether you will let them range freely in your garden. If you plan to let them range, be aware that they can be destructive creatures that will pull up plants, peck vegetables, and make a mess. If you plan to pen them, you will need to consider enrichment, the pecking order, and keeping the pen clean. These things deserve consideration before you get your chickens, and we'll look at each in the following chapters.

What Are The Pros And Cons?

There are several advantages to owning chickens, but some disadvantages too. The key benefits include the fact that you can enjoy access to the freshest eggs without having to worry about the welfare of the chickens, and you will have a constant supply, so you will rarely run out. You may also enjoy sharing eggs with your neighbors or even selling a few.

Many people find that owning chickens is enormously rewarding and enjoy looking after these quirky birds, which can have excellent personalities and may be surprisingly affectionate if you rear them yourself. You can create a profound bond with a chicken; they are more intelligent than most people give them credit for. Little is as engaging as a flock of birds rushing to meet you when you step out of your front door.

The downsides of chicken ownership include that you may have to deal with sick birds sometimes, and you can't easily go on vacation for more than a few days unless you have responsible neighbors or friends to call on. You may find that they damage your garden if you don't keep them penned, and you might also have to deal with bullying problems among the flock.

Another disadvantage is that chickens can be pretty noisy birds, even if you don't keep a rooster. You must check whether your city allows you to keep chickens, as some forbid it. You must be prepared to be woken up most mornings by the "egg song," which may not suit late risers.

Furthermore, chickens don't retain their egg-laying productivity throughout their lives. A young bird will lay almost daily throughout the spring and summer, but as your birds' age, they will stop laying regularly and possibly stop entirely, which means that the bird begins to represent a cost. You will either have to accept that and let it live out its life as a pet or cull it – which is uncomfortable for many people who don't want to do either.

What's An Organic Chicken Vs A Non-organic Chicken?

If you wish to raise organic chickens, either for yourself or so that you can sell the eggs, you will need to get an official classification from the USDA. You must prove that your chickens are fed on 100 percent organic feed, allowed outdoor access, and not given antibiotics. These requirements do not apply to non-organic chickens, which can be kept indoors and may be given antibiotics and non-organic food.

If you just want organic eggs for yourself and your family, you won't need official classification, but you should follow the same guidelines and avoid feeding your chickens on non-organic corn, feed, or treats.

You will also need to consider what pesticides you use in your garden if you plan to let your chickens free-range or even if they are penned. Pesticides can blow in on the wind and may contaminate your chickens' food if you use them on your land. Bear this in mind when you are raising chickens.

Why Should You Raise Chickens?

There are many reasons that you might want to raise your chickens. For many people, the ethical issue is an essential one. Although great strides have been taken to make chicken farming more humane, there are still significant issues. Some people question whether commercial farming can genuinely meet the egg production needs of the growing population. It is hard to imagine the amount of space needed to give our factory chickens the truly ideal lives that we would like them to lead.

Raising your chickens can be ethical and may also be more environmentally friendly. It benefits your garden in many ways, giving you manure, providing pesticide-free insect control, and reducing the food miles of your eggs to zero. It is undoubtedly an eco aspect, especially if you can source corn and straw locally to further reduce the food miles. More and more people are looking at community farming, growing food on their land, and changing how we approach our food for the better. Raising chickens is one aspect of this.

A sense of independence comes with raising your chickens and gathering your eggs. You don't have to keep popping to the store to get eggs when you want to bake, and you don't have to fill your fridge up with box after box just to get you through the week.

Of all the livestock you could keep, chickens are probably among the easiest, and they are a great way to test the waters and try your hand with animals before you attempt something more challenging. They can take a backyard homestead to a new level, giving you an essential and unique food item that brings enormous flexibility to your cooking.

How Do You Choose A Breed?

Choosing a breed of chicken can be challenging, and the first thing you should do is assess your climate and the temperature extremes that occur with summer and winter. Chickens are hardy birds, but choosing ones suited to your environment and likely to survive and thrive is vital. If you get cold temperatures, you'll need to choose a different breed to those that cope well with the heat.

You should also think about the breed's productivity. Some chickens look pretty but lay a few eggs. Others lay far better and are usually a good choice if you plan to depend upon your flock for egg production. You should take temperament into account too. Some chickens are much more content to be penned than others, and some breeds are known for being docile and even affectionate, while others can be aggressive. Knowing what you value most in your flock will help determine which birds suit you best. Some people also consider the colour of the eggs to be vital and choose a mixture of breeds to get some variety; This might be relevant if you consider selling the eggs, as colorful eggs can attract consumers.

In terms of climate, birds that do well in hot environments include:

- Leghorns
- Penedesencas
- Andalusians
- Some that do well in cold climates include:
- Cochins
- Barred Rocks
- Buff Orpingtons
- Some of the best for egg production are:
- Rhode Island Reds
- Sussex
- Barred Rocks
- Australorps

- Delawares

They can all reliably lay 5 or 6 eggs a week in their prime. If you're looking for birds that are known for being friendly, choose:

- Silkies
- Cochins
- Faverolles

As you can see, there's already quite a lot to think about, but hopefully, that's got you excited to learn more and start choosing some chickens to welcome to your home. Many people love picking out their flock and selecting birds that will be perfect for their setup, but before you get started, it's crucial to learn more about the logistics of looking after chickens.

We will start the first chapter by looking at what chickens eat at different stages of their lives, as good nutrition is critical for a bird that produces such rich food almost daily. Keep reading to learn more!

1
What To Feed Chickens

"It's become more readily apparent that we need to be growing our own food and growing more things organically."

-Nell Newman

In this chapter, we'll start looking at providing good nutrition to your chickens at all stages of life. A chicken's needs will change as it ages, so it's important to know what your bird needs are at all times, so you can be sure you're meeting them.

Even if you feed adult chickens, not chicks, you need to know what they eat. To form healthy, nutritious eggs, they must have the correct blend of food. If you don't give your birds what they need, they will likely stop laying or lay infrequently and produce eggs that lack richness, flavor, and vitamins.

Before we start, it's worth noting that most chicken feed can be purchased in different forms, including pellets, crumbs, and mash; This refers to the feed's size, not it's content or intended chicken age. Pellets are the biggest form, followed by crumbs, and then mash. Some chickens will eat any kind, but you may find that your chickens get used to the variant you give them, and they may not eat other types once they have adapted.

With that in mind, let's find out how to feed chickens from the point of hatching to adulthood. We'll also touch on the other things chickens need to stay healthy.

Starter Diets

From the moment they hatch, chicks can eat independently, and as they are birds, not mammals, they don't depend on their mothers for milk. Mother hens may help their chicks to feed by locating grubs for them, scratching back the dirt, and encouraging them to peck around, but the babies can and should be given food immediately after hatching.

This usually means providing a starter diet, which you can use until the chicks are 8 weeks old. A starter feed will give them everything they need to develop healthy bones and immune systems and minimize the risk of health issues.

Starter feed is usually around 20 percent protein, which is far more protein than adult chickens consume and supports the rapid rate of growth these young birds undergo. Chicks grow much more rapidly than many other baby animals, and their food needs to reflect this.

You can purchase both medicated and unmedicated feeds. The medicated version will protect chicks from a disease called coccidiosis, which kills many babies otherwise. Suppose you get your chicks vaccinated against coccidiosis. There's no need to give them a medicated feed, and you shouldn't do so because it will undo the effects of the vaccine and leave your birds vulnerable to infection. If you don't have vaccinated chicks, you may find that this feed is the best option. Coccidiosis should be taken seriously, as it can quickly lead to the bird's death.

Most chicks eat around 1 or 2 ounces of food daily until they are about 8 weeks old, but you don't need to worry too much about measuring it. Chicks don't eat more than they need. Besides, it's not excessive to put extra in a pen. However, you don't want food to hang around for more than a few days, or it may get dirty and become a source of mold that might be dangerous to the chicks.

Avoid feeding chicks any treats for the first 8 weeks. They do not need treats, and the nutritionally dense starter feed will give them the best diet. If you feed them treats, they will fill their small stomachs with less valuable food, which results in them not getting as much nutrition as they could otherwise do, which may affect their growth.

Grower Diets

Between 8 weeks and 16 weeks your chicks should be eating a commercial grower feed with a slightly reduced protein level, reflecting the slowing down of growth. It's best not to keep feeding them their starter diet after 8 weeks, or they may begin to gain too much weight, and they will not get the proper nutrients for their age.

The feed will contain many of the same things as starter feed in other ways, with omega-3 and plenty of vitamins to ensure that the chicks remain healthy. As the chicks grow, they will begin to eat more daily food and should be given about 80 gm of food per week. Again, they rarely overeat, so you don't need to worry about giving them more food than they will eat in a day.

You should avoid giving chicks treats at this stage. Stick to the basic feed, and don't offer your chickens anything else until they are older. It might be tempting to start adding things like peas and sweetcorn to their diets, but again, this can cause issues if the chicks start eating this rather than their other main diet. Resist the temptation and keep your little chickens on their correct diet to stay as fit and healthy as possible.

Finisher Diets

You are not likely to be giving your chickens finisher-feed because this is intended for fattening chickens before killing them. It is high in protein and energy and is a complete feed, but you will not generally be using it for backyard birds, especially if you want to promote good egg-laying.

Don't mistake a finisher feed for food you give your young chickens as they reach adulthood; it isn't. You can go straight from a grower diet to a layer diet as soon as your chickens are old enough.

Layer Diets

A layer diet is intended to give chickens everything they need when laying eggs. It's important not to give it to chickens younger than 18 weeks old unless they have started laying because it has a high calcium level. Calcium ensures that the chickens can produce strong eggshells, but if you start feeding it to them too early, the additional calcium could damage their kidneys.

Reserve the layer feed until your chickens are 18 weeks or laying, and then swap them onto it. Again, it is a complete feed, and your chickens don't need treats, but at this stage, you are allowed to start offering treats if you want to. However, you should ensure that your chickens eat plenty of their complete feed daily and not fill up on treats. You can do this by not offering treats until later in the day when the birds mostly fill their crops up on their standard feed and will not be tempted to over-eat treats.

Layer feed is lower in protein than finisher feed, and the two feeds are intended for growing chicks, so bear this in mind. Your adult chickens do not need as much protein as chicks still growing, so make sure you swap the food at the appropriate time. You may find that your chickens switch more quickly if you choose a food that has the same consistency (e.g. pellets, crumbs, or mash) as the feed they have been eating.

Other Food Options

If your birds are not laying, you might wonder what you should feed them when they reach adulthood. The answer is that you can choose a commercial chicken food with less calcium than the layers feed. If you feed roosters and non-laying hens on a layers feed, they may get too much calcium. You should also avoid starter and grower feeds, as these are too high in protein for adults.

However, it should be noted that many people feed their whole flock on the same food – usually layers – without worrying about the calcium content. Getting certain flock members to eat particular things can be challenging, and you must ensure that your laying hens are getting the proper diet. If your rooster eats layers of feed, it is likely to be okay, and many backyard chicken owners find that this keeps things simple.

When your chicks are young, you don't need to worry about differentiating between roosters and pullets. Both will thrive on the same food, which means you can keep it simple.

Making Natural/Organic Feed

Although there are many commercial options that you can try, you might also be interested in making your chicken feed. You need to understand what your chickens need at different stages of their lives to ensure they are getting all the necessary vitamins and minerals. A chicken not getting the proper nutrients from its diet is much more likely to get sick, so getting the food right is critical.

It's important to note that while your chickens can benefit from free-ranging and picking up grubs, worms, slugs, insects, and more, this doesn't count as a complete feed, no matter how much free-ranging they do. Your chickens need a full feed mixed by you or a commercial outlet to stay healthy.

So, what does chicken feed need to include if you want to make your own? Assuming that you are making it for adult chickens, you can mix ingredients like:

- Peas
- Wheat
- Mealworms
- Sesame seeds
- Sunflower seeds
- Oats

You can make your chicken food reasonably cheaply by buying these ingredients in bulk which is a great way to ensure you can offer your chickens organic food if you want to, without paying large amounts for the premium commercial brands.

There are plenty of other options for making your feed, so look up recipes online to find one that suits your situation and the ingredients you can access. You might also like to try something like this one:

- 5-10% Fish meat (offers chickens omega-3 and protein)
- 2-5% Kelp (promotes healthy gut bacteria, add vitamins and minerals)
- 10% Oats (provides protein; you can substitute oats for barley if you prefer)
- 20% Peas (provides protein)
- 30% Wheat (improves digestion and provides carbohydrates and protein)
- 30% Corn (source of carbohydrates)
- Mineral salts (required if your chickens do not free-range)

Try to choose whole grains and opt for organic ingredients where you can. Don't just try feeding your chickens on corn and scraps from your kitchen because you will not be able to keep your birds healthy, and they will end up deficient in multiple nutrients. Although many people like to feed their chickens kitchen scraps, this doesn't represent a healthy and balanced diet. Kitchen scraps can be used as treats but shouldn't be a regular part of your chickens' diet.

Similarly, corn is a great feed and very affordable but must be given in moderation because it is heavy in carbohydrates. Too much corn will lead to overweight, unhealthy, and unhappy chickens.

If you are not experienced, it's best not to mix your chicken feed when you first start because you may not recognize the symptoms if your birds lack a particular nutrient. As you become more experienced, you are more likely to detect a problem if it occurs.

For those who want to create their feed, keep a close eye on your chickens during the transition and the period shortly after. If you notice that your chickens lose glossiness, shed feathers, show a lack of interest in their food, or other issues begin to occur, make sure that you double and triple check your recipe to ensure that your chickens are getting everything they need. Consider feeding them commercial and homemade foods while they get used to the swap.

To make a starter feed for your chicks, you must be even more careful. Deficiencies during the early stages of life could be dangerous and have long-term health implications.

A good recipe for starter feed is:

- 5 lb. of processed wheat
- 5 lb. of processed oats
- 6 oz of sunflower seeds
- 5 lb. of processed split peas
- 3 oz of kelp meal
- 2 tablespoons of brewer's yeast
- 3 oz of fishmeal

Again, if you use a homemade feed for young birds, you need to be hyper-vigilant and watch for any signs of issues. If you don't pick up on problems quickly, your chickens risk serious health issues, so be on your guard. If you notice problems, swap your chicks back onto a commercial feed, or correct the balances in your feed if you don't think you've got them right.

You should also think about how you are going to mix the feed. If your chickens are un-fussy eaters, you may be able to mix it all and give the birds the mix simply – but this won't work in most cases. The chickens will pick through, sorting out the pieces they like and leaving the pieces they are less keen on. Some birds may eat more of the mixture, while some may leave the majority and only take their favorite treats; This can lead to deficiencies you aren't aware of.

You may therefore wish to grind up the feed. You can get your grinder or source a local mill that can mix the feed and grind it for you. You can decide how fine you need it for your birds; if they are used to a mash, they may not eat a coarser feed, so bear this in mind. The more refined it is, the harder it is for them to pick bits out, too.

What Else Do Chickens Need?

It's imperative to ensure that your chickens are getting grit at all times, although very young chicks may manage without for a while, especially if they are eating an excellent feed. However, you can purchase both adult grit and chick grit; ideally, you want to ensure that chick grit is available to babies so they can eat it if they want to.

Grit is a critical element of your bird's food and serves two purposes. Firstly, it helps birds to grind up their food. Bear in mind that chickens do not have teeth. They break things into small pieces by pecking little bits off at a time, but this still leaves relatively large chunks in their crops, and breaking these down can be challenging.

Grit will help the chicken break up the food by tumbling and grinding around it, slicing through chunks and turning them into small pieces. Grit is insoluble and is usually made up of small stones. For chicks, it may just be flakes of stone.

Chicken owners who only give their birds commercial feed and never permit them to free-range do not have to provide their birds with grit because commercial feed is very soft and can be broken down just by the chickens' digestive systems. However, most chickens are given at least some greenery to peck at and any that free-range will pick up a wide range of foods.

That means that they need grit. Free-ranging chickens tend to source some of this naturally for themselves, picking up tiny stones from the ground and swallowing them, but it is still a good idea to provide your birds with a source of grit so they can eat what they need stay healthy.

If you don't give your chickens grit and eat foods other than their standard mix, there is a risk that they will get a crop impaction, which can be fatal. You should always ensure a supply of grit that your birds can eat whenever they want.

Also, laying chickens requires a second kind of grit – oyster shells; This is soluble grit and works slightly differently. You can provide just oyster shells to all your birds, which will do the same job as insoluble grit, although less effectively. On the whole, it's best to provide both kinds if you can.

The oyster shells are there to keep your hens' calcium supply up. They need a lot of calcium to form their eggs' shells, and if you don't provide it, you'll find that the shells end up weak and thin and break very readily.

Whether your chickens are free-range or not, it's a good idea to provide them with calcium in the form of oyster shells, as this will ensure that they can form viable, healthy eggs. They will pick up some calcium-rich foods as they roam, but having a constant supply allows them to create consistently solid shells and ensures they never face a deficiency.

It might surprise you that chickens can eat oyster shells, but these will gradually dissolve in their digestive system, breaking down and boosting their calcium levels.

Some give their chickens dried crushed eggshells, which serve the same purpose, but there is a slight risk that your chickens might end up associating these with eggs and pecking the eggs themselves; This is a frustrating habit that can be hard to break and may spread through the flock. It shouldn't happen if you crush the eggshells first, but be aware of the risk before deciding.

What Treats Can Chickens Have?

Treats are a great part of chicken ownership, especially if you're an animal lover and take pleasure in spoiling your pets. However, it's imperative to employ a few rules regarding chicken treats. Like humans, chickens can get overweight and suffer from health problems if they eat the wrong things, and also, like humans, they have a fondness for "junk food." That means you must be careful about what you give to your birds, when, and quantities. Treats of any sort should make up no more than 10 percent of a chicken's diet; the rest should come from its main feed.

You should not give your chickens any treats at the start of the day. It is best to wait until they have eaten their fill of the mash or pellets so that they start their crops off with a good meal. Most chicken owners let their chickens eat from their feeders for an hour or so before letting the chickens out to roam, as this encourages the birds to fill up on their proper feed before they start foraging and picking up treats for themselves. During this time, avoid giving them any kitchen scraps or other treats.

Once they have eaten their "breakfast," you can start feeding your birds the things they particularly enjoy. A whole range of foods is suitable for chickens, as they are omnivorous and eat many different things. Treats can be a great way to enrich the lives of a bored flock, especially if they aren't able to forage. Try feeding your chickens things like:

- Bananas
- Oatmeal
- Cherries
- Mealworms
- Cottage cheese
- Wholemeal pasta
- Corn
- Watermelon (this is great for keeping them hydrated in the summer)
- Pumpkin
- Scrambled egg
- Apples
- Pears
- Berries of all kinds, including strawberries, raspberries, blueberries, and more
- Cabbage
- Cauliflower
- Cucumber
- Squash
- Peas

- Brown or wholemeal bread
- Grass (but *never* give your chickens grass you have cut yourself; they need to peck small amounts at a time, or it could get tangled up in their crops, cause an impaction, and kill them)
- Grapes (halved for safety)
- Live yogurt
- Sunflower seeds
- Fish

Note that you should pay attention to the sugar content of the treats you offer and avoid giving too much of any one thing. For example, if your birds eat a lot of watermelon one day, choose non-sugary treats for the next few days; This will reduce the risk of them getting overweight or suffering from digestive issues.

You should also be aware that some treats are much healthier than others. White pasta and white bread will not hurt your chickens, but they contain empty carbohydrates that cause your chickens to gain weight and do not offer much nutritional benefit. Most chicken owners, therefore, avoid these things.

You should limit dairy products. Chickens enjoy things like cheese, and it's thought that they benefit from eating live yogurt, but too much of these things can cause diarrhea. If your flock suffers from this, avoid dairy products until their gut bacteria has balanced and their droppings have normalized.

You should avoid foods like avocados, nuts, potato peels, green potatoes, and citrus fruits (which chickens don't like and will rarely eat). You should not give your chickens spoiled foods, as these could contain dangerous molds that might make your birds very sick. Onions, garlic, raw rice, raw beans, and sugary treats like chocolate should all be avoided.

Chickens are not discerning about their diets and will eat almost anything you offer, as well as things they find around the garden. Take the time to remove anything you don't want them to eat, including non-edibles that could be mistaken for food. Do not keep cleaning products or poisons anywhere your chickens could accidentally access.

If you notice your birds becoming overweight, cut back on the treats. It's easy to spoil chickens because they take such pleasure in their food, but an overweight chicken is at risk of health problems like an overweight human. You can tell if a chicken is overweight by weighing it and looking at averages for the breed or feeling for the keel bone – the bone that runs vertically down the chest.

You should be able to find this bone with your hands, but it should not be prominent. If you can't feel it, the chicken is overweight. If you can feel it very clearly, the chicken is too thin. In a healthy chicken, it should be lightly padded by fat but detectable.

How Do You Keep Chickens Hydrated?

Ensuring your chickens always have enough to drink is crucial, particularly in the summer. Your birds will use water to stay cool, so they should always have plenty available inside their coop and outside if they are allowed to free-range.

You may see your chickens drinking from water buckets, pools, or other standing water, but you should always provide fresh water. You need to refresh the water regularly, and where possible, you should put drinkers in shady spots to keep the water cool.

In really hot weather, you may wish to put a block of ice in the drinker to ensure that the water stays cold and pleasant for the birds to drink. You may also wish to add electrolytes to the water, which can help keep your chickens cool. Some owners add frozen treats such as berries or sweetcorn. Making a block of treats in ice and leaving it in a shady spot will also give your birds something to peck at that will help them stay cool. However, feed treats in moderation as chickens don't need to eat as much when the weather is hot.

In really cold weather, ensure you regularly check that the water supply is still liquid and break up any ice. If you are not available much during the day, it can be tricky to keep water unfrozen. Some people find that adding a ping pong ball will break the tension on the surface and make it harder for the water to freeze. The ping pong ball will disturb the water, keeping it moving and stopping it from turning to ice.

Using a larger trough can help to keep the temperature up, and you can try putting water inside the hen house, where the temperatures are likely to be higher. If you're struggling, look into a chicken waterer; this device is designed to keep the optimal temperature of the water. However, it does need a power supply, so you may be unable to add it to your chicken coop if you don't have electricity.

Making sure your chickens have unfrozen water is critical, so find ways to deal with this if you are not available to check on the drinkers during cold weather.

Summary

In this chapter, we've covered:

- The different diets that chickens need at the various stages of their lives, including starters, growers, finishers, layers, and how to make your feed if you would rather mix it yourself.

- The importance of giving your chickens grit, even when they are small.
- The treats that you can give to your birds, as well as a few things to avoid.
- How to keep your chickens hydrated at all times, including in the summer and winter.

In the following chapter, we will look at how to take care of chickens, their habits, and the pecking order. We will also touch on chicken first aid, plus common diseases and parasites that plague birds.

2

Looking After Chickens: Common Behavior And Care

"My mom used to call us 'free-range kids,' like free-range chickens. We roamed the countryside."

-William Moseley

Chickens are pretty famous for some crazy behavior, like running around the farmyard when their heads have been cut off, but what are they truly like if you sit and watch them? Understanding any animal can be a challenge, and a lot of people find birds particularly difficult to fathom – so in this chapter, we're going to look at some of the common chicken behavior that you might see, as well as the diseases, problems, and injuries that might plague your flock from time to time.

A good chicken owner will have a strong sense of why their birds behave as they do and will recognize what their actions signify. If you don't understand your chickens, at least to some degree, it's very hard to take care of them well, so let's explore how and why chickens act the way they act, and what the different behavioral quirks mean.

Why Do Chickens Dust Bath?

If you have ever watched chickens, especially on a sunny day, you have probably observed that they often turn themselves upside down in a patch of soil and start rolling around in a manner that seems surprising for a bird. They will toss the dirt up through their feathers, kick, roll, and turn, and often coo with apparent pleasure at the same time.

This can be somewhat confusing behavior the first time you see it, and it's frustrating if it happens in the middle of a newly dug flower bed, but it's pretty important to the chicken's health and well-being. Chickens do not wash in water and doing so could result in them getting very chilled, so the dust bath is an alternative that helps them stay clean and knock parasites out of their feathers.

The soil or sand they bathe in helps absorb oil from the feathers, and will dislodge critters or other dirt embedded there. Chickens choose clean, loose soil so that it doesn't stick to them, and they can spend hours dust bathing when the weather is good.

You can and should make a dust bath for your chickens, especially if they don't get to free range frequently. If you do this, you will need a large container, several inches deep, that you can place in a dry spot and fill with soil or sand. You can also mix in diatomaceous earth, dried lavender (which will help to repel pests), and wood ash if you have any available; This makes an excellent mixture for killing external parasites and cleaning the chickens' feathers. You can opt for other herbs, such as rosemary, thyme, or mint. These all help to repel insects and are safe for your birds.

Be aware that the chickens will likely throw the dirt all over with enthusiasm, so it's worth getting a box that's deep enough to keep at least some of the soil in. You should top it up and refresh it regularly so they can continue bathing like this, but you don't want them to kick the contents straight out.

You will probably find that free-ranging hens dig their dust bath somewhere that suits them, especially if you don't provide one. They will generally scratch out a shallow ditch in the ground and settle into it, shaking the soil up through their feathers. If there is room, most chickens choose to dust bath with other flock members; they seem to enjoy this social aspect. You may hear cooing or even the strange purring noise that chickens make when they are really happy.

I often find our chickens rolling around almost on their backs, apparently blissful at the combination of the sun and the soil on their feathers. They groom themselves, peck dirt off each other, and there's a certain level of peace among them that you rarely see at other times. They love this most of all in spring, but I've seen them bathing throughout the year.

It's a good idea to provide your chickens with a covered area, even if they generally prefer your flower beds. This ensures that they always have somewhere that they can retreat to for a bath if they start feeling grubby. The drier the soil is, the more effective the bath will be; your birds will not bathe in mud.

Some chickens dust bath a lot more than others, but you should check on the bath every week or so and see whether it needs cleaning out. Remove droppings and top them up with soil, sand, ash, diatomaceous earth, and herbs as needed. This ensures it serves its purpose and keeps your hens in good condition.

How Do You Stop A Chicken From Eating Eggs?

In the introduction, I mentioned an issue that some chicken owners run into with their birds deciding to eat their own eggs. This can be a major problem; unfortunately, it's a habit that often spreads through the flock because the birds learn from each other. If you have one hen that discovers eggs are an appealing food source, you'll find that the others soon start doing the same. Frustratingly, it can be very challenging to stop this, but here are a few methods that you might find helpful.

Firstly, check that your chickens are getting a sufficient amount of protein. Eggs are high in protein, so if your chickens are particularly determined to eat them, it may be because they are lacking in other parts of their diet. Boost their protein intake if possible and see if this cures the issue.

Secondly, ensure your birds are getting enough calcium; This will strengthen the egg-shells and make it harder for them to peck them open. Thin shells are more tempting targets and the chickens can break them to get at the insides with little effort.

Another option involves putting a fake wooden egg or a golf ball into the nest box. This may help to convince the chickens that eggs aren't food; they will not get a reward for pecking at this. However, it will likely only work with a chicken that has only recently discovered eggs are edible. Other birds may not easily break the habit just because they encounter an inedible egg.

You can take this further by blowing a chicken egg and piping some English mustard into the insides. Most chickens are not fond of mustard and will not enjoy the taste if they peck this egg open; This may deter them from trying future eggs more effectively than the wooden egg.

Keeping the nest box dim could help too. If the chickens can't see the eggs, they are less likely to eat them. They will simply lay and leave the box, rather than hanging around and inspecting its contents.

Furthermore, you should remove any broody chickens from the nest box, as these can cause congestion. If a bird keeps sitting in the box, your others may not be able to get in to lay, or may find that it is more cramped than normal; This increases the risk of an egg getting broken and eaten. Give broody chickens a separate dark box if you want them to be able to incubate eggs, or keep removing them from the nest box until they stop trying to incubate eggs.

A fundamental prevention method is removing all real eggs from the hen house as early as possible. Hens generally lay in the morning, and most will have finished by around 10. Try to go out as soon as possible, collect up all the eggs, and take them away; This reduces the opportunity for the egg eater and may help stop the habit from spreading to other flock members.

If you really cannot get a hen to stop eating eggs, you may want to consider a rolling away nest box. This is designed to encourage the egg to roll out of the box and into a separate container when it has been laid, taking it out of the hen's reach. It's probably the most extreme/expensive method, but it can be effective if you have multiple egg-eating hens or a habit has set in. Once a chicken has become an established egg eater, getting them to stop using other methods is very tricky, so try to step in as early as possible.

Note that prevention is much better than cure when it comes to this habit, and you can reduce the risk of your chickens picking it up in a few different ways. One involves removing eggs from the house as soon as possible after they have been laid, and never giving your birds whole eggs or anything that looks similar to an egg.

Another involves ensuring that your nest box is sufficiently cushioned so the birds are unlikely to break the eggs in the first place. Usually, egg eating habits arise because a chicken has trampled on an egg and decided that the insides look tasty – and they will soon learn that breaking the eggs brings a food reward. Cushioning the box makes it less likely that an egg will get broken, which reduces the risk of the chickens seeing them as food.

What Does Mating Behavior Look Like?

If you're keeping both male and female birds, you need to know how to recognize mating behavior. This will help you understand the dynamics of your flock and give you an idea of which birds are likely to be laying and turning broody in preparation for chicks. You should keep an eye on this, particularly in spring, when most chickens mate. This is a good time of year, as it allows time for the eggs to be incubated and hatch, and the young chicks will have a full season of feeding and foraging before the cold weather comes.

Mating behavior can vary depending on the dynamics of your flock. Many chickens perform a courtship dance, but this may be skipped in dense flocks where roosters have the opportunity to mate with many different hens. A rooster can mate as many as 30 times a day, sometimes even more, and mating is most common in the early hours of the morning and in the late afternoon.

If the mating dance is performed, it starts with the rooster dropping a wing down and dancing around this dropped wing in a circle. If receptive to the rooster, the hen will crouch down, dipping her head and body; This indicates acceptance and makes it easier for the rooster to get onto her back.

The rooster will then grab onto the back of the hen's head or her comb and perform a brisk walk on her back. He will dip his tail to the side of the hen's tail, spreading out the feathers and bringing the cloacae into contact. This is the point at which the sperm crosses from the rooster to the hen, and she is fertilized. There is no penetration with chickens.

The rooster will then crow away while the female resumes her previous activity.

Roosters may also perform other behavior in an attempt to win the females. They will call the female they are courting over to a treat and then pick up and drop the treat repeatedly to attract the hen's attention. The rooster may also make a "tuk-tuk" sound as the hen inspects the treat. This treat-giving is rarely a prelude to mating but is part of the courtship behavior and seems to be an aspect of winning over females.

If you have multiple roosters in your flock, one will probably be considered the leader – usually the biggest. He wins his position through fighting, and rooster fights can be surprisingly aggressive, especially during mating season. Other roosters may attempt to win females but will often be chased off by the larger male or even the females. They do sometimes manage to mate, but this is rare. Older hens are often aggressive toward a young male and may do him serious injury in some cases, so be aware of this when introducing new birds to your flock.

Once a hen has been mated, you should check her for any injuries, especially if your rooster is inexperienced. Long spurs and over-mating can also cause issues. If your hen has been injured, check out the section on chicken first aid below. She should be removed from the flock for a few weeks to recover.

In general, chicken mating is straightforward and unremarkable. Still, it's worth watching the flock's behavior in spring and watching for any problems, especially if you have multiple roosters or inexperienced ones.

Why Do Chickens Roam?

If given a chance, chickens love to roam around your garden, but they rarely go out of sight of their coop. This is because they know that the coop represents safety from predators, shelter, food, and the rest of the flock. If they are going to roam further, they will usually do so in pairs or groups. Two of our girls love visiting our neighbors (who fortunately do not mind!) because they can stroll around there easily. Still, they only began doing this when they were well established on their territory and felt comfortable. They also tended to go together!

If you are going to allow your chickens to roam, there are some things you need to think about. I'm a big advocate for permitting roaming where possible because I think it enriches the birds' lives, ensures they can supplement their diet with a range of treats, and makes them happier. It also provides free pest control for your garden and brings a lot of pleasure; they look so picturesque exploring, scratching, and busying themselves about the place. However, having roaming chickens does bring some drawbacks.

Chickens are destructive. They aren't aggressive birds, but if they spot a tasty morsel in a flowerbed, they aren't going to worry about digging up your petunias or prize roses; they will scratch away until they can get their prize. They will also peck at and eat any plants that take their fancy, sometimes to the point of destruction. They will scratch up your grass, overturn your plants, and leave droppings all over your patio. The answer to these problems is to create a fenced area where you are happy for your chickens to roam freely. This can still be filled with grass, plants, and other enrichment activities, but it won't be the things that you especially care about.

We haven't done this with our birds, although we have occasionally fenced them into certain areas for safety (when we first had them, to prevent them from roaming too far, for example). There are several reasons, one being that our garden is difficult to fence. Another is simply that we like to see them around the place. However, we also accept that they will tear up plants and make holes in the lawn, and we have to protect anything we don't want them to ruin. It's worth it to watch them engage in natural behavior and live their lives to the fullest.

So, how do you get chickens started with free ranging? It's important to wait for a few days before you do. When you bring your chickens home, give them at least 3 days to settle into the coop before letting them out. They will be busy learning about their new home during this time, and don't need to explore new areas. This period will also ensure that they start viewing their coop as a place of safety, meaning that they will run back to it if a predator threatens them.

The first day you let your chickens out do so in the late afternoon or early evening. They will automatically return to the coop when the sun begins to set so they can roost, which is a good way to ensure that their free-ranging is limited for the day. Employ this method for a few days before letting them out in the daytime.

To let them free range for the first time, open the coop door and wait for them to head out on their own. It may take a bit of time, but that's fine. Carrying them out is likely to cause alarm and could result in the birds running off.

You should have some particularly tempting treats to hand when you initially let your chickens roam, so that you can coax them back to you if necessary. Before we let ours out the first time, we spent about a week training them to come to a specific noise, always rewarding them with food. We rarely have an issue if we need to locate them now, as we can simply call them back and reward them with a treat, just as you would with a dog. This is well worth doing with your flock.

You need to take safety precautions for your chickens if they are allowed to roam in your garden. Think about local predators and how your birds will fare. Roosters will fiercely defend their flock from various predators, but even so, you should take steps to prevent things like foxes, coyotes, stoats, and other predators from getting near your birds. There are few foolproof methods, but fencing your garden well and keeping your birds shut in during dusk and twilight will help to reduce the risks.

What Is The Purpose Of Preening?

You are bound to see your chickens preening fairly frequently, which is a good sign. This is simply another method of cleaning themselves. Feathers serve several important functions: they provide insulation from heat and cold, and they are reasonably waterproof to stop your chickens from getting wet. However, they won't work well if they are not clean.

Preening removes dirt and debris, helps to reduce the presence of pests, and re-oils the feathers, ensuring that they remain waterproof. Chickens have oil glands near their tails, and they will gather oil from here before preening – so don't worry if you see your chickens pecking at their tails frequently. They are simply re-waterproofing their feathers.

You will see your chickens preening all parts of their bodies, sometimes for long periods. They often do this in the afternoon, when they have fed well and feel sleepy. They will frequently sit in groups to preen, which helps them to watch out for predators, and they may even preen each other at times. This is a group bonding activity, and birds particularly close to each other may increase their bonds through this kind of grooming.

If a chicken doesn't preen properly, you will notice that its feathers take on a greasy, dirty look. This is often a sign that there is something wrong with the bird. It may be sick or injured, in which case it will no longer have the motivation to look after itself. Make sure you check any birds that seem to have stopped preening or look particularly scruffy.

Why Do Chickens Scratch?

Scratching is an extremely common behavior for chickens, and you will see mother hens teaching their babies how to do this as soon as they are old enough. Chickens scratch the ground for several reasons, but most commonly, they are foraging for food.

Chickens have powerful feet, and scratching at the ground overturns the soil, tears up plants, and exposes insects and grubs beneath the surface. A chicken will scratch at any bit of bare soil that takes its fancy or grassy areas if it thinks there may be something good to eat under. It doesn't do this only when it sees a worm or another insect; chickens instinctively scratch at any bit of ground when hunting for food.

Scratching unearths worms, woodlice, beetles, centipedes, and other insects may also turn up seeds and other bits of plant matter that the chickens can eat. Chickens are voracious predators and feed on almost anything they can find. Scratching is their best method of foraging – so they do it a lot, particularly if they can find bare ground, such as flowerbeds.

You should be aware of this if you're going to allow your chickens to free-range because this behavior can be quite damaging, and it's something that they will do almost constantly when foraging. Our lawn has quite a few bare patches that represent favored scratching spots, and now that the chickens have removed the grass, they can easily overturn the soil to search for food.

It is surprising how strong a chicken's legs are, and how easily they can pull up even established plants when they think something is worth getting. If you do not let your chickens free-range, they will still scratch at most materials as a natural behavior and on the hunt for insects that may have crawled into their pen. Things like wood chip and straw allow them to exhibit this behavior but keeping your birds on a hard surface such as concrete or gravel may deter them from scratching and isn't recommended.

Scratching is also part of a chicken's social bonding. They scratch when they are around members of their flock and only when they are feeling comfortable. You will often see two chickens scratching at the same bit of ground together, enjoying each other's company. The whole flock may scratch in one place if they find that it has plenty of grubs in it. They won't share the spoils, however!

Sometimes, chickens will dig at the ground with more purpose, and will remove chunks of soil to hollow out a nest or dust bath (particularly if you have not provided one). Some chickens like to lay in more secluded places than a nest box, and will dig themselves a little spot somewhere they deem safe, which can be frustrating. If this happens, check whether you have provided enough nest boxes for the size of your flock.

When I was young, we had a game hen that would scrape out a little hollow under a bush to lay. Sometimes, there would be ten eggs or more before we found where she was hiding, so if one of your birds isn't laying in the box, take some time to look around and see if you can find a hollow where the chicken may be going instead. This will often be under a bush or behind a shed, usually where it is dark, shady, and quiet.

What's A Pecking Order?

You may have heard of a pecking order before, but if not, this is the term used to refer to how chickens construct their social order. Chickens have a surprisingly strong hierarchy; every bird within a flock has a specific place that rarely shifts up or down (unless new birds are added or birds are removed).

The pecking order determines how the chickens behave. It dictates which chicken gets the first pick of treats, roosting spots, or dust bath position. The high-level chickens will always get the first pick of anything, while low-ranking individuals will have to wait their turn or miss out entirely, depending on the scarcity of the resource.

A pecking order tends to be pretty fixed once a group of chickens has been established, so you rarely see squabbling among a flock. Occasionally, a small skirmish may break out, especially if a particularly coveted treat is on offer. Still, for the most part, the lower-ranking chickens keep out of the way of the high ranks, and do not squabble. This results in a fairly harmonious situation.

The chickens at the top of the pecking order often take on responsibility for the other birds too, and may call them to share in treats; This depends on your bird and the dynamics within the group, but it isn't uncommon for the "head" chicken to treat the others somewhat like chicks and allow the others to feed first, even though it has the right to the first pick if it chooses.

A rooster will almost always be the head of the group if you have roosters, but in female-only flocks, there will still be an established leader. Female-only flocks may be more harmonious, and male-dominated flocks can get out of control during the mating season, so you may have to step in if your hens are injured. Ideally, you want at least 10 hens to every rooster, or possibly more; This helps keep a good balance and prevents the hens from being hassled too much.

If you have a large flock, you will probably find that they naturally split themselves into smaller groups, especially while foraging. Depending on the dynamics, there may be one rooster per group or groups of just hens. Each bird will know its position in the pecking order and is unlikely to try to fight it. Young roosters may scrap to try to elevate their positions, but on the whole, most birds are peaceful most of the time.

You can minimize disputes in your flock in a few different ways. The overall goal is balance. If every bird has a roosting spot, a place at the feeder and drinker, a spot in the nest box, and room to scratch around, there isn't likely to be much conflict.

You need at least 3 inches of feeder and drinker space per bird, and preferably more. Have multiple feeders and drinkers, and put them in the middle of the coop so all of the birds can get to them. For every 3-4 birds, you should have 1 nest box, and each bird needs at least 8 inches of roosting space. If they aren't fighting for basic resources, you will find that your chickens are reasonably peaceful unless you have a treat that they particularly love!

The only other time you are likely to see major disputes among your chickens is when a bird or multiple birds are added to the flock. Adding birds to your established flock can be challenging, and will often disrupt the pecking order while the birds get used to each other and work out where their new rank is.

This is particularly difficult if you add just a couple of birds to a large flock, or if you add much younger birds. The established flock will bully the newcomers, possibly to the point of being dangerous. It isn't unheard of for them to kill an individual if you don't step in. You will need to work hard and spend a lot of time on your introduction if you are going to do this, and it's really better not to add just one or two birds to a big group.

Letting the birds free range together before you pen them together, or penning the new birds in a separate but connected area may help. Overall, it's challenging for experienced chicken owners to successfully add new birds to their flocks.

How Do You Help An Egg Bound Hen?

Egg binding can be a problem in any hens, and it occurs when the egg does not pass from the shell gland to the vent. This means that the egg remains inside the chicken at the final stage before being laid, and it can kill a hen in 2 days if it isn't treated.

Egg binding is commonest among young or overweight birds or birds that are laying year-round due to unnatural lighting conditions. It may also happen if your chicken eats too much protein, is deficient in calcium, is stressed, or has a poor diet. Some birds are also genetically predisposed to egg binding. Essentially, it can happen to any bird, so knowing how to deal with it is important.

Firstly, let's look at the symptoms. There are a few ways to tell if a hen is egg-bound, but the common symptoms include:

- Lethargy
- Straining
- Staying in the nest box
- Not producing eggs
- Liquids dripping from the vent
- An egg-shaped lump near the vent

If you see any of these signs, you need to take swift action because your bird will die quickly if you don't get it to pass the egg. If possible, take your chicken to an avian-friendly vet with the expertise to help. However, if you don't have a vet available, some home remedies can help. Only use these if other options are not open to you; be aware that the chicken may die if you are unsuccessful.

You should bring the chicken into the house and place her in a bowl of warm water. Put some Epsom salts in the water and allow the chicken to soak herself for about 20 minutes, ensuring that the vent and lower body are submerged. While she is soaking, gently rub her abdomen with your hand to try to massage the egg and shift it around. Be careful, as you don't want it to break inside her; this can lead to an infection.

If your chicken is reluctant to stay in the water bowl, check that it isn't too hot, and place a light towel over her head. Chickens tend to go still and quiet when they are in the dark, which may encourage her to stop trying to escape.

When the soaking time is up, lift her out and gently dry her with a towel. Do not allow her to get chilled before her feathers have completely dried; keep her indoors. You can use vegetable oil to lubricate her vent, and massage her abdomen a little more.

Next, set up a hospital cage for her; This should be warm, dry, and dark. Many people use dog crates with towels over them. Use an eyedropper to give the hen 1 cc of liquid calcium and some Nutri-Drench (or other rich vitamin supplements), and then leave her for an hour in the quiet and dark.

Repeat the process with a warm soak and a massage if she has not passed the egg by the hour is up. Keep trying until the bird can lay the egg, or get her to a vet when you can.

Egg binding cannot always be prevented, but keeping your chickens to a good weight, limiting treats, and providing good quality food will help. You should also avoid lighting your coop in winter, as forced laying throughout the year often contributes to this problem.

Basics Of Chicken First Aid

Ideally, if you keep chickens, you should find a bird-friendly vet you can call whenever something is wrong with one of your birds. However, this is a challenge for many people, so it's a good idea to know some of the basics of treating chicken injuries before you get your flock. Where possible, always seek expert veterinary care; the below information is intended for instances in which you cannot easily take your chicken to a vet.

The first thing you need to know is how to recognize when a chicken is sick or injured, so let's cover some common symptoms you should always be on the lookout for. You need to take action if you see a chicken that is:

- Lethargic
- Droopy
- Disinterested in food
- Hiding from you or the flock
- Limping
- Inactive
- Not laying as expected
- Pale around the comb/wattles
- Standing or sitting in a strange posture
- Producing unusual droppings
- Suffering from open wounds

You should have a first aid kit built up in advance to be ready whenever you need it. Chickens can easily get hurt and suffer from many sicknesses, so don't wait to organize this. Your first aid kit should include:

- Anti peck spray
- Antibacterial paste
- Anti-mite treatments
- Antibiotic ointment
- Epsom salts
- Aspirin
- Petroleum jelly
- Nutri-drench
- Electrolytes

- Diatomaceous earth
- Vitamin E with selenium
- Disposable gloves
- Droppers
- Towels
- Self-adhesive bandages

It is preferable to take your chicken to a vet if this is an option, rather than treating the bird yourself. However, the above supplies will ensure that you can step in if your chicken is ill or injured, and a vet is not an option.

How To Care For A Sick Or Injured Chicken

If you are dealing with a sick or injured chicken, the first step is to bring the bird indoors or transfer it to a hospital cage. Unfortunately, chickens can be vicious and may pick on any flock member they detect weakness in, even killing them. Isolating a bird prevents bullying and diseases from spreading among your flock.

The hospital cage will generally be small (as it is not intended for active birds) and should have food, water, and bedding available unless there is a specific reason to exclude these. Many people use a dog crate as a hospital cage. Once you have a hospital cage prepared, let's look at how to treat injuries, and then we'll move on to caring for a sick chicken.

You should use a clean towel and gentle pressure if your chicken is injured to slow the bleeding. Bleeding wounds can look worse than they are. Keep pressure on the injury until the bleeding stops, and then clean and bathe the wound with warm, sterile water and a clean cloth. Assess the injury. You may need to trim the surrounding feathers to get a good look at it. Deep wounds must be treated with diluted bleach, water, and baking soda.

Keep the bird isolated and keep checking on the wound daily. If the bird shows signs of infection, you may need to use antibiotics, but these should be avoided if no infection appears. You should keep your chicken well-fed and add electrolytes and vitamins to its waters for a couple of days. These will help it overcome the shock and rebuild its tissues.

Keep the bird hydrated with water on a spoon if necessary; water is much more important than food, although the bird needs to start eating again within a few days to recover. You can give your chicken aspirin in its drinking water if it is in pain. Do not pour water down your chicken's throat unless you have been shown how to do this by an expert. You may choke it.

Once the chicken's injury has completely healed, gradually reintroduce it to the flock by penning it alongside them or letting it free range with them; This should help it to resume its natural place. If the bird does not show signs of recovery, you may need to take it to a vet.

If treating a sick chicken, your approach will vary depending on the sickness, but you should isolate the bird from the flock again. Keep it warm, minimize stress levels, and consult a vet if possible. Read the following section for more specific advice on treating common illnesses.

Common Chicken Diseases

Infectious Bronchitis: This disease quickly spreads through your flock and results in sneezing, wheezing, and coughing. Birds should be vaccinated against it.

Thrush: this is similar to the disease that human babies can get, resulting in a white ooze inside the crop and an increased appetite. Treat the bird with an anti-fungal medicine from the vet.

Avian Influenza: the symptoms of this include respiratory problems, diarrhea, and potentially swelling around the face/wattles. There is no cure for this, so you will need to kill affected birds and sanitize all areas before getting a new flock. Be cautious as this disease can spread to people.

Fowl Pox: this causes lesions on unfeathered parts of the bird and sometimes in the mouth. Birds can be vaccinated against this disease.

Marek's disease: the symptoms of this disease are tumors and paralysis. This is a viral disease, and carriers must be isolated and euthanized. However, chicks can and should be vaccinated.

Newcastle disease: you may see breathing difficulties, nasal discharge, and wheezing with this illness. Again, vaccination is a good prevention method and good sanitary practices.

Chicken Parasites

Chickens are also vulnerable to several parasites, so here are a few to look out for.

Coccidiosis causes weight loss, loose droppings, and potentially blood in the droppings. It is a parasite that damages the chicken's gut wall. You can vaccinate your birds or use a medicated feed for chicks. Keep food areas clean and dry to minimize the transfer risk of this disease.

Mites: there are three major kinds of mites, including scaly leg mite, red mite, and northern fowl mite. All of these will feed on your chicken's blood and can cause anemia and plucking. Use a mite repellent and give your chickens rich feed to boost their energy levels.

Botflies: these will lay their eggs in the chicken's skin, and the larvae will burrow into them; This is painful and dangerous. Keep an eye out for botflies and keep the pen clean and sanitary.

Worms: your chickens can get internal parasites like other animals, and you should treat them for worms regularly; This minimizes the risk of the various kinds of worms they can suffer from.

Most external parasites can be avoided by providing a dust bath for your chickens, as this will allow them to clean their feathers and dislodge the parasites. Clean the coop regularly too.

Summary

In this chapter, we've covered:

- Why chickens bathe in dust and what you need to provide.
- Egg eating and how to prevent it.
- Chicken mating habits.
- Roaming, preening, and scratching, and what these behaviors are for.
- The intricacies of a pecking order.
- How to help an egg-bound hen.
- How to perform chicken first aid, and the tricks for caring for sick and injured birds.
- The common diseases and parasites that chickens may suffer from.

In the following chapter, we will look at how to house chickens and some top tips for cleaning them out.

3

How To House Chickens

"Home is where we should feel secure and comfortable."

-Catherine Pulsifer

As the quote above reminds us, home is one of the most important things in life – and this is true for your birds just as it is true for you. A well-designed coop makes a big difference to chicken ownership and can ensure that your birds are happy, safe, and less likely to get sick. With that in mind, let's look at coops, what they should include, and whether you should buy or build your coop.

Why Is A Coop Important?

The term "coop" can sometimes be confusing because some people refer to the whole cage, complete with the run, and others use it to refer only to a house. I will use "coop" to mean the whole cage, and refer to a "house" when I mean just the area that your hens sleep in and lay their eggs in (as the nest box tends to be adjoined to the sleeping quarters).

A coop is necessary for a whole range of reasons, and it provides your chickens with:

- Shelter from hot and cold weather.
- Safety from predators.
- A spot to gather.
- A place to lay their eggs.
- A sense of safety.
- A place where they can get food and water.
- A place where they can be confined when necessary.

You may decide that you do not want a coop. You only want a house, but remember that this can be a major problem if you need to pen your birds for any reason – and many things might require penning. For example, avian flu outbreaks can mean you need to keep the birds in. A sudden predator spike, a bout of dangerously bad weather, visitors with dogs, or other issues may also come up. Even if you never intend to keep your chickens penned, I would strongly suggest having a coop where you can safely confine the chickens if necessary.

Your chicken's house will usually be located inside the main coop, and if you set it up correctly, this can provide your chickens with a double layer of protection. The outer coop will keep most predators away, while the house is usually extra secure and should foil all but the most determined predators.

Some people wonder if they need a house and a coop, but I would generally say that the answer to this is a firm yes. A house is confined, fairly weatherproof, safe from predators, and easier for the birds to keep warm with their body heat when winter comes. It also gives access to the nest box, and we'll look at the need for this in more detail in a moment.

I would therefore say that in almost all circumstances, you need a house and a run – forming the full coop. You can use many variations, and a coop can follow almost any design you like, but if you are going to keep a happy and healthy backyard flock, you must have a chicken coop.

Do You Need A Nest Box?

Next, let's look at the purpose of the nest box. Your chickens will lay their eggs whether or not you give them a box, so you might be wondering why you should bother. The answer is that it can be a great way to ensure that all the eggs end up in the same place (or at least most of them). You can then easily gather the eggs at a time that is convenient to you. The box will prevent the eggs from being broken or stolen by other animals.

Your chicken house should have a nest box attached so the birds have somewhere quiet, dark, private, and safe to lay. This is their preferred situation, so if you don't provide it, they are pretty likely to just go off and lay elsewhere in a spot that they find comfortable. They also prefer to lay above ground level, so the nest box should be elevated.

For medium breeds, a nest box should be at least 12 inches tall, 12 inches wide, and 12 inches deep. If you have large breeds, allow more space. You can go a little smaller for small breeds, although not much. Remember that you will often end up with more than one chicken in the nest box at once.

A nest box should be lined with a padded material of some form or another. The cushioning underfoot will reduce the risk of the eggs getting broken and encourages the chicken's nesting instincts. You can use various materials, and there is much debate about the best. Your options include:

- Straw
- Pine shavings
- Hay
- Shredded newspaper

There are other options too, but these are the top ones. We favored straw, but it stays wet, so if one of your birds poops in the box, you'll need to clean it out. Fortunately, this is often an isolated area. We were wary of hay, as the chickens occasionally get their feet tangled up in the strands.

You can also add lavender or rosemary to the nest box to repel mites and keep it fresher. Even if you do this, the box should be cleaned out reasonably often to ensure the bedding is fresh and free from bugs.

Always check whether a material is suitable before using it, as some are thought to cause respiratory problems. Sand, for example, is okay as long as you use coarse sand, but play sand may get into your chickens' lungs. I suggest sticking to straw, as we found this successful, but feel free to experiment.

You usually need a nest box for every 3 or 4 birds. This minimizes the risk of the box being blocked up when one of your birds wants to lay. If you have a flock of more than 4, make sure you have 2 boxes. If you don't have enough space for them, they will lay in random places in your garden. It is worth noting that chickens will often have a favorite nest box and refuse to lay in the other one, but if you provide 2 boxes or more, you will have done your best at least!

What Is The Roosting Bar?

Chickens instinctively perch at night, and they will be miserable if you don't provide a roosting bar. You should always provide more roosting space for your flock, so they can spread out or bunch together as they choose. They will often sleep close together during the winter. The chickens on the outside tend to be the weaker flock members, and if you don't provide enough space, these will be pushed onto the floor.

Perching allows chickens to keep their feet warm, because they will tuck their breast feathers over their feet and legs, which helps them maintain their warmth. Higher perches are good for chickens that can fly well, such as bantams, whereas larger chickens need lower perches. If you don't provide perching space in your house, your chickens may search for other roosting options, such as in bushes or trees, as they dislike sitting on the floor to sleep. A grounded chicken is vulnerable to predators, so they instinctively seek height for safety.

Enclosed Runs

If you aren't going to let your chickens free-range full time (or often even if you are), it's a good idea to have an enclosed run where you can let your chickens roam in safely. This is usually attached to the house and may contain the feeders and drinkers, plus the covered dust bath.

If your chickens will not be free-ranging, this run needs to allow a minimum of 1 square meter per bird – preferably more than this. This is the smallest space you can keep chickens in; if you have large birds, they will need more room. Giving your chickens too little space increases the risk of disease and aggression among the flock. They will quickly destroy the ground they are on, and may turn on each other due to frustration or boredom.

An enclosed run needs to be safe from predators of all kinds, so you should research the threats in your local area and ensure that your run can withstand these. For example, if you have foxes, wolves, coyotes, bears, or other animals capable of digging, you will need to bury the metal mesh that makes a run at least a couple of feet underground to prevent them from going under it.

You will also need to enclose the top so that nothing can climb over and birds of prey cannot swoop down on your flock. Covering all or parts of the run with weatherproof material will help keep the ground drier and pleasanter for the chickens, stopping feeders and dust baths from getting wet.

You should make a point of regularly checking that the run is in good condition. Any breakages should be mended immediately, as predators can take advantage of the smallest opportunity. Your run must be extremely durable if you have strong predators like bears in your local area.

You also need to think about what you will spread at the bottom of the enclosed run so that your chickens aren't paddling in a muddy puddle, but we'll cover that toward the end of this chapter.

Buying Commercial Coops

If you buy your coop, take some time to check out the different options. There are many different designs, and various materials to choose from.

Plastic coops have become popular because they are easy to clean and sterilize, but wooden coops often look prettier. Things like mites can be more of an issue in a wooden coop, because the material is porous, so be aware of that when you make your selection.

You should also do some research into the customer reviews. It's worth buying a coop that gets good reviews and will last well, as cheap coops will often cost you the difference in repairs – and there's a risk of predators breaking in and killing your flock. A well designed coop can make a world of difference in chicken keeping, so bear this in mind when you're choosing, and take your time over the decision.

Read some reviews on available coops in your area, and weigh the pros and cons. A commercial coop will often come with everything mentioned above, such as roosting bars, nest boxes, feeders and drinkers, and more.

A few things to look out for include:

- Good ventilation.
- A nest box.
- Well insulated.
- Easy access for you and chickens (especially to the nest box so you can collect eggs).
- Predator-proof.
- Some windows/way of letting in natural light for the chickens.
- Enough space for your intended flock.
- Easy to clean out.

Making Your Own Coop

Many people like to make their coops because this lets them design it however they like. If you're making your own, you can fit it to your garden, add elements you need, and do away with things you don't want. You will generally be building the coop from wood and strong metal mesh, although you can use other materials if you prefer.

You can find a lot of chicken coop designs online, but let's run through a few of the major things you need to consider before you start, and probably before you even get the materials!

Size: this will be based on the number of birds you have, and you need to think about it both in terms of the house and the run. Let's start with the run.

Your run cannot be "too big" regarding the chickens' welfare because they'll take as much space as you can offer. However, a huge enclosed run will be expensive to build and difficult to maintain, and there's a heightened risk of predators finding a weak point. You may also find it takes a long time to clean out. You should therefore consider the size of your flock and your yard, and design the run accordingly.

Do leave space for additions, as you never know if your flock might grow, and it's easier to fence off a bit that you don't want them to use than it is to add more secure run space. The amount of room you need depends on the size of your birds and their breed to some degree, but if your chickens are not allowed to free-range, you should allow for a minimum of 10 square feet per bird. Four birds would therefore need a 42-square-foot run. Don't get more birds than you have room for because they will be unhappy and fight.

If you plan to let your chickens free-range regularly, you can get away with a lot less enclosed space, and you only need about 4 square feet per bird. However, bear in mind that if you then do have to pen them, they will be miserable, so be as generous as you can with the space.

A large house can be a problem in winter because the birds won't be able to keep it warm. A house that is too small has obvious drawbacks. You should therefore design your house around your ideal flock size. You need to consider several things, including the size of your birds, how often you can clean the house out, and whether you are keeping roosters (which generally need more space). Go a little bigger rather than too small, especially if you plan to breed the birds.

There aren't many recommendations for this, but generally, allowing about 3 square feet of space per bird should be fine. With smaller birds, like bantams, you can scale this down.

All of your chickens must fit comfortably in the house, and you should ideally have more than one entrance so that they don't have to queue up to get in and out. If the house is elevated, add a ramp so they can choose to walk rather than fly.

Materials: wood tends to be the most accessible building material, and you can use strong metal mesh for the open part of the coop. Choose the mesh grade according to the predators you are protecting your chickens from; many animals can bite through thin metal, so you'll need to research how thick the mesh needs to be.

Remember that you should provide sheltered areas in your open run. Your chickens will not be happy if they are constantly exposed to gales and blizzards, making their food and dust bath wet. Strong tarpaulins can be a great way to provide sheltered spots that the chickens can go into when the weather is bad.

Ventilation: your house must be ventilated or the birds cannot survive in it, because it will fill with carbon dioxide, ammonia, and moisture. When you are designing your house, ventilation will be a critical element. Your house needs approximately 4 feet of ventilation in winter and even more if possible in summer. Of course, you want to be careful not to make your coop so airy that the birds can't keep it warm with their body heat.

Ventilation needs vary depending on things like how frequently you clean the coop out and how hot the environment is, how low the roof is, and how many chickens are in there. If you are using online instructions, follow their guidelines for making ventilation, but also check the coop once it is in operation and see whether it feels damp or smells unclean. This should help you to determine how well the ventilation is working. Do not cover up the ventilation holes of the house, even if the weather is cold in winter.

Insulation: to keep your birds warm in winter and cool in summer, you should consider providing insulation. You may not need to do this if you live in a temperate environment, but it might give you more peace of mind, and it means you won't need to worry about your chickens if a cold snap hits or a heatwave starts.

One of the easiest ways to add insulation when building your coop is to use spray foam or fiberglass insulation in the roof. This provides a layer of protection that will stop heat from being lost to the outside or entering the coop. However, you must cover both of these materials with ply so the birds cannot interact with them. They may peck at and eat insulation, and this could kill them.

If you are concerned, you can add a thermometer to your chicken coop and use this to check that your birds aren't getting too hot or too cold. Avoid using heaters or lights in the coop, even in icy weather; the fire risk is simply too high, and many people have lost their flocks. In general, chickens are very tolerant of cold weather and will simply puff up, fluff their feathers over their feet, and huddle together if they are cold at night.

You can buy insulating jackets for some hen houses, but this will depend on your house design, and it risks interfering with the ventilation. Remember, if the coop can't ventilate, it will get damp inside, massively decreasing the temperature. Generally, as long as the coop is dry and not too large, the birds' body heat will be enough to keep it warm.

However, you should also position the coop to be naturally sheltered from winds, extreme heat, and extreme cold. Nearby trees or shrubs will help to reduce any gales and may also provide shelter from precipitation. If the coop is near other buildings, it may also stay warmer.

Food and water: you need to put feeders and drinkers in the coop – preferably multiple ones. You can buy free-standing options or ones that hook onto the side of the pen. There are many different designs, all with pros and cons. Many feeders dispense just a small amount of food at once and keep the rest stored, so it doesn't get wet in the rain. They may have separate points to encourage the birds to spread and reduce squabbling.

If you want to keep things simple, you can just give your chickens food and water in buckets, but this does have a few problems. You will need to clean the buckets regularly to prevent the food from spoiling and the water from growing algae, and there's a risk of them getting knocked over and spilt.

If you want hard-wearing feeders and drinkers, metal may be the best option, but plastic can have its advantages too. It is slightly insulating, so it may prevent the water from freezing, and it can look more attractive.

Dropping boards are another critical element of designing your coop which you should consider. You can make cleanup much easier for yourself if you add some boards that slide in under the roosting bars. This is usually the part of the house that gets messiest, so cleaning this daily and then doing occasional deep cleans of the rest of the house can massively cut down on the chore of cleaning without compromising on the hygiene of your chickens.

If you make these boards from plastic or another easy-to-clean substance, you can lift them out, hose them off, and minimize the need to clean the rest of the coop. Wooden boards will also work but may be a little harder to clean. Make the boards light, so they are easy to handle, and ensure that they overlap so droppings won't fall between them.

You don't have to make dropping boards for your chicken house if you want to maximize the simplicity, but it makes a huge difference to cleanup.

Chicken Tractors

If you've never come across chicken tractors before, you might be baffled by the name – but these are a cool invention and bring a different element to chicken keeping. We had one for our last flock, and while it wasn't perfect, it was a fun idea that was practical, aesthetically pleasing, and enhanced the quality of life our chickens enjoyed.

A chicken tractor is a movable pen that can be pushed around your yard, so the birds get fresh space regularly. It incorporates a house and an enclosed run, so your birds have everything they need. This can make keeping a penned flock in a reasonably small space easier because you can constantly supply new ground. They can then scratch around, peck at the plants, and be moved on when they've "finished" on a spot which is also ideal if you want the birds to fertilize different areas of your garden, as their droppings will be spread with minimal work.

Admittedly, in our situation, we ended up letting our birds free-range anyway. Still, having a movable coop was ideal for the days we were busy or away, because we could put them on some fresh ground and know they would have at least a few days of fresh food and scratching opportunities. We always felt happier knowing they were in an interesting new spot with insects to hunt, worms to dig up, and fresh plants to peck. So, what are the pros and cons?

Let's start with the pros!

- Your birds can be moved around, so your backyard won't get ruined in one area and have a better quality of life.
- Everything is contained in one neat, fairly small area.
- You don't need to clean out an enclosed run because you're constantly moving the coop.
- There's a reduced risk of diseases because your chickens aren't staying near their feces for more than a few days.
- You don't have to deal with flies being attracted to the coop.
- Vermin are less likely to get into the coop.
- You can take the coop to sheltered spots when the weather is bad.
- You can dedicate less space to the coop without compromising your chickens' welfare.

Those are quite a few advantages, but no setup is perfect, so let's look at the disadvantages:

- They are often quite expensive and aren't easy to make unless you're pretty crafty.
- They may be less secure than a fixed coop, so they might not be suitable if you have big predators in your area.
- You have to move them regularly, which is an additional chore.
- You can only house a few chickens, or the coop must be too big to be easily movable.
- You can't hook electronics up to them.
- You can't easily add a dust bath, and feeders/drinkers must be hooked onto the sides or moved separately.

A chicken tractor might be ideal if you only want to keep a few chickens. Our last flock of 4 did beautifully in our tractor, and we loved its flexibility. The only downsides worth noting are that it was heavy to move with one person, and if you put it on bumpy ground, there was room for predators to burrow in under the edges. Overall, we loved it.

Predator Protection

Protecting your chickens from predators is an essential aspect of owning them, and although I have touched on it briefly, it deserves its section.

The first thing you should do is to make a list of the common predators in your area. You can do this by considering the animals you know live in the state or by researching predators local to your area online. Write them out and consider how you can safeguard your chickens from them.

For example, to guard against certain predators, you will need to prevent them from going under the fencing you have for your chickens, which may mean digging the wire into the ground to be around 12-24 inches deep. You can also create a "skirt" around the pen, which means they cannot dig alongside it. It will involve using heavy-duty mesh and strong wood for other predators.

If you have animals like bears and badgers local to you, you'll need to put a lot of time and energy into chicken protection. Even a strong pen may not hold up to these predators, so you may wish to purchase a reinforced commercial one or use metal poles to increase the structural integrity. Predators may break into the pen by sheer brute force if you don't do this.

One alternative for dealing with particularly strong predators is to protect the coop with an electric fence. This is an expensive option, but may be the only choice if you are likely to see bears or badgers in your backyard. Most people, however, do not need to go to these extremes.

Aerial predators are easy to deal with when your chickens are in their coop because you can ensure that the top is fully enclosed, and your chickens will be out of reach of birds of prey. However, consider this if you were thinking of building an open-top pen.

When dealing with foxes, be aware that they are cunning creatures. They will exploit any weakness they can see, and although they do not have much brute strength, they can crawl through surprisingly small gaps and are powerful diggers.

Foxes will, unfortunately, kill as many birds as they can if they get into your hen house; This is not for the sake of destruction; if you do not disturb the fox, it will take away all the carcasses and bury them. However, it's not what you want to happen to your chickens, so make sure your pen is entirely fox-proof and shut your birds in before dusk when foxes are often active.

Things like stoats and weasels can slip through tiny gaps; a weasel can get through a ½ inch hole! Although small, they can kill your entire flock. You need to check there are no easy entry points for them and shut the chickens in the house at night when these predators are most active.

Rats can bite through thin wire, so you may wish to choose a thick mesh for your pen. They are not an enormous threat to chickens during the day, but they will steal eggs and may attack chickens while asleep, so you want to rat-proof the pen if you can. They will also steal the chickens' food and may pose sanitation risks.

Snakes are an additional risk in some places, so you may wish to create a boarded base around the bottom of the pen, with mesh above it. This will prevent the snakes from getting into the pen.

Even things like neighboring cats and dogs could threaten your chickens if they have a high prey drive or are particularly hungry, so be aware of this and keep your chickens safe. The best defense is to ensure they are all in their house at night and shut the door. They should be safe from most predators except cats, dogs, and birds during the day (unless you have daytime foxes).

Of course, when your chickens are not in an enclosed run, they are vulnerable to anything that happens to them. You need to weigh this risk and consider mitigating it when deciding whether to let your chickens free-range. If you have a lot of birds of prey and small chickens, you might lose too many of your flock to let the others free range.

Fencing your yard securely will go some way to preventing predators from getting at your chickens, but it's unlikely that you will be able to protect them from predators unless you keep them enclosed. You will probably have to accept that you will likely lose a few birds if they spend all their time out of their pen.

What Bedding To Choose

Unless you have a chicken tractor, you need to think about the bedding that goes in the enclosed run. Because chickens will soon scratch up the grass in their run, it's important to put down a layer of something dry so that they aren't just wading around in the mud. The commonest options include pea gravel, sand, wood shavings, and wood chip.

I would recommend not using pea gravel. From what I've seen, birds do not like it very much and it doesn't allow them to exercise their natural scratching behaviors to the same degree. Our last flock came from a place that kept their birds on pea gravel, and it took them a few weeks of being on grass before they even realized they could scratch. Pea gravel is a lasting option but not great for the birds.

Coarse sand is easy to clean because you can simply rake droppings into it, and they will be covered up, so they don't attract flies; This is much easier than picking up and removing droppings, and many prefer it. However, you will need a relatively thick layer of sand that will stick to your shoes when wet. If you don't have a covered run, it may wash away in heavy rain.

Wood chips are a great option and should only need topping up every 6 months; they are natural, so they will just decompose into your soil. They keep your feet cleaner, too. Don't confuse wood chips for bark chips – bark chippings are unsuitable for chickens.

Wood shavings are another good choice, but only if your run is covered, or they will turn soggy, wash into the ground, or blow away. We occasionally put straw in our run to keep the chickens off the ground when it is particularly wet or snowy, so this is another good option to decompose naturally.

Keeping The Coop Clean

You will already know that chicken coops need cleaning out like all pets and livestock. That's true for the house and the enclosed run, although if you have a chicken tractor, you won't need to clean the run. You will still need to clean the house. Many chicken owners do a "deep clean" once or twice yearly but do spot cleans every day or a few days to keep the house tidy and minimize the risk of spreading parasites and diseases.

Being prepared for the amount of work involved with owning chickens is essential. Cleaning doesn't have to take long, but it does need to be done reliably and regularly.

Let's start with the run. How you clean this will depend upon the bedding you have used, and whether the enclosure is open to the elements. An open enclosure will be self-cleaning because of the rain, but you may need to help it along sometimes. If you have wood chips, pea gravel, or something similar, you can wash droppings through them using a hose or watering can.

You can rake droppings into the ground, where they will decompose naturally, or use a scoop to shovel them out and remove them from the pen, as you would with used cat litter. You may want to choose a chicken-safe disinfectant and sanitize the area semi-regularly to minimize the risk of parasites attacking your birds.

How often you need to change things like wood chip will depend on your environment, the size and concentration of your flock, and the general setup. Remember that a dirty pen invites problems like flies, increasing the risk of disease.

If your pen is sandy, you can rake droppings into the sand and change the bedding only when it is needed. You will probably get a fairly good idea of how frequently bedding needs changing once you own the birds; sometimes, you can just hose the current layer down and add fresh bedding on top, but it does depend on the situation and how large your flock is.

The inside of the house will also need cleaning regularly. The dropping boards should help because you can simply remove these once per day, remove the droppings, and slot them back into place. This will keep the house clean for much longer, reducing the need for a full clean-out.

The nest box needs to be cleaned whenever it is dirty. The frequency will depend on how many boxes you have and the habits of your flock. If one or more of your birds insists on sleeping in the box, it will need cleaning more frequently. Change the bedding and add fresh herbs whenever you feel it is getting dirty. This will keep the eggs you harvest cleaner too.

You can also do spot cleans, picking up large or messy droppings. However, you will still need to do full cleaning from time to time, and you should do at least one annual "deep clean" where you sanitize everything.

For this, remove all bedding and loose components from the house. Scrape the inside of the house, remove all the droppings you can, and then scrape the loose components clean. You can use water inside the house on a hot day, so spring and summer cleans are popular. Spray and scrub everything with detergent, and then rinse it well. Do not use bleach in the chicken house. You can use something like vinegar to sanitize, which is much safer for your birds. Rinse it thoroughly to ensure that your birds aren't inhaling it once they return to the house.

Clean every component as thoroughly as possible, and allow them to dry. You can use this as an opportunity to inspect the pen for any damage (although you should also do this at other times, as annually is not enough). Repair any holes, fix any breakages, and make any necessary adjustments to your coop.

Once everything is clean and dry, you can put it all back together. Add fresh bedding to the nest boxes and let your birds enjoy their clean home! Some people do this twice a year, but it is best to do it in the hot months so that the house can dry thoroughly before night falls and the temperatures drop. You don't want to make the house wet during the winter.

Summary

In this chapter, we've covered:

- Why you need a coop.
- What the nesting box is for.
- The purpose of the roosting bar.
- Why you should use a dropping board.
- The pros and cons of enclosed runs.
- Purchasing a ready-made coop and what to look out for.
- How to build a coop from scratch.
- What a chicken tractor is.
- How to protect your birds from predators.
- Cleaning out the coop.

In the following chapter, we will look at bringing chicks home for the first time and how to care for them.

4

Homing Chicks

"When the nest becomes too small a bird is ready to spread its wings and fly."

-Matshona Dhliwayo

Bringing chicks to your home for the first time might just be one of the most exciting parts of owning chickens, and it's so important to get it right. Chicks are vulnerable to all sorts of problems. They are utterly defenseless against predators, so if you will have success with your new household members, you need to ensure that you provide them with the right environment. In this chapter, we're going to find out how!

It's important to note that you should be quarantining any animals you bring into your home for a set period (usually 4 weeks). As you are unlikely to be introducing the chicks to your flock until they are several weeks old, this isn't likely to be an issue, but bear it in mind, mainly if you introduce older birds. Many chicken diseases are contagious, and you don't want new members to introduce illness to an otherwise healthy flock.

To decrease the chances of something spreading, you should wash your hands before going between your flock and the chicks, or vice versa. Clean any equipment or tools used with both flocks, and take all the precautions to limit the risk of transmitting diseases.

Where Should You Buy Chicks From?

Before you purchase your chicks, make sure that you take the time to do adequate research about the place that you intend to buy them from. Read reviews and ask around. If you know anyone who has purchased birds from there before, find out their experience. Talk to the staff and find out whether they seem knowledgeable and ask them about things like vaccinations. All these things should give you an idea of whether they are a good source for chicks.

More and more people are taking an interest in the welfare of their animals, but there are still plenty of places that are motivated by profit and do not treat chicks well – beyond what is needed to ensure that they survive. Ethical issues aside, you are much more likely to get happy, healthy chickens with good layers from chicks that have been well cared for, so check the retailers out thoroughly. If possible, you should visit the place before buying chicks and inspect the birds' conditions and the level of care they receive. Decide whether you are happy with what you see before purchasing any birds.

You can also buy chicks via mail order, although this has the disadvantage of never seeing the facility, they were hatched in. Because of this, you should take particular care to do your research, read reviews, and find out as much as you can before placing an order. If you find mixed reviews, be wary.

If you do this, you will probably have to wait until spring is underway, partly because more chicks are hatched in spring. The retailer needs to ensure that weather-related mailing delays are unlikely and that the chicks will not suffer from cold temperatures while in transit. Until nighttime temperatures are reliably over 40 degrees F, chicks can't be shipped, and no reputable company will try to ship them because the chicks are at risk of losing their lives.

If you live in a freezing state, you may not be able to get chicks in the mail. I would recommend collecting them yourself if possible, anyway, as this involves less stress for the chicks and reduces the risk of something going wrong. You can find local farms simply by entering your area into a search engine and looking for chicks, and this should also give you some reviews. Furthermore, if you pick the chicks up in person, you can talk to the staff about their needs and get any questions you may have answered; This is a much pleasanter experience overall.

You can buy chicks as young as a day old or wait until they are a little bigger and have slightly more strength. The benefit of getting chicks young is that you can establish strong bonds with them, and you get the fun of watching them grow. Rearing your chicks can be good fun, but it is pretty challenging, so you'll need to be well prepared – which leads to the next thing I want to cover.

Getting Prepared

Before taking on a brood of chicks, you need quite a bit of equipment to give them the best chances of survival. You have to have all of this ready in advance, and you should get:

A brooder: this contains the chicks in a small area, keeps them safe from drafts, and protects them from injuries (we'll look at this in more detail shortly).

Feeders and drinkers: these must be small enough for your chicks to use comfortably. The feeders can be any small, shallow dish from which your chicks can pick up food, but you need to pay attention to the drinkers. Chicks can drown in just a little water. It would be best if you had a very shallow dish, or you fill the bottom with marbles or clean stones so that the water level is not deep; This should reduce any risk of the babies drowning. As with adult birds, ensure enough feeders and drinkers to accommodate all the chicks you have bought so there is no squabbling and they can all get enough.

A heat lamp: chicks need warmth. In the wild, they would spend a lot of time sheltering under their mother and huddling with each other. Their ability to maintain the correct body temperature is poor, especially in the first few days. You will therefore need a reliable heat lamp that can keep them warm. They should be kept at 95 degrees F for the first week, and then you can decrease the temperature by 5 degrees per week. You should reach around 65 degrees F or a little higher by week 9. Most chicks get their proper feathers between 7 and 12 weeks old and can start managing their body temperature.

Bedding: as with adults, you can choose bedding options, but the best is pine shavings. These are fairly inexpensive, absorbent, and easy to clean, making it much simpler to keep the brooder clean and hygienic. You can also chop up straw or use crushed corn cobs. You can use shredded paper with older chicks, but it's too slippery for newborns. Bedding needs to be changed daily, and any wet parts should be scooped out and replaced frequently, so choose something inexpensive. Wet bedding causes a mold risk, so be cautious about removing damp areas as soon as possible.

Feed: don't get your chicks until you have suitable feed for them, just in case something goes wrong. Chicks can't eat the same food as the adults! You can purchase a chick starter feed (check whether you need medicated or unmedicated before buying). You can give them this dry or mash it with a little water to make it like oatmeal. Remember that chicks need a lot of protein at this stage, so you do need the right food if they are to thrive. Without chick feed, they will likely fail to gain size and weight as they should.

You may also want to get some electrolytes and probiotics if one of the chicks starts looking unwell. You can use these with healthy chicks to give them a boost or just give them to any chicks that appear sickly; This may help get them back on track, so it's a good idea to have some to hand just in case.

This should be all that you need for chicks most of the time.

How To Build A Brooder

Building a brooder is a straightforward, easy, and does not have to be expensive! A brooder is there to keep your chicks safe and contained, so something as simple as a cardboard box could suffice if you have a sturdy one. However, cardboard is liable to get wet if you don't line it with something, which can cause mold problems, so it isn't ideal. Cardboard boxes are also a fire hazard if you use a heat lamp. A cardboard box will work in a pinch, but better options exist.

Many people use plastic boxes, but be aware that you will need to cut the lid to allow airflow; you don't want to put the chicks in a sealed box, or they will quickly die. You can use a reasonably small box to start with, but make sure you give the chicks more space as they grow. Chicks need around 6 square inches of space each for the first few weeks and then should be moved to a larger container. You usually can see from their behavior when they need more space because they will start to peck at each other and squabble.

So, how do you build a brooder? If you use a plastic box, start by taking the lid and a sharp knife and cutting out a rectangle inside the lid; This will make it easy for you to get chicks in and out and allow you to keep an eye on them. It will also make it harder for them to kick bedding out of the box. If you are making a brooder with older chicks in mind, you will need to cover this hole with a grid so the babies can't fly out.

Next, you usually need to line the box. If your brooder is made from something slippery like plastic, you must put down a non-slip liner before adding the bedding. Walking on smooth surfaces can cause health problems such as splayed legs (more on that shortly). Even cardboard may cause splayed legs, so you'll need a non-slip mat in almost all containers, followed by plenty of bedding. Cut the mat to size and set it in the bottom of the brooder, and then add layers of bedding on top.

The bedding will help keep the chicks clean and dry, absorbing the wetness from their droppings. You want a deep layer to do this without the water going through to the bottom of the box, but not so deep that you will be wasting lots of material when you change it. Often, one to two inches should be sufficient.

Once the brooder is ready, you need to decide if you will use a heat lamp; This is highly recommended, as chicks are far less likely to get sick if they are kept warm, and even normal room temperature isn't sufficient for them. Unless you have them alongside another heat source, you ideally want to use a heat lamp.

However, it needs to be highly secure because it could cause a fire and kill the chicks if it falls. The lamp is – by definition – very hot, so treat it as a potential fire hazard. Many people chain theirs, so it is suspended above the brooder, radiating heat but not touching the box. This is critical if the box is made of anything that could catch fire or melt. Take heat lamp security seriously and do not take any risks with it.

Your chicks should also have a space they can move into to get away from the warmth if they are getting too hot, so position the lamp near one end of the box rather than in the center.

The chicks can then decide whether they are hot or cold and move accordingly. This gives you a good indication of whether the enclosure's temperature is right; if they are all huddled right under the lamp all the time, they may need to be somewhere warmer. However, if they are spread around the opposite edge of the brooder or are panting and holding their wings up, you might want to lower the temperature. You can reduce the temperature by lifting the lamp further from the box or increase it by putting the lamp closer – but make sure it doesn't touch the box.

The brooder should be placed somewhere warm (above 50 degrees F) and away from direct sunlight. Ideally, it should also be easy for you to see so you can keep an eye on the chicks as they grow and change. Many people put brooders in their kitchens or living rooms, but the best spot depends on your home and habits. It should also be out of reach of pets and children (even the most well-meaning children should be supervised when around chicks).

The Day They Arrive

When your chicks are due, you must ensure that everything is ready for them. That means turning the heat lamp on a few hours before reaching you so that the brooder will be warm and cozy; This is particularly important if they are likely to have been traveling in cool weather, as they may need to warm up.

It is less important if the weather is warm and the brooder is in a snug location, but it's still a great way to ensure they get the best possible start. Keeping consistently warm will reduce their disease risk, so try to do this. If you cannot turn the lamp on, use a timer switch or put it on the night before.; This means the box will be warm as soon as you put them in it.

You should also set up the feeders and drinkers and ensure you have plenty of bedding prepared. Ideally, you should ensure you will be around a lot for the first few days to keep an eye on the chicks and detect any issues; This may mean taking time off work or rearranging other commitments.

When the chicks arrive, take the box into the room with the brooder and set it on a flat, stable surface. Open it and take the first chick out. Dip the chick's beak gently into the water before you place it in the brooder so it learns where the water bowl is. Next, let it go inside the brooder and allow it to explore.

Do this for each chick, so you know they have found the water bowl. If you aren't sure whether they will find the feed, put all the chicks in the brooder and then use your finger to scratch the feed lightly. They will likely move over to investigate what you are doing and start scratching themselves. This should trigger their instinct to peck about, and they will begin feeding.

You can leave them to settle in, but it is good to be available and check on them frequently, especially on the first day. If any have been injured by transit or have got sick, you are more likely to pick up on it quickly if you are checking on them, and then you can take action to deal with the problem.

How To Spot Sick Chicks

You should be hyper-vigilant for signs of disease, especially in the early days. There are a few things that will help you to determine if a chick is sick. The first of these is their behavior. A sick chick will often sit in the corner of the brooder with its head and eyes closed and will not respond much to its surroundings. It may also sneeze or huddle close to the heat lamp while the other chicks seem warm and comfortable.

Its droppings may also become very wet, and its breathing might become heavy. If you notice particularly wet droppings in the box, take some time to survey each chick and make sure they behave as you would expect. Chick poop does tend to be pretty watery, but if it is excessively so, it shows something is wrong.

Watery eyes are a further sign that something is wrong with a chick. Keep an eye out for this; if you see it, take the chick out of the brooder to inspect it. Make sure the brooder is clean and check for any signs of mold that may be causing this. A clean brooder is the best way to ensure your chicks stay healthy.

Those are the commonest signs that something is wrong – but how do you know what? Let's look at the major chick diseases, what symptoms they cause, and what you can do about them if you see them. Some of these will overlap with the section about illness in adult chickens.

Infectious bronchitis: A chick sneezing, lethargic, and watery-eyed may have infectious bronchitis. You might also see gasping, coughing, wheezing, and nasal discharge. Sometimes, you may hear a bubbling or rattling noise as the chick breathes.

As the name suggests, this can quickly spread through the brooder, so check on the other babies for signs of illness if you are concerned. You can reduce the risks of this by raising the brooder's temperature by a few degrees and offering the affected chicks warm mash. Isolate sick chicks and clean feeders and drinkers regularly to reduce the reinfection rate.

Chicks can be vaccinated against infectious bronchitis, so consider this, especially if you are concerned about it. It often shows up when the birds are stressed, so do check whether other conditions are causing issues for your birds.

Marek's: If your chick is limping or struggling to move, it may be suffering from Marek's disease. A warm brooder with good ventilation can reduce your chicks' chances of developing Marek's. Still, it is a dangerous disease that kills both adults and chicks, particularly affecting children between 12 and 24 weeks old. Some forms of Marek's are more deadly than others, and you should consider vaccinating your chicks against it if possible. Be very wary of introducing chicks that have had Marek's to an otherwise unaffected flock.

Aspergillosis: A chick gasping or convulsing may have Aspergillosis, a fungal disease that often affects the respiratory system. The bird may also seem lethargic and may not be growing as it should. It's likely to lose its appetite but will be very thirsty. A clean environment and good ventilation can make this disease less likely to occur, but there is no known treatment once it has started. This is partly why keeping the chicks in a warm, dry container is so critical to clean it regularly to reduce the risk of spreading fungal spores.

Rot gut: Rot gut can lead to symptoms such as listlessness, particularly smelly diarrhea, and lack of interest in the surrounding world. It usually appears in chicks between 2 and 5 weeks old and tends to be caused by overcrowding. As long as your chicks have enough space and you are regularly cleaning out their box, it should not occur. Antibiotics may be able to cure it.

E. coli: If you see a chick with breathing difficulties, diarrhea, coughing, and a lethargic manner, it may have been infected by this bacteria. It has a high death rate, especially among newly hatched chicks, and it is difficult to treat because of many different strains. Hygienic living conditions are your best defense against this bacteria.

Brooder pneumonia: If your chick is drinking a lot, gasping for air, and not interested in food, it might be suffering from brooder pneumonia. This is another fungal disease that can spread quickly through your chicks, and it usually occurs anywhere between day 7 and day 40. It will kill around half of the affected birds. Unfortunately, there is no cure, so you must ensure the brooder is kept clean and sanitary to minimize the risk of this fungus spreading.

Splayed leg: This is also known as spraddle leg, and it can occur if your brooder is too slippery or for a few other reasons (overcrowding, vitamin deficiencies, injury, difficult hatching, or inconsistent incubation). It results in the legs twisting out from the hips, and they will stay in that position, rendering the chick unable to walk until you step in and correct the problem.

You can avoid spraddle legs in many cases by ensuring your chicks have a good surface to walk on. Kitchen towels will work, but newspapers are slippery and should be avoided.

If spraddle legs occur, you must brace the leg back in the correct position as soon as possible. Fast correction increases the chance of the chick being able to walk normally as an adult. You can use all sorts of things to brace the leg, but a proper bandage is the best option. Wrap the chick's leg below the knee joint, not too tightly (you don't want to cut off the blood flow). Do this on both legs, and then cut another piece of bandage and bind the legs in a slightly wider than normal stance so that they are beneath the chick's body and able to support it.

You can also use a hair tie or an elastic band to hold the legs together. Make sure the bands are not tight. Your chick should look like it is wearing loose handcuffs. Separate the chick from the others, so it does not get picked on, and keep it in a warm box with food and water and close supervision.

It can take days for a splayed leg to cure itself, but 2 days is usually sufficient if you have noticed and corrected the splay quickly. Keep adjusting the brace daily and check on the chick's progress. Gradually, its muscles should strengthen and recover its ability to stand up and move around normally. It can go back in with its fellows once it has had the brace off for 24 hours without any issues.

Pasting up: This is not necessarily a disease, but it is something to watch out for as it can harm the chick. It happens if the chick's droppings don't get expelled as neatly as they should and instead stick to the chick's vent and end up drying there. Chicks may not manage to clear this themselves, but fortunately, it is pretty easy to resolve. As soon as you see it, wet a cloth with some warm water and gently wipe the droppings away. If they have dried, you may need to hold the chick against the cloth for a few minutes to loosen them.

Keep working until the chick's back end is clean again, and then place it under the heat lamp and keep an eye on it. You want to check that it dries off, fluffs up, and doesn't get chilled, but this should be all it needs. Do not leave the chick with dried droppings stuck to it, as this can lead to various complications.

Other things to watch out for include messy droppings, panting, and shivering. If your chick is unwell, it will likely stay in one place, possibly with its eyes closed. Isolate chicks that show signs of disease and treat them accordingly.

Handling Your Chicks

You should make a point of regularly handling your chicks and getting them used to your touch; This is a great way to make it less stressful for them if you need to treat them for anything, and it builds a bond that will last into adulthood. If you teach your chicks to trust you, they will carry this trust as they grow, making it much easier to deal with your flock.

If your birds trust you will not hurt them, they will likely come when called and permit you to pick them up. Although most adult chickens do not particularly enjoy being handled, some get very tame and will sit on your lap, allow you to pet them, and more. There are many reasons that this is beneficial, including treating the chicken's ailment. Administering medication is much easier if the chicken is not panicked by being held.

It's also pleasant! Part of owning chickens should be the pleasure you get from them and having a good bond with your flock is a great way to make the most of their presence in your life. You should handle the chicks very frequently and get them accustomed to you. If you only pick them up when you need to administer medicine, they may come to distrust you, so make handling, patting, and touching part of the daily routine if you can.

Handling The First Few Weeks

You might be wondering what to expect when the chicks have settled in and started to get accustomed to their new home. Until they are a few days old, chicks will do little except eat, flap, poop, and sleep. However, they quite quickly become active and will explore the brooder, preen each other, peck and scratch, and essentially behave like miniature chickens.

Let them out of the brooder if you don't mind a mess. Make sure the room is safe and warm, and there are no crevices they can enter. Pick up anything they shouldn't eat from the floor, and shut any pets out of the room before doing this. Next, allow the chicks to explore!

Once the chicks hit about 3 weeks old, you can start teaching them to roost. Drill a hole in 2 wooden blocks and insert a sturdy wooden dowel between the 2 so it stands a short distance from the brooder floor. The chicks will start to hop onto it and gradually learn to balance. They will probably fall off a lot initially, but they will master it, and then you can replace it with a higher one.

You can also take your chicks outside in a fenced area to let them peck at the grass and feel the sun on their wings. If you do this, make sure you choose a sunny day, so they don't get chilled, and don't leave them unattended!

How To Introduce Chicks To Your Flock

When your chicks are old enough, you can start introducing them to the rest of the flock – but this needs to be done with care, so you don't cause any issues. The older birds may not like the newcomers, as they will disrupt the pecking order and may be seen as competition.

You should not introduce chicks until they are at least 6 weeks old; even then, you must do so gradually. Ideally, wait until your chicks are between 8 and 12 weeks before adding them to the flock. Make sure you do so in a group so the chicks have some companionship and safety in numbers rather than being singled out.

One of the most effective ways to introduce chicks is on neutral ground, where both parties can retreat if they choose to. If your chickens are free-range, this is the ideal time to introduce them to the chicks. Plenty of distractions discourage them from attacking the chicks, and they are likely to be interested in other things, so their focus won't be on the new birds. They will have time to start getting used to them.

You may wish to place the chicks in a carrier, such as a cat or a dog carrier. Your hospital cage may also work. Put this outside with the rest of the flock, and let the birds start getting used to each other. When they can see and smell each other and begin interacting, they will start to accept each other. Make sure the chicks are safe from the older hens if they decide to attack them.

It is best to be present for this introductory session to see how it goes. The success will depend on a lot of different factors, including the personalities within your flock. If you have laid back or mothering hens, they may take easily to the new flock members, but others will not be so welcoming.

You can gradually introduce your new chicks over the next few days and weeks. If possible, start letting the birds free range together. With lots of other enrichment and plenty of space to distract them, most won't bother fighting unless some particularly coveted morsel gets unearthed; This is an excellent way to gently and gradually encourage them to accept each other.

Don't pen the birds together until they are harmonious. Once they have started to get used to each other, you may want to put the pullets in the main pen but fenced off from the adults.

Alternatively, put them all together but provide some area of refuge for the youngsters if they need to escape. A cardboard box with a small pop hole that the young birds can fit through but the older ones can't is one option that should work well.

You can also put the chicks in pen to explore while the older chickens are foraging or consider putting the chicks in the house after dark so that the chickens wake up to them and there is no squabbling. When the birds are anxious to get out, fill their crops, and lay their eggs, they are less likely to pick on the younger birds.

You should monitor the situation closely for at least a few weeks so you can step in if a bird is getting bullied. Make sure that there is still plenty of space for the flock, and check you have enough feeders, drinkers, nest boxes, and perching spots for everyone, which should increase your chances of happy chickens. You will soon have a harmonious flock again, but it could take a month or so.

Summary

In this chapter, we've covered:

- How to source your chicks.
- Preparing for chicks and everything you need to have ready.
- How to build a brooder.
- What to do when your chicks arrive.
- Signs that your chicks might be unwell.
- The first few weeks of chick ownership.
- How to introduce chicks to the rest of the flock.

In the following chapter, we will look at how to deal with eggs, including tips on getting hens to use a nest box, collecting eggs, storing eggs, selling eggs, and more!

5
Dealing With Eggs

"A hen is only an egg's way of making another egg."

-Samuel Butler

Finally, in this chapter, we will look at the primary reason many raise chickens, eggs; This is probably the critical factor in choosing to get a backyard flock. Unless you plan to raise the chickens for meat, it's essential to know as much as possible about this process, how to handle the eggs, and what you should do with them – besides eating them. I will explore a few techniques for helping you maximize the harvest you get from your chickens!

Training Hens To Use Their Nest Box

You might expect that your young hens will know how to use a nest box since hens do look for quiet, dark, private places to lay eggs in automatically – and sometimes, you will be correct. At other times, you'll find your hens are more reluctant and lay in random places, which is much more likely to occur when they are young and inexperienced, as they can get "caught short" and find themselves laying almost anywhere.

One of the best ways to prevent this is to keep your hens in their pen until they have laid, as they are much more likely to retreat to the nest box if they aren't wandering around the garden and having fun. You can also place a fake wooden egg or a golf ball in the nest box to encourage them to lay alongside it.

Take the time to ensure your nest box is safe and meets its requirements. Darkness, privacy, and safety (so being elevated from the ground) are the critical criteria, and if your nest box does not meet these, the chickens will look for another spot. Ensure that these boxes are ticked, and the chickens will almost certainly decide that it is a safe place to lay in.

You also must ensure that you have enough nest boxes for your girls. If they find the box occupied, they will start laying elsewhere, which can become a habit. You should ensure they almost always have room to get into the box and provide additional boxes if you run into crowding issues. Even a cardboard box with a pop hole will work as a temporary solution, provided it has some straw and is elevated from the ground and stable.

Finally, make sure that the nest box is always scrupulously clean. Hens instinctively know that their babies need a clean environment to thrive in, and they will not lay in a nest box that isn't clean and tidy. Make sure there is a deep bed of straw (or your chosen nesting material), so the birds can set their egg on something soft. They may dig themselves a little hollow and lay in this.

You may find that some of your hens are keen to sleep in the nest box; this almost invariably causes it to get dirty much more quickly. If this happens, you may want to create a board that lets you close the nest box off once the birds have finished laying; This will stop it from becoming a bedroom but sometimes result in a hen not being able to access it when she wants to lay, so it is essential to find a balance.

If you do all these things, your hens should be in the box, although this may not always happen 100 percent of the time. If you let them out earlier than expected, but in general, their instincts will guide them to the box if it meets all their criteria for a suitable laying spot. Be patient if it takes a few weeks and you occasionally find an egg in an odd place when your birds are young – this is pretty normal and should go away as they become more seasoned layers.

How Often To Collect Eggs

You should be collecting eggs from your chickens daily. There are several reasons for this. Firstly, it ensures that your eggs are brought into a cool and controlled environment quickly, reducing the risk of them being contaminated by food-borne bacteria. If they sit in a hot hen house for days, they will rapidly become unsafe to eat.

This is even more of a problem if the chickens poop in the nest box. Bacteria may spread from their feces and into the eggs. Promptly removing the eggs reduces the risk of this occurring.

Removing the eggs reduces the risk of a chicken accidentally standing on one or deciding to sample it. If you leave the nest box crowded with eggs, it's almost inevitable that one will get broken, and then it's only a matter of time until one of your birds discovers she has a tasty breakfast waiting for her. Taking the eggs away will minimize the risk of this occurring and hopefully prevent the egg-eating problem, which – as we discussed earlier – can be a challenging habit to break.

Thirdly, collecting the eggs prevents hens from broody when you don't want them to. If there's nothing to sit on, it's less likely that one of your hens will decide to sit. It can still happen, of course, but if you don't want hens blocking the nest box, staying all day indoors, and ceasing their laying, it's a good idea to discourage them by promptly taking eggs away. You will also decrease the chances of rats or other vermin finding and eating the eggs, which could be a big problem.

It's generally a good idea to collect eggs around mid-morning. Most of your hens will have laid by this point, as they tend to lay from early morning onward. The nest box should therefore contain that day's offerings, and you can go out and get them all at once, rather than having to make several trips. If you have a large flock, you may wish to collect eggs twice a day to prevent the nest boxes from getting too full.

Occasionally, a hen will lay later, but it's pretty unusual, so this is generally the best way to ensure you get all of the eggs once before the day has had time to get hot. Some people collect their eggs at around 10 in the morning, while others will wait until noon. If you have to wait longer, this will be fine, but if you can get them mid-morning, this is the best option.

How To Clean And Store Eggs

Storing your fresh eggs properly is critical. You may sometimes end up with a lot of eggs to get through, so you want to ensure that they are being kept in the best possible way to last for a long time. There is a lot of ongoing debate about the best ways to store eggs, and whether they should be washed first, so you should be cautious about this process. Do some reading and decide for yourself on the best method, but I recommend the option below, which involves dry cleaning your eggs.

Eggs have a protective layer on the surface of their shells that prevents bacteria from penetrating the shell and compromising the egg inside, called the bloom. It is intended to protect the chicks, but it does a good job of keeping the egg fresh and safe to eat, too, so you should make use of it

If you wash the egg, especially in cold water, you will remove this layer and compromise the egg's safety. You may even push bacteria into the shell. I would therefore suggest that you dry clean your eggs instead; This is only necessary for eggs that have dirt or poop on them, and it involves using something lightly abrasive to clean them. A rough kitchen towel will work. Simply rub any visible marks off the egg using the towel, and then they are ready to store.

Sometimes, if an egg is mucky, you may want to wash it despite the bloom. You can do so, and you should use tepid water a little warmer than the room temperature and the egg. Place the egg under the running faucet when it has reached the optimum temperature (but make sure it won't get any hotter, or you risk raising the egg's temperature too much). Running water will help ensure that bacteria gets washed away rather than lingering on the shell.

Use a cloth to buff the egg's surface until you have got the contamination off the shell, and then wipe it dry with a paper towel. Place it to one side to fully dry, and then it can be stored. Do not immerse eggs in warm water or try to soak them, as there is a high risk of contamination if you do this. Cold water should be avoided because it will cause the pores to contract and suck in bacteria as they do so, contaminating the inside of the egg.

Wet washing should be sufficient to get the egg clean enough to store, but you may wish to mark any eggs that have been wet and then use these up more quickly. They will no longer have the protective antibacterial bloom and may go off faster. Using them up sooner reduces the risk of food waste or food poisoning.

Once you are satisfied that the eggs are sufficiently clean, they can be stored in the fridge. Wipe out the container you use to keep them in before storing a fresh batch, and then put each egg inside, marked with the date that it was collected from the hen house. Use the oldest eggs up first to continually replenish your supply.

Checking Your Eggs Are Organic

Your eggs won't be organic just because you have chickens in your backyard instead of in a factory; you need to give your chickens the right kind of feed. That means buying an organic blend and ensuring that any treats (e.g. corn) are organic too.

You can get organic chicken feed from various places, and if you want to raise organic chickens, this will be a must. It isn't possible to have organic eggs if your chickens eat a standard, non-organic commercial feed. Consistently giving them organic feed is critical. Do not mix it with a non-organic feed to make it go further.

It's also worth considering what else your chickens might be eating. The treats you give them need to be organic, so check that you are purchasing the right corn. If you feed your chickens scraps, e.g. vegetables from your kitchen, these must also be organic. Anything that has been grown using pesticides (or at least those not acceptable for organic farming) will need to be kept away from your birds, or you will contaminate the eggs.

You should also consider what you use in your garden and what your chickens might have access to. For example, if you grow your vegetables and use pesticides but then allow the chickens to browse in that area, your eggs probably will not count as organic, as the birds are bound to pick up some artificial chemicals from that area. Even if you keep the chickens away from that space, using certain pesticides may mean that your eggs are not organic because pesticides can spread a long way in the soil and on the breeze.

The best way to ensure that your eggs are organic is to purchase organic feed for your chickens, limit their treats to organic foods, and keep any pesticides and plant treatments that aren't considered safe for organic farming out of your garden. You probably can't control what your neighbors use; hence, there is still some chance of contamination, but you will have minimized this as far as possible. Avoid medicines such as antibiotics where possible, and remember that these make eggs non-organic too.

If you mix your chicken feed, consider this for every ingredient. If you cannot source an organic version, you may not be able to use that particular ingredient unless you are happy to compromise on the organic nature of the eggs; This can be challenging; therefore, you may look around for suppliers. Fortunately, organic feed is becoming more and more readily available, so you may be able to get the ingredients you want without too much trouble.

Organic feed is almost always more expensive than non-organic, even if you make it yourself. Still, many people are keen to turn away from commercial pesticides and work more harmoniously with nature – so at least consider this possibility when choosing what to feed your flock.

What To Do During An Egg Shortage

You will likely find that your backyard flock does not produce a particularly steady supply of eggs, no matter how large. Hens will slow down their egg production in fall and winter as the daylight hours decrease, and many will stop laying entirely.

You can counteract this by adding lights to your chicken pen to increase their daylight hours artificially, but this can contribute to other problems and may cause stress and unhappiness in the flock. It also requires electricity and increases the fire risk, so I would advise letting your hens have a break during the colder months. You will likely still get some eggs – just fewer.

At other times, your flock will stop laying for less obvious reasons, so if this happens, take some time to assess them. *Are they getting enough food and water? Are they stressed by overcrowding or poor conditions? Are any of the birds sick?*

Sometimes birds will stop laying after a shock, such as a predator attack, and sometimes they just take a short break even if nothing is wrong. Often, Chickens that are molting will not lay, as they need the calcium to rebuild their feathers. A molt lasts between 8 and 16 weeks, often in the fall.

Older chickens will gradually lay less and less, so be aware of this. Some hens will stop laying as they age, which is frustrating, but just part of owning chickens. There's nothing you can do about this. However, you can often correct the flock's conditions to encourage them to get over a predator attack. Making them feel safe, providing excellent food, and boosting their health with vitamins can encourage them to resume laying.

If you are suffering from an egg deficit, you might be wondering what you can do about it. One option involves using store-bought eggs again to fill the deficit, but the other is storing your eggs well to maximize their longevity. You will frequently have gluts of eggs, particularly if you have a large flock, so maximize these in the following ways:

Organized usage: Always date your eggs when you bring them in. You can do this with a pencil; it takes only a few seconds. It will let you use eggs up correctly, ensuring that your freshest eggs always go to the back of the supply and the older ones get used up first; This means you can make eggs last for as long as possible.

Chill them quickly: Collect eggs, clean them if necessary, and put them in the fridge as soon as possible; This reduces the time they are at room temperature, massively slowing the spread of bacteria and making them last much better. Eggs stored in the fridge can last up to 3 months, which means you can sometimes get through the laying deficit without needing to buy any eggs, as long as you keep them properly and have enough. Some people even say that you can keep them for 6 months, so you can start employing the float test (below) if in doubt.

Store them correctly: Store eggs with the point end down. That might surprise you, as many people store them the other way up, but the rounded end has an air sac, and it's thought that having this at the top can help minimize evaporation and moisture loss.

Check whether they are fresh: By employing the float test, you can check how soon eggs are likely to need using up. If you have forgotten to date an egg or aren't sure if it is okay to eat, place it in a container of cold water. If it floats to the top, air has penetrated and become rotten. If it sinks, it's fresh. If it floats around the middle of the container, it should be used up soon as it starts to turn bad. In general, rotten eggs also have a very unpleasant smell when broken.

Keep chilled eggs in the fridge: Don't move eggs from the refrigerator to the counter. Although it can be okay to store eggs at room temperature for a while, you shouldn't do this once the eggs have been refrigerated. The temperature change can cause them to sweat, which helps to introduce bacteria into the egg and compromises it.

Freeze your eggs: Did you know that you can freeze eggs when you have a glut? You may not be able to fit all of the eggs in your fridge, or you might simply have more than you think you will use – so consider freezing them. An egg can keep almost indefinitely in the freezer, so having frozen eggs will get you through the no-lay period, but you can't freeze them in their shells and limit their usefulness.

To freeze eggs safely, you should lightly stir the yolks and whites up with a fork or whisk (you don't have to do this, but it results in a better texture when you thaw the eggs). Add a little salt to eggs if they will be used for savory meals and a little sugar if they are intended for baking; This stops the yolks from becoming gelatinous when frozen. 1/8th of a teaspoon per egg should do.

Place the eggs in a muffin tray, ice cube tray, or other small container and put them in the freezer until they have fully frozen. When frozen, they can be transferred to a larger container to save space. Note whether they are sweet or savory, date the container, and keep it in the freezer until you hit an egg shortage.

Frozen eggs are not quite as good as fresh ones, particularly if you wish to do something like frying them – and obviously, you cannot make boiled eggs using this method. However, they are surprisingly flexible. This is an excellent way of preserving your eggs without dedicating a lot of fridge space to them and having a limited number of days to use them.

If you do all these things, you should find that you can weather egg shortages very well without going to the grocery store to correct the issue!

How To Sell Eggs

If you have excess eggs, you may like to sell them. You need to check your local and state laws before doing anything else. You may not be permitted to sell eggs from backyard chickens in some states. In others, you may need a license, permit, special permission, or proof that you meet specific hygiene and chicken welfare criteria. If you want to sell eggs labeled as organic or free-range, you will almost certainly have to do these things, as your claims must be certifiable.

In some states, you may be allowed to sell your eggs. You should check this, as laws vary from place to place and are subject to change. If in doubt, get advice from local officials before you try selling your eggs. You don't want to risk getting into trouble for breaching the law. Federal laws are currently relatively simple and state that labels must include:

- A "sell by" date of 30 days after the eggs are laid
- Warnings about safe consumption
- The seller's contact information

The law also stipulates that eggs must be refrigerated correctly; This is all that is necessary to comply with current national laws but do check for updates or more local laws superseding this. You should also make sure that your eggs are clean and presentable. You do not need to grade eggs unless you sell them commercially in the US, but you should put "ungraded" on the box. Be aware that in some states, the egg boxes must be new, whereas other states permit the reuse of boxes provided they are clean.

If you find out that you can sell your eggs, the best place to start is often at a farmer's market or local farm shop. Check out the area around you and find out if an opportunity is available. You might also sell at a roadside stall, at the end of your driveway, or on your property. You will need to think about how you will collect the money for your eggs, how to prevent theft, and how to deal with things like accidental damage or customer complaints.

Selling eggs can be a nice little extra income and may help keep your flock going if there is a market in your area. How viable it is as a business or a side business will depend heavily on your region. There will be some costs, including refrigeration, boxes, and possibly certification or permits if necessary. You might also have to pay for a stall or entry to the market.

Weigh these things before deciding whether to sell your eggs commercially. Many backyard flock owners are reluctant to take on the extra trouble of doing this, but it is often easier than you think, and it's well worth looking into if you find that your flock is producing more than you need. Giving eggs away to friends and family often only goes so far, and a little extra income from your birds can be nice!

Hatching Eggs And Candling

You may decide that rather than buying chicks for yourself from another company, you would instead hatch your own – especially if you have a rooster in your flock. Hatching eggs have the potential to be great fun, and it's a great learning activity for children and adults alike. It certainly has its challenges, and you need to be prepared for chicks not to make it if you try this, but it's worth considering as a great activity and a way to expand your flock.

Note that you cannot get chicks from your hens if you don't have a rooster. Hens will lay eggs regularly with or without a mate, but these eggs will always be infertile and have no chance of hatching. If you want chicks, you must either buy fertile eggs online or purchase or borrow a rooster. Since roosters can be a drawback in a flock, you might want to just borrow a farm's rooster for a few days. He will fertilize the hens and can then go home. If you have space for a rooster, however, consider getting one. Many out there need homes, so it should be easy to find a rescue if you would like to.

If you are going to do this, I would highly recommend getting some books specifically about raising chicks, as there is so much to know – but for now, let's look at some of the basics of hatching eggs and handling them.

What candling is: Candling is a process that you will use multiple times when attempting to incubate eggs and hatch chicks. The phrase derives from a time when a candle would have been used, but now, we generally use a bright torch for this purpose, as it's handier and safer. You will need to candle any egg you wish to hatch before putting it in your incubator. If you are going to let a hen hatch her eggs, you may still want to candle those she is sitting on before she settles to brood (she may not like this, so wear gloves when removing eggs from beneath her).

To candle an egg, you need to hold it to bright light, such as a torch or a spotlight. The light will shine through the egg, illuminating the shell; This has various purposes, but you are initially looking out to check that the egg's shell has not been damaged. If you can see any cracks, even very minor ones, the egg should not be placed in your incubator or under a hen.

Bacteria get in through these cracks, compromising the chick and turning the egg rotten. There is a risk that it will explode, and rotten eggs smell unpleasant. You may sometimes want to candle eggs before storing them, again to check for cracks, but this technique is generally only used when you want to hatch chicks.

Candling will also be used later in the process, because it helps you determine whether the egg is fertile and whether the chick is developing. It essentially allows you to see through the shell, getting a glimpse of the baby inside.

Hatching chicks: Once you have checked that the eggs are free from cracks, you can put them in the incubator, and they should be turned about 5 times per day for the first 1 to 18 days. This turning prevents the chick from getting trapped between the yolk and the shell, which may kill it.

You can mark the eggs with a pencil on one side, so you know whether you have turned each one or not. Always incubate a minimum of 6 eggs so that if you have some failures or some chicks do not make it, you still have a few to keep each other company; a lone chick is unlikely to survive.

Your incubator should ideally be set to a temperature of 100.5 degrees F and must never be allowed to fall below 99 degrees F, or the babies will die. The relative humidity in the incubator should be between 50 and 55 percent for days 1-17, then raised to 70 percent on day 18. The ventilation will need to be increased after day 17.

You should always wash your hands before touching the eggs to avoid spreading unnecessary bacteria to them. Apart from turning them, it's best to leave them untouched for the first few days. However, if you do wish to candle them again, you can usually see whether they are fertile or not by day 3, as veins will start to spread throughout the egg, and these will show up when you shine the torch through it.

Over the next few days, if you keep candling the eggs, you will see the chick's vague outline growing inside the shell. It's terrific to do this with children and ask them to note what changes they see.

When day 18 comes, you can stop turning the eggs, as the chick will be inhabiting most of the space and is no longer at risk of getting trapped. Leave each egg with the largest end facing upward. Keep the temperature and humidity steady.

Most chicks will hatch on day 21, and you should have the brooder ready and waiting for them. If the eggs have got cold at any point, it may take a few more days, as their development will have slowed. When the chicks start hatching, do not get involved. It is unfortunately easy to hurt a chick by pulling off bits of shell, as blood vessels may still be attached to it.

It usually takes up to 7 hours for a chick to fully emerge from its shell, but it can take a full 24 in some cases. Don't interfere, even if the chick seems to be struggling. If a chick can't make it alone, it may not be strong enough to survive independently, even if you get it out of the shell.

The chicks will start peeping as soon as they have hatched, encouraging the others to start hatching, so leave them in the incubator. Keep the temperature up, and only lower it to 95 degrees F once all of the babies have hatched. Give unhatched eggs up to 23 days to hatch.

Candling eggs throughout incubation: You can candle eggs at any time during the incubation period, but it is recommended that you don't do so 3 days before hatching unless you need to check something. The eggs should be left alone at this stage. Don't keep eggs outside the incubator for more than 30 minutes, and minimize the time spent outside, as cooling the eggs can slow their development.

Candling should show the gradual growth and development of the chick, and you may also hear the chick peeping inside the egg. The air pocket (the lightest part of the egg when you shine a torch through) shrinks as the chick grows.

You can sometimes spot problems or indications that the egg is not fertile. A few things to watch out for include:

- A ring inside the egg with no veins or few veins.
- A distinct blood spot with no veins or few veins.
- No sign of life after 10 days.
- Lack of development when compared with other eggs in the clutch.

These things might indicate that the egg will not hatch, but don't throw it away too quickly. Candling is far from an exact art; it can be hard to accurately tell what's going on. You may simply be looking at the wrong angle. Unless you know that an egg has gone bad, leave it in the incubator to see if it starts developing.

Summary

In this chapter, we've covered:

- How to get your hens to use their nest box.
- How often you should collect the eggs.
- How to clean eggs and the best storage method.
- What makes your eggs organic.
- What stops your hens from laying, and how to deal with egg shortages.
- Selling eggs and what this involves.
- How to breed your chickens.

Conclusion

"The key to everything is patience. You get the chicken by hatching the egg, not by smashing it."

-Arnold H. Glasow

Hopefully, you know everything you need to start your backyard flock! There are few things so wonderful as watching your chickens scratch contentedly around the yard, safe, happy, and fluffy. There isn't much that tastes better than a home-laid egg you've collected just that morning from a warm, snug nest box. Backyard chickens are a joy that many people should sample at least once in their lives!

They are also a wonderful experience for children. They create excellent learning opportunities and helping to care for them will encourage your child to establish respect for animals, an understanding of them, and a sense of empathy and caring. Chickens are intelligent birds that will develop a deep bond with you if treated well, especially if you have had them since they were young.

We love keeping chickens in our household; they create a sense of contentment and satisfaction that it's hard to get from other parts of life. There is something about them that is solid, reassuring and feels deeply rooted in a simple life where food was grown at home and given a greater sense of importance than in many other contexts. I am a firm believer in the value of any food you can make for yourself, and a backyard flock is a fantastic option for individuals from all walks of life to try.

If you have a bit of space in your backyard and want to share it with chickens, it isn't too hard to get started. You may even be able to get a coop second-hand. Many rescues offer chickens saved from the egg industry, or you can select chicks or point of lay birds. Whatever you do, you will love having these feathery creatures pecking around your home. There is little more picturesque and country cottage than a flock pecking and scratching about!

During our years of chicken keeping, we've had rescues, point-of-lay birds, chicks (both our own and purchased birds) and a variety of others that have ended up with us at one time or another. All have been wonderful in their ways, full of charm, quirkiness, and strong, unique personalities.

I highly recommend chicken keeping to anyone looking for a way to increase their connection with their land and food. Chickens are the simplest livestock you can keep, and investing your time and energy into their welfare is a superb way to feel satisfied with life. They take work and are a commitment, but the rewards they bring far outweigh the drawbacks.

If you aren't sure whether chickens could be right for you and your family, see if you can help at your local farm for a few weeks and get to know the birds there. You will likely be paid at least in eggs, and you'll get to watch these beautiful birds and see how intelligent and fascinating they are. From there, it's not much of a jump to taking on your flock, and I can guarantee that the eggs from your birds will taste nothing short of amazing!

RAISING GOATS FOR BEGINNERS

BOOK 8

The Only Backyard Homestead Guide You'll Ever Need For Naturally Raising Goats For Milk and Meat in 7 Steps

BY

BRADLEY STONE

Introduction

"Until one has loved an animal, a part of one's soul remains unawakened."

-Anatole France

If you have ever thought about keeping goats, you aren't alone – many people now are looking to move animals into their backyards, and goats are among the most popular options. It may sound somewhat surprising because we don't tend to talk about goats as much as other animals, like cows, sheep, pigs, chickens, and more – but it's thought that there are around 1 billion goats in the world and about 2.55 million goats in the United States alone.

That's a lot of goats!

Of course, many belong to commercial farms rather than backyards. Nonetheless, it's clear that goats have a significant role to play in our modern world and offer an enormous amount of valuable resources.

Humans have kept goats for centuries because they are beneficial animals, hardy and intelligent. They are used for meat, fiber, and milk – which can then be used to make cheese or butter. Goat's milk does have quite a different flavor from cow's milk, but many people find it delicious, and it contains more calories, which is good from a nutritional perspective – as long as you aren't trying to lose weight.

Anyone who is looking to make their lifestyle more sustainable and become more self-sufficient is bound to at least consider goats as part of this plan; This is partly because goats can be kept on a smaller piece of land and in much smaller herds than cows. It is quite unfeasible for most backyard farmers (although by no means all) to keep a herd of cattle for milk and meat, but keeping a couple of goats can be much more manageable. Additionally, goats will provide you with fiber, which puts them a step ahead of cattle, especially if you want to go all the way with sustainability by creating sustainable clothing and food. Raising goats might sound daunting, but by the end of this book, you'll know what to do and how these fibers can be used! Goat fiber is becoming increasingly popular, and its market is constantly growing.

If you are an animal lover, there's even more reason to keep goats. They are charming, quirky creatures with a high degree of intelligence – which can be both a blessing and a curse. You are probably already aware that the goat is almost always the trouble-maker in children's stories; it's always the one climbing over the fence, nibbling at the washing, or getting into the vegetable garden. We might laugh over that sort of thing, but there's a reason that the stereotype exists!

It is essential to recognize that goat farming is a challenge. Goats are amazing creatures that are hardy and tolerant, but they are by no means "easy" to keep. Rearing any animal can be difficult, but there are a lot of things that you should know about farming goats before you get your first goat – and that's what I'm going to talk you through today. I hope I can set you up for success and ensure you have everything you need to keep your goats happy and healthy.

In this book, I will talk you through all there is to learn about keeping goats. We'll cover choosing the suitable goats and building a bond with them, how to house your goats and what they need, and feeding them. We will also look at goat care, including the basics of healthcare, grooming, castration, and more.

Once you've got the basics of looking after your goats down, we'll start learning about harvesting from them, and this will touch on getting fibers, getting milk and making cheese, and finally, how to butcher a goat; This will set you up for success with your herd, so let's start looking at how you choose a goat!

1

How To Choose Goats & Getting To Know Them

"Animals are such agreeable friends—they ask no questions; they pass no criticisms."

-George Elliot

This chapter will cover several topics, including the main reasons for keeping goats and the best kinds of goats for the various materials you can harvest from them – meat, milk, and fiber. Some goats are suitable for all 3, whereas some are more specialized, so it's crucial to think about this.

Why Should You Keep Goats?

We have already briefly touched on some of the advantages of keeping goats, which are the three things that you can harvest from them – meat, milk, and fiber. If you are trying to live off the land and become independent from civilization, all three of these things become very important (although some people choose to do without meat and even dairy). Goats constitute a significant advantage for anyone who wants to become more self-sufficient, and they have a few other uses too!

The first and perhaps the greatest benefit besides the materials they produce is their ability to clear weeds. If you have a herd of goats and a patch of land that you wish to clear, you can pen the goats on the land, and they will quickly clear large areas for you. Therefore, it is important to note that goats are keen eaters and can quickly tear up plants. They love eating weeds and brambles, so they are fantastic for preparing an area for other plantings – although you will need to keep them out of that area once your desired plants are in place.

Goats can also be used as pack animals; they are strong and can transport large, heavy items. They will eat food on the road and can even be trained to pull a cart. They have been popular for centuries because of this feature. Therefore, people utilize them around farms and homesteads to pull items around. You may have to invest some time and energy in teaching them certain things, but they are helpful labor if you do this.

They will also provide dung, which can be rotted into manure, added to compost heaps, or even used as fuel for fires. Goat dung may not be the most appealing fuel, but it is eco-friendly, and you might find you're willing to give it a go. Gathering goat dung can be relatively easy since you'll be mucking out their barn or living quarters fairly frequently – so you won't be out looking for firewood in winter. If you would rather use it to enrich your garden, it remains excellent and will provide you with wonderfully good fertilizer to help your vegetables.

Goat hide can also be useful, and if you harvest your goats for meat, you may want to look at tanning further along the line. Goatskin rugs and drums are used in some countries across the globe, and things like goatskin gloves are seen as luxury items. If you are interested in utilizing sustainable, completely natural materials, this is a great aspect to look into later, as it will let you use an otherwise wasted product.

Furthermore, goats are fairly inexpensive to keep – although you should consider vet fees in advance and ensure you can cover these if you need to get one of your goats treated for sickness. Vets can be expensive, and things like medication and vaccinations must be part of your budget. However, goats are not as expensive for daily living as many other farmyard animals.

They are browsers and will nibble whatever plants are available. You still need to supply them with food, but they will supplement it themselves. They also don't need much beyond a sheltered spot and some (really strong) fencing, so the setup shouldn't be prohibitive. However, fencing is a vital aspect to consider, and we'll cover it more in the next chapter.

What Are The Best Goat Breeds For Meat?

There are a lot of goat breeds out there, and if you are feeling daunted, it may help to narrow down your focus and think about what you really want from your goat. If you plan to harvest meat from it, choosing a breed that will give you a good quantity of usable, pleasant meat is critical.

Some of the best breeds for this include:

- *The Kalahari Red:* this is a robust breed that will cope with minimal care and attention, and it's an excellent breeder. The females can produce kids every eight months, keeping your herd to a good size.
- *The Kiko:* this New Zealand breed is large and produces a lot of meat for its body weight. You don't need to supplement its feed as much as you do for some breeds, like the Kalahari Red, which makes it easier and cheaper to keep.
- *The Australian Rangeland Goats:* These are highly popular in their home country and are known for being extremely hardy, so they are ideal for goat keepers who want an easy time.
- The Boer: this is said to be the best breed for producing meat. It is high in quality and provides fleshy briskets and excellent ribs. These goats are pricier, but most keepers consider them worth the extra cost.

What Are The Best Goat Breeds For Milk?

Having a dependable goat when it comes to milking is critical, and it also helps if the goats are friendly and easy to tame. There are many breeds you can choose from, including:

- *The LaMancha:* these are known for being affable and gentle, and their supply is generally reliable. They are easy goats to manage and ideal for first-time keepers.
- *The Saanen:* this large breed is great if you have plenty of space and offers a very high supply of milk – up to 3 gallons a day. They also provide good meat, and they are friendly.
- *The Anglo-Nubian:* you can get about a gallon of milk daily from an Anglo-Nubian, and many say it has a delicious flavor. However, you should be aware that these goats can be loud and lack some of the patience and sweetness of others on this list.
- *The American Alpine:* these goats aren't as prolific in milk production as the Saanen, but they are still excellent. They can also produce milk for up to 3 years without rebreeding, which has made them a popular option.

What Are The Best Goat Breeds For Fiber?

Choosing with care if you want fiber from your goats is critical because this varies massively from breed to breed. If you plan to sell the fibers, ensuring you know what goats you are buying is even more vital. Top options include:

- *Angora:* if you are familiar with the term "mohair," you may already know that it can only be got from Angora goats. It is much sought-after and has superb durability and beauty. Other breeds have been crossed with Angoras, including goats such as the Pygora and Nigora.

- *Altai Mountain Goat:* you are certainly also aware of the term cashmere, which can be taken from many different breeds, including the Altai Mountain Goat. These goats produce a lot of fiber, usually black or gray, and are well worth keeping.
- *Don Goat:* this breed also produces cashmere, and it can be used for meat, too, making it a popular option for farmers who want multi-purpose animals. These goats create a high quantity of fiber, and it is usually of superb quality.
- *Zalwali Goat:* another cashmere production option, the Zalwali produces meat, milk, and fiber. Most are black, some have white speckles, and they look unique.

Where Should You Buy A Goat?

If you are going to buy a goat, it is crucial to do some thorough research first, and I would always advise buying one locally; This allows you to inspect the farm, the conditions, the animals, and the person keeping them. You will get a sense of how well they are being cared for, whether any in the herd are sick, how much space they have, and how lively they seem. These things will all help you to choose well.

You can also look at reviews online to understand the farmer and their reputation. If possible, ask around locally about people's experiences. Try asking the farmer why they are selling the goat, how old it is, whether it has had kids, whether any diseases have been present in the herd, and what sort of temperament the goat has. Choosing with care gives you much more chance of getting healthy goats that will produce well.

Avoid sales rooms where you have no opportunity to meet the farmer or inspect the goat's previous living conditions. You can pick up excellent animals this way; however, it's much safer to buy from a reputable breeder whose conditions you can inspect personally for your first herd.

How Do You Know Which Goat To Buy?

Once you have narrowed down what kind(s) of production you intend to focus on, you might be wondering how to choose your goats. There are a few things that you should look out for, including:

- Does the goat walk steadily, with no limp or wobbliness?
- How bright at the goat's eyes?
- How do the hooves look and smell? A foul smell around the hooves could indicate rot.
- How does the coat look and feel? Is it smooth and free from dirt?
- How do the goat's teeth look? They should be sound, with none missing.
- Is the goat a good weight? Can you see protruding bones, particularly around the ribs

and hips?

- How does the goat respond to you? Is it nervous and trying to back away? Is it aggressive and keen to bite or kick? Does it allow you to approach and respond positively to the sound of your voice?

These things should make picking some individuals out of the herd easier. Remember that you should never keep just one goat. They are social animals that need at least one other companion.

How Do You Get Your Goats Home?

Before you go to buy goats, you should know how you are going to get them home. You will need to know how many goats you are transporting and have a suitable means of carrying them; This will usually involve buying or renting a livestock truck or trailer.

The vehicle must be ventilated, protected from the wind, and safe for the animals. You need to ensure you have sufficient space for as many goats as you buy and the ability to separate any vulnerable animals (e.g. pregnant or nursing goats and kids) from the rest of the herd.

If you are going to drive the goats home yourself, ensure that you are sufficiently practiced in handling the vehicle before you start. Your animals' lives are at stake, and your responsibility is to get them home safely.

How Do You Determine The Value Of A Goat?

There are a lot of factors to consider when determining the value of a goat, including:

- The breed
- The sex
- The age
- The condition
- Any illnesses/scars/disfigurements/issues
- The number of goats you are purchasing at a time
- Where you live and the current market demand

Although the market fluctuates a lot, it's a good idea to look at recent goat sales in your area and see what the prices are like. In general, does will cost between $75 and $400, bucks will cost between $110 and $550, and wethers (castrated male goats) will cost between $130 to $520. Kids are usually in the range of $250. Some goats cost $800 or even more.

However, the factors mentioned above will make a massive difference to the price of the goat, so the above figures are very rough guides. If you are buying a whole herd of goats at once, you are likely to pay less per goat than if you buy them individually. The more desirable the breed, the more the goat will cost.

How Much Does It Cost To Keep Goats?

The cost of goat keeping will also vary somewhat depending on the price of supplies in your area. Still, once all your setup is in place and you are just paying for the basic ongoing costs, each goat will probably cost you something like $25 per month; This includes basic vet fees, such as worming.

If you can feed your goats on pasture and let them forage for themselves, the costs will probably go down, but remember that it is better to overestimate your costs and set some aside for unexpected fees (such as repairs to fencing, veterinary care, and so on) than to underestimate your costs. Make sure you can afford to keep a herd of goats before you get them – it can easily add up, especially if you want a large group. A couple of goats might only add around $600-$800 to your yearly costs, but a herd will be thousands. Do these sums and check that you know these costs before you start.

Summary

In this chapter, we've covered:

- The advantages of keeping goats.
- The top goat breeds for the different harvests you might take.
- Where you should get a goat.
- How to choose a goat and how to find out its value.
- How to get your goat home.
- The general costs of starting a goat herd.

In the following chapter, we will look at how to house your goats and the kind of fencing they will need.

2

Housing Your Goats

"There is nothing more important than a good, safe, secure home."

-Rosalynn Carter

Before you get goats, you need to have an appropriate shelter for them – and that means you'll need to build some structure. Goats need to have a warm, dry, safe space to retreat when the weather is terrible, or they will be miserable. A shelter also protects your goats from predators if anything in your area might attack them, especially overnight. If this is the case, ensure your shelter is secure and can be locked at dusk so the goats are protected.

If you don't give your goats sufficient shelter, they will likely seek it for themselves, even if this means climbing over fences or forcing their way into buildings they shouldn't be in. Goats do not like wet and cold weather, so you must provide them with ways to stay dry to keep them happy and healthy.

With that in mind, let's look at everything you need to know to ensure that your shelter is suitable for your goats.

What Size Should The Shelter Be?

The size of the shelter will, of course, depend on how many goats you plan to keep, but you should allow a minimum of 2.5 square meters per goat –ideally, more like 3-4 square meters. If each goat has an individual stall, it needs 4 square meters of space. Remember that if you plan to enlarge your herd at any point, it's better to have a too big shelter than to end up trying to increase the space of one that is too small.

However, you don't want the shelter to be enormous because it will be harder for the goats to keep warm if there's a lot of excess space. Roominess is necessary, but your shelter can be too big. If you plan to put your goats in a large barn or anything similar, you should consider partitioning it or adding some insulation so that your goats can stay cozy when the weather is cold.

Your goats should be able to access their outdoor grazing space from this area so they can come and go as they please. If you have to move your goats to their grazing area, consider whether it's possible to build the shelter there, as they will need to be able to get out of bad weather.

You should also make sure that the shelter is windproof and dry. However, it is vital to ensure that ammonia can escape so that the goats don't suffocate. If there isn't enough ventilation, your barn may become dangerous.

Repairs should be done promptly to keep your goats happy and warm. If you plan to pen goats separately, note that they prefer to be able to see each other and make allowances for this.

How Do You Muck Goats Out?

Keeping the goat pen clean and dry will be critical, especially when the weather is hot. If you don't regularly clean the area, your goats will be more vulnerable to worms and parasites, so cleanliness is critical.

Unfortunately, this is more challenging because goats are quite messy animals, and they can't be trained to use a particular area for their toileting needs. That means you will need to clean the pen out regularly – something you should be aware of before taking on a herd. Even one or two goats can make a surprising mess, although they will be easier to clean than a whole herd.

There are many ways to clean goats out, and you will probably develop your methods as you gain experience. As long as the pen is clean, that's all that matters. Some people clean their goat pens daily, and you will probably find this necessary. You can walk around the shelter when you check on your goats in the morning, picking out droppings and messy patches and removing them from the shelter. How you clean your goats out will depend to some degree on the material you use for their bedding.

Because goat droppings are small, mucking them out isn't like mucking out a cow or a horse. You generally need to scoop droppings out using a shovel or something similar – especially if you have used shavings for your goat bedding. If you have used straw, you may find that a pitchfork is the most effective tool for removing soiled patches.

You will occasionally want to do a full clean to remove all the old bedding and replace it with new bedding. Some people do this about three times a year and usually do one of these deep cleans before winter. You can then keep spot cleaning and add more clean bedding gradually throughout the winter; This will insulate the goats and keep them off the cold ground. The more bedding you add, the better insulated the goats will be, so deep bedding is a great way to keep them cozy in the winter.

Some people also put lime down on the floors of their goat shelters, as this will help to keep them sterile; This can be done after a full clean-out before you put down fresh bedding.

How Do You Keep The Floor Dry?

It is crucial to keep the floor dry in your goat pen, as this will help to reduce the risk of any issues with mold and fungus. The bedding will likely get wet because your goats will urinate and defecate in it – and it will also be kept warm by the goats' body heat; This will create a suitable breeding ground for parasites, flies, and other nasty creatures that attack your goats.

You, therefore, need to keep the floor as dry as possible, and this involves choosing an absorbent material that can easily be scooped out or removed. Many people use sand and straw on the pen's floor, but sand is more permeable and may be easier to see when it needs cleaning. Sand is probably the most effective way of keeping the pen dry.

Keeping the feeder and waterer above the ground is another way to minimize mess. Goats are fairly messy eaters and drinkers, and elevating these areas will help to reduce these issues. You may also want to put a tray under the drinker to catch drips, but this is optional.

What Sort Of Bedding Do Goats Need?

You can use a wide range of bedding options for goats, but the commonest include:

- Pine shavings
- Straw
- Sawdust
- Wood chips
- Sand
- Pellet bedding
- Cedar shavings

Pine shavings are particularly popular because they are absorbent, soft, and usually very cheap. They also reduce odors, and they are extremely easy to scoop out when they get wet.

Straw is also popular, partly because this is what you feed your goats. It won't matter if your goats throw straw all over the floor if you use this for the bedding too. Straw is usually easily accessible but not as cheap as pine shavings in most places. It's also a bit less absorbent and may be trickier to clean.

Sawdust can be suitable for goats, and it is often very cheap or even free if you have a local sawmill. It is generally odor free and highly absorbent, so you might find it great for a herd of goats since they will produce a lot of urine. You can scoop it out with a shovel quickly.

Wood chips are also easy to find and lightweight. They aren't always as cheap as other bedding options, but the chips can easily be scooped out. They are absorbent and should keep your goats happy and clean.

Sand is a great way to improve drainage and keep the goats dry. However, you should make sure that you provide another bedding on top to give your goats insulation.

Pellet bedding might be a great choice if your goats are keen to eat their bedding and you're concerned about this. Pellets are not appealing to goats and are generally cheap and easy to get. They are also absorbent, so they will keep the pen dry.

Cedar bedding is also a good option because it is a pest repellent. However, if your goats are prone to eating their bedding, you might want to avoid it because it's toxic in large quantities.

You can choose from a wide range of beddings, so find out what's cheap and available near you, and try it out. If you dislike one kind of bedding, try another and see how it goes.

What Do You Need For Milking Goats?

The shelter you provide to your goats should have a suitable spot for milking them in. You need to stand up comfortably in all parts of the shelter, particularly in the milking area. You will need to add a milk stand – either purchased or homemade. Stands will usually be made of metal or wood. Metal stands are better because they generally have a mesh, so spilled milk will drain away rather than make the surface slippery. Wooden stands are sometimes rather slippy once milk has been spilled on them.

Your milking stand should be easily accessible, but not beside the other goats, as this may cause distractions and make it harder to milk the goat. It needs to be easy for your goats to jump onto and easy for you to sit. The area should also be as easy as possible to clean, which means you can minimize the dust in it.

What Do You Need For Breeding Goats?

If you are going to breed goats, you will need to have a separate area for your doe to be in during the last few weeks of pregnancy, and this should be easy to clean and snug (although it must still be ventilated). The doe must be kept at an appropriate temperature, so ensure the space is cool in the summer.

You may need a space where you can pen your doe with a buck for some time while they mate, especially if you are borrowing a buck from another herd; This should be big enough for both to be kept comfortable.

Your doe should be treated very gently following the mating, as it takes about 2 or 3 weeks for the embryo to implant. Increase the quality of your doe's feed once you know she is pregnant; alfalfa hay may be a good option (we will look at goat food in more detail in the next chapter).

You will need a kidding stall for your doe, which must be easy to clean and protected from the elements. You should choose clean straw for the bedding because the kids may inhale shavings or fine wood chips. These bedding will also stick to the little ones when they are first born and wet. Your doe can be moved into this stall weeks before you expect the baby to be born, and it usually helps to put a companion in with her. A companion will keep her calm and happy, but you don't want the whole herd barging around your doe, or she may get stressed out by them.

You should also make sure you have some colostrum on hand in either powdered or frozen form before the baby is born. The baby needs this in the first few hours if it is going to survive, and while the mother will usually be able to supply it if something goes wrong, it's imperative to have access to some.

It's a good idea to have the phone number of an emergency vet to hand, especially when you are inexperienced in breeding goats. If something goes wrong, accessing an expert is critical to look after your animals and could save both the mother and the baby.

How Do You Protect Your Goats From Extreme Weather?

You may worry about your goats when the weather gets either hot or cold, and it can be challenging for them.

Hot weather is usually easier to deal with than cold weather. As long as your goats have access to plenty of water and shade and their shelter is well-ventilated, they will generally cope well with hot weather. They may be more lethargic than usual, but for the most part, they should manage. You can help them by adding ice to their water, freezing treats for them to lick at, and ensuring their shelter is breezy by opening doors or windows.

Don't rush to shear your goats in the summer because their coats are insulating. Spring shearing will allow them to grow enough wool to protect their bodies from the heat, but if you shear them in summer, they will be vulnerable to overheating and sunburning.

Winter can be trickier, as goats need to be able to access outdoor spaces pretty much all year round if possible, but you might be concerned if it's freezing hard. Although goats are tough creatures, they aren't impervious to the cold. They have thick undercoats, but it can take a while to acclimate to the cold when temperatures first drop.

If your goat's undercoat is good and it is eating well, it is likely to tolerate cold weather extremely well and may not be cold even when standing in the snow. Artificial coats are often not effective for keeping your livestock warm because they can compress their hair and may stop them from developing a well-insulated natural coat.

You should ensure that your goats eat a high-fibre diet when the weather is cold. Hay will help them to generate plenty of heat because they can ruminate and keep themselves warm for a long time. However, your goats won't eat if they can't find water, so you need to ensure that their drinking water does not freeze, or at least that it gets defrosted quickly. Sometimes, this will involve carrying buckets of water out for your goats several times a day, especially if you live in a frigid climate.

Ensure your goat's shelter is waterproof and as windproof as possible without removing the ventilation. You want to ensure that your goats are always dry and that windchill is kept to a minimum. Your goats will press together for warmth if they are cold at night, which helps keep their body temperature high.

If you want to keep their shelter warmer, consider looking into the deep litter method, which can warm the pen a little. The deep litter method involves adding clean bedding on top of the old bedding, and as the waste in the old bedding decomposes, it will produce heat. Your goats will usually be cozy enough if the shelter is dry.

If you have any vulnerable goats during winter (kids, pregnant females, or sick herd members), you may need artificial heat to protect them from the cold. However, this is usually only in serious situations.

What Do You Need For Fencing?

Goat fencing is one of the things that you need to pay the most attention to. Goats are known for their ability to escape from almost any area, and you must be able to keep your goats contained. If they escape, they are likely to cause damage and may get hurt, especially if they can get to a road. You may be liable for any damage they cause, so be aware of this problem and ensure you are going to be able to contain your goats before purchasing them.

Goat fencing needs to be at least 4 feet tall, and if you keep tall goats, it needs to be 5 feet, or they will jump over it. You can use a wide range of materials, although many people like to opt for mesh because it's strong and reasonably effective. You can also use wooden pallet fencing or welded fencing; as long as the fencing is strong, it should work for goats. However, you must ensure you avoid all barbed wire fencing because your goats are likely to damage their faces, ears, and possibly legs while trying to get over it.

Your fencing also needs to be free from holes, which is one of the reasons that mesh is good. Ideally, you want 2-inch x 4-inch mesh squares. Goats are very good at finding holes and weaknesses. If they want to escape either from loneliness or boredom or because they want something on the other side, they can be determined. You should ensure that your goats cannot jam their heads through the holes in your fencing, as they may get stuck and injure themselves – so be aware of this.

What Are The Different Types Of Goat Fencing?

The two main kinds of goat fencing are electric and non-electric. Electric fencing is much more expensive because it has an ongoing cost, but it can be effective for keeping goats in if you have determined escape artists. Your fencing should have around 4500 to 9000 volts, and you should be aware that your goats are very likely to know if you turn it off. They will escape if you don't keep the fencing electrified since electric fences don't tend to be secure without electricity and are usually just horizontal wires.

If you are going to buy non-electric fencing, the options include:

- Cattle panels
- Galvanized wire steel mesh fence
- Woven wire fence
- Welded wire fence

- Pallet fence
- Goat fence

Remember that the larger the area you plan to keep your goats in, the more you will need to spend on fencing. Take the time to think about the price of setting up the fencing, the maintenance, and any ongoing costs (like electricity) before you decide how many goats to keep and how much space you can give them.

Fencing can be expensive, but it's important to remember that buying cheap, unsuitable fencing isn't going to be cheaper in the long term. Make sure you have the funds to contain your goats and don't be tempted to buy unsuitable fencing just because the price is low.

Summary

In this chapter, we've covered:

- What size shelter your goats will need.
- How to deal with manure.
- How to keep the shelter floors dry.
- The sorts of bedding that goats like.
- The setup you'll need for milking.
- The setup you'll need for breeding.
- How to protect your goats when the weather is bad.
- Everything you need to know about fencing!

The following chapter will examine what goats eat and how to feed them!

3
What Do Goats Eat?

"Ask not what you can do for your country. Ask what's for lunch."

-Orson Welles

Thinking about what your goats are going to eat is another important part of dealing with a herd, and while goats are known for being adventurous eaters, you can't just feed your goats random foods. Ensure your goat's diet will maximize their health and minimize any risk of medical issues, so let's look into what goats eat, what quantities they need, and how to feed them.

Goat Digestive Systems

You may find it easier to understand your goat's needs if you learn more about a goat's digestive system. A goat is a ruminant, like sheep and cattle, which means they have four stomach chambers. These are known as the Reticulum, the Rumen, the Omasum, and the Abomasum. These stomachs all have slightly different functions.

First, the goats chew their food, passing into the Reticulum. Here, microbes begin breaking it down, passing into the Rumen, where further microbes can break it down. Food goes back and forth between these two chambers several times during digestion. Because plants are so fibrous, it's important for animals that live on things like grass to have this ability to break them down gradually.

However, goats also "chew the cud" at this stage. Food particles enter the Reticulum and are sorted into small and large pieces. Pieces that are small enough will pass into the Rumen, while large bits will be regurgitated into the mouth for further chewing.

To begin with, goats don't chew their food sufficiently because they often eat while on the move. Eating like this means they can store food in the stomach for chewing later when they have more time, freeing up their mouths to collect more material. This lets them eat more quickly while they browse, and it also makes it easier for them to keep an eye out for predators because they can chew with their heads up.

When the first two stomach chambers have broken down food, it is sent to the Omasum, which filters it and reabsorbs the water. From here, it goes to the Abomasum, the closest to the sort of "stomach" you might be familiar with. Acids and enzymes are added to the food to break it down into something that can move into the small intestine, where the nutrients are extracted and passed into the bloodstream. Finally, waste has the water extracted by the large intestine, and the goat gets rid of the solid waste in droppings.

Understanding this process will help you better plan what your goat eats and when and why your goat might be chewing away hours after being given a meal!

What Are The Nutritional Needs Of A Goat?

It's critical to make sure you understand the nutritional needs of your goats before you get them, as feeding your goats the wrong things or in the wrong quantities could seriously impact their health. No matter what picture books suggest, goats have specific diets and can't live on fresh laundry! Goats need:

- *Long fibers:* these help the Rumen to work efficiently and are usually gained by eating plant matter.
- *Supplements:* your goats must get enough minerals from salt licks and other supplements.
- *Concentrates:* milking goats or youngsters may need you to supplement their diet with concentrates.

Most goats eat around 3 to 5 percent of their body weight daily. For a 40-pound goat, this would equate to around 1.2 pounds of food. For the most part, your goats may be able to browse for their food, but you will likely need to supplement this, especially during the winter. Your goats should always have access to hay, even if you want them to browse. Goats will rarely eat food once it has fallen on the floor, so bear this in mind and keep your hay rack elevated.

Hay And Grain

Hay and grain will usually be the mainstay of your goats' diet (or grass, if they are out foraging). Each goat will consume at least a pound of food per day unless you have pygmy goats, so ensure you provide this. If your goats are foraging, you should still provide them with hay they can fill up on and supplement their foraged food. Place a manger inside the goat shelter, so the hay stays dry.

There are several different kinds of hay, including:

- Alfalfa
- Fescue
- Meadow grass
- Timothy
- Orchardgrass
- Clover
- Brome
- Bermuda grass
- Bluegrass
- Oat hay

All of these offer different degrees of protein, fiber, and total digestible nutrients (TDN), so spend some time looking at the recommended portions for your goats. Alfalfa and clover hay have the highest percentage of protein (19 percent and 15 percent, respectively), while bluegrass and brome provide the most crude fiber (40 percent and 35 percent, respectively). For goats that are milking or youngsters, alfalfa might prove the best option, but it may be too high in calories for your other goats.

You may also wish to provide grains, but remember that long-stemmed plants will help your goats digest their food, and they shouldn't have a lot of grain in their diets. Few goats can tolerate more than 5 percent of their food as grain. Goats that require more energy (such as milking goats and youngsters) may benefit from grain feed, but other members of your herd may not require grains. Remember that, like any other animal, a goat that gets too many calories in a day will get fat, so keep an eye on the high-calorie foods that your goat consumes and limit these if necessary.

If you are going to give your goat grains, opt for whole grains, and choose things like wheat, oats, barley, soybeans, and corn. Be aware that most goats love grains, so you should limit these and consider reserving them as treats.

Free Choice Minerals

Your goats should have access to a mineral block that they can lick at any time. They require calcium, salt, phosphorus, zinc, copper, magnesium, and selenium. The best way to provide these is through a granular mineral source with 50 percent trace mineral salt and

50 percent dicalcium phosphate; This should give them everything they need.

You may also want to supplement your goats' vitamin intake to keep them healthy. They are more likely to be vitamin A and D deficient than other vitamins. Goats can make their own B vitamins and vitamin C and K, so they should not need these. If your goats are not free foraging, they are more likely to be deficient in vitamin A. If they don't get enough sunlight, they will struggle with vitamin D. If your goats are out in the fields daily, you are unlikely to need to give them vitamin supplements.

Free Choice Baking Soda

You might be surprised to learn that your goats could benefit from being given access to baking soda, but it's true. Baking soda can help to prevent bloat, which is sometimes deadly. Of course, wild goats wouldn't be eating large amounts of baking soda, but they would also eat a lot more twigs, shrubs, and weeds than domestic goats tend to. Your goats will live on a richer diet with a lot more grass, and this can upset cause stomach upsets and lead to gas buildup – bloat.

You can see if your goat has bloat by checking whether its abdomen is distended on the left side and whether it feels tight and hollow. If your goat seems to be in pain, it may suffer from bloat, which is sometimes fatal.

Baking soda will help balance the pH levels in the goat's stomach and minimize the risk of bloat. Offer baking soda in a separate feed dish, away from other foods, so they can eat it when they need it and ignore it when they don't.

Scraps From The Kitchen And Garden

Goats can eat various scraps from the kitchen and garden but stick to fruits and vegetables. Suitable options include:

- Banana peels
- Carrots
- Greens
- Raisins
- Pumpkin seeds
- Apple skins
- Blueberries
- Salad
- A little bit of bread

Almost all vegetables are okay for your goats to enjoy, but ensure you keep these scraps low in quantity. Your goats don't need to be eating large quantities of "human food", and you should avoid anything with salt or sugar added. Do not give your goat meat or dairy scraps; goats have evolved to be healthy on plant-based foods, and other foods may make them ill.

You can give your goat plant scraps from your garden but avoid azaleas, lily of the valley, rhubarb leaves, milkweed, nightshade vegetables, and plants high in oxalates. In general, goats are good at working out what they should and shouldn't eat, but you still need to pay attention and only feed your goats safe foods. If in doubt, don't give it to your goat!

Summary

In this chapter, we've covered:

- The different parts of a goat's digestive system and how these systems work.
- The nutritional needs of a goat.
- Feeding your goats hay and grains.
- Free choice minerals.
- Free choice baking soda.
- Kitchen and garden scraps.

The following chapter will explore how to care for your goats.

4

Caring For Your Goats

"The greatness of a nation and its moral progress can be judged by the way its animals are treated."

-Mahatma Gandhi

It would help if you had a good idea of how to care for your goats – because, like all animals, they are vulnerable to various issues, and you must be able to address these when they arise. In this chapter, we'll cover all the basics of goat healthcare.

Brushing Your Goats

Goat grooming is an important aspect of goat care, which may surprise you – but like other livestock, goats benefit from being brushed. Brushing can help you bond with your goats and improve their coat health, as well as allow you to check your goats for any medical issues. At the minimum, you should brush your goats out near the end of spring when they start shedding for the summer.

You can get a firm-bristled grooming brush for the first part of the process. Run this along the goat's body in the same direction as the hairs in firm sweeps. It will remove dirt and dust from the coat, and you'll feel if there are any bumps or injuries. Start at your goat's neck and work your way down the animal's back and sides.

Swap to a soft brush to finish off the brushing and distribute the naturally produced oils through the coat. These will protect it and make it glossier.

Many goat owners find brushing therapeutic, and it's a great way to build up your relationship with your flock. This will make them more docile and easier to handle.

Goat Hoof Care

You will also need to inspect and trim your goats' hooves occasionally. You should keep an eye out for foot rot. You can use a hoof pick to remove dirt and manure from the hoof, which needs to be trimmed. This is even more important if your goat is mostly kept on soft surfaces.

The goal of trimming is to ensure that the hooves' sides, walls, and heels are flat with the sole. This makes it easier and more comfortable for your goat to walk. You should get a veterinarian to show you the proper method for trimming so that you are not at risk of injuring your goats.

What You'll Need For Grooming

To groom a goat, you should have some basic supplies. These include:

- A hoof trimmer
- A tail comb
- A curry comb
- A hard brush
- A soft brush
- A bath mitt (for occasional washes)

If you plan to show your goats, you may also want things like clippers and possibly accessories, but these are the basics. Some animal-friendly shampoo may help if your goats are adventurous and you often need to wash them.

Tattooing Goats

Tattoos are a reliable means of identifying your goats. If you want your goats to be accepted to the herd books of the American Dairy Goat Association (or a similar body), you must have them tattooed. Almost all goats are tattooed on the ears, and you must use the sequence assigned with your membership identification number. This tattoo must go in the right ear where possible. You can use the left ear to identify individuals within your herd.

To tattoo a goat, you should:

1. Clean the site thoroughly and tie the animal so it can't escape.
2. Insert the symbols into the pliers and press the rubber pad firmly over them. You must check the pad is correctly in position.
3. Test that the symbols are correct by marking the tattoo on paper.

4. Ink the goat's skin.
5. Locate the veins or cartilage in the goat's ear and place the symbols between them, running parallel to it.
6. Punch down to imprint the ear, and then immediately apply more ink and rub it in for at least 15 seconds.
7. Clean the equipment and allow the ear to heal.

Goat Shearing

You should first check for specific information about shearing your goat, as it may vary depending on the breed. Most goats should be sheared once a year, however.

You may want to get a professional with the proper equipment to shear your herd if it is large. Shearers can cost upward of $300 if you want electric ones. You can use hand shears for a small herd, but it is hard on your back.

Before shearing your goats, you should treat them with an insecticide a few weeks in advance. Keep the goats dry for 24 hours before the shearing, and make sure they are clean, making it easier to deal with the wool. Clean out the shelter and add lots of fresh bedding. Without their coats, they will be more vulnerable to infections and parasites, so cleanliness is important.

To shear a goat, you should:

1. Secure the goat.
2. Remove any debris from the coat using a hairdryer.
3. Start shearing at the front of the goat's belly, moving backward toward its udder/scrotal area.
4. Work upward along the goat's sides, going from the back leg to the front leg, until you reach the spine.
5. Shear the legs, starting at the bottom.
6. Shear the neck, from the bottom of the throat upward.
7. Shear the goat's back, starting from the crown of the head and going back to the tail.
8. Remove any remaining hair and release the goat.
9. Separate any stained fleece from the other fiber, and store the fiber in a paper bag with a date and information about the goat.
10. Clean the area and then start with the next goat.

Goat Leash Training

Getting your goat to walk on a leash can be extremely useful, and it's not as difficult as it might sound, as goats are intelligent animals. If you plan to show your goat, it's important to teach it to walk on a leash, but even just around the farm, this can help manage the goats.

Try the method below:

1. Collar your goat and allow it to get used to the collar. The collar should go around the top of the goat's throat, near the jaw.
2. Attach a lead and walk a few steps, giving gentle tugs. If the goat follows you, reward it and keep walking, rewarding it every few steps. Gradually increase how far your goat must follow you to earn a treat.
3. If the goat won't follow you, show a food reward and encourage it verbally. Goats respond well to voices.
4. Don't let your goat go past you. Use a verbal command and turn in the opposite direction if it tries.
5. When you have completed the session, remove the collar and leash. Keep up training until your goat reliably walks with you on a leash.

Basic Healthcare

You need to be able to spot signs that your goats are ill, and there are a few critical health indicators that you should keep an eye out for. Your goats should always:

- Have bright, clear eyes
- Move around comfortably and easily
- Have good appetites
- Show engagement and alertness
- Have glossy coats

Unfortunately, goats are good at hiding the symptoms of illness, and you may not notice anything is wrong until it's too late. Knowing your herd well and trusting your instincts are essential aspects of caring for your goats. If you are concerned about one of your goats, you should contact a vet as soon as possible. However, if you are unable to contact a vet, you should:

1. Isolate the goat from the others.
2. Put the goat somewhere that is warm, dry, and not stressful. Ideally, it should still be able to see members of its herd or at least be somewhere familiar.

3. Give it access to clean hay and fresh water.

If your goat has a physical injury, you will need to strap or immobilize this until a vet can be found. For medical problems, see the section on Health Issues at the end of this chapter.

Vaccinating Your Goats

Goat vaccination can go a long way to preventing illness in your goats. You should get an experienced goatherd or a vet to show you how to vaccinate your flock. If you have a small herd, you will probably only need to vaccinate your goats against *clostridium perfringens* types C and D and tetanus (CDT). The rabies vaccine isn't approved for use on goats, but it may be recommended by your vet if rabies is common in your area.

Goats should be given an annual CDT booster, while pregnant does need a vaccination at 4 months, and kids need it at the 1 and 2 month marks. If you give your goats rabies vaccines, these must be done annually.

Talk to your vet about other vaccines if you have a larger herd; they can offer advice specific to your situation.

Deworming

You want to avoid worms in your goats, but current advice is to limit the use of deworming medication as much as possible. Few dewormers are approved for use on goats, and many worms are becoming resistant – so talk to your vet before choosing a deworming medication.

You can prevent or reduce the risk of worms through good environmental management.

Tricks include:

1. Rotate your pasture areas and put goats on land that hasn't been grazed for 70 days.
2. Use dewormers around 2 to 4 weeks before kidding. This will reduce the infection of newborns.
3. Keep goat areas sanitary and clean, and be careful about feeders and waterers.
4. Isolate new flock members for at least 30 days and treat them with 2 different dewormers.
5. Increase how much your goats can browse rather than grazing.
6. Keep your goats healthy; this increases their resistance to parasites.

None of these will completely eradicate worms, but they will help limit their presence in the herd, and medication can be used as a secondary measure.

Goat Castration

Where possible, castration should be taken on by a vet or experienced goatherd rather than a beginner. If done incorrectly, it could be dangerous, painful, and inhumane. However, if you know what you are doing, you can castrate a male kid at home. Ensure the kid has had a CDT vaccine before castration and operate in a clean environment.

You have a few options for castrating a male kid, but the rubber ring is generally considered the least painful option and should be done at around 8 to 10 weeks old. The ring is applied to both testes (in most cases) and usually causes minimal discomfort.

Health Issues

Although goats are hardy creatures, there are many issues that they can suffer from, and it's worth knowing what to look out for. Remember, if you are in doubt, you should always consult a qualified veterinarian for proper advice about diagnoses and treatment.

- *Clostridial Diseases:* this is known as bloody scours or Enterotoxemia Type C. It has two main forms and is often related to indigestion. It can affect kids and adults and may result in death. Good cleanliness will reduce the risk of this disease, but the CDT vaccine is the most important guard against it.
- *Soremouth:* this is a viral skin disease that results in blisters and scabs on the lips. It can also affect the udder and teats and sometimes the place where the hooves join the skin. It reduces your goat's willingness to eat and makes it vulnerable to other diseases. It also makes it hard for mothers to feed. You can vaccinate against it, which is contagious to goats and humans, so be cautious when dealing with it.
- *Pneumonia:* this can be viral or bacterial, or both, and is usually a result of stress or poor conditions. It will result in a painful cough, a fever, and breathing problems. A vet will need to prescribe this treatment because it can take different forms.
- *Footrot:* this is caused by warmth and dampness, affecting the hooves. In the form of foot scald, it only affects the area between the toes and is easy to treat with improved conditions. Virulent footrot attacks the horny tissue in the hoof and is much harder to get rid of. Taking good care of your goats' hooves and providing a good environment will reduce the risk of footrot. Quarantine any new animals, as an outsider often introduces footrot. Some vaccines may help.
- *Mastitis:* this affects female goats, and it's a bacterial infection that can cause udder damage. It can result in heat, swelling, pain, and milk that looks strange. Sanitary con-

ditions help reduce the risk of mastitis, but you must talk to your vet about treatments.

Those are just a few of the diseases and issues that your goats may suffer from, but with the guidance of a vet or experienced goatherd, you should be able to avoid most of them. Goats kept in good condition and not stressed are far less likely to suffer from health problems.

Summary

In this chapter, we've covered:

- The basics of caring for your goat's coat and hooves.
- Grooming supplies.
- How to tattoo your goats.
- How to shear your goats.
- Training your goats to walk on a leash.
- Basic healthcare needs for your herd.
- Vaccinations, deworming, and castration advice.
- Some common health issues to look out for.

The following chapter will look at how to shear your goats.

5

Shearing Your Goats

*"I do not believe in God. I believe in **cashmere**."*

-Fran Lebowitz

If you plan to keep your goats for their fibers, you need to know how to harvest them in a sustainable, efficient way that causes no harm to your goats. We briefly discussed shearing in the previous chapter, but we will explore how to do it in detail in this one.

Fiber Goat Associations And Registries In The USA

You may wish to join an association or registry if you produce and sell fiber from your goats. Registries will offer several advantages, giving you information about standard breed requirements. In many cases, only purebred goats can be registered, and you may have to prove that your goats meet the breed standards.

There are a few registers for fiber goats, including:
- The Pygora Breeders Association (for pygora goats)
- The Colored Angora Goat Breeders Association
- The American Colored Angora Goat Registry
- The American Angora Goat Breeders Association

Note that if anything about your ownership changes (e.g. you buy more goats or sell some of your goats), you should update your information with the registry.

General Shearing Tips

There's a lot to learn when it comes to shearing your goats. The best way to learn is hands-on practice, but you may also benefit from watching videos of it being done or talking to professional shearers. Don't worry if you don't get it straight away, but prioritize your goats' happiness and safety. If your goats are stressed out or harmed by the shearing process, it will be much harder to get them to stand still for it in the future – so be careful!

Remember, before shearing a goat. It would be best if you did in-depth research into how that particular goat's fibers should be harvested, as it differs from breed to breed. Cashmere goats are often combed rather than sheared. To ensure you get the best possible product from your goats, tailor the information below to suit the breed you are keeping.

We have already discussed the shearing method above, so let's now look at tips to maximize your success with this process. You should:

1. Keep your animals dry for 24 hours before shearing them. Wet fleece cannot be stored, and wet goats are a nightmare to shear.
2. Avoid feeding your goats the night before shearing. This means that the Rumens will be empty, making the process less stressful for the goats and the shearer. Less water can also be a good idea; dehydrated goats are easier to shear.
3. Try to shear off long lengths of wool, as these are more valuable and produce more yarn.
4. Get additional hands around if possible – this will make it much easier to corral the goats and shear them.
5. Use a sorting table for the fleece to easily remove the dirty bits that need to be thrown away. You can bounce the fleece against the table to remove the second cut and shake off any loose debris.
6. Work on getting your goats to trust you. Having a good bond with your animals will make an enormous difference in how easily you can handle them when shearing.
7. Bag the fleece and ensure you add all the information to work out which goats produced what fleece and when. Bagging the fleece on the day is extra work, but it will save you time and energy in the long run.

You should be prepared for shearing day to be a long day unless you have a very small herd. It is a lot of work, and it takes hours to shear goats.

How To Groom A Cashmere Goat

Again, get some hands-on experience with professionals before you do this for yourself. Some goats love combing, which makes the process easier, while others dislike it. If you have a goat that hates being combed, work mostly while the goat is eating or provide lots of treats to keep it distracted. The more you comb your goats, the more they should get used to it. You can comb them throughout the year, collecting up the fibers.

You will then need to remove the guard hairs, mats, debris, and other bits and pieces until you are left with just the soft fiber. Several kinds of goats can produce cashmere, but the quantities will vary enormously, and if you want to harvest it, you need to choose ones that are good for fiber.

How To Find A Shearer

You will probably want to find a shearer for your herd unless you just have a couple of goats because shearing is hard work that can be tough on your back. It's pretty physical, and many people consider it a skilled job that professionals best do.

You should talk to people in your area to get ideas about who to hire for shearing and take the time to look at the reviews. If you can, talk to the company about their process and ask how they minimize stress for the goats.

There is a big difference between a lousy shearer and a good shearer. If your goats are badly sheared and handled roughly, they will be much harder to shear in the future. Be careful, and change firms if you aren't pleased with the results.

The Terminology For Fiber Goats

You may find it helpful to learn about the different kinds of fiber that your goats can produce. These include:

- Type A: this is a mohair-like fiber that is usually 6 inches or longer and feels silky and smooth. It is generally considered the highest quality.
- Type B: this is usually a blend of fibers like mohair and cashmere, and it is usually curly and around 3 to 6 inches. The guard hair is more prominent.
- Type C: this is fine and may be accepted as commercial cashmere in some cases. It needs to be at least 1 inch long but is usually less than 3 inches. The guard hair is coarse and easy to separate.

Summary

In this chapter, we've covered:

- The associations and registries you might wish to join.
- Tips for shearing your goats.
- How to groom a cashmere goat.
- How to find a shearer.
- The terminology of fiber goats.

In the following chapter, we will look at getting milk from your goats and how to make cheese so you can enjoy some delicious food!

6

Milk And Cheese

"Drinking your milk and talking at the same time may result in your having to be patted on the back and dried for quite a long time afterwards."

-A.A. Milne

Many people want to keep goats for the milk and cheese they produce. While goat's milk isn't necessarily healthier than cow's milk, some people prefer the taste, and it is certainly easier to keep a herd of goats than to keep a herd of cows. Goats are far more suited to a homestead than cows are. With that in mind, let's consider how you can collect milk and make cheese from your herd.

Milking Equipment

Before you start milking your goats, you will need the right equipment, or you'll find that you struggle. Here is a checklist of things you may need:

- A milk bucket: this needs to be stainless steel so it can be sterilized. A 6 quart bucket is fine for most goats.
- A supply of cloths: when you have finished milking, you will wipe the udders with a warm, clean cloth. Some people use disposable wipes, but it's cheaper and more eco-friendly to have some washable cloths. Make sure you use a clean one for each doe.
- Teat dip: this reduces the risk of infection after milking the goat. You can use iodine or chemical dips.
- A strip cup: this is a stainless-steel container with a mesh at the top. You use it to collect the first few milk squirts to check for any chunkiness. This milk should be discarded as it has a high level of bacteria.
- Milk filters are disposable filters used to get dust and hair out of the milk. You can use a cheesecloth, but it will need to be boiled between each use.

That's about it, apart from your milking stand!

Getting Ready For Milking

Setting up a routine for milking your goats is a good idea. Being consistent helps your goats stay calm and know what's happening. You can milk once or twice per day. Always make sure the area and all of the equipment are clean before you start.

You should try to milk your goats at the same time every day, and don't switch the side from which you milk an individual. Wash your hands and the udder and try to milk the goats in the same order every time. Usually, the head of the herd will go first.

Milking A Goat

Once your goat is set up at the stand, you can sit beside it and milk it. You will probably use your whole hand for a large goat, but for a small goat, you may use three fingers. Never pull on the teats, as this does not produce milk and will hurt the goat. Your hand should be about 2 inches up the udder, not at the bottom of the teat.

To milk, a goat, wrap your forefinger and thumb around the teat and gently squeeze it. This will produce milk. Squirt the milk into the strip cup first and then into the bucket until the milk stops coming. At this point, gently massage the udder for a minute or two. This encourages the rest of the milk down into the teats.

Resume milking until the flow stops again, and then you're done. The more quickly you can milk your goats, the fewer issues you will have with them getting bored and restless. You will get much quicker and more efficient with practice.

If possible, get someone to show you how this works and practice on someone else's goats before getting your herd. Once you've finished milking, clean the goat's udder, and then you can filter and store the milk. Make sure your goats have food and water before you leave them.

Pasteurizing Goat's Milk

You may want to consider pasteurizing your goat milk, especially if you wish to keep it longer and ensure it is safer to drink. Pasteurizing reduces the number of bacteria in milk so that it stays fresh for longer and is safer to consume.

It is relatively easy to pasteurize milk yourself at home. If you don't want to buy expensive equipment, you can do it on your stove, although a pasteurizer may be worth purchasing if you have a large herd. Make sure the milk has been filtered before you pasteurize it.

To pasteurize milk on your stove, you will need a large stainless-steel pan, a thermometer, a timer, some ice, and a spoon for stirring. You should add the milk to the pan and place it over medium heat. Stir it frequently, and keep stirring as the temperature increases, or the milk will scorch and stick to the bottom of the pan.

Use your thermometer to check how hot the milk is, but don't let it touch the bottom of the pan, or it will give you an inaccurate reading. The temperature of the milk needs to reach 165 degrees F. Once it does, you should set your timer for 15 seconds and make sure the temperature is maintained for this long.

Next, remove the pot from the heat and place it in an ice bath to start chilling the milk immediately. Decrease the temperature to 55 degrees F. Keep the water cold by topping it with more ice if necessary, as the milk is cooling.

Sterilize some jars and then use these to store the milk in your refrigerator. These will keep far better than just ordinary bottled milk.

Making Goat's Cheese

One of the best things about keeping goats is that you can make your cheese – and goat's cheese is a delicious food many people enjoy eating. Cheese is also a great way to store excess milk, liven up your diet, and make more from the product you are harvesting. Goat's cheese is delicious on bread and can be used in various recipes. If you are living off the land, being able to produce your cheese is a beautiful thing that will enrich your diet.

You might feel a little daunted by making your own cheese, but remember that goat's cheese doesn't need to be matured for months before being eaten, the way some cheeses do. The process can be surprisingly simple, and you don't need an enormous amount of equipment.

As with pasteurizing goat's milk, you will require a thermometer and a large pan. You also need cheesecloths, lemon juice, vinegar, salt, and herbs. Use the recipe below.

Ingredients:

- 1 qt of goat's milk
- 2 tablespoons of white vinegar
- ½ teaspoon of salt

- 1/3 cup of lemon juice
- Dried herbs (optional)

Method:

1. Place a colander in your sink and line it with 3 fine cheesecloths.
2. Place a heavy-bottomed pan over medium heat and add the milk. Begin heating it very slowly, stirring frequently.
3. Heat it until it reaches 180 degrees F (don't touch the thermometer to the bottom of the pan when measuring).
4. Remove it from the heat as soon as it reaches 180 degrees F and add the lemon juice to the pan. Stir gently to combine.
5. Add the vinegar and stir gently to combine, but don't mix it too much. Leave it for 30 minutes.
6. You should see some specks of curd forming. Ladle the milk into the cheesecloth and add the salt, stirring gently.
7. Tie the ends of the cheesecloth together using string, and then suspend it above the sink. Many people hook it over the faucet, but you can take other approaches.
8. Allow the cloth to hang for around an hour so the liquids can drip.
9. When the hour has passed, take the cheesecloth down, untie it, and place the contents on a cutting board to shape them. Your cheese is now ready. It should be stored in the fridge until you are ready to eat it. Add the herbs at the time of eating.

Summary

In this chapter, we've covered:

- What equipment is needed for milking a goat.
- How to prepare for milking, and how to milk the goat.
- Pasteurizing goat's milk.
- Making goat's cheese.

In the following chapter, we will look at goat meat and how to harvest it.

7

Goat Meat

"Understand, when you eat meat, that something did die. You have an obligation to value it – not just the sirloin but also all those wonderful tough little bits."

-Anthony Bourdain

How To Breed Goats

If you are going to breed your goats, you need an uncastrated male and a female goat. Unlike many domesticated animals, goats naturally breed during a specific season, as the days get shorter at the start of fall. The gestation period for a goat is around 150 days, so by mating in the late summer or fall, the goats ensure that the kids will be born when spring comes. This allows them to grow throughout the summer. Although some large institutions do use artificial insemination and hormones to encourage their goats to mate at other times of the year, you will almost always be breeding your goats in the fall.

Males are sometimes ready to mate when they are over 3 months old, although for many, it's when they reach about 5 months. Keep them separate from the does until you are ready for mating to happen. Most can breed after 4 months old, as long as they weigh more than 80 pounds, but it's better to wait until they have reached at least a year old. You should learn the signs that a doe is in heat and a buck is in rut before you start pairing them up.

Put a doe and buck alone in an enclosure and leave them for a few hours to mate. This is usually all that it will take. She is pregnant if your doe doesn't go back into heat about 21 days later. It would be best if you increased the nutrients in her diet about 6 weeks before she is due to give birth. Your doe should mostly eat grain before she gives birth but make the switch gradually.

2 weeks before the birthing date, move the doe into a birthing stall, and keep her calm. You should aim to be present for the birth and make sure that you have a vet on hand. Some

goats will have twins or triplets, while others will just have 1 kid. Talk to your vet beforehand about what to expect, what problems to look out for, and what supplies you should have ready. As mentioned earlier, having some colostrum in frozen or powdered form is very important, as this will save the baby's life if the mother won't or can't feed it for any reason.

When You Should Butcher A Goat

Most goats are butchered before they turn a year old, depending on what kind of meat you want. If you want kid meat similar to lamb, the kid should usually be butchered when it is around 3 to 5 months old. By this time, it will weigh between 25 and 50 pounds. Kid meat is sometimes known as Cabrito.

Older goat meat is not as tender as kid meat, but it generally has a better flavor and more juice. To produce it, you will usually slaughter the goat at around 8 to 10 months old, and this kind of meat is known as Chevon. It is a good idea to learn more about the specifics of the breed you keep because the process does vary between breeds.

Knowing the approximate timings will help you figure out how many goats you need to keep to supply yourself and your family with meat. Of course, the amount of meat you will get depends heavily on the goat breed, but this calculation is something you should consider.

Take into account:

- How many you have, and what the chances of twins or triplets are.
- Whether you plan to harvest kid meat or adult goat meat.
- How much space you have for raising the kids to butchering age.
- How much meat you will get from the goat.

Considering all these things will help you figure out how big your herd needs to be and how much meat you will get from it each year.

How To Butcher A Goat

The most important thing to consider when it comes to butchering your goat is the humanity of the butchering process. If you are not experienced in this, you may want to think about getting some experts to do the butchering for you. It is crucial to ensure that the goats don't suffer unnecessarily during the process. A professional should show you how to do this before you attempt it at home; the descriptions below are intended for information only. If you have not got hands-on experience, make sure you get some before attempting to slaughter a goat on your own.

Some people prefer to use electric stunners that cause a heart attack; This may be one of the easiest options, and these stunners do not tend to be expensive. Alternatively, you can stick the jugular vein by immobilizing the goat, grasping the jaw with one hand, and inserting the knife behind the jaw. Draw it through the pelt so that it severs the vein and the carotid arteries, which will help you to achieve a complete bleed, which makes the carcass easier to deal with. Use a bowl to catch the blood and minimize the mess.

Next, you will need to skin the carcass using a sharp knife. Start at the forelegs and then do the hind legs. Remove the animal's feet and then start separating the skin from the body by pushing your fist against the pelt; This will loosen it and allow you to pull it away across most of the body. The head should then be removed, and the internal organs stripped out. Be careful when removing the anus, so you don't puncture the intestines.

You can finish stripping off the pelt and then rinse the carcass in lukewarm water before processing it.

Assessing Meat Quality

There are no official quality grades for goat meat, and the USDA doesn't offer guidelines. It is lean red meat, containing fewer fats and more unsaturated fatty acids than other red meat. However, because there are no grading guidelines, it can be tricky to assess the meat quality.

You should ensure that the meat is unbruised by ensuring that your goats are handled humanely and the butchering process is completed with care. Bruising can affect the flavor of the meat and may result in more wastage if it is serious. With good care, you can ensure that your meat is high quality, even without guidelines from the USDA.

How To Store Goat Meat

Once you have harvested your goats, you will need to store the meat properly to minimize wastage and ensure that you don't miss out on the rewards for your hard work. The easiest way to store goat meat is to portion it up and freeze it, just as you might do with meat from the store.

Removing any bones before freezing is best to use your freezer space more efficiently. Goat meat should be wrapped in waxed paper and then in a layer of aluminum foil or a freezer bag to minimize the airflow and prevent freezer burn. Make sure you are freezing it in small enough portions to be useful to you.

Next, label and date the bag so you know exactly what is in it and how old it is. Goat meat should be used up within 3 or 4 months of freezing. Although you can keep it for longer, it may degrade in terms of taste and texture.

You can temporarily store goat meat in the fridge, but you should only do this for a couple of days, especially if it has been ground. Cuts will last longer but will still need to be used within a few days.

There are other options for storing goat meat, which might appeal if you don't have a freezer, or you lack the space to store the meat properly. Drying and salting have been used for centuries to preserve meat, and when done properly, they will allow you to store the meat at room temperature for a long time.

However, because of the risk of bacteria, it's a good idea to take a proper course in these preservation techniques if you want to use them, especially for large quantities of meat. It will be critical to get it right to avoid wastage and minimize the risk of food poisoning.

Summary

In this chapter, we've covered:

- Goat breeding and how to do it.
- When goats should be butchered.
- The process of butchering a goat.
- How to assess the quality of meat.

How to store goat meat.

Conclusion

"To the goats, all people are equal, except for those who have treats."

-Karin Tidbeck

Raising goats is a fascinating world that many more people are now looking to step into and learn. Goats are exciting creatures; their intelligence and wiliness set them apart from sheep and other commonly farmed animals like cattle. They are considered one of the oldest kinds of livestock and show many different personality quirks. Some goats are stubborn, some are affectionate, some are aggressive, and some are placid.

There is no doubt that goats are intelligent creatures and that they respond to you depending on how you treat them. Many people who keep goats find that they become very fond of their animals and learn a lot from watching them and caring for them. They are more rewarding than sheep, easier to care for, and generally far more characterful than almost any other creature you might put in your backyard – but they are a lot of work, too, and you shouldn't underestimate this.

Goats are hardy creatures but require a lot of care and attention, and you can't afford to neglect them. You must be available to muck them out, provide food and clean water, and milk them at least once a day. You can't just go off for a month's vacation when you have goats. You need to be there for them – but they will return the favor with rich, sweet milk, beautifully soft fibers, or delicious meat. You will also derive a lot of pleasure from the work you invest in your goats, and you'll probably find that you learn a great deal from them.

You should do plenty of thorough research before taking on goats. As well as reading this book, it's a good idea to talk to current goatherds, get more details about the breeds you are thinking of rearing, and visit forums to ask any questions you might have. This will mean you can hit the ground running with everything you need to know to succeed!

Thank You

It means the world to me that you chose my book when there are dozens of books out there.

I appreciate you picking this book and making it to the end.

Before you leave, I want to ask a tiny favor that would make a massive difference to me. **Can you consider leaving a review on the platform, please? Your review is the easiest and best way to support independent authors such as myself.**

Your feedback will help me to continue writing books that get you results. It would mean so much to see your review, and I personally read every one.

>> Leave a review on Amazon US <<

>> Leave a review on Amazon UK <<

Food Preservation and Canning For Beginners

I. *Food Waste FAQs*. (n.d.). USDA. Retrieved November 10, 2021, from https://www.usda.gov/foodwaste/faqs

II. Nummer, B. A. (2002). *National Center for Home Food Preservation | NCHFP Publications*. National Center For Home Food Preservation. Retrieved May 2002, from https://nchfp.uga.edu/publications/nchfp/factsheets/food_pres_hist.html

III. *National Center for Home Food Preservation | USDA Publications*. (2015). National Center For Home Food Preservation. Retrieved November 14, 2021, from https://nchfp.uga.edu/publications/publications_usda.html

IV. *National Center for Home Food Preservation | NCHFP Publications*. (2017). National Center For Home Food Preservation. Retrieved November 14, 2021, from https://nchfp.uga.edu/publications/nchfp/factsheets/sterilizing.html

Off-Grid Living

- Riviera.L (2020, January, 9), Ecopyschology: How Immersion in Nature Benefits Your Health. YaleEnvironment360. https://e360.yale.edu/features/ecopsychology-how-immersion-in-nature-benefits-your-health

- Simply Self Storage Staff, (2018, June, 11th), Living Off the Grid - Your Guide to Self-Sufficient Living. https://www.simplyss.com/blog/living-off-grid/

- Off Grid World, (2021, May, 1st), Anybody Can Live Off the Grid: Is It Right for You? https://offgridworld.com/anybody-can-live-off-the-grid-is-it-right-for-you/

- Elemental Green team, (2021), 10 Eco Building Materials Revolutionizing Home Construction. https://elemental.green/10-eco-building-materials-revolutionizing-home-construction/

- Dodrill, T. (2019, May, 10th) Is It Illegal to Go Off the Grid in Your State? Ask a Prepper. https://www.askaprepper.com/is-it-legal-to-go-off-the-grid-in-your-state/

- Rejba. A. Living Off the Grid in the USA -IS It Illegal? The Smart Survivalist. https://www.thesmartsurvivalist.com/living-off-the-grid-in-the-usa-is-it-illegal/

- Schwartz. D. M. (2021), Best States to Live Off Grid: All 50 States Ranked. Off-Grid Permaculture. https://offgridpermaculture.com/Finding_Land/Best_States_to_Live_Off_Grid__All_50_States_Ranked.html

- Rejba. A. (2021), Where is the Best Place in the World to Live Off the Grid. The Smart Survivalist. https://www.thesmartsurvivalist.com/where-is-the-best-place-in-the-world-to-live-off-the-grid/

- Rejba. A. (2021), Living Off the Grid In Canada. https://www.thesmartsurvivalist.com/living-off-grid-in-canada-is-it-illegal/

- Rejba.A (2021) what Should I Know Before Living Off the Grid In Australia. The Smart Survivalist. https://www.thesmartsurvivalist.com/what-should-i-know-before-living-off-the-grid-in-australia/

- Davidson, J (2021, January, 5), Off-Grid Water Systems: 4Proven Ways to Bring Water to Your Homestead. Tiny Living Life. https://tinylivinglife.com/2021/01/learn-how-to-build-off-grid-water-system/

- Drinking. Water Team (2019, August, 23) Drinking Water and Human Health. https://drinking-water.extension.org/how-does-a-well-actually-work-to-supply-drinking-water/

- Solar Energy Industries Association. (2021) Net Metering. https://www.seia.org/initiatives/net-metering

- Sunbadger team, (2020, December, 30th) How Does Solar Energy Work: Ultimate Guide To Solar Energy in 2021). https://sunbadger.com/how-does-solar-energy-work/

- GreenMatch, (2021, March, 29), Solar Thermal Panels.https://www.greenmatch.co.uk/solar-energy/solar-thermal/solar-thermal-panels

- Nunez. C (2019, May, 13), Hydropower Explained. National Geographic. https://www.nationalgeographic.com/environment/article/hydropower

- Llyod, D. (2014, December, 11) Wind Energy: Advantages and Disadvantages. Stanford Edu. http://large.stanford.edu/courses/2014/ph240/lloyd2/

- Office of Energy Efficiency & Renewable Energy. How Do Wind Turbines Work? https://www.energy.gov/eere/wind/how-do-wind-turbines-work

- Office of Energy Efficiency & Renewable Energy. Biomass Resources. https://www.energy.gov/eere/bioenergy/biomass-resources

- Rycroft. M. (2019, January, 30th). Biomass Gasification for Large Scale Electricity Generation. EE. Publishers. https://www.ee.co.za/article/biomass-gasification-for-large-scale-electricity-generation.html

- GreenMatch. (2021, September, 09), Advantages and Disadvantages of Biomass Boilers. https://www.greenmatch.co.uk/blog/2015/10/advantages-and-disadvantages-of-biomass-boilers

- Solar News. (2019, November, 15th), Benefits of Solar Powered Air Source Heat Pumps. Energysage. https://news.energysage.com/benefits-of-solar-powered-air-source-heat-pumps/

- Power. M. (2020, July, 27th), Pros and Cons of Solar Powered Air Conditioners. Green Builder. https://www.greenbuildermedia.com/energy-solutions/pros-and-cons-of-solar-powered-air-conditioners

- Nubie, S, Off-grid AC: 9 Forgotten Ways the Ancient Romans (And Everyone Else) Stayed Cool. Off the Grid News. https://www.offthegridnews.com/how-to-2/off-grid-ac-9-forgotten-ways-the-ancient-romans-and-everyone-else-stayed-cool-1/

- Browne, P. (2016, July, 12). How You Can Stay Cool Like an Ancient Roman. The Local. https://www.thelocal.it/20160712/roman-chill/

- Office of Energy Efficiency & Renewable Energy. Geothermal Heat Pumps. https://www.energy.gov/energysaver/geothermal-heat-pumps

Off-Grid Solar Power

I.   Grist. (2021, April 8). *If everyone used as much energy as Americans, we'd run out of oil in 9 years*. Retrieved December 13, 2021, from https://grist.org/article/if-every-one-used-as-much-energy-as-americans-wed-run-out-of-oil-in-9-years/

II.   *How much energy do solar panels produce for your home | YES Energy Solutions*. (n.d.). YES Energy Solutions. Retrieved December 19, 2021, from https://www.yes-energysolutions.co.uk/advice/how-much-energy-solar-panels-produce-home

III.   Ritchie, H. (2020, November 28). *Renewable Energy*. Our World in Data. Retrieved December 20, 2021, from https://ourworldindata.org/renewable-energy

IV.   *How much energy do solar panels produce for your home | YES Energy Solutions*. (n.d.). YES Energy Solutions. Retrieved December 19, 2021, from https://www.yes-energysolutions.co.uk/advice/how-much-energy-solar-panels-produce-home

Prepper's Long Term Survival Bible

I. Infoplease. (2020, August 5). *Living Off the Grid*. Retrieved March 19, 2022, from https://www.infoplease.com/math-science/earth-environment/living-off-the-grid

II. *Making Water Safe in an Emergency*. (2022, January 27). Centers for Disease Control and Prevention. Retrieved March 21, 2022, from https://www.cdc.gov/healthywater/emergency/making-water-safe.html

III. Hunter, J. (2020, November 30). *The Pyramid of Wilderness Survival Food*. Primal Survivor. Retrieved March 21, 2022, from https://www.primalsurvivor.net/wilderness-survival-food/

Backyard Homestead Handbook

I. B, M. (2022, January 23). *15 Surprising Vegetable Garden Statistics (2022) | Home Garden*. Cooped Up Life. Retrieved April 10, 2022, from https://coopeduplife.com/vegeta-ble-garden-statistics/

II. Hirt, H. (2020). Healthy soils for healthy plants for healthy humans. *EMBO Reports*, *21*(8). https://doi.org/10.15252/embr.202051069

III. Schmutz, P., & Hoyle, E. H. (2022, March 15). *Canning Foods at Home | Home & Garden Information Center*. Home & Garden Information Center | Clemson University, South Carolina. Retrieved April 15, 2022, from https://hgic.clemson.edu/factsheet/canning-foods-at-home/

ix   Larkin, M. (2019, May 24). *10 things that could potentially kill you on your next camping trip and how to protect yourself.* Insider. Retrieved February 13, 2022, from https://www.insider.com/things-to-watch-out-for-when-camping-2019-5

x   Schlesinger, S. A. (2022, February 8). *Cardiopulmonary Resuscitation (CPR) in Infants and Children.* Merck Manuals Professional Edition. Retrieved February 14, 2022, from https://www.merckmanuals.com/professional/critical-care-medicine/cardiac-arrest-and-cpr/cardiopulmonary-resuscitation-cpr-in-infants-and-children#

Made in the USA
Middletown, DE
11 August 2024

58938217R00320

Raising Goats for Beginners

I.   Clur, K. (2022, May 4). *How Many Goats Are There? (US & Worldwide Statistics in 2022)*. Pet Keen. Retrieved June 19, 2022, from https://petkeen.com/how-many-goats-are-there-statistics/#1_There_are_around_one_billion_goats_in_the_world

Survival Medical Handbook

i   *Food Waste FAQs*. (n.d.). USDA. Retrieved November 10, 2021, from https://www.usda.gov/foodwaste/faqs

ii Nummer, B. A. (2002). *National Center for Home Food Preservation | NCHFP Publications*. National Center For Home Food Preservation. Retrieved May 2002, from https://nchfp.uga.edu/publications/nchfp/factsheets/food_pres_hist.html

iii *National Center for Home Food Preservation | USDA Publications*. (2015). National Center For Home Food Preservation. Retrieved November 14, 2021, from https://nchfp.uga.edu/publications/publications_usda.html

iv *National Center for Home Food Preservation | NCHFP Publications*. (2017). National Center For Home Food Preservation. Retrieved November 14, 2021, from https://nchfp.uga.edu/publications/nchfp/factsheets/sterilizing.html

v   Grist. (2021, April 8). *If everyone used as much energy as Americans, we'd run out of oil in 9 years*. Retrieved December 13, 2021, from https://grist.org/article/if-everyone-used-as-much-energy-as-americans-wed-run-out-of-oil-in-9-years/

vi *How much energy do solar panels produce for your home | YES Energy Solutions*. (n.d.). YES Energy Solutions. Retrieved December 19, 2021, from https://www.yesenergysolutions.co.uk/advice/how-much-energy-solar-panels-produce-home

vii Ritchie, H. (2020, November 28). *Renewable Energy*. Our World in Data. Retrieved December 20, 2021, from https://ourworldindata.org/renewable-energy

viii *How much energy do solar panels produce for your home | YES Energy Solutions*. (n.d.). YES Energy Solutions. Retrieved December 19, 2021, from https://www.yesenergysolutions.co.uk/advice/how-much-energy-solar-panels-produce-home